D0305469

OVER THE TOP

OVER THE TOP

Adrian Flanagan

Weidenfeld & Nicolson

LONDON

First published in Great Britain in 2008
by Weidenfeld & Nicolson

1 3 5 7 9 10 8 6 4 2

© Adrian Flanagan 2008

All rights reserved. No part of this publication may be
reproduced, stored in a retrieval system, or transmitted, in
any form or by any means, electronic, mechanical,
photocopying, recording or otherwise, without the prior
permission of both the copyright owner and the above publisher.

The right of Adrian Flanagan
to be identified as the author of
this work has been asserted in accordance with the
Copyright, Designs and Patents Act 1988.

A CIP catalogue record for this book
is available from the British Library.

ISBN-13 978 0 297 85079 3

Typeset at the Spartan Press Ltd,
Lymington, Hants

Printed and bound in Great Britain by
CPI Mackays, Chatham, ME5 8TD

Maps by Peter Harper
Illustrations [on p. 53–55, p. 89] by Oxford Designers & Illustrators

Weidenfeld & Nicolson

The Orion Publishing Group Ltd
Orion House
5 Upper Saint Martin's Lane
London, WC2H 9EA

The Orion Publishing Group's policy is to use papers that
are natural, renewable and recyclable products and
made from wood grown in sustainable forests. The logging
and manufacturing processes are expected to conform to
the environmental regulations of the country of origin.

www.orionbooks.co.uk

For Louise, Benjamin and Gabriel
and
In memory of Christian, Tracey and Alexandre Foures

LONDON BOROUGH OF HACKNEY	
91300000003386	
HJ	10/11/2008
910.4109	£16.99
	SHD

CONTENTS

08 August 06
Barrabas wintered
in Nome

Nome

28 October 05
Depart Hamble
River 13.53.34

England

01 November 05
Swept overboard

08 May 06
Arrive in Honolulu
to repair mast

Honolulu

Hawaiian Islands

Atlantic Ocean

27 November 05
Hit by tropical
cyclone

Equator

Pacific Ocean

Recife

29 December 05
Tracked by
pirate vessel

Rio de Janeiro

19 January 06
Whale encounter

03 January 06
First antipodal
point

Juan Fernandez
Archipelago

Santiago

Buenos
Aires

15 January 06
The 'big' storm - spinnaker
lost and steering cables fail

28 February 06
Barrabas completes westabout
rounding of Cape Horn

Falkland Islands

Cape Horn

Southern

18 February 06
Two capsizes
damage the mast

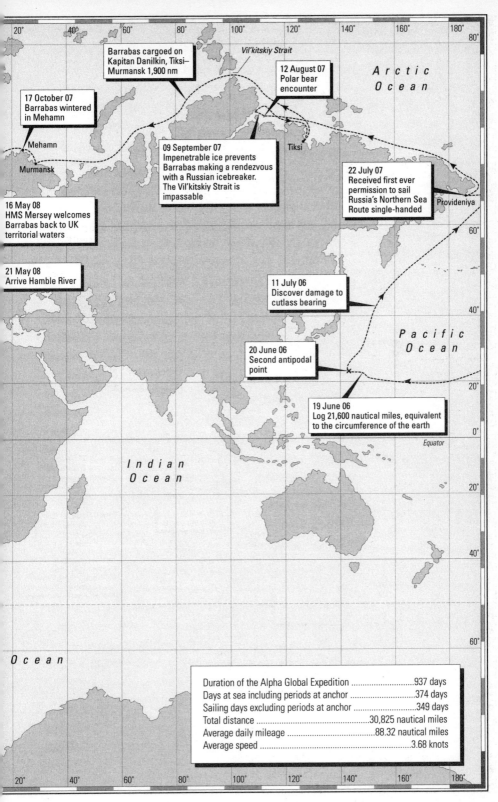

17 October 07
Barrabas wintered
in Mehamn

Barrabas cargoed on
Kapitan Danilkin, Tiksi–
Murmansk 1,900 nm

Vil'kitskiy Strait

12 August 07
Polar bear
encounter

*Arctic
Ocean*

Mehamn

Murmansk

09 September 07
Impenetrable ice prevents
Barrabas making a rendezvous
with a Russian icebreaker.
The Vil'kitskiy Strait is
impassable

Tiksi

22 July 07
Received first ever
permission to sail
Russia's Northern Sea
Route single-handed

Provideniya

16 May 08
HMS Mersey welcomes
Barrabas back to UK
territorial waters

11 July 06
Discover damage to
cutlass bearing

*Pacific
Ocean*

21 May 08
Arrive Hamble River

20 June 06
Second antipodal
point

19 June 06
Log 21,600 nautical miles, equivalent
to the circumference of the earth

Equator

*Indian
Ocean*

Ocean

Duration of the Alpha Global Expedition	....	937 days
Days at sea including periods at anchor	....	374 days
Sailing days excluding periods at anchor	....	349 days
Total distance	....	30,825 nautical miles
Average daily mileage	....	88.32 nautical miles
Average speed	....	3.68 knots

Route of the Alpha Global Expedition

You will pass through storms and heavy rains and at times you may suffer defeat. The essence of a creative life, however, is not to give up in the face of defeat, but to follow the rainbow that exists within your heart.

DAISAKU IKEDA

This is a seriously difficult objective.

SIR ROBIN KNOX-JOHNSTON

PROLOGUE

You are alone. You have only seconds left to live or more precisely, only seconds remaining after which your death will be imminent. What thoughts might go through your mind?

Not long enough, you may think, for the massive database of your life experience to reassemble itself into an order of merit.

Time slows. Seconds stretch, hammered flat on the anvil of oblivion, each end reaching towards infinity.

Alpha Global Expedition, Day 5
Tuesday 1st November 2005
49°.09.58′ North, 06°.50.38′ West – Western Approaches, English Channel

Dawn's grey light seeping in from the east makes little impression. Storms have raged through the night. A train of deep depressions spiralling down from Iceland is slamming into the west coast of England. The narrow confines of the English Channel heap the seas into marauding waves, monsters as high as a double-storey house. Near hurricane-force winds screech through the rigging. I have been bashing into these gales for three days. Bad weather was predicted, but not to this extent, not this severity.

It's been five days since I departed from the River Hamble on my attempt to sail the first single-handed *vertical* circumnavigation of the earth. My route is planned to take me westabout Cape Horn, from the Atlantic Ocean to the Pacific Ocean then, over the top of Russia, through the North Polar region. For now, I am somewhere off the south coast of Cornwall. Relentless headwinds neutralise meaningful progress. I've eaten little food and hardly slept. To cap it all, seawater has fouled my freshwater tanks.

At 8.00 am, the wind suddenly dies to 16 knots. The sea calms enough for me to get to the foredeck safely. This is only a respite while the eye of the storm passes over. The trailing part of the system will hit soon. I take the opportunity to rig the storm jib and set up the self-steering gear: a wind vane attached to a servomechanism that connects to an auxiliary rudder via a shaft. The rudder is made of dense nylon but does not float. As a precaution, in case the securing pin fails, I tie a lanyard through the rudder's carrying handle and make it fast to a strong point on the transom. The lanyard is a two-metre loop and I let it fall into the water and trail behind the boat.

Within five hours, the weather has gone berserk. Wind speeds reach 50 knots. One yacht 15 miles east of me sets off its emergency beacon and an air–sea rescue helicopter flies out to pick up the crew. I listen to the frantic radio exchanges. It is the first of three 'mayday' calls I hear that morning.

The boat takes a wave bow on, riding high, her nose pointing skywards. She comes off the wave with a tremendous crash. A loud cracking sound ricochets from below and I think my yacht has split herself open. I duck down the companionway steps. I use both hands to grip, to prevent myself from pitching forward or being flung backward or hurled sideways. In the dim light below decks, I feel relief wash over me. There is no water rushing in, drowning my boat. I go to the fore cabin. Eleven fuel cans weighing a combined 220 kg have smashed through the storage cage. The stench of spilt diesel percolates the cabin. I gybe the boat so the sails are backed against the rigging and then lash the wheel hard over in the opposite direction so that the sails and rudder are working against each other. The boat stops in the pounding seas. I set about sorting out the mess. My first priority is to stow the fuel. I lash two cans alongside the ones already in the aft deck fuel cages, one either side. I make space for three more in the lazarette. There is room for the remaining six cans in the cockpit, forward of the wheel, which makes getting to and from the cabin awkward in the difficult conditions.

The necessity of maintaining a radar watch in the busy shipping lanes has confined me below decks for most of the time since dawn. I am safer below, and dry. In the early afternoon, I come on deck. My mission is simple and quick: to alter course 15°, which means adjusting the self-steering vane. The control line is a continuous loop running from a cog on the Hydrovane, the self-steering assembly, to a small block, which I have clipped to the guardrail on the starboard side level with the cockpit. I plan to be on deck for 10 seconds, no more, sufficient time to eyeball my horizons for nearby shipping and to tug on the self-steering control line. I am dressed in two T-shirts and a pair of longjohns as base layers, an all-in-one fleece-lined mid-layer, heavy-duty oilskins and sea boots. I am not wearing a lifejacket or a safety line.

For the moment, the large cuddy – a tubular steel framework clad in transparent sheets of tough transparent polycarbonate – protects me from the elements. I clamber over the six fuel cans in the cockpit, scanning the forward horizon. A turbulent, cold, grey sea stretches away. I turn to look sternwards. All clear. Now the adjustment. Bent double beneath the cuddy, I step onto the starboard cockpit seating to get past the wheel, planting the sole of my left boot onto the starboard side deck. My thighs brace intuitively to counter the pitching deck. With my left hand, I reach towards the control line clipped to the guardrail, bending at the waist, facing backwards. Just as I am reaching, a wave hits the boat on the port side, heeling her over at an acute angle. The starboard toe rail dips below the surface. Water rushes over my left boot.

I never see the wave that sweeps over the bow. Perhaps the seas have lifted the yacht and then she digs her bows into the water. Perhaps a second wave has hit the boat on the starboard side in the confused cross chop. I will never know exactly what happened. There is no noise of water charging up behind me, or perhaps the wind has torn away the warning sound. My fingers never make it to the control line.

The impact when it comes is immensely powerful; a vice-like grip against the back of my left leg and the exposed part of my upper body leaning out past the protective screen of the cuddy. The water knocks me over and picks me up, my body flat, parallel to the deck and four feet above it. Then I am swept over the guardrail. My arms are flailing, trying to propel me back on board, trying to grab a handhold. Through the foaming maelstrom of water, I see parts of the deck, the main block and the cockpit winches flit away to the right. Then I see the bare steel of the hull and through the green lens of sea the blue nameplate of the boat, white lettering spelling out B A R R A B A S. The water releases its hold and I plunge into the sea, completely submerged. When I break the surface, the nameplate is directly above my face. I am completely separated from the boat.

This is what goes through my mind:

- Death is a certainty. Okay, this is it, aged 45.
- I see my French friends, Christian and Tracey Foures and their 10-

year-old son, Alexandre, all killed in the Boxing Day tsunami the
previous year.

- The angelic faces of my two boys, Benjamin and Gabriel, smile at
  me.
- The startling green eyes of Louise, my ex-wife and expedition
  manager, twinkle with love or sympathy – I'm not sure which,
  perhaps both.
- Drowning is too unbearable to contemplate. I will strip down to my
  base layer and let hypothermia claim my consciousness before the
  sea takes me down.

Despite the frigid water, I feel warm and irrationally calm. I surmise
afterwards that in this moment of extreme danger, the adrenalin
pumping into my system has shut down core functions and diverted
blood to the muscles of my arms and legs, bringing warmth. My vision
sharpens to the acuity of an eagle. Perhaps the calm that I feel is part of
this primeval fight/flight response or perhaps it is the simple realisation that the game of life is up. Maybe I even feel some measure of
relief. I cannot be certain.

These thoughts and sensations come unbidden, fused like wax
crayons suddenly exposed to intense heat, their colours mingling in a
kaleidoscope of finality.

PART I
Beyond the Horizon

CHAPTER I

The Seed

On a late April afternoon in 1976, I pressed my forehead against the small oval of Plexiglas as the great 747 swooped over the tower blocks clustered on the eastern side of Hong Kong's Kai Tak International Airport. Bamboo poles strung with laundry bristled from tiny balconies, plastic chairs and flowerpots littering rooftop gardens. Traffic streamed through the shadowed canyons between the high-rises. Beyond the urban concentrate, ships cluttered the harbour: British frigates, container carriers huddling around Kowloon's main terminal, tankers moving regally to and from the refinery. Past the harbour, Hong Kong Island rested in the green velvet of the South China Sea.

As soon as the aircraft braked for the last time after landing, I was out of my seat and brushing past the passengers sitting next to me. I wanted to be first at the door when it opened. I dropped the overhead locker, grabbed my small hand luggage and quickly strode to the rear door. Through the small window, I could see the stairway truck approach the aircraft. After 24 hours in the air from London with stops in Rome, Bahrain, Bombay, Rangoon and Bangkok, the moment I had been waiting for had arrived. A flight attendant threw some levers. A hollow knocking announced contact of the stairway against the fuselage. A hiss of gas sounded the final equalisation of pressure between the clammy atmosphere of the cabin and the outside. Then the door swung open. The smell of salt and seaweed, the aromatic scent of frying duckling, avgas and diesel fumes, jasmine, camphor wood and charcoal all mixed and cooked and carried on the humid air rushed at me; the smell of the Orient. I breathed deeply and then stepped out onto the platform.

The cacophony inside the terminal building was close to deafening. Hundreds of jostling Chinese shouted and waved at travel-weary friends and relatives hauling suitcases and pushing trolleys. Overhead,

rows of strip-lighting bathed the crowds in a bright, bluish hue. I
spotted my parents among a group of other *gweilos* at the far end of
the arrivals area. The contrast to northern England's pastoral, rolling
farmlands, where I went to boarding school, was stark. This was quite
literally another world and my brief forays into it during school holidays were always adventures.

The squadron of butterflies released in the pit of my belly at that
first whiff of promise continued to flutter and tingle as we drove from
the airport in soundproofed air-conditioned comfort along the bustling
streets. On the sidewalks, hordes of people moved purposefully, ser-
enaded by the entreaties of shopkeepers. The traffic ebbed and flowed,
honked and hooted in a night awash with the iridescence of multi-
coloured neon. We drove through the cross-harbour tunnel to Hong
Kong Island itself and climbed the steep, twisting roads towards
the residential belt of apartment buildings that ranged along the mid-
levels.

We lived in a new block called Cliffview Mansions, on the 18th
floor. From the glass-wrapped balcony, the breathtaking view of Hong
Kong's downtown district and the harbour rolled away to Lion Rock
on the mainland, rising like a great monolithic guardian. Past Lion
Rock, the border with communist China lay hidden in the folds of the
dark hills.

I opened a sliding window and leaned out against the balustrade.
Despite the jetlag and my tiredness, I had, even then, a sense that
something was about to change.

Several days later, I was alone in the apartment. With my 'O' level
examinations the following term, I had plenty of work to do, but the
drudgery of study was beginning to weigh me down. I needed relief. I
padded across the drawing room towards my father's study. Ordered
rows of books on mahogany shelves covered one wall. I scanned the
titles and authors' names. At school that term, I had devoured the
fiction of A J Cronin: *The Keys to the Kingdom*, *The Spanish Gardener*,
The Judas Tree, *The Citadel*. I had recently read James Clavell's novels:
Tai Pan, *King Rat*, *Noble House* and *Whirlwind*. Leon Uris, whose book
Mila 18 I remember still, was a favourite author of mine. I was looking
for a novel, perhaps another Leon Uris.

The previous weekend, we had taken the company boat to Lantau
Island. A 40-foot cruiser and ostensibly a cross-harbour working boat,
the *Esso Victoria* and her three crew were available to Exxon's senior
executives for recreational use. I loved 'going on the boat', swimming

in protected bays, exploring coves and hidden beaches, making landfall in the dinghy and walking among the rocks or along grassy tracks to remote temples. It was with my recent experience of the sea that my eye lingered on the spine of a book depicting a stormy seascape. The author's name, Francis Chichester, was vaguely familiar and the book's title, *Gipsy Moth Circles the World*, promised adventure and escape. I took the book down, glancing at the cover picture.

During a previous business trip to Burma, my father had bought an unusual chair made from lacquered strips of indigenous hardwood, slung back and mounted on rockers. I ambled across to the rocking chair still examining the picture on the front of the book. A grey and brooding sky, an avalanche of high waves and isolated among them a sailing boat carrying a small triangle of canvas at its bow. A solitary figure was just visible. The scene, this tiny figure dwarfed in the immensity of the ocean, captivated me. I studied that picture for a long time and then opened the book at a photographic section.

The first photograph showed a ketch-rigged yacht heeled over under full sail. A peculiar sensation fizzed through my body. I was looking at the picture but I could *feel* it as well, as if I was there, on the boat, sensing her movement though the water, the wind brushing my skin, the sun's warmth on my back, the tang of salt air in my throat. The rocking movement of my seat enlivened the sensation.

The pictures of Chichester himself held the most fascination for me – washing on deck, making a sail adjustment, taking a sun sight, stitching a sail, bandaging his injured right elbow. These showed a man occupying his own, unique world, away from the push and pull of other people's influences, opinions and actions; a world of his own creation, the ultimate expression of his own force of will.

I turned the pages to the beginning of the first chapter, entitled 'The Dream', and started to read and quite soon the seed of my own dream split from its pod and fell to take root in the fertile soil of my adolescent imagination.

Each day at 5.15 pm, I would walk from the apartment along Conduit Road and then take a narrow pathway cut into the hillside towards the Ladies Recreation Club, a country club set high above the energetic heart of Hong Kong, with floodlit tennis courts, indoor and outdoor pools, squash courts, bars and restaurants. My father usually arrived at the club at around 5.30 pm from his office and together we would go to the indoor pool and spend an hour lapping up and down. But on this particular day, I was oblivious to time,

interrupting my reading only to switch on the desk lamp as afternoon
wore through to evening.

We had dinner, lamb chops, at eight o'clock.

'Where were you?' my father said when I sat down at the table.

'Reading.'

He must have assumed I meant studying.

'I borrowed one of your books,' I said, wanting to share my
discovery. Bowls of peas and mash passed back and forth. 'Gipsy Moth
Circles the World, Francis Chichester's book.' The conversation moved
on to golf and my father's workday and other trivia. How could my
parents not be interested in this? My father must have read the book,
why else was it in his study? I wasn't hungry. Chichester's world, the
world of the endurance adventurer, was clearly one that only a few
could understand. I excused myself from the table, lay on my bed and
continued my travels in this new universe of the lone voyager.

I consumed every word, down to the itemised lists of stores Gipsy
Moth IV had carried outbound from the UK to Sydney, then home-
bound to Plymouth. As dawn cracked the eastern sky, I felt exhausted
and elated. Chichester's story was not simply one of sailing. The
dreaming, the planning and the preparation as much as the execution
brought the whole expedition into the realm of high adventure:
challenge, discovery, exploration, the path to self-knowledge and self-
realisation. That Chichester had originally planned to circumnavigate
by air rather than by sea was pivotal – he had not let circumstances
that had ended his attempt to fly round the earth deflect him from his
goal. That had been in 1931 following a near-fatal crash. He set off on
his round-the-world voyage on Gipsy Moth IV in 1966, 35 years later at
the age of 64. His ability to keep faith with himself inspired me. To sail,
powered by nature's engine, to be in the open wilderness of the
oceans, to be as one with a boat in an endeavour that would strain
every sinew, challenge every concept, expose every weakness, call on
every asset and demand total commitment was to me simply irresistible, the fullest definition of adventure I could imagine. Perhaps it was
my naivety or my adolescence, but it seemed to me entirely reasonable
and necessary that a man (that's how I thought of myself) should find a
way to measure himself completely.

I stood at my bedroom window looking down towards the harbour
in the burgeoning light of a new day. In that private moment I knew
that one day, I too would set out to sail a single-handed circumnavigation of the earth. I was 15 years old.

Like Chichester, more than three decades would pass before I finally stepped aboard my own yacht in pursuit of that dream.

At the end of the holidays, I flew back to boarding school, Stonyhurst College, in England, set among the cool, green hills of Lancashire's rolling farmlands. It was a relief after the hectic bustle of Hong Kong. My mind was a jumble of crammed facts and figures: chemical formulas, mathematical equations, Latin and French vocabulary – in preparation for the upcoming exams. Behind all that jagged knowledge, my dream of sailing around the world played like soft music. I shared a room with three other boys. One of them, Roger, listened as I spoke about my aspiration late into the night.

'Where's it coming from, this thing with the sea?'

I shrugged in the darkness. 'Don't know. It's just there.'

It was the same question my father would ask several times in the years that followed. I could *feel* the reasons, but words failed me when it came to trying to explain them to other people. Perhaps there was some biological predisposition to adventure. My father was born in Bangalore in 1931. At 15, he was dispatched to boarding school in England and did not see his parents again until he was twenty-three. He went to London University to study chemical engineering but bunked out halfway through, took a ship to Kenya and found a job with Standard Vacuum Oil, later to become part of Exxon Mobil. It was certainly a maverick action.

I was born in Nairobi several years later on 1st October 1960. I learned to swim before I could walk. My father had a thick green towelling dressing gown. He would take the belt, tie it round my bulging tummy and 'walk' me round the edge of a pond in the garden, suspending me in the water.

As he climbed the greasy pole of corporate life, my father's job took him to far-flung places. He abhorred the weather in England. I think his choices were an unconscious attempt to reclaim a fractured childhood and re-immerse himself in the colonial lifestyle he had known as a boy.

In 1965, we sailed on a P&O ship to Hong Kong. I remember the ship, the voyage, the thrill of being at sea and the excitement of arrival in a strange and mysterious place. After three years, we upped and moved to Japan, by sea again, this time on a Dutch ship, the *Boissevain*. After living in Yokohama for three years, we moved on to Bangkok, to a large colonial mansion surrounded by high walls and green expanses of lawn in Soi Yen Akart, in the heart of the city. I loved the heat, the promise held in a tropical dawn, the Buddhist temples, the gentle countenance of the people. But mostly, I loved the sea. Exxon owned a beach house on the coast at Pattaya, on the Gulf of Siam, two hours' drive from the city. At 10 years of age, I had started going to boarding school in England, Saint John's Beaumont, a preparatory school near Windsor Castle. To my young eyes, the contrast with the life in Africa and the Far East I had known until then was stunning. I enjoyed boarding, the independence of it, but was always buoyed by the prospect of returning to Bangkok and our weekend trips to Pattaya.

After a second, longer stint in Hong Kong, my parents retired to South Africa while I went to medical school in London for two years, then had a brief sojourn in the military, training with the Parachute Regiment and spending a year at the Military Academy, Sandhurst, before rejoining my studies and emerging eventually as an osteopath. I moved to private practice in Yorkshire, but the idea of crunching people's spines for a living quickly palled. I returned to London. Before long, I had started my own business in food distribution, got married and fathered two children. Despite the accumulating responsibilities of family and business life, my aspiration to sail around the world never waned, but it had been derailed by life.

I was restless, unfulfilled and bored. A question started to recur. Why had I allowed myself to be swept along a path that was clearly the wrong one?

CHAPTER 2

The Pioneers

Louise came into my study. 'What're you doing?' She took a seat in front of the desk.

My laptop was open. I gave a defensive half-shrug. 'Nothing much.' I had been daydreaming: Thailand, 1971. I was 11 years old – my first sailing experience. We had gone down to the beach house at Pattaya for the weekend. From somewhere, my father had acquired a Sailfish. The flat, plywood hull was nine feet long, painted bright red with a square foot well and a slit in the centre to take the daggerboard. A slim mast supported a single sail, and the rudder and short tiller hung from sprockets at the stern.

The small craft did not look particularly seaworthy and I felt myself torn between apprehension and the thrill of taking the boat out on the water. I was surprised because my father had never shown any interest in sailing and I wasn't certain that he knew much about it. Nonetheless, I helped drag the Sailfish across the soft sand.

I looked back towards the house, one of four situated on a small bay called Palm Beach. Rocky spurs at either end of the beach protected the bay. The Sailfish floated off the bottom and I clambered aboard. A tiny electric buzz prickled my skin. While my father held onto the stern of the Sailfish, he explained the basics of sailing and then we were off. At the first practice tack, the Sailfish flipped onto its side and I spilled into the sea. We both swam round to the underside of the upturned hull, stood on the daggerboard and righted the boat. This happened several more times. As we got further from the beach, past the embrace of the bay, my edginess grew. Although I was a competent swimmer, the impenetrable indigo of deep water colluded with my imagination to conjure monsters from the depths. I must have said something because my father lashed me to the mast for safety, confident now in his ability to keep the boat upright. At the next tack, the

Sailfish flipped again, trapping me. Panic buzzed along my sinews and my lungs began to heave involuntarily for breath in the soundlessness of underwater. Suddenly, I was pulled from the water as the Sailfish righted. After that, we sailed the small craft more successfully and eventually found our way back to the beach. By this time, I was cold and afraid. I did not venture out again, preferring to play in the turquoise translucence of the shallows.

The next day, reports reached us that local prawn fishermen had caught a 20-foot great white shark just a little further up the coast.

Louise stood up, reaching across the desk towards a pack of cigarettes. I closed the Word document I'd been working on, a new diary. I'd just written the first entry:

Friday 28th November 2003
Today I have made a decision – to sail a solo circumnavigation along a route never previously achieved, west around Cape Horn and through the Russian Arctic.

This has been a long-held ambition (since 1976). I was 15 years old. I am now 43. It's 'now or never'. I have cash to part-finance the voyage and with my impending separation from Louise, a mind now urging me on.

I have two young sons. To them alone, I am responsible. Such an undertaking, with the inherent dangers of injury or even death, defines the most reckless action a parent could consider. Equally, I have only one lesson to teach my boys: above all else, they must be true to themselves . . . it will be only a short time in the totality of their lives . . .

The purpose that had loitered so restlessly over the years, suppressed and shaped by time and circumstance, had finally asserted itself. The realisation that at last I had made the commitment left me feeling altered. The phantasmal apparition of a dream, beautiful and labyrinthine but no more tangible than wind-blown smoke, was suddenly real.

It was too early to tell Louise. The setting wasn't right. Our house was too full of the memories of a marriage that had foundered, not calamitously or abruptly, but which had ebbed insidiously towards the abyss. My difficulty was not commitment but contentment, and the wellspring of that discontent was my desire to sail alone around the world.

Louise left to pick up the children from school. I sat for a long time listening to the quiet hum of the house. Beyond the windows, lawn spread away towards wooded slopes. A watery sun spilt weak light onto the grass. I went out and wandered among the trees, remembering the summers here, a wide hammock slung between two sturdy trunks, playing with the boys, the air ringing with birdsong and the magical peals of children's laughter, the gentle rustling of the leaf canopy rising high above. Now, in late November, the place was denuded. An Arctic wind blew in from the north. The sunlight dwindled and died. Lights came on in the house casting cosy oblongs of warmth in the darkness. I sat among the fallen leaves watching the moving figures of my wife and sons behind the windows, listening to the muted clanking of pots and pans, the sounds of children, shouted instructions and mild reprimands that carried no teeth. I savoured this moment of comfortable domesticity, a situation I had grown accustomed to but which, like the diminishing view from a speeding train, would soon be lost to me. The course of all our lives would change. My journey had begun.

From the time I stumbled on *Gipsy Moth Circles the World*, I scoured libraries and bookshops for any literature I could find by the pioneering solo circumnavigators and discovered a world of adventure and daring peopled with eccentric misfits, wanderers and romantics, a tapestry woven with tales of bravery, bravado, competitiveness, fear and wonder.

The first circumnavigation of the earth was completed by the surviving crew of the *Victoria*, one of a five-ship Spanish convoy under the command of Ferdinand Magellan, which sailed from Seville on 10th August 1519 in search of a westward route to the Indies.

Ferdinand Magellan was born in the spring of 1480 into the lower Portuguese nobility. By the age of 10 he was a page at court and in 1505 at the age of 25, he sailed to India to install Francisco de Almeida as the Portuguese viceroy. The expedition did not go well. Magellan fell out of favour with Almeida, accused of illegal trading with the Moors. When Magellan returned to Portugal, he was ostracised by the court.

Portuguese explorer Bartolomeu Dias had already rounded Africa's Cape of Good Hope in 1488 and 10 years later, Vasco da Gama discovered the sea route from the Atlantic Ocean to India, arriving in Calicut on 20th May 1498. The Republic of Venice had gained control over much of the trade routes between Europe and Asia. Portugal hoped to use the new sea route to break the Venetian trading monopoly.

Spain and Portugal, the dominant naval powers, had signed the Treaty of Tordesillas on 7th June 1494, to divide the world in two. The dividing line ran through the Atlantic. Spain gained lands to the west. Lands to the east, including Africa and India, went to Portugal. If Spain was to challenge its rival in the lucrative spice trade, sea routes to the west, if they existed at all, needed to be found.

Against this background of political and economic tensions between Spain and Portugal, Ferdinand Magellan offered his services to King Charles V of Spain.

Magellan's small fleet comprised four carracks (three- or four-masted ships): *San Antonio*, *Concepción*, *Victoria* and *Santiago* and the two-masted caravel *Trinidad*. The fleet reached Rio de la Plata on 10th January 1520. Magellan ordered the *Santiago* down the coast on a scouting expedition. She was wrecked in a storm. On 21st October, off Cape Virgenes, Magellan noticed that the waters were salty but penetrated deep inland and concluded that he had found the elusive passage that would lead them to the Spice Islands. Magellan sent two ships ahead, *Concepción* and *San Antonio*, but the *San Antonio* deserted on 20th November and returned to Spain. The three remaining ships reached open water on 27th November 1520. Ferdinand Magellan proclaimed, '*We are about to stand into an ocean where no ship has ever sailed before. May the ocean be always as calm and benevolent as it is today. In this hope I name it the Mar Pacifico.*'

Sailing northeastwards, Magellan reached the Philippines on 16th March 1521. On the morning of 17th April 1521, he was killed on Mactan Island fighting the indigenous forces led by Lapu-Lapu, a local chieftain.

Juan Sebastián Elcano took over command of the expedition. He had 115 men left, too few to man the three remaining ships. Elcano ordered the *Concepción* to be burned to ensure it could not be used against them. The fleet, reduced to *Trinidad* and *Victoria*, fled westward. After reaching the Moluccas (the Spice Islands, now part of modern Indonesia), they traded with the Sultan of Tidore. The two ships, laden with valuable spices, attempted to return to Spain by sailing west but the *Trinidad* began to take on water. The *Victoria*, not large enough to accommodate all the surviving crew, sailed on. Several weeks later, *Trinidad*, by now repaired, attempted to return to Spain via the Pacific route but she was captured by the Portuguese and wrecked in a storm while riding at anchor. The *Victoria* rounded the Cape of Good Hope and arrived in Spain on 6th September 1522. She had sailed 43,400 nautical miles. Only 18 of the original 237 men who started the expedition were on board, including Elcano. These were the first circumnavigators.

More than 350 years after the trailblazing voyage of Magellan's *Victoria*, Joshua Slocum, an American sea captain, made the first single-handed circumnavigation of the earth in a 37-foot sloop-rigged fishing boat named *Spray*. Slocum's father made leather boots for the local fishermen. Joshua worked in the shop but yearned for a life of adventure at sea. He ran away from home at fourteen by hiring himself as a cabin boy and cook on a fishing schooner, but he soon returned home. In 1860, after the death of his mother, Joshua, then 16, left home for good. At Halifax he joined a merchant ship bound for Dublin as an ordinary seaman.

From Dublin, he crossed to Liverpool, joining the British merchant ship *Tangier*, bound for China. During two years as a seaman, Slocum rounded Cape Horn twice, landed at Batavia (now Jakarta) in the Dutch East Indies and visited the Moluccas, Manila, Hong Kong, Saigon, Singapore and San Francisco. Slocum quickly rose through the ranks to become a chief mate on British ships transporting coal and grain between Britain and San Francisco. His first blue-water command, in 1869, was the barque *Washington*, which he took across the Pacific, from San Francisco to Australia and home via Alaska.

Shortly before Christmas 1870, the *Washington* put in to Sydney, Australia. There he married Virginia Albertina Walker on 31st January 1871. Virginia was an American whose New York family had migrated west to California during the 1849 gold rush and eventually continued on, by ship, to settle in Australia. She sailed with Slocum, and, over the next 13 years, bore him seven children at sea.

In Alaska, the *Washington* was wrecked when she dragged her anchor during a gale, ran ashore and broke up. Slocum saved his wife, the crew and most of the cargo, using the ship's open boats. Impressed by Slocum's leadership, the owners of the shipping company gave him command of the *Constitution*, which he sailed to Hawaii and the west coast of Mexico.

His next command was the *Benjamin Aymar*, a merchant vessel in the South Seas trade. The ship's owner, strapped for cash, sold the vessel out from under Slocum, and he and Virginia found themselves stranded in the Philippines. There, in 1874, under a commission from a British architect, Slocum organised native workers to build a 150-ton steamer in the shipyard at Subic Bay.

In payment for the work, he was given the 90-ton schooner *Pato*. He sailed her as a general freight carrier along the west coast of America and in voyages back and forth between San Francisco and Hawaii.

Virginia died in 1884. Two years later Slocum married Henrietta Elliott. In 1887 at the age of 43, Slocum's next command, the 140-foot three-masted barque *Aquidneck,* was wrecked en route to Montevideo. He sold the wreckage, paid off his crew and built the *Liberdade,* a 35-foot junk-rigged boat which he described as a cross between a 'Chinese sampan' and a 'Cape Ann Dorie'. With Henrietta and two of his sons, Slocum sailed the *Liberdade* 5,000 miles to Washington DC. It was then that the idea of sailing around the world took hold. In 1892, a friend, Captain Eben Pierce, offered Slocum a ship, which he said, 'needed some repairs'. Slocum went to Fairhaven, Massachusetts, to find that the 'ship' was a rotting old oyster sloop propped up in a field. He rebuilt the boat and named her *Spray*.

On 24th April 1895 at the age of 51, he set sail on his epic voyage from Boston, Massachusetts.

I had resolved on a voyage around the world . . . a thrilling pulse beat high in me. My step was light on deck in the crisp air. I felt there could be no turning back, and that I was engaging in an adventure the meaning of which I thoroughly understood.

Slocum navigated without a chronometer. Instead, he used the traditional method of dead reckoning for longitude and noon sun sights for latitude. When Slocum arrived in Gibraltar, British naval officers warned him of the dangers from pirates so he sailed back westwards across the Atlantic and through the Magellan Strait to the Pacific Ocean.

Slocum normally sailed *Spray* without touching the helm. Her sloop rig and long keel made her inherently capable of self-steering. More than three years later, on 27th June 1898, he sailed into Newport, Rhode Island, after more than 46,000 miles.

In 1902, Slocum settled on a small farm on Martha's Vineyard in Massachusetts, but he could not adapt to a life on land and was soon sailing *Spray* to ports along the US eastern seaboard during summer and to the West Indies in winter.

On 14th November 1909, at the age of 65, Slocum set sail for the West Indies once more. He had decided on a new adventure – to sail up the River Orinoco. It was to be his last outing. Whether *Spray* collided with a ship or sank following a whale strike remains a mystery. Slocum was never seen again and no wreckage was ever recovered.

The Americans remained at the forefront of single-handed circumnavigations. Harry Pidgeon circumnavigated from 1921 to 1925 and again from 1932 to 1937 aboard *Islander*, both times westwards via the Panama Canal. Edward Miles sailed eastbound via the Suez Canal from 1928 to 1932, breaking his voyage to return to America and build a second boat, *Sturdy II*, after fire destroyed the original. The French also took to long-haul single-handed sailing. From 1923 to 1929, Alain Gerbault in *Firecrest* sailed around the world westwards via the Panama Canal and from 1936 to 1938, his countryman, Captain Louis Bernicot, sailed a route similar to Slocum, westwards via the Magellan Strait.

It was not until the Second World War that an Argentine, Vito Dumas, recorded the next benchmark voyage after Slocum, the first solo voyage to include a rounding of Cape Horn. Dumas was not the first single-handed sailor to double the Horn. Earlier, in 1934, he befriended a young Norwegian, Al Hansen, at the yacht club in Buenos Aires. Hansen was preparing his boat *Mary Jane* for a westward passage around Cape Horn. He set off in April and certainly made it past Cape Horn, but *Mary Jane* was wrecked on the jagged rocks of Chiloé Island off Chile's west coast. Hansen's body was never found.

Vito Dumas was born on 26th September 1900, the son of Italian immigrants. Raised in poverty, Dumas was tough, both as a sportsman and in business, prospering as a cattle farmer and trader. He spent his spare time racing yachts off Brazil and Argentina.

Greatly influenced by Joshua Slocum, Dumas wanted to sail around the world. No single-handed yachtsman had yet incorporated a rounding of Cape Horn. This was to be his great challenge. His route would take him past the other two great capes of the southern hemisphere: Africa's Cape of Good Hope and Australia's Cape Leeuwin. In 1933, Dumas commissioned Manuel Campos to design a yacht for the dangerous voyage ahead. The result was a 32-foot, ketch-rigged wooden

boat with a canoe stem and stern based on the small whaling boats
that plied the Patagonian coast. Dumas named her *Legh II*, the initials
of his mistress.

The Great Depression forced Dumas to abandon plans for the
voyage and with the onset of war, he was forced to sell the boat. By
early 1942, at the age of 42, Vito Dumas was nearly broke but he was
restless and still determined to sail *Legh II* around the world. He
eventually found her in the ownership of the original buyer. Friends
loaned him cash to buy the boat back. Relying on charity to equip
and stock the yacht, Dumas finally set sail on 26th June. He stopped
three times, at Cape Town, Wellington and Valparaiso. The weather
en route was monstrous. During the first stage, a cracked plank
threatened the survival of his boat. He fixed it repeatedly with canvas
and red lead. A deep abscess in his right arm was causing almost
intolerable pain. He was at the point of amputating his arm when he
fainted. When he came to, he found the wound had opened. Pus was
seeping out. He cut out the infection with a knife leaving a hole in his
arm three inches wide. The wound slowly healed. Later during the
voyage, Dumas fell through a hatch, breaking a rib. With Cape Horn
abeam, a massive wave strike flung him across the cabin. He shattered
his nose.

To combat the cold, Dumas stuffed newspaper down his clothes. He
only carried one tool, a screwdriver, and had no radio to avoid accusa-
tions of spying. In the wilderness of the Southern Ocean, he developed
the technique of running before the seas, a ploy that the great Frenchman Bernard Moitessier would later use in the South Pacific. Dumas
suffered malnutrition, the beginnings of scurvy and hallucinations,
mainly because he refused to fish, his fervent belief in the sanctity of
life overriding even his own survival.

Dumas was an engaging character, a painter and musician as well as
a businessman and adventurer; despite having little money when he
arrived in Cape Town, he left a few weeks later on 14th September
with his kitty intact. He spent most of his time on shore in the
company of a wealthy young widow. In Wellington, New Zealand,
the Meadows family took him in and in Valparaiso, the Chilean navy
overhauled *Legh II* at no charge. He arrived home on 7th July 1943 to a
hero's welcome.

The Joshua Slocum Society of America awarded Vito Dumas the
Slocum Prize in 1957. Two years later, in 1959, he received the Cruising
Club of America's Blue Water Medal. He died on 28th March 1965.

Winds and currents are largely consistent in the directions they sweep around the world. The trade winds span a wide band centred on the equator and blow in a generally westwards direction. Further north and south, the prevailing winds are westerlies, blowing from west to east. Circumnavigators using the Panama Canal sailed westwards, moving downwind in the trade wind belt. Even though Joshua Slocum sailed westwards through the Magellan Strait against the prevailing westerlies, he would have been reasonably sheltered in the strait. Once clear of land on the Pacific side of the Magellan Strait, Slocum sailed northwest to hook onto the westwards-moving trade winds. Vito Dumas, sailing at much higher latitudes in the Southern Ocean, had travelled eastwards with the prevailing westerly winds blowing from behind.

After Vito Dumas's triumphant return home in 1943, Americans Alfred Peterson and Bill Murnan and Frenchmen Yves le Toumelin and Jean Gau each circumnavigated, all via the Panama Canal and all downwind, sailing westwards, between 1948 and 1957. The next benchmark voyage would be a westbound circumnavigation via Cape Horn, *against* the prevailing westerly winds.

Marcel Bardiaux was born 10 years after Vito Dumas, in Clermont-Ferrand in the Auvergne region of France on 2nd April 1910. Bardiaux's father was killed days before the end of World War I. Bardiaux, his mother and younger sister moved to Paris. The young Bardiaux was sickly and spent five years in a religious orphanage before going to work to supplement his mother's meagre war pension. Like Joshua Slocum, Bardiaux ran away at 14 and tried to join a ship at Le Havre, but the police returned him to his mother. Working as a joiner, plumber and puppet-maker, Bardiaux found time to make a canoe, which he paddled on the Seine. By the age of 19, he had become the French and European kayak champion.

In 1929, Bardiaux met Alain Gerbault in Paris. Gerbault had just completed his circumnavigation aboard *Firecrest*. It is probable that this meeting with the first Frenchman to sail around the world fired a dream in the young Bardiaux. He served his military conscription in the navy and, as a reservist at the outbreak of war, was interned in Germany. He escaped, evading his captors by hiding in a river using a metal breathing tube.

Back in Paris, Bardiaux came across the plans for a Bermudian sloop designed by Henri Dervin, 30 foot in length, 8′10″ wide and displacing four tons. He must have heard about Vito Dumas's voyage in the

Southern Ocean. That same year, 1943, he started construction of his yacht in a first-floor workshop at Nogent-sur-Marne, cutting and forming the ribs for the boat with lumber scrounged from dumps and assembling them into frames on paper patterns. The wartime scarcity of materials extended the build period to six years. Finally, on 29th July 1949, with the help of friends, he hauled *Les Quatre Vents* through the cobbled streets of Perreux on two truck axles and launched her. After months of fitting out, Bardiaux sailed from Paris on Sunday morning, 1st January 1950, on a voyage that would cover 68,000 nautical miles westwards around Cape Horn, take eight years to complete and make more than 500 port calls en route.

Approaching Cape Horn, *Les Quatre Vents* rolled in heavy seas, destabilised by the weight of ice on deck and in the rigging. Bardiaux finally passed the longitude of Cape Horn at 12.30 pm on Monday 12th May 1952. After anchoring off Hermit Island, he backtracked, passing between Lennox Island and Navarino Island and into the Beagle Channel, eventually arriving at the Chilean naval base in Ushuaia on 16th May.

Like Slocum, Bardiaux sailed northwest in the Pacific to pick up the easterly trade winds. He rounded the Cape of Good Hope into the Atlantic Ocean and sailed to the West Indies and then Bermuda before the final long leg, across the Atlantic to France.

In 1960, Marcel Bardiaux began construction of a second yacht. *Les Quatre Vents* had been a *wet* boat. This time, Bardiaux wanted a boat that would be strong and dry. He decided to build her of stainless steel. It took eight years. He named her *Inox*. Over the next 30 years, Bardiaux sailed 400,000 nautical miles on *Inox*. She ran aground on the northeastern coast of Canada in 1996. Bardiaux spent a year repairing the damage. *Inox* returned to France in 1997. Marcel Bardiaux died on board his boat in February 2000, in the harbour at Redon. He was 89 years old.

When I first read Marcel Bardiaux's story, my pulse quickened. Even more than his amazing circumnavigation, the idea of a stainless steel yacht seemed fantastic. Could I find such a boat? It seemed unlikely, even impossible.

All these sailors were writers. Joshua Slocum penned the classic *Sailing Alone Around the World*. Vito Dumas wrote his story of the first east-about circumnavigation in *Alone Through the Roaring Forties*. Marcel Bardiaux titled the book of his circumnavigation *Aux Quatre*

Vents de l'Aventure. Each story seemed to be a rung in a ladder reaching ever upwards towards greater challenges.

Nineteen men had sailed solo circumnavigations before Francis Chichester set out from Plymouth, England, on 27th August 1966. Chichester set himself a number of challenges. He wanted to record the fastest voyage around the world in a small boat and to do so by way of Cape Horn. He assessed the time taken by the clipper ships from Plymouth to Sydney, Australia, at 100 days – he wanted to beat that time. By planning to make only one stop in Sydney, he would achieve the longest single-handed passage ever made by one man alone at sea and beat the record of 7,400 miles held by Vito Dumas.

When Chichester returned triumphant to a welcoming crowd of 250,000 people at Plymouth on the afternoon of 28th May 1967, he had accomplished all but one of his goals. His voyage to Sydney had taken 107 days, a week longer than the magical 100 days he had sought. I doubted very much that he cared about this. To me, his greatest achievement was in the entirety of the voyage. Chichester had raised the bar and raised it high. By completing his circumnavigation with only one stop, the challenge became obvious. Could one man, alone, sail around the earth without stopping?

Contenders began emerging before Chichester had even made it back to Britain. Eric Tabarly, a French naval officer, had dominated the 1964 transatlantic single-handed race. Chichester had inspired the race four years previously, when he set a wager with four friends to race across the Atlantic westwards from Plymouth's Eddystone Lighthouse to the Ambrose lightship off New York Harbor. The prize was to be half a crown. In preparation for the 1968 race, more than forty sailors registered interest, Tabarly among them. The race, sponsored by the *Observer* newspaper and known internationally by the acronym, OSTAR, had the effect of hauling ocean racing into a new era of hi-tech one-design boats funded by commercial sponsorship deals. Tabarly was building a new boat, a monster 67-foot trimaran. Speculation was already rife that Tabarly, a national hero and winner of the Legion d'Honneur for his 1964 victory, might be considering a solo non-stop circumnavigation in the new boat following the 1968 OSTAR. Success would eclipse Chichester and shift the widening focus on long-range sailing to France.

In Britain, talk spread like wildfire at boating and yacht clubs and in the pages of the sailing press. This centrifuge gradually teased out nine men who would vie for the chance to claim an iconic place in sailing

history. In March 1967, while Chichester was still two months from
home, one such conversation took place at a house in Downe, Kent,
the home of the Knox-Johnstons. Their son, Robin, a 28-year-old
merchant seaman, was on leave before joining his new ship *Kenya* as
first officer. Over breakfast one morning, Robin's father suggested
that a solo, non-stop circumnavigation might be the last great sailing
prize.

Robin Knox-Johnston had joined the British India Steam Navigation
Company after failing the Civil Service Commission's examination for
entry to the Royal Navy. Some years later, while stationed in India, he
saw plans for a sailing boat in a yachting magazine and sent off for
them. The plans that arrived were of another boat entirely, a stubby,
canoe-stern craft based on a Norwegian lifeboat to a 1924 design by
American William Atkin.

Knox-Johnston had the boat built anyway, of Indian teak using
traditional methods and tools. He named her *Suhaili* after the south-
easterly winds that blow in the Gulf of Arabia. *Suhaili* was launched
using a coconut while the artisans who had built her sang ancient
chants to bring her good fortune. With his brother and one other
crew, *Suhaili* sailed from India to South Africa in stages. In November
1967, they took her on an 8,000-mile non-stop voyage from Cape Town
to England, taking 74 days.

Knox-Johnston had one major problem. Was *Suhaili* a suitable boat
for a round-the-world voyage? Ideally, he wanted a steel boat, and a
steel boat of sufficient size would cost in the region of £5,000 – a huge
sum and one far beyond his reach. Despite writing 50 letters, Knox-
Johnston could not attract a sponsor.

With interest gathering, the *Sunday Times* newspaper eventually
stepped in as race sponsor, offering a Golden Globe trophy for the
first to finish and, because competitors would set sail on varying dates,
a £5,000 cash prize for the quickest finisher on elapsed time.

Knox-Johnston tried to convince his employer to sponsor his entry
in the Golden Globe race. They declined. Time was pressing and
money was tight. If he was going to attempt the voyage, he had no
choice but to do so in *Suhaili*. This had its advantages: he knew the
boat inside out, she was tough and she was seaworthy.

Knox-Johnston departed on 14th June 1968. Two other competitors
had already left: John Ridgeway on 1st June and Chay Blyth one week
later on 8th June. Six others followed, with race favourite, the hugely

experienced Frenchman Bernard Moitessier, setting sail on 22nd August.

Of all the lone sailors who shaped my own decision to sail a single-handed circumnavigation, Bernard Moitessier most clearly epitomised the independent free spirit I longed to become. He was not only a sailor, but a writer, thinker and philosopher who had achieved a unity with the sea that provided him with purpose and meaning, where he could exist on a plane that simply did not offer itself in any land-bound life. I too wanted to be in such a place, if only for a short time: a place where I governed myself, where my survival depended absolutely on my own abilities and self-reliance, a place where the only laws were nature's laws. I wanted to be in a place of such immense power and humbling beauty, of tranquillity and isolation as to be the only place where I could fully understand all that I had been, all that I was and all that I might become.

Bernard Moitessier was born in Saigon on 10th April 1925 into an affluent family. His childhood was idyllic and privileged – home was a colonial mansion with wide verandas, sweeping lawns and servants. He was a talented linguist, becoming fluent in Vietnamese and Thai, and learned to sail with the local fishermen. The cultural influence of the Orient, with its emphasis on holism and a reverence for nature, made a deep and abiding impression on Moitessier, but set up an inner conflict with the rigidity and bureaucracy of French colonialism. During the Japanese occupation of World War II, he was imprisoned. Later, he was drafted to fight the Viet Minh in a brutal war against which he instinctively rebelled. His father wanted him to take over the family import business, but he refused, escaping to sea in a junk, *Marie-Thérèse I*. She was wrecked on Diego Garcia. A British corvette took him to Mauritius He built a second boat, *Marie-Thérèse II*, and sailed her to the Caribbean via Durban, where he met Marcel Bardiaux in 1953. In the West Indies he suffered a second shipwreck. Broke, Moitessier returned to France. He wrote the first of his five books, *Un Vagabond des Mers du Sud*. He was a student of the solo sailing pioneers and had read books by Slocum, Pidgeon, Bernicot, Gerbault and Dumas.

His own book caught the attention of a well-known naval architect, Jean Knocker, who approached Bernard with a plan to design a new boat. Hearing of the plan, Jean Fracaul, owner of a metal-working firm and a sailor himself, offered to build the new boat for just the cost of the materials. The result was a 39-foot ketch, which Moitessier named *Joshua* in honour of Joshua Slocum.

Moitessier's first passage around Cape Horn from west to east came in 1965. He was sailing with his wife, Françoise, from Moorea in the South Pacific to Gibraltar. In mighty seas, Moitessier streamed warps astern to slow *Joshua* and to try to hold her stern to the waves. The danger of the boat capsizing or pitchpoling (somersaulting) was very real. *Joshua*, he realised, was a trade wind boat, out of place in these high southern latitudes. Exhausted after hours at the helm, Moitessier suddenly recalled reading of Vito Dumas's technique for running before the seas. He shouted down to Françoise to find *Alone Through the Roaring Forties* and locate the relevant passage. She did and read aloud to him. Dumas had carried sail to generate boat speed downwind, angling the stern of *Legh II* 15° to 20° to the approaching combers. Moitessier tried the technique. *Joshua* responded beautifully, heeling over as the waves swept beneath her hull. He immediately cut the warps streaming astern and *Joshua* settled.

After Moitessier's departure on the Golden Globe race, the final entrant to leave was Donald Crowhurst, sailing on 31st October within hours of the *Sunday Times* deadline. The two men could not have been more different. Against Moitessier's experience and instinctive feel for the sea, Crowhurst was a relative novice with little grasp of the realities of single-handed ocean sailing. He hoped that his participation in the Golden Globe race would bring fame and money and with that, his failing business at home would be saved. It was a desperate gamble that would end in tragedy.

After his departure on the Golden Globe, Knox-Johnston found trouble early. Close to the Canary Islands, *Suhaili*'s keel had worked loose. The remedy required Knox-Johnston to go over the side and caulk between the planks – difficult enough underwater without breathing equipment, more so with the boat bobbing about but, with a predatory shark circling in the depths, the job took on a huge element of danger.

Later, the gooseneck attaching the boom to the mainmast smashed and he had to fashion a rope-binding to hold the rig together. He lost use of his radio so no one at home knew where he was or even if he was safe until a sighting off the coast of New Zealand set everyone's mind at ease. With Cape Horn still to come and Bernard Moitessier closing the gap in *Joshua*, Knox-Johnston had it all to do, but his lead over Moitessier was still substantial.

After rounding Cape Horn for the second time, the Frenchman decided to abandon the race and continue east. His reasons for doing this will remain forever secret. Perhaps the ignominy of coming second to Knox-Johnston was too much. Perhaps the contrary pull of yin and yang that had made him restless throughout his adult life led him away from prostituting himself on the altar of fame and adulation. Perhaps Moitessier was simply uncomfortable with the idea of seeing the purity of the environment he loved reduced and diminished by a race that held at its heart, in his opinion, nothing more than the licentious greed of newspapers. Whatever his reasoning, it was un-doubtedly complex. Some claim that Moitessier made the first single-handed non-stop circumnavigation because he crossed his outward track first but it was Knox-Johnston who arrived home first, crossing the finish line at Falmouth at 3:25 pm on 22nd April 1969 after 313 days at sea, the only competitor of the nine starters to finish. In so doing, he became as iconic a seaman as his own heroes, Frobisher and Drake, before him.

Donald Crowhurst sailed out into the Atlantic and proceeded to radio in false reports suggesting his outstanding progress. Many com-mentators believed him to be a serious contender for the £5,000 prize money on offer. Sir Francis Chichester, sitting on the judging panel, had his doubts. Crowhurst never left the Atlantic. At some point, de-feated by a conscience unable to accommodate the lies, Crowhurst stepped off his trimaran, *Teignmouth Electron*, and into oblivion. A British ship, *Picardy*, spotted the abandoned yacht on the morning of 10th July 1969. Crowhurst had made his final entry in the logbook two weeks earlier on 23rd June.

Knox-Johnston donated his prize money to Crowhurst's widow.

Nigel Tetley, a Royal Navy officer and one of Knox-Johnston's fellow competitors, almost made it. His trimaran, *Victress*, similar to Crowhurst's *Teignmouth Electron*, broke up and sank in the North Atlantic on 21st May 1969, barely 1,000 miles from England. Despite plans to sail another solo circumnavigation and attain the closure that had so narrowly eluded him, Nigel Tetley hanged himself in February 1972.

In my opinion, Robin Knox-Johnston's feat during the Golden Globe is without peer in single-handed sailing and perhaps the tragedy that befell others bears testament to the true test of a solo circumnavigation – one as much about mental resilience and spiritual strength as of seamanship.

★

I first met Sir Robin Knox-Johnston at the London Boat Show in January 1999. His company, Clipper Ventures, organised a round-the-world race to be sailed in identical 67-foot sloop-rigged monohulls. I joined up for the 2000 race, sailing the trans-Atlantic leg from the United Kingdom to Havana via Vilamoura on the south coast of Portugal. It was an opportunity to get blue-water experience without finding, preparing and equipping a boat myself.

Knox-Johnston struck me initially as gruff and acerbic, but I quickly put these traits down to an inherent shyness and he must have been aware that I, like so many others drawn to the sea and sailing, held a view of him similar to that of a penitent genuflecting at the altar of an altogether higher being. Although this was a position he might only reluctantly relinquish, it must have been awkward for him at times. I had learnt from my reading over the years that the great adventurers of rock and water shared several common characteristics, notably a bent towards introversion and a self-effacing demeanour. Outwardly, these behaviours masked a deeply rooted stubbornness, a utilitarian approach to problem solving, an over-reaching determination to achieve a goal once set and a desire for solitude that might strike most people as unusual, if not odd. The manifestation of this complex ran a high risk of misinterpretation.

Rather than engage Sir Robin in protracted conversation, I chose instead to observe and learn.

Louise and Benji, who was not yet two, flew out to Vilamoura to meet the boat. We had finished last in the fleet of eight. Morale on board was low. At the re-victualling stage, shore crews piled boat provisions on the dockside, similar piles for each boat. We found that our pile had been raided and our cheese taken by another crew. Louise decided to take the matter up with Sir Robin.

'It's not my problem,' Sir Robin said, enjoying the confrontation with the wife of one of the crew but keen not to let the matter escalate too far.

'You can't allow *Liverpool* to go to sea without cheese!'

'*Liverpool*'s crew is responsible for their provisions and it's up to them to get their act together.'

Louise blanched. 'That's unacceptable! You're not seriously suggesting that my husband and the rest of *Liverpool*'s crew sail across the Atlantic Ocean without any cheese, are you?'

Sir Robin was at a loss for words, visibly taken aback.

'You're in charge here, Sir Robin, and you need to sort this out.'

Sir Robin slowly shook his head, arms crossed. '*Liverpool*'s crew will have to deal with it.'

With that, Sir Robin ambled off and I joined Louise on the dockside. I felt a confusing mix of embarrassment and pride at Louise. Did she not know who he was, what he had done? Did she have any idea at all?

'Are you nuts?' I said to her.

'You're not going to sea without cheese. Come with me.'

Louise marched into town. She found a delicatessen and bought a huge block of Cheddar weighing several kilos. I lugged it back to the boat. Everyone on board cheered. When she spotted Sir Robin, she went over. 'Here,' she said presenting the bill. 'You have to pay this.'

Sir Robin looked at the bill, then at Louise. He seemed to gauge her then nodded sagely. He handed the bill back. 'Send it to the office. They'll settle up with you.'

So we went to sea with our cheese (and Sir Robin reimbursed Louise).

During the second phase of the Atlantic crossing, Vilamoura to Havana, we passed through one truly horrific storm. The anemometer showed wind speeds exceeding 100 mph as we joined with the storm, passing between two enormous pillars of cloud that seemed to touch the surface of the sea and spiral upwards to the heavens. The sea became a maddened confusion of broken water. I was on watch at the helm. I drove that boat for six hours, sailing directly through the eye signalled by a ring of blue sky far above. I came off watch shaking with exhaustion and fear.

The Atlantic crossing had taken six weeks, slowed by several periods of calms that lasted for days. Twice squalls overtook the boat with winds accelerating from 10 knots to 50 knots in a matter of seconds, shredding spinnakers both times. Calms can be the hardest tests. Frustration builds, tempers fray, with hours spent making minute adjustments to the sails to tease out a few precious metres.

Perhaps the most valuable knowledge I gained was not to do with sailing but with myself. I did not enjoy long-haul sailing with other people. Being in a confined space under a degree of pressure starts to peel away the rind of conformity. Soon, psychological debris litters every nook and cranny on board. I tranquillised myself by finding some quiet part of the deck, sitting so that I could not see anyone else and pressing my hands over my ears to block their noise. In that cocoon, I imagined myself alone. Whenever I practised, my spirits soared.

Chay Blyth retired from the Golden Globe race, his borrowed boat unequal to the task of sailing the Southern Ocean. A former para-trooper, Blyth had rowed the Atlantic in 1966 with fellow soldier John Ridgeway. Although Chay Blyth had never sailed before, Ridge-way's entry in the Golden Globe had convinced him he could do it too.

Hugely competitive, Blyth watched Knox-Johnston sail home to glory. In the aftermath of the Golden Globe race, he toyed with dif-ferent ideas for a grand adventure. One was to kayak up the Amazon. Another was to sail alone around the world *westwards*. That meant not only tackling Cape Horn but doing so *uphill*, against the prevailing winds and currents that drive the Southern Ocean eastwards around Cape Horn from the Pacific side to the Atlantic side. Sir Francis Chichester told him he was crazy.

Chay Blyth has never made any pretence about enjoying sailing. Every bit as tough as Moitessier, his motivations were very different: his instincts were commercially driven. He wanted to establish himself and he decided on the long voyage, persuading the British Steel Cor-poration to sponsor a new 59-foot ketch-rigged yacht.

Blyth sailed from the River Hamble on *British Steel* on 18th October 1970. At Cape Horn, ferocious storms beat him back. Summoning all his resilience, he made it round. Even worse conditions awaited him further west while he was still deep in the Southern Ocean approach-ing the Cape of Good Hope. He returned to England on 6th August 1971, tying up at the Royal Southern Yacht Club after 292 days alone at sea. Whatever his motivations, Chay Blyth achieved one of the great pioneering single-handed circumnavigations.

From the time of Slocum's boat *Spray*, the tracks of yachts carrying single-handed sailors now criss-crossed the earth. Those tracks, includ-ing the Vendée Globe racers, were west–east or east–west. I wanted to challenge myself as Chichester had done, to feel as Moitessier had done, to hone my seamanship skills as Knox-Johnston had done and to push at the boundaries as Chay Blyth had done. I also wanted a true adventure. To my mind, true adventure requires a unique aspect, something that's never been done. No one had sailed a north–south route around the polar regions. To my knowledge, no one had even attempted a *vertical* circumnavigation.

So that's what I'd decided I was going to do.

CHAPTER 3

Reckless Endeavour

I had sufficient money to make the voyage but not enough to minimise the risks. To go with the best boat for the job and a decent rescue plan, I needed to raise funds. My personal network was too narrow to rely solely on individual contributions. To draw sponsors, the project had to promise and deliver a value outcome and that meant television.

Most of my time was spent researching the best way forward, worst-case scenarios, sponsor target groups, timetabling and scheduling. It was a massive undertaking. Everything became a jumble in my mind, getting the boys settled in their new home with Louise when we sold the house, starting Benji at his new school, Ashfold, where he was due to begin the following month and, added to that, I had to think about finding somewhere to live – should I buy or rent?

Who would manage the shore-side operation? I would need someone to manage a website during the voyage, handle the media (if the media took an interest in what I was doing), but more crucially, get spare parts out to distant ports if I had to stop for repairs. I began work on a sponsorship strategy and to consolidate the project on paper – film people would want to see some kind of proposal. I had a mountain to climb and with each passing hour, the summit receded further into the distance.

I stepped up my physical training programme and on Wednesday 17th December 2003, went out cycling on a punishing two-hour circuit. By evening, I was dog-tired. That night I dreamed so vividly that I later recalled every detail.

I was walking along a dim country lane (in England) when suddenly an enormous male lion appeared in front of me. I felt afraid, but continued to walk towards the lion, skirting past him and then running up the lane and over the brow of the hill. Suddenly, I found myself in a field. Sensing the lion approaching from the rear, I sprinted across the field and leapt a fence topped with barbed wire. A lioness materialised on the opposite side of the fence. I walked towards her, removed a shoe and hit the lioness on the nose. She retreated. The male lion ambled up to the fence. I tried the same trick with him but he backed away annoyed. The dream ended with me astride the male lion, clutching a handful of his tawny mane.

I searched through a book of dream interpretations. To dream of a lion indicated a great driving force, which I took to mean my desire to achieve a circumnavigation. The interpretation went on to suggest that if I tamed the lion (presumably my riding on the lion's back) then the quest would be successful. I took encouragement from this early and positive portent.

The dismal round of 'Thank you but no thank you' began just before Christmas. I knew it would be all too easy to allow despondency a foot in the door. I submitted a documentary proposal to the BBC and received a prompt reply – they thought this an exceptional expedition but could not find room in the schedule (two years down the line!) to accommodate a documentary.

Of the eight independent production companies I had shortlisted, several went to second stage but these positive initial responses ultimately marinated into rejections.

I trawled the internet for boats. Like Knox-Johnston, a scarcity of money and time precluded a new-build boat, but there were good boats about and I found one lying in Gibraltar, a French-designed Trireme 38. Without sponsorship, the £75,000 price tag was above my budget.

Into my clogged agenda, I had to find time to gain the Royal Yachting Association's practical Yachtmaster's ticket as a refresher and to cover subjects such as diesel-engine maintenance, which until now, I had not needed to know. If I could study for the Yachtmaster exam with a decent instructor, might the instructor agree to act as shore support? I checked out RYA instructors and found a one-man band called Charlie Sailing on the south coast. Charlie Tait and his wife had completed a three-year circumnavigation and he was an advocate of steel boats.

A lot of email communication passed between Boatshed, the brokers in Gibraltar selling the Trireme, and myself. The broker suggested an opening offer of £65,000, but it was too early to commit

money. I wanted to see the specification sheets and then I'd think
about getting over to Gibraltar to look at the boat.

After Benji started at Ashfold, I decided it was time to tell Louise.
Louise was actively looking for a house to buy and I was beginning to
have difficulty keeping the project contained.

Louise and I first met in London in April 1996. I was running my
own company, Flanagan's Supermarket Direct, an early foray into the
grocery home shopping market that was to explode with the dotcom
boom of the late 1990s. Louise worked for a local magazine. She visited
our south London offices to discuss advertising ideas. On 11th June, we
went on our first date and on 18th October the following year we were
married in Oxfordshire. It was a difficult time. Although the company
was working in association with a major British supermarket group,
persuading shoppers to change their buying habits to remote ordering
was proving difficult. The company was losing money.

Deceit among my fellow directors in a boardroom awash with
arrogance and avarice led quickly to hostility and recrimination. Six
months after my wedding, I left the company I had built and took a job
as director of business development at the British College of Osteo-
pathic Medicine, from where I had graduated in 1988, but my residual
anger at what had happened at Supermarket Direct continued to
simmer. It was shortly after this unhappy episode that I dislocated my
right shoulder and went into hospital for remedial surgery. I con-
tracted the superbug, MRSA. During two months of convalescence at
home, I began writing a novel, *Cobra*. I also thought about gaining
blue-water experience and investigated Sir Robin Knox-Johnston's
Clipper Ventures.

My ambition of sailing a circumnavigation was not new to Louise –
much of our conversation during dinner on that first date centred on
the plans each of us had. At the time, she had listened. Over a year
later, she confessed that she had dismissed what I'd said as a fantasy
that would be dissolved quickly by marriage and children. Soon after
my recovery from the MRSA infection, Louise gave birth to Benjamin.

The Fox and Hounds was a cosy pub set high in the Chiltern Hills.
'What's the occasion?' Louise asked, sipping at a glass of wine.

'Several things – getting divorced.' The words came out wrong, sounding glib. My mind was elsewhere.

Louise clinked her glass against mine. She knew what I meant – a toast to getting divorced without rancour.

'And?' she questioned, setting her glass down.

'And what?'

'Several things, you said.'

The food arrived. After the waitress had journeyed back and forth to our table ferrying salt, pepper, mayonnaise and a refill for my empty beer glass, I launched my offensive.

'I'm going to do it – the circumnavigation. I don't have a boat yet, but I've found some possibles. I may fly out to Gibraltar to have a look at one. I've been in touch with documentary makers and there's some interest.'

Louise laid down her knife and fork. She looked at me for a long moment. 'You're crazy!'

'Maybe. But I'm going to do it anyway.'

'You're absolutely out of your bloody mind!'

'How's your food?'

'What about me, the children, school fees, have you thought about any of that?'

'I've thought about all of that, yes.'

'It's completely bloody selfish and irresponsible.'

Irresponsible. The same word Knox-Johnston's mother had used in 1969 about her son. His voyage had teleported him into a world of wealth, glory and fame. The queen had knighted him. His five-year-old daughter seemed to have survived unscathed and he remarried the woman who had divorced him. I wasn't after material gain. I simply wanted to feed a hunger that would not go away.

I nodded. Sipped beer. 'You're right,' I said.

'But you don't care?'

'Of course I care.'

'You could bloody well die!'

'I could get hit by a bus crossing the road tomorrow.'

'And how are you going to pay for it?'

'Film, sponsorship.'

'And if none of that materialises?'

I had sold my London apartment. The proceeds would buy the boat. I wasn't yet sure about the rest of the costs, but my belief was unshakeable.

'I'll find a way,' I said. It was lame, but also the truth. 'If I am meant to do this, it will happen.'

I felt a little foolish. I had constructed a budget and I was some way short of the required funding.

'Look, none of this should come as much of a surprise,' I said.

'I thought the Clipper thing had got this out of your system.'

'It didn't.'

Louise was eating mechanically. I poured her more wine to take the edge off. She was shaking her head. 'You don't know anything about sailing, well okay, a bit, but you don't have the experience to do this.'

Now, on this point, she was right. I had never sailed single-handed but single-handed sea trials constituted part of my preparation plan. How did I explain that it was about feel, the assessment of my skills, the ability to develop? People had stood at the summit of Mount Everest without ever having seen snow.

'I told you about this before we got married, before we had the children.' Our second son, Gabriel, had arrived two years before on 18th October, our fourth wedding anniversary.

'Well, you should have done it then, before they were born, or do it later, after they've been through school.'

'I wanted to, remember?'

'I didn't believe you. I thought it was all pie in the sky.'

'Just because you thought that doesn't mean to say it was. It isn't – and if I leave it till after the boys are through school, I'll be too old.'

'Chichester's your big hero . . .'

'So?'

'He was in his sixties, right?'

'I can't wait that long.'

We talked around the subject through the rest of dinner, the best part of two hours.

To her eternal credit, Louise finally said, 'If you have to do this, then okay. If you really have to, then I'll support you as best I can.'

I smiled, as much to hide my guilt as to show relief.

'There is one condition,' Louise said.

My smile vanished. 'Only one?'

'I'm being serious.'

'Shoot.'

Louise's eyes filled with tears. She blinked away the excess. 'You have to promise.'

'Okay.'

'I mean it.'

'Okay, I promise.'

'You wear a lifejacket with a safety harness. Whenever you're on deck you wear a bloody lifejacket and make sure you're strapped on!'

I grab at the boat, kicking to raise my body out of the water. By some miracle, the shock cord securing the spray dodger to the guardrail has slipped beneath the middle finger of my right hand. It's a thin line, 4 mm diameter. The forward momentum of the boat quickly takes up the slack in my arm, tugging through my shoulder joint, hauling me through the water. The cord tensions. How long will it hold? Come to that, how long will my shoulder hold? The drag is twisting my body round so that I am facing backwards, my arm stretched up and out behind. The dislocation and surgery have left my right shoulder weakened. Either the shock cord or my shoulder is going to fail. No question. It is a matter of when and which will go first. Either way, it will be the end. I try pulling myself towards *Barrabas*, crooking my arm at the elbow to save the strain through the shoulder. The lactic acid burn comes quickly. It's no good. I have to straighten my arm and I feel the shoulder beginning to rip.

I am now level with the transom. Two brackets protrude beyond the edge of the aft deck. These brackets are designed to take the bridle lines for the drogue and capable of withstanding many tons of tensile force. If I can reach the starboard bracket, I would have a secure hold.

I lunge for the bracket, bringing my left arm out of the water. Kicking is hard and ineffectual in my waterlogged boots. I miss the bracket by the width of a hand. The effort yanks at my shoulder. It is going. At best, I have one more attempt. The shoulder will not tolerate any more. I am becoming exhausted, strength flowing out of my body. Before I went to Sandhurst, I attended an officer selection course at Browning Barracks, headquarters of the Parachute Regiment. I trained for three months. The physical testing was hard, very hard, but nothing like this. I repeat the manoeuvre, giving it everything I have. My fingertips brush past the bracket. Now I have nothing left. Cold is beginning to bite. My shoulder will fail at any moment. The shock cord has frayed, its outer sheath ruptured. A few rubber bands are all that are holding me.

Then I see the lanyard trailing through the water behind the Hydro-vane rudder. I can scarcely believe it – a lifeline! I stretch towards it with my left hand and close my fingers tightly round it. Then I release my tenuous, one-fingered grip on the shock cord. Pressure through my right shoulder evaporates. I actually laugh at the relief, swept aft of *Barrabas*, bodysurfing behind her. My right hand finds the lanyard. Now I have a two-handed grip.

Barrabas slows momentarily and I move past her transom, my body twisting round so that I am facing backwards once more. Quite suddenly, quite mysteriously, I feel a pressure against the back of my thighs, my buttocks, the small of my back. It is shaped and solid like an armchair. I lose all sense of where I am relative to the boat, or of my predicament. I begin to travel backwards or perhaps the boat has built speed and is simply going past me. My mind scrambles. I am unable to assimilate what is happening. Clear of the transom, I slide sideways on this cushion of water, around the self-steering assembly towards the port side. I have been gathered up by another wave. Air trapped in my oilskins may be giving me added buoyancy. In an instant and with infinite gentleness, I come to rest, sitting on the sugar scoop while *Barrabas* bucks and lolls and surges on the angry sea.

I sit there disbelieving, uncomprehending, shivering.

Delivered.

CHAPTER 4

What if . . .

The broker in Gibraltar sent the specifications of the Trireme. She was robust and well equipped. Her underwater profile was near ideal, ticking many of the boxes on my wishlist. Her deep 'V' bow would be an effective wave-cutter. The fin keel lowered the centre of gravity, aiding stability and sea-keeping qualities. A skeg-mounted rudder added strength and protected the prop. The main disadvantage was the short keel. The boat would struggle to make a decent tacking angle going upwind. Topside, her decks were flush to the hull, allowing breaking water to spill off quickly. The low-profile coach-house minimised windage and a centre cockpit allowed quick access to all points on deck and greater security in big weather. At 38 feet, she was manageable single-handed but still had sufficient waterline length to produce decent speed (the longer the waterline length, the faster the hull speed). Constructed entirely of mild steel save for the aluminium rig, the Trireme 38 was near perfect. She lacked a cuddy to protect the helm, solar panels, a wind generator and support bars around the base of the mast, but I could add these.

Should I commit personal funds ahead of winning any sponsorship or go ahead with financial commitments and work to secure sponsorship funding later? I decided to go to Gibraltar and have a look at the Trireme. I booked a flight for 8th March 2004, then emailed the spec sheets to Charlie Tait and asked for his opinion.

I bought a copy of David Lewis's book, *Ice Bird*. A New Zealander by birth and medical doctor by training but a restless spirit by nature, David Lewis was the first to solo to Antarctica and his boat was steel, 1/8th inch plate all round. It was interesting reading given that I would inevitably encounter pack-ice conditions in the Arctic, along Russia's Northern Sea Route. In his book, Lewis also raised the question that everyone asks themselves at some point in their lives, *'What if?'*

In 2002, Louise and I considered the possibility of emigrating to New Zealand, principally to secure a better quality of life for the children. In January 2003, we flew to Auckland. The two weeks we spent there were among the happiest we had together and we returned to England resolved to take things further. Medicals were conducted, applications filled, supporting evidence compiled. In August, the New Zealand government approved our application. If Louise was prepared to give it a go, then I would sacrifice my aspirations for a circumnavigation – a small price to keep my family together. In the end, Louise didn't feel that we were strong enough together to survive the move. We abandoned the plan and decided instead on divorce. During the time we were in Auckland, David Lewis died.

One evening in late March 2004, Louise said, 'I've been thinking about your sailing.' Her eyes were downcast. 'It's very irresponsible.'

'I know it is; at least I can appreciate that argument.'

'What am I going to do?'

We had come quickly to the crux. 'Listen, it's still some time away. I'm not going to be here one minute and gone the next.'

She seemed sad, lost almost.

'I want to read you something.' I fetched *Ice Bird* and found the page I wanted, explaining who David Lewis was. I waited a short beat so I had her full attention and began to read. ' ". . . there is a compulsion to question and explore and to refuse to be satisfied with accepted explanations or assumed limitations placed upon endeavour. The imperative is present in individual men and women – in varying degrees, of course. The chosen or cursed ones are devil-driven; the call comes to them and they must answer." '

I looked at her for some reaction, but Louise stared at me for some sort of explanation.

'I guess I'm cursed,' I said. 'The truth is I've got no choice. What's the alternative? Every day to be regretting that I didn't fulfil myself in the way I need to, so that I can live in the moment and not always in some other time, unable to focus on the task at hand, be it job, children or whatever, and doomed to living with the misery of failure.'

'What failure? You can get a job.'

'I've got a job.'

'I mean a long-term job.'

'Listen, I don't really expect you to understand because it's not the kind of thing you aspire to. You can't feel it. It's a bit like men and pregnancy. We can't feel it. We can imagine it perhaps, but it's not the same thing.'

'That's a stupid analogy.'

'Maybe, but you get the point. Look, if I'm hard about it, the divorce is your choice. If that's what you want, you have to take the consequences. You have to adjust to a new life on your own. It's nerve-racking for you, but it's temporary. The thing here is the children.'

'I know. That's what I'm talking about.'

'When they are men, I'll ask them what they would have had me do. I'm confident now of what their answers will be. So I'm going to go.'

'And if you don't go?'

'Then I'll spend the rest of my life asking myself the same question over and over and never finding the answer.'

'What question?'

'*What if . . .*'

Le Breuil-en-Auge is a sleepy Normandy village with a strip of tarmac running through it linking Deauville and Lisieux. From the village, a thin road meanders up the hillside among the trees like a frozen stream and tops out into open farmland. At the apex of the hill, a driveway curves through flat lawn fringed with high hedgerows to a picturesque house of classic Normandy design – native *colombage* of exposed timber frames in-filled with brick and whitewashed plaster sitting on a plinth of local stone and set beneath a steeply pitched slate roof.

We visited as often as we could, not for the place but to see Christian and Tracey Foures and their two sons, Alexandre and Louis, who spent weekends recharging here after their busy work and school week in Paris.

It all started in 1998, six months after Louise and I were married. Our honeymoon had been a disaster. We'd opted for a European road trip. With the implosion of my position at the company and suffering a ragged combination of stress, depression and upset, Louise decided we needed to regroup. We flew to the Maldives. At Mahé Airport, an attendant from the hotel led us and two other couples to a small quay nearby where a pristine launch waited, its twin diesels humming in the gathering heat of morning. To escape the exhaust fumes, we climbed to the flying bridge while the other passengers headed for the cabin.

Several minutes later, a head popped up sporting a thatch of unruly hair, wrap-round shades and a wide grin. A slender, arrestingly attractive woman followed him. The man made a comment in French and Louise, a fluent French speaker, struck up a conversation with him. The Frenchman introduced himself as Christian. His wife Tracey was English. We became friends immediately during the forty-minute transfer to Kuda Huraa, a fourteen-acre island of tropical splendour.

Our weekends in Normandy were to become a highlight of our lives in the ensuing years and we quickly fell into a practised routine centred on culinary extravaganzas. Most notable were the Plateaux des Fruits de Mer sourced from the Saturday market in Deauville and lavished with Tracey's homemade mayonnaise.

On this cold February evening, Christian and Tracey's welcome was as warm as the log fire roaring in the grate.

With the children exhausted with excitement and asleep upstairs, Christian slung a giant rib-cut of beef onto a wire tray to cook over the open fire. The wine was uncorked and Les Rosbifs and Les Grenouilles settled in for the evening.

With Christian's English halting at best and my French close to non-existent, Louise and Tracey switched easily between languages as double-act interpreters. As the story of my intended voyage unfolded, Christian was at once incredulous, awestruck, envious and delighted. He insisted on breaking open the champagne.

'C'est magnifique,' Christian kept exclaiming, endlessly refilling my glass. Together, the four of us slid inevitably and inexorably towards comfortable drunkenness in a way that is only possible with friends who are deeply loved and implicitly trusted.

The weekend was just what I needed to take my mind off the project and get away from the mounting stresses of getting divorced, moving house, ensuring the welfare of the children as best we could, buying a boat and committing myself to a venture that seemed increasingly improbable.

Three days later, we said our farewells to Christian and Tracey. It would be the last time I saw them.

I picked up the phone at the third ring.

'Charlie Tait here.'

'You get the spec?'

'Yep. Solid boat. Good blue-water hull. Well equipped.'

I liked his economy. 'What about the price?'

A slight hesitation. 'Bit on the high side is my opinion.'

I nodded. 'That was my feeling.'

'Got anything else?'

I had been continuing my searches. 'Ever heard of Reinke?'

Charlie grunted.

'Reinke Super 10, 37 feet, based in Devon, launched 1985.'

'Bit old.'

'My thoughts too.' I thanked Charlie and rang off. The Reinke looked good on the surface, mainly because her price tag was less than £40,000. However, Charlie was right. She was pushing twenty years of age and she had an aft cockpit. Ideally, I wanted a centre cockpit, like the Trireme.

Louise had been busy house-hunting and found a suitable property in her preferred village of Chearsley, across the Vale of Aylesbury from our house. She burst into my office clutching a wad of interior design magazines.

'I got this for you.' She handed me a copy of *Yachting World*. I took it, thanked her and thumbed through the glossy pages. We talked houses for 10 minutes. I had recently decided on a new-build complex – no chain, ease of purchase, nothing needing fixing. 'Your place is too far from me,' Louise said.

'Twenty minutes?'

'You can do better.'

'Okay, you find a better one, I'll have a look.'

'I have,' she said, standing. 'Let's go.'

We drove to Ludgershall, a 'horseshoe' village and supposedly one of the best examples of its type in the country. The house was semi-detached, three bedrooms, five minutes to school, ten from Chearsley. The sellers were planning to emigrate to Portugal. Whichever house I went for, it was only going to be a base while I planned the voyage, trained for it and then actually sailed around the world. I put in an offer and by six o'clock that evening the deal was agreed.

The *Yachting World* magazine was a £2.50 gift, but the gesture was far more telling and infinitely more valuable. It demonstrated a measure of acceptance on Louise's part. For that I was grateful.

The whole problem of some kind of shore-support operation had been occupying much of my thoughts. In *Yachting World*, I saw a two-page spread advertising the United Kingdom Sailing Academy in Cowes on the Isle of Wight, offering a variety of courses. The professional skipper training caught my attention. Seventeen weeks' duration and fully residential, the course was expensive but offered everything I needed to cover from time on the water to re-familiarisation with radio procedure, diesel engine maintenance, electrics, navigation – a consolidation of my disparate experiences, an extension of that knowledge and the possibility that I might persuade them to provide my shore base. Shirley Robertson had run her 2000 Olympic campaign from there and gone on to win gold in the Europe class.

I discussed the option with Louise after the boys were in bed. She still bristled every time I brought up the sailing, but I had a longer-term strategy. What if Louise acted as my shore support? This was more wild fantasy than realistic possibility, but Louise could bring so much to the project, an outlet for her outstanding organisational abilities (which I'd witnessed that very afternoon) and her previous public relations experience and, the children, by extension, would be more closely involved. There were downsides. Louise had no experience of sailing. She had never managed a project like this and more immediately, her inclination towards the venture and me was likely to become hostile if I pushed too hard. I tried to dismiss the idea. She would *never* agree to it.

I didn't fly out to Gibraltar. By March 16th, I had made two firm decisions. First, the Trireme was too expensive and though I might eventually raise sufficient sponsorship to stretch my boat budget, I didn't want to overspend at this stage. Second, I would attend the UKSA in October.

The day I had been dreading crept slowly out of the future until one day, I woke up and it had arrived: Wednesday 7th April – moving day, the end of my marriage and the break-up of the family. It was a tragic day for little Benji and Gabriel. I hoped more than anything that Louise and I could make a better go of things apart than we had managed together. One question circled endlessly in my mind – would my voyage, with all its attendant dangers and absences, shatter the delicate balance of our friendship?

CHAPTER 5

Great Circle

I spent the next few weeks settling into the house in Ludgershall, patiently waiting for the shock of my altered situation to hit. Maybe the relief of being free to get on with the job in hand was overriding my sadness. Who knows? The mind is a complex machine. The pain of it all would manifest itself down the line but for the moment, I was content to focus on the boys and the voyage.

I concentrated my internet search for a boat in France and Holland, the biggest European markets for steel yachts which, if I was going to venture into the ice, was the only material to go with – aluminium was too soft and fibreglass a non-starter. Late in the evening on Monday 17th May, I sat back with a feeling of quiet excitement. I was looking at my computer screen, at a picture of a Flot 40 Mk II, built in 1990 and lying in Lorient on the Brittany coast. After searching through hundreds of boats, this one fitted the bill. I emailed asking for specifications and more pictures. It wouldn't take a lot of work to adapt her for my purposes. She did have an aft cockpit, but much depended on the build quality and whether I believed she was strong enough to withstand the pummelling of a 30,000-mile passage through some of the most treacherous waters in the world.

I bought a DVD of *Touching the Void*, Joe Simpson's survival ordeal on an Andean mountain. In a peculiar way, the film underscored the enormous risk I would be taking when I set out on my circumavigation. Joe Simpson really thought he had bought it on that mountain. His fear was palpable and the chances of rescue non-existent.

Chichester admitted to being terrified prior to his voyage around the world. I was truly terrified as well. My misgivings were unnerving me. I began to dwell on the awesome scale of what I was proposing for myself – the organisation, planning and training, but much more than that, the sheer scale, duration, difficulty and danger of the undertaking.

I had to decide on a start date to bring perspective to timings and costs. My choice of route was fundamental to when that date would fall. The advantage of heading south from England lay in the greater experience I would have of the boat by the time I arrived at the Bering Strait to tackle the Arctic. However, this option created another monstrous challenge – Cape Horn.

Simple geography determines a circumnavigation of the earth. A definition might be a route that approximates a great circle by containing at least one pair of antipodal points.

A great circle is any line around the earth defined by a plane that passes right through the centre of the earth. For example, all meridians of longitude (which pass through the North and South Poles) are great circles. The equator is the only line of latitude that is a great circle (all other lines of latitude, either north or south of the equator, are called small circles.) A great circle does not have to be a meridian of longitude but can be on a plane angled any which way, providing the plane passes through the centre of the earth. It follows then, that to sail a circumnavigation, I had to finish at the point where I started, always moving in generally the same direction.

Sailing south from the start meant I would have to finish by sailing back to that point from the north. Following a great circle route necessitates crossing the equator twice (going in opposite directions each time) and bisecting all meridians of longitude.

In *Gipsy Moth Circles the World*, Sir Francis Chichester described the essential element of a 'true' circumnavigation as a track where '. . . the vessel passes through two points on the earth's surface which are diametrically opposite each other . . .'

The best way of visualising antipodal points is to imagine a globe pierced with a stick passing through the very centre of the sphere. The entry and exit points are antipodal. The reasoning for at least one pair of antipodes on the vessel's track resides in shaping the track to conform as closely as possible to a great circle – a perfect ring around the earth. Land masses prevent a perfect track over water, so antipodes approximate an actual track to a great circle. The more pairs of antipodes along the track, the closer the track conforms. Many circumnavigations ignore this fundamental rule, but for me it was an essential requirement, backed by historical precedent:

Magellan's *Victoria* (1522) – two pairs of antipodes along the route
Sir Francis Drake's *Golden Hind* (1580) – four pairs of antipodes

Joshua Slocum's *Spray* (1898) – five pairs of antipodes
Sir Francis Chichester's *Gipsy Moth IV* (1967) – two pairs of antipodes
Sir Robin Knox-Johnston's *Suhaili* (1969) – two pairs of antipodes
Chay Blyth's *British Steel* (1971) – two pairs of antipodes

Over one hundred finishers of the Whitbread (now Volvo) Round-the-World races (circumnavigations of Antarctica with runs down and up the Atlantic) and the Jules Verne record-holders could be classified as 'near misses', together with most if not all of the finishers of the BOC (now Vendée Globe) single-handed round-the-world challenges, under Chichester's determination of a true circumnavigation.

The final requirement of a circumnavigation is that the distance travelled should be at least 21,600 nautical miles, equivalent to the distance around the circumference of the earth. This requirement inevitably results by adhering to the antipodal principle.

Vito Dumas's epic voyage in 1942/43 did not technically conform to a circumnavigation. The track of *Legh II* was confined to the southern hemisphere. He did not cross the equator. Consequently, there were no antipodes along the track of *Legh II*, which meant he sailed a distance less than the circumference of the earth. In fact, he sailed a total distance of 20,000 nautical miles.

To bisect every meridian of longitude, I would have to round Cape Horn westwards, from the Atlantic side to the Pacific. Cape Horn is the most feared stretch of water on the planet – the currents move east and the prevailing winds are from the west. To go westwards, I would be sailing into the teeth of the weather, effectively 'uphill' as Chay Blyth had done, rather than running downhill with the wind behind. To take on this challenge with my very limited experience was arguably crazy (I spoke to Sir Chay Blyth about my route. That's when he told me Chichester had said he was crazy. Sir Chay looked at me, shrugged and raised his eyebrows. I knew what he was silently saying. '*I went ahead and did it anyway.*') However, the decision became a matter of elimination. To bisect every meridian and transit the Arctic via Canada's Northwest Passage meant going round the Cape of Good Hope, the southern tip of southern Africa. But – and this was a big *but* – would a route that missed out Cape Horn leave me with a gaping chasm of discontent? I didn't have to think for long. Yes, it would. So, if it was sensible to leave the Arctic phase until the latter part of the voyage, then a westward rounding of the Horn became inevitable.

I considered the reverse option, of travelling north to tackle the

Arctic first. This would mean a June departure, which would not leave enough time to prepare properly, unless I delayed until 2006 and my finances wouldn't stretch to that. A north-first route would also necessitate an eastwards, downwind rounding of Cape Horn to bisect every meridian. If I was going to accept the challenge of the Horn then I wanted its full measure, crazy or not. Only a handful of single-handed sailors had ever achieved a westwards rounding of the Horn (Marcel Bardiaux and Sir Chay Blyth among them). I wanted to be included in that group.

I needed three months to get to Cape Horn by mid-summer in the southern hemisphere. My start date was therefore set for sometime in October 2005.

Now I had to create an identity for the mission. Ideas for names had been chasing around my mind for some time. A circumnavigation was clearly *global*. If successful, I would achieve the 'first' vertical, from which I deduced the word *Alpha* (and even if I wasn't successful, the attempt was a 'first'). To conjure the thrill of adventure I came up with *Expedition*. My great hope was christened: the Alpha Global Expedition.

Wednesday 2nd June was blisteringly hot. I visited the UKSA in Cowes. After a tour round the facilities, I had a long chat with the chief instructor, Francis Knight. Elements of the 17-week course that were not directly relevant to me could be substituted with more useful material. Francis seemed perplexed. I told him only that I had a specific mission in mind for which the course at UKSA was a training step. Francis generously accepted that without probing further. Another reason why the UKSA appealed to me was that my time there would serve as a preparatory period for Benji and Gabriel to get used to my not being around quite so much. At least they'd be better equipped to handle my actual departure when it came.

On Monday 7th June, I met my accountant to set up a limited company in the name of Alpha Global Expedition Limited. The process threw out an unexpected opportunity.

Despite trying to ignore the possibility of Louise helping me on the expedition, I couldn't. She'd be perfect. Before we were married, she had worked in the hotel trade, in public relations, rising to represent some of the finest hotels in London. She was extrovert, capable, quick and a natural communicator.

I asked Louise if she would act as company secretary. She agreed. Perhaps this reflected a softening in her attitude towards the expedition and me. And, perhaps, if I trod carefully, I might eventually persuade her to get more involved.

On 16th June, I packed up the car and headed for France. *Ninae*, the Flot 40, was immediately recognisable with her broad yellow hull strip. She looked squat and solid as if hunched on the water in permanent anticipation of an elemental onslaught. She had never strayed far from her home waters so although the boat was older, her low mileage showed in her condition.

I spent a couple of hours going over the boat, above deck and below, looking at systems, lifting floor boards, inspecting the bilges and the inside of the hull plating. I could see no sign of rust, no water, no damage. The interior was beautifully fitted out and fully insulated. The professionally fitted electric, electronic, engine and plumbing systems looked to be in similarly good condition.

We took the boat out into the bay, hoisted sails and I spent 40 minutes playing with her. The helm was heavy and because of her weight, she could not point close to the wind without losing considerable speed but, with the wind abeam, she made 4–5 knots in a 12-knot breeze. So performance was okay. However, more importantly, my feeling towards the boat, that inexplicable chemistry, wasn't there. Despite her good condition, her inventory, the meticulous build quality and her undeniable strength, I felt a grudging reluctance emanating from *Ninae*. My initial euphoria was evaporating and I left Lorient disappointed to begin my search anew.

Back in England, I drove into London for a meeting with Generate Sponsorship, a small agency marrying sponsors' money with suitable events. To approach bigger brands with credibility, I needed the help of people who knew their way round and could tap into their contact database, prepare a proposal document in the right format and press buttons with potential partners. My problem was cash flow and my dilemma acute; unless I invested in a professional sponsor document with a qualified contact list, I reduced my chances of success.

The UKSA left a message for me on Wednesday 21st July – if I had a boat, they had a berth for her. Well, I didn't have a boat, but the UKSA's willingness to provide berthing, if and when I did find a boat, was a great relief.

With no sponsorship and cash flow strained, I had to consider one final option: release equity in my house. This option had always been off-limits, but pitted against this sentiment was the question of my commitment. Lance Armstrong, the great American road cyclist and Tour de France champion, had a saying, 'Go hard or go home.' It pretty well summed the situation up. This expedition represented much more than just an adventure and an achievement in its own right. It was a statement about my life, my principles, beliefs and character. Did I have the conviction and the courage to follow those beliefs? Did I have the guts to follow a dream or, by giving up, did I consign myself to the garbage bin of mediocrity?

This whole challenge was about so much more than getting on a boat and sailing it. The journey to get to the start line was proving every bit as arduous. I hated burdening other people with my problems, but I found that I did: my parents, Louise. I could have faced bald facts – I did not have sufficient funds, I did not have enough experience, I did not have enough time. Equally, I could borrow the money, get on with it, see if sponsors materialised and if they didn't, well . . . I'd find a way!

Or would I? Instead, I descended into crisis, paralysed by indecision. At the same time, I suffered a delayed reaction to the divorce and, for the first time in my life, I spiralled into a deep depression. On top of this, a friend with whom I had entered a property deal two years previously had bunked out and was now refusing to pay £16,000 owed to me. I had been relying on this money. Now, my cash flow was groaning under ever greater strain. My father was encouraging delay. I found myself thinking that I should forget the October 2005 departure.

My efforts at generating sponsorship did not yield results and Generate's work to secure corporate sponsorship had come up empty. By the end of the summer, cash flow was desperately tight. The only solution was to mortgage the house and borrow the money.

I seemed to have gone nowhere. I even thought about abandoning the expedition altogether. Had I just gone round in a great big circle?

CHAPTER 6

Barrabas Found

A new chapter of the Alpha Global Expedition began on Monday 4th October, my first day at the UKSA. I spent Saturday with Louise and the children then, at 11.00 am on Sunday morning, Louise took the boys off to a birthday party at our friends, the Laidlaws. Sam Laidlaw, chief executive of Centrica, would come to play a pivotal role in the expedition.

I packed up and left, after first locking myself out of Louise's house while my computer and wallet were still inside. I clambered over the side gate, tried to force the kitchen door, breaking the glass in the process and finally got in through the landing window. It was not an auspicious start. For the first time since the divorce and through all the tribulation of the last two months, I felt alone.

I stayed with my aunt Rosemary on the Isle of Wight on Sunday night and at 10.30 am the next morning drove to the UKSA. All the new arrivals were apprehensive in the unfamiliar surroundings, but I felt pleased to be making progress towards the mission objective. Refamiliarisation with all things marine was refreshing and revitalising. Conversely, being away from the boys was tough. After one month at the UKSA, I'd made a flying visit back for Gabriel's birthday on 18th October and had a weekend with them. Both children had adapted quickly to the changes. Louise worked hard to smooth the transition for them, despite an ongoing simmering antipathy between us. The children's ability to get on with their lives according to the prevailing circumstances settled what might have been a showstopper.

Among the other members of my crew on 'Starboard 5', Chris Elliott at 48 was the oldest. He'd lived in France for 25 years. A complex man capable of great sensitivity, softly spoken, courteous and likeable, Chris was the first to approach me and introduce himself during that first day at the UKSA. Chris was married to a French woman but after 10 years, they were now flirting with divorce. He was at the UKSA to train for a career change from his previous life as a freight agent. We had the 'divorce' conversation early on and as a result established a kind of bond. I could not know then that Chris's input would change the course of the Alpha Global Expedition.

Nick Musgrave was exactly my age. A former management trainer with Citibank, he was in New York during the 9/11 catastrophe. That experience, together with the humdrum tone of his existence, persuaded him to leave his job, sell his apartment and look for a new direction.

None of the Starboard 5 team or anybody else directly connected to the UKSA knew of my plans. Chris had twigged something mainly because I was always asking the instructors about steel boats and short-handed sailing. Despite my uncertainties about *Ninae*, I was having a spectacular lack of success at finding another suitable boat and like the dismal hankerings of a man after an old girlfriend, I called Bretagne Yachting, the broker in Lorient. *Ninae* had been sold. I was philosophical. What I was really hankering after was the Trireme I had found in Gibraltar a year before (which had also been sold).

During a weekend break, Chris went to France and returned with a clutch of French sailing magazines.

'I've found you a boat!'

'Really,' I said, trying to sound enthusiastic. How could he have found the right boat if he didn't know my plans?

Chris flicked through the magazines and placed one on my desk. 'Here,' he said, his finger tapping at one of the photographs in the brokerage section.

I recognised the boat immediately. It was a Trireme 38! But her hull was bare metal even though the caption described her construction as 'acier' – steel. Bare steel would rust. I assumed a print error in the caption. She must be aluminium, I thought. Aluminium or not, Chris had inadvertently come across *exactly* the right boat. I sat back, stunned.

There was a telephone number next to the picture. 'Can we call and find out?' I handed Chris my mobile.

The boat's owner, Bernard De Castro, answered. Chris began talking in faultless French.

'Ask him about the material – is it aluminium?' I whispered.

I heard Bernard laugh. 'Non, non,' he said. 'C'est Inox.'

My mind reeled. Inox! Stainless steel!

Marcel Bardiaux, 1960. He had built a stainless steel boat. I never

Barrabas

wind cups

VHF aerial

wind direction indicator

tricolour

forestay

40'

upper spreaders

11'6"

mast

batten sleeves

radar scanner

reefing cringles

reefing pennants

lower spreaders

mainsail

deck light

shrouds

spinnaker pole

backstays

headsail

lazy jacks

inner stay

leech

boom

rudder

skeg

anodes

stem

rubbing strake

bow

hull

keel

www.alphaglobalex.com

Barrabas – deck layout

aftdeck

sidedeck

foredeck

iridium satellite
telephone aerial

stern light

dodger

winch

block

self-steering
rudder

satellite
receiver

engine

wind generator

solar panels

self-steering vane

'grab' rails

cuddy

central hatch with
storm bars

boom breaker

liferaft

'granny' bars

guard rails

unsinkable dinghy

dinghy lashings

windlass

navigation lights

pulpit

anchor

headsail furling
gear

tricing line

cleat

toe-rail

tiller emergency steering post

lazarette

binnacle

sink

spot light

head

chart table

electrics isolation switch

stool

inverter

port side saloon seating/berth

day tank

saloon table

aft cabin

deck fuel cans

companionway steps

galley

drying cupboard

oil drum

gas cylinder

20-litre fuel cans

starboard side saloon seating/berth

power tools

watermaker

forecabin

tool boxes

vice

anchor locker

anchor chain

Barrabas – section view

thought I'd find such a boat. Never! And yet, out of nowhere, here she was, magically placed before me, a small colour photograph in a French sailing magazine. I thought too of Bernard Moitessier, Alain Gerbault, Louis Bernicot, Yves Le Toumelin and Jean Gau, the great French single-handed circumnavigators. The heritage was right, the 'Frenchness' was right!

I knew with that peculiar, inexplicable certainty that I had found the boat to partner me on my voyage around the world.

Bernard De Castro sent detailed specifications of *Barrabas* and more pictures. The price, 125,000 euros, was way over my budget, but she had everything I was looking for: granny bars at the mast, a stern frame supporting solar panels and wind generator, a large cuddy protecting the helm and companionway, six gel batteries as opposed to four on the Flot 40 and diesel-fired heating. All this would have cost 15,000 euros to add to the Flot 40. Given that the Trireme was two years younger, had a stainless steel hull and mast, a superior under-water profile and a practically brand-new engine – a powerful 60hp Lombardini diesel with less than 65 hours' running time – and *Barrabas* looked like a fair deal by comparison. I studied the pictures and the data long and hard. Bernard, a master welder, had taken six years over the build. It was obvious that *Barrabas* was over-engineered and in-credibly strong. She ticked every box. What appeared as scratches on the bows turned out to be a remarkable feature – etchings of Neptune hurling a trident with a sea dragon rearing up behind, worked into the steel with an angle grinder by a French sculptor. The attitude of the cuts were varied to reflect light differently creating a 3-D effect.

Over the following fortnight and after many telephone calls to Bernard with Chris acting as interpreter, the time had come to make an offer. If *Barrabas* was the boat for the mission, I had to secure her. Bernard told us he was travelling from his home in Burgundy to Montpellier on the south coast of France where he kept *Barrabas* to see two other potential buyers.

The time had also come to tell Chris about the Alpha Global Expedition. He listened with bewilderment that transformed to elation when he realised that his contribution had been crucial. It was import-ant that Bernard knew what might be in store for *Barrabas*. Chris called him. To our surprise, he had already put off one of the other potential buyers (who must have been dithering) on the basis that he felt I was serious. Now he was thrilled at the prospect of *Barrabas* sailing a circumnavigation. I agreed the asking price, subject to survey. It was a massive leap, but buying *Barrabas* felt right. The boat would keep me safe and bring my goal within reach. The responsibility on her would be huge. She had to be up to it. But I knew she would deliver, even though I had never set eyes on her. I remembered seeing *Ninae* for the first time. I'd felt deflated, my heart didn't skip a beat, my pulse didn't quicken. The relationship had to be strong, passionate. I felt that with *Barrabas*.

I had pledged money and with that pledge, the project came alive. I booked return flights to France for Chris and myself to have a look at the boat early in the New Year.

With Christmas approaching, I was keen to get away and have some time at home with the children. Louise and I gave Benji his sixth birthday party on Sunday 2nd January at Chearsley Village Hall. Afterwards, I heard Benji say to Louise, 'I am so happy Daddy could come to my party.' He then looked at her and asked, 'Will Daddy be at my next birthday?'

'Your next birthday is a long way off, Benji,' Louise said. I looked at Louise and felt a void open within me. Here in a land-locked English village, the idea of sailing around the world seemed so ludicrous, so far removed from the basic reality of life.

Travelling back to the Isle of Wight on the last ferry that night, I felt homesick for the familiarity of Louise and the boys. A thought kept replaying in my mind . . . *commitment is following through on a decision long after the mood has changed.* I wrote something similar in a card I left for Louise. These moments of indecision were part of the endeavour – never give up, just keep going.

The Starboard 5 crew met up at breakfast and we moved onto the UKSA's catamaran for the fifth sea phase. I was skipper and decided to use wind and tide to sail to Portsmouth. We moored up for lunch before sailing across the Solent into Bembridge. The weather was cold and blowing Force 6, the catamaran's limit. My cell phone had been ringing, but with the diesels running, I hadn't heard it. The boat's cell phone rang. I answered, then handed the phone to James Mitchell, the instructor. He listened and then offered the phone back to me.

'Hello,' I said.

'Adrian, it's Sarah.'

'Everything okay?' I asked the UKSA receptionist.

'Louise rang – there's nothing wrong with the kids, she said to tell you that straight away, but could you ring her back urgently.'

I hung up and punched in Louise's number.

The instant Louise answered, I knew that something was terribly wrong.

'Adrian?' Her voice was weak from crying.

'What's up?'

'Where are you?'

'Out on the water. You okay?'

'There's no easy way to say . . .'

'Just tell me what's happened.'

A momentary silence then Louise said, 'Christian, Tracey and Alexandre have been killed.'

My hand dropped and I felt my throat constrict. Louise's voice sounded tinny. I raised the phone back to my ear. They had decided on a last-minute Christmas holiday to Thailand for a week. They were on the beach after breakfast when the tsunami hit. Louis, their younger son, had miraculously survived. Details were sketchy. She knew no more than that. My immediate thought was to get back to Louise as fast as humanly possible.

Someone produced a cup of sweet tea. I went on deck. The shocking deaths of our friends were incomprehensible, but their families . . . their grief was unimaginable. And as for Louis . . .

James called Red Funnel Ferries and asked if they could hold the 5.30 pm sailing from Cowes to Southampton. We bombed across from Bembridge and made it back to the UKSA at 5.20 pm. I jumped off the boat, sprinted to my car and got to the ferry terminal at 5.40 pm. The boat was waiting. I drove like a maniac and finally arrived at Louise's house at 8.20 pm. It was a long, difficult and painful evening that left us both wrung out.

Next day, I took Benji to school, the beginning of the new term, and then I drove to Southampton Airport. By some strange irony, Chris and I were flying to France that afternoon.

Port Camargue near Montpellier was an enormous, purpose-built marina development, the largest of its type in Europe. The weather was clear and sunny. Chris knew exactly where to go following Bernard's instructions.

We parked up.

'Nervous?' Chris asked.

I didn't reply immediately, just nodded. I was more excited than nervous. 'Let's go,' I said taking a deep breath.

Barrabas was impressive – meaty and beamy, her hull sides flared just behind the foredeck like the nostrils of a panting racehorse. She radiated solidity, strength and integrity. I sensed an instant chemistry as if *Barrabas* knew why I had come.

Bernard de Castro greeted us effusively. A small man in his sixties with the physique of a jockey and a swarthy complexion pointing to his Spanish ancestry, Bernard bristled with energy. He was not in any way extrovert and the language barrier prevented me from getting to know him better but I could tell he was honest. No one who could build a boat like this could be anything but honest – the toil, the dedication, the craftsmanship, the care and attention to detail. These were hallmarks of strength and fortitude, qualities instilled in *Barrabas*'s construction, every bit as tangible as the welds and steel of her hull. I liked him immediately. Bernard wanted to know more about the Alpha Global Expedition, specifics on the route, the ice, Cape Horn.

'This is exactly the type of voyage that *Barrabas* was built for,' Bernard said. I wondered whether he dreamed of sailing a circum-navigation. If he couldn't do it then perhaps seeing the boat he had spent six years building go around the earth might, in some vicarious way, be a fulfilment of sorts.

Bernard had created *Barrabas* with a 'belt and braces approach' as he put it, over-engineering the rig and deck fittings to a specification suitable for a yacht twice the size. Internally, the bilges were clean and dry with no signs of corrosion. As for visual appeal, *Barrabas* was striking: the artwork on the bows, the gleaming metal of her sides and her sleek, classically French lines.

I had researched stainless steel. Its obvious advantage is that it does not corrode at the rate or to the extent of mild steel. Chromium in the steel mix reacts with atmospheric oxygen forming a tough film of chromium oxide on the surface, protecting the metal beneath. Bernard gave me the grade of steel he'd used: 316 L (Ti) – low carbon content (<0.03%) with titanium. During welding, carbon atoms can migrate towards the heat source (carbide precipitation) creating areas of weakness, which ultimately become brittle and fracture. Other elements such as molybdenum introduced into the steel mix prevent carbide precipitation, but the best carbon 'anchor' is titanium.

To stop external carbon contaminating the hot steel during welding, Bernard had used inert argon gas. I studied the welds above and below the waterline. There was no evidence of corrosion or precipitation.

Prohibitive cost rules out stainless steel as the material of choice for boat-building. Bernard had managed it because he worked for the French stainless steel manufacturer Ugine. The company supplied the

material at an affordable price and tested every piece for purity. As a
master welder, Bernard defrayed otherwise exorbitant labour costs by
doing all the work himself.

The multi-chine hull had various plate thicknesses – the lower two
chines were 4.25 mm and the upper two chines 3 mm. Deck plating
was also 3 mm. The famous French naval architect François Charpen-
tier designed the Trireme 38 as a mild steel boat but because of the
greater tensile and compression strength of stainless steel, Bernard was
able to reduce plate thicknesses and save a significant amount of
weight. The result was that *Barrabas* was lighter and stronger than the
design specification.

The other huge advantage of stainless over mild steel is its malle-
ability. On impact, stainless is more forgiving and will bend and fold
before tearing and splitting. In ice-strewn waters, this property was
critical, particularly in the absence of specific ice-strengthening modifications to the hull.

Below deck, the finish was not to the same standard as the construction and fell some way short of *Ninae*, but my primary concern
was with the build quality, safety and practicality rather than internal
aesthetics.

We spent the rest of the afternoon going over the boat, Chris inter-
preting between Bernard and me. At 6.00 pm, we left Port Camargue
and found a hotel in Grau du Roi. I woke at 4.00 am thinking about
Barrabas and the commitment I was about to make. On top of this, my
mind was full of the tragedy that had befallen our friends, but somehow their deaths were acting as a spur, forcing me to realise even
more clearly that nothing in life is certain and that to dally is to waste,
to prevaricate is to squander and to dream but not to act leads only to
regret.

The following day we picked up where we'd left off, checking
through the boat's systems, with me constantly firing questions and
Chris doing a masterful job as interpreter. We ate lunch together in a
nearby restaurant where the conversation continued with talk of parachute anchors, maximum angles of heel, other technical points and
something else that intrigued me.

'How did you come up with the name, *Barrabas*?' I said.

Bernard nodded as though he'd expected the question. 'I was a
young man, conscripted to fight in Algeria . . .'

The French military drafted the 22-year-old, an anti-authoritarian
but a good soldier, assigned him to Special Forces and dispatched him

to the desert in a small troop to gather intelligence. At a deserted oasis, he found and read a book, *Barabbas: The Story of a Believer Without Faith*, written in 1950 by Par Lagerkvist, a Swedish writer who moved to Paris and lived in France and Italy. The book won the Nobel Prize for Literature in 1951. Bernard admired Barabbas's maverick character. '. . . When I built the boat, she was a maverick also. It seemed right that I call her *Barrabas* too.'

'Do you still have the book?'

Bernard nodded. 'Oui. It's on the boat.'

'If I buy the boat, will you let me have the book?'

Bernard smiled then shook his head. 'Non,' he said.

I understood his need, a part of her that he could keep for ever.

Chris had to get back to England. I drove him to the train station in Montpellier and returned to the boat for lunch with Bernard, a boeuf bourguignon made by his wife, Odette. I was a bit anxious given that Bernard's English was as bad as my French, but over a bottle of Merlot we managed, with the help of an electronic dictionary, to talk about the boat, my plans for her and the expedition. Lunch lasted an hour and a half. We talked about the deaths of my friends Christian and Tracey, our approaches to getting the most out of life, my reading of Chichester's book when I was fifteen and his plans. 'Perhaps I will build another boat, this time from aluminium,' he confided. After-wards, Bernard went off for a couple of hours so that I could have time on my own with *Barrabas*.

It was a beautiful afternoon. I climbed to the top of the mast, poked around below, had a nap in the back cabin (which Chris later decided was an 'embryonic' experience) and just existed with *Barrabas*. I imagined myself sailing her (I couldn't take her out on the water because there wasn't a breath of wind) and felt comfortable with the prospect. *Barrabas* seemed to be saying to me, calmly, devoid of any hysteria, 'Let's do it. I'm ready.' I got the feeling that the boat, like a thorough-bred, was straining at her mooring lines wanting the big challenge to prove herself and win the fulfilment which, like me, she sought.

'Are you still interested?' Bernard asked when he returned.

'I've been sleeping in the aft cabin.'

He laughed, seemed unsurprised and understood that *Barrabas* and I had already established an intimate bond. We discussed details of the purchase transaction, agreed a price and a completion date of 31st January. He then asked, 'How can I be certain?'

'Parce que je dis,' I said.

Bernard raised his eyebrows, his mouth turned down at the corners, he cocked his head to one side and gave a small Gallic shrug and, with that, we shook hands and the deal was done.

It was late January 2005. The Yachtmaster practical examination was imminent. I had to knuckle down. A few days before testing, my mother called from South Africa. Victoria, the housemaid, had recently died of an AIDS-related illness. Her partner, Selby, employed by my parents as a gardener, had come to the house the day before and committed suicide on the forecourt by swallowing weedkiller.

It was all I could do to stay focused.

We picked up the external examiner, Mike Hindley, a former test pilot, from the harbour master's quay at Warsash on the River Hamble. After watching two of the others being put through their paces, I realised Mike wanted to see confidence. We were in Wootton Creek on the north shore of the Isle of Wight when it became time for my examination. I barked orders for a stern spring and bow line, slipped the bow, drove back on the stern spring, forcing the bow out and swung round in a tight circle, heading back out of the Wootton channel. The car ferry to Portsmouth was leaving dock. I hesitated to let her go and noticed a small look from Mike who was perched in the companionway. I knew what that look meant. I gunned the engine to get in front of the ferry. This met with a nod of approval from Mike. I ordered sails up and set course. Mike called me down below. A plane had gone down (hypothetically) and wreckage had been observed. Solent coastguard needed our help. Mike gave me a position on the chart to locate. I found a couple of transits, talking out loud and plotting them on the chart. When I was just about to make the transit, Mike called off the exercise. Now, just outside the mouth of the River Medina near Cowes, he asked me to pick up one of the mooring buoys close by which I did under headsail. Mike simply said, 'Good, well done, you've passed,' and promptly transferred the role of skipper to Nick Musgrave.

Back at the UKSA, I went to see the chief executive, David Green. Ever since her voyage around the world, *Gipsy Moth IV* had been on display at Greenwich, mounted on a concrete plinth next to the famous clipper ship *Cutty Sark*. For years, she'd been trammelled by thousands of feet, exposed to the elements and suffered the vagaries of acid rain. By 2004, she was a wreck. In partnership with *Yachting*

World and the Maritime Trust, the UKSA acquired *Gipsy Moth IV* for '£1 and a gin and tonic' in return for a complete restoration. The UKSA was to be her new home.

David immediately grasped the Alpha Global Expedition's marketing potential for the UKSA and the hook-in with the *Gipsy Moth IV* restoration project. He reiterated the UKSA's willingness to offer *Barrabas* a berth.

The previous 48 hours had been momentous. After years of thinking and dreaming and months of planning and training, three major events occurred almost simultaneously – on Monday 2nd February, with the final transfer of monies to France, I had become the new owner of *Barrabas*; on Tuesday, I acquired my Yachtmaster ticket and on Wednesday, I secured the backing of the UKSA as my campaign base.

Barrabas and *Gipsy Moth IV* would be stablemates.

CHAPTER 7

The Gypsy

I drove to the Camper & Nicholson yard in Gosport. It was early February 2005. David Green had organised a press function for the *Gipsy Moth IV* restoration project and invited me along. *Gipsy Moth IV* was laid up on blocks, her hull stripped exposing the cross-ply construction, revolutionary in its day. To touch the hull of the most famous small sailing yacht in the world, the stuff of my boyhood dreams and the embodiment of the spirit that I had sought to make real for so long, was tantamount to a spiritual experience. I also met Chichester's son, Giles, which was as close as I would get to Chichester himself, and I came away re-energised.

Before finishing at the UKSA, I asked Nick to help me crew *Barrabas* back to England. He agreed to join me on *Barrabas* in Montpellier in mid-March. I used the intervening time to begin the refit preparations.

My biggest concern was the communications, navigation and weather systems. Costs would be high and I needed an expert to source hardware, programme the computers and supervise installation. I found Tim Thornton on the web at Marine Computing International. Tim would come to play an indispensable part in the Alpha Global Expedition.

I retained Generate Sponsorship to source supply sponsors from a shortlist that I'd compiled – work that could be ongoing while I was sailing *Barrabas* back to the Cowes. By Wednesday 9th March, I'd done as much as I could to get the various balls rolling towards sponsorship and the refit. Louise drove me to Stansted Airport. When we said goodbye, her voice held a tremor.

'Be careful,' Louise cautioned.

It was great to see *Barrabas* again. On board, I slept well, feeling that same sense of embrace as when I'd met *Barrabas* for the first time in January. I had the next few days to familiarise myself with the boat before Nick arrived. I took an hour to figure out how the head (toilet) worked, went shopping for provisions and decided to go through *Barrabas* from stem to stern to sort through tools, spares and gear and discard rubbish.

Louise called on Friday morning.

'Is there some part of you that doesn't quite believe that I'm actually going ahead with this project?' I could hear the excitement in my own voice.

'Now you're in France, the reality is beginning to sink in, yes.'

She was worried about being left with the children and not having me around as a support system.

'It'll be okay,' I said. 'I'll be back before you know it.' I knew something that Louise did not – that she was strong, much stronger than she believed herself.

That conversation was pivotal. Up until then, Louise's attitude to me and the expedition had been detached and critical. That hostility seemed to be dissolving. She was beginning to believe that I could and would do this and, more importantly, she was beginning to accept that my commitment was real. I felt closer to her then than I had for a very long time.

Chris called.

'You still good for tomorrow?' I asked.

'No. I've got two job interviews, so I'll be with you Sunday.'

On Saturday morning, I worked my way through the engine and electrical systems and then drove to Montpellier to collect Nick from the airport.

Chris arrived at the yacht club on Sunday at 11.00 am. Nick and I drove across to meet him and together the three of us had lunch at a quayside café. Back at the boat, we telephoned Bernard at his home in Burgundy and went through my long list of questions that I'd complied during my familiarisation with *Barrabas*.

Chris left early on Monday morning. My telephone rang. It was Louise. She was tearful. Christian and Tracey's bodies had been identified in Thailand and returned to France. The funeral was taking place that afternoon in Honfleur. Alexandre's body was still missing. We all assumed he'd been swept out to sea.

Nick and I went through the topsides. We spent time scraping the hull as best we could with a makeshift scraper on the end of a pole.

'Is there a plastic water bottle I could cut in two to see under water?' I asked Nick, pulling items out of the lazarette.

'Or we could go buy a face mask,' Nick said.

'Bernard must have used something to see underneath.'

I reached into the lazarette and pulled out a bucket stuffed with rags.

'Nah,' Nick said. 'He wouldn't have thought of something like that.'

I emptied the bucket and lo! Bernard had cut the bottom out of the bucket and screwed in a Perspex pane, caulked with a silicone sealant. We laughed like drains. Bernard, it seemed, had thought of everything!

We woke to thick fog on Wednesday 16th March, but the weather was favourable for our departure the next morning. The voyage to England would be a test, an opportunity for me to gain an understanding of *Barrabas*, her sailing abilities, her sea-keeping qualities, her idiosyncrasies. The learning curve would be steep. How would I handle *Barrabas*? Our bond would be forged during the next few weeks.

Over the following days, Nick and I enjoyed good sailing towards the Iberian islands, feeling secure on *Barrabas*. On Sunday 20th March, with dolphins cavorting in front of the bow, we sighted the mountainous silhouette of Mallorca through the heat haze. It was a magical moment for me. *Barrabas* and I had travelled our first steps together. I called Louise and the boys. Passing the Canal de Mallorca with winds gusting to Force 5, *Barrabas* screamed along under full sail, our speed over the ground nudging 11 knots. I was amazed. There are no currents in the Mediterranean Sea, so her speed was being generated without assistance.

After the initial flurry, the winds died so we motored much of the time, which meant stopping in port to refuel. On approach to Gibraltar, *Barrabas* sailed into the 'Vendiale', a seasonal westerly wind. The sea state became agitated, with steep, breaking water, the first heavy weather we had encountered, but *Barrabas* stayed composed. I was quickly developing a keen sense of the boat and getting a measure of her mood.

'How does she sail?' I'd asked Bernard at our first meeting.

'Treat her well and she will behave. Treat her badly and she will bite!' he said, grinning.

We arrived at Marina Bay, Gibraltar, to refuel, re-provision and get our laundry done. I could see that Nick was tired. A decent night's sleep in port would do us both good. We slipped out of the marina the next day, then anchored off Algeciras to await the tide that would carry us through the narrow strait between Spain and North Africa.

The weather turned foul off Cape Saint Vincent, Portugal's south-western corner. Force 8 winds ripped around the headland, churning the seas to white water. *Barrabas* stayed steady and solid under shortened sail, not rising to the temptation to ride high over the waves and slam her bows. We trundled up the Portuguese coast in light winds, mostly under engine. It meant another refuelling stop, and south of Cape Finisterre and with no charts, we tentatively put into Camarinas. It was a beautiful spot, an enclosed bay surrounded by verdant, forested slopes dotted with white sandy beaches.

We moored up at the Camarinas Club Nautico, eventually locating the yacht club manageress, Carmen Rodriguez. I bought two Cokes and noticed her take what looked like a crème caramel out of the oven. Speaking in halting French, I joked that this was our lunch. Carmen grinned, placed chicken curry and rice in front of Nick and myself, followed by the dessert, which turned out to be a delicious cheesecake.

Going past Cape Finisterre, light following winds provided an opportunity to see how *Barrabas* performed under spinnaker, but ominously we were picking up radio warnings of a Force 10 storm moving into the area. Barometric pressure began falling and by the early hours of Friday 9th April, winds had accelerated to Force 9. Nick had been hand-steering since 2.00 am – five hours by the time I came on watch at 7.00 am. I could sense immediately that *Barrabas* was overpowered. Nick was screaming through the wind that he had almost broached twice.

'Heave-to now,' I yelled.

'Too dangerous!'

I yelled at him again to gybe the boat. 'Do it now!'

Barrabas came round beautifully, the sails crossing the deck, opposing the force of the rudder turned in the opposite direction and she stopped amongst the seas breaking all around us. Amidst the fury of the storm, *Barrabas* was an oasis of calm. Nick lashed the helm and we quickly shortened sail.

At 4.00 pm, we raised the storm staysail. As night fell with no let-up, I decided to run a 30-minute watch system to combat fatigue. What an introduction to the boat's ability to handle rough weather! She behaved magnificently, never slamming her bows on the big waves towering 30 feet above the deck. The storm eventually blew itself out by the following morning. Neither of us had slept for 30 hours. I ordered Nick below to rest. Ten minutes later he appeared at the companionway looking sheepish.

'I've blocked the bloody head!'

I grinned at him. 'It'll be dirty work.'

He spent 20 minutes slopping out the toilet into a bucket. A wave hit the boat heeling her over. A barrage of cursing came from below. The bucket, full of effluent, had slid away from Nick, hit an exposed frame and spilt its contents all over the floor and into the bilges. He gamely spent the next two hours cleaning up, sluicing out, washing floorboards, filling and evacuating the bilges while I steered through the aftermath of the storm. The heads had blocked because he'd used it without water in the bowl. I decided to take the pump apart myself and learn the system. Nick had done enough. It took me another hour.

Through our various trials, my primary concern with *Barrabas* was her inability to sail close to the wind. That limitation could affect our attempt at Cape Horn with the wind coming at us in monstrous conditions. It was a concern that would sit and fester for the next 10 months.

In the early morning of Monday 11th April, off Île d'Ouessant close to the northwestern corner of France, the engine suddenly died. During my watch from 2.00 am to 7.00 am, I had monitored the fuel situation, revising my consumption estimate from 3 litres per hour to 2.5 litres per hour. Instead of refuelling the tank at 6.00 am, I'd decided to leave it until after breakfast. There was no wind and the tide was taking us towards the rocks near the coast.

I broke out the reserve fuel, bled the engine to rid the fuel system of any trapped air and restarted the engine. It gunned and died. After five attempts, the engine was refusing to start. We were now only half a mile from the treacherous rocks of Île d'Ouessant.

Nick kept watch while I went below to strip the fuel system. A blockage in the fuel feeder pipe from the tank was obstructing fuel flow. I blew it back, taking in a mouthful of diesel in the process, but cleared the blockage. This was our last chance to get the engine started otherwise I would be forced to call for help. The engine fired first time, but when I pushed the throttle forward, increasing power to 1,800 rpm, she began to sputter and complain. It had been a narrow escape. While Nick helmed, I sat at the chart table, designing a more robust fuel system – more filters and a secondary fuel tank – to ensure that I didn't lose use of the engine like that again.

That night, in dense fog, we crossed the shipping lanes of the

English Channel, navigating with radar. At one point, 17 ships were within three miles of our position.

At dawn, the English coast was a welcome sight; peaceful Dorset countryside rolling down to a still and languid sea. I wondered what it would feel like to see the English coast at the end of a circum-navigation and for a moment, I dreamed. After a brief stop in Wey-mouth to take on more fuel, we made it into Cowes at 2.00 am on Thursday 14th April and picked up a mooring buoy at the entrance to the Medina River, the same buoy that Mike had asked me to pick up during the Yachtmaster examination. After breakfast the next morning, I motored *Barrabas* downriver and tied up at the UKSA.

My first voyage on *Barrabas* had ended after 2,000 miles. It had been quite an undertaking, but I never really stopped to think about that. It was only afterwards that I realised the passage had really been a trial: a crash course in heavy weather tactics, emergency reefing drills, sys-tems maintenance and radar navigation in the hardest school of all – the open sea.

The *Oxford Mail* published an article about my upcoming voyage while I was sailing *Barrabas* back from France. BBC Radio Oxford picked up the story. Louise drove me to the studio for an interview with Anne Diamond, once a national TV presenter and now hosting the breakfast show. The follow-on was that BBC regional TV wanted to send a film crew to the boat. Although media attention was beginning to build, I still had no sponsorship funding.

With the Alpha Global Expedition unexpectedly launched in the media, the immediate necessity was to organise an expedition website. I wanted the expedition to benefit charity so that the voyage wasn't solely, and I guess selfishly, serving my own personal aspiration. A website would act as a channel for donations, as well as an information source to the wider world and the media. I nominated two charities – Save the Children and the Oxford Children's Hospital – one a global organisation to reflect the global nature of the voyage and the other, an important paediatric centre close to where I lived near Oxford.

Generate had been busy with the list of suppliers I'd provided. There were expressions of interest from Hydrovane, DMSTech and GUL. I spoke to all three companies and arranged to drive down to the GUL factory in Cornwall to pick up sail clothing in anticipation of the BBC film crew.

Tuesday 26th April turned out to be a lovely day, perfect for the long drive down to GUL's offices. En route, I pulled off the M5 motorway for coffee and sandwiches. I was sitting in the car putting sugar in coffee and unwrapping food when a loud rap on the window startled me. I turned to see a woman in her sixties standing by the driver's door. I assessed her quickly – peroxide blonde hair, bad teeth, threadbare clothing – but she radiated a certain energy. Perhaps she just wanted directions.

The engine was off so the electric windows weren't working. I opened the door.

Her eyes were a piercing blue. 'You're going to live to 92,' she said without hesitation.

The woman had my attention. 'And . . .' I asked.

'You'll be in good health all the way through – perhaps a little illness at the end.' The woman paused. 'D'you mind talking to a gypsy?'

'No,' I said, shaking my head.

The woman took hold of my right hand in her left and her right index finger began an intricate dance around my palm. 'Of your two sons, one is very gifted.'

I didn't say anything, giving her no clue. I wasn't wearing a wedding ring.

'This journey you're planning – it'll be the best thing you ever do.'

That stunned me.

The gypsy went on. 'You're worried about something?'

'Lots of things – money mostly.'

Her finger went back to its dance. 'You'll be getting some money.' The gypsy searched skywards for a moment. 'In August.'

'How much?' I was trying hard to keep my tongue from my cheek.

The gypsy thought for a moment. '£28,000,' she said and began to turn away.

'Wait a sec.' I scrabbled in my pocket, found a ten-pound note and pressed it into her hand. I could ill afford it, but something compelled me. The gypsy looked at me for a moment, not smiling, then turned and wandered away among the parked cars.

I carried on to the GUL factory. In the factory shop, I tried on oilskins and mid-layers and came away with two sets of each that GUL agreed to sponsor.

More than three months later, I would have reason to think of the gypsy woman again.

★

Tim Thornton's company, Marine Computing International, had imploded. A client had reneged, bringing about a cash crisis for the small firm and, in the aftermath, Tim had lost his three staff to other job offers. I drove to the MCI office on a small industrial estate near Southampton to find Tim sitting among a chaos of strewn papers and abandoned desks. Despite the inauspicious start, Tim's enthusiasm for the Alpha Global Expedition was undisguised. As a yachtsman, meteorologist and technophile, his expertise was obvious. We discussed the specifications for the weather and communications systems and I left Tim with instructions to design the system architecture.

By mid-May, it was time to go to work on *Barrabas*. The Medina Yard on the Isle of Wight, located just up-river from the UKSA, was owned by Sir Peter Harrison, the money behind Team GB, which had challenged for the America's Cup in Auckland in 2003. Craig Nutter, a former Team GB crewmember, managed the yard. As an experienced sailor, Craig recognised the unique nature of my impending voyage and did what he could to accommodate my limited budget. With *Barrabas* safely in her cradle, I spent nine hours with the jet-wash cleaning her undersides (a yard record!). I enjoyed being there – the people, the place and the atmosphere; and Cowes, the centre of the British yachting scene, was home to every imaginable boating service and supplier.

My first stop was Spencer Rigging, the oldest established riggers on the island. I'd decided to replace all the standing rigging – the array of steel wire stays that support the mast. Mark Spencer agreed 'to do something' on price and promised to get Ray Field, his most experienced rigger, to do the work. The rigging loft was like a stage set, harking back to the days of square-riggers with its tarred wooden floors and smell of caulk. As a modern-day addendum, centre-fold spreads papered almost every square inch of wall space.

Richard Pierrepont of RHP Marine was next on my list. His services company could provide battery installation and electrics as well carrying out the modifications to the engine fuel system I had designed during the trip back from France.

Louise telephoned me on Friday 20th May.

'I was with Bob and Tina at their new art gallery in Thame and we came up with a publicity idea.'

I was curious. Tina Hadley was a professional photographer whom we'd commissioned for our wedding and the boys' christenings.

'I talked to Bob and suggested that he sponsor the AGX [Alpha

Global Expedition] by donating a limited-edition print as a raffle prize for people donating to the AGX charities with £5 or more. Local press are interested. On the back of it, the gallery gets good exposure. What do you think?'

'I think it's great,' I said, feeling elation far in excess of the benefits of a little local publicity. Was Louise becoming 'engaged' in the expedition? She had never referred to the voyage as the 'AGX' before.

We talked about the boys' upcoming half-term break and agreed for the three of them to come to Cowes. Louise found a B&B place on the net, Busigny House on Castle Road in the old part of Cowes, set up on the hillside overlooking the town and the mouth of the Medina River. I went to check it out and met Sally Warwick, the owner, whose second husband had been one of the fatalities in the tragic Fastnet Race of 1979.

Louise and the boys arrived on Friday 27th May. We spent a wonderful time together, taking the boys to the beach, going for walks along the seafront and visits to arts and crafts centres, riding on the steam railway and eating bowls of moules marinière at a beachside restaurant at St Helen's. At the weekend, we visited Sam and Debbie Laidlaw at their holiday home in Bembridge. Sam took a real interest in the expedition, driving over to Medina Yard to have a look at *Barrabas*.

It was a great few days and a chance for me to take my mind off the daunting amount of work that I needed to complete on *Barrabas*. Antifouling turned into a big job. Layers of epoxy primer, tie-coats and antifouling added and removed unequally over the years had left *Barrabas*'s hull surface uneven below the waterline. The only way to get the paint off was to sandblast the hull using small-bore Olivine grit. The problem was that if I took the hull back to bare metal, I'd need more paint than I'd planned. I spoke to Darren Gittins at Blake Paints. Darren spoke to his technical department and came back with a spec for stainless steel – three layers of epoxy primer, a tie-coat and two coats of antifoul. He reduced the price on the epoxy, provided the antifoul at no charge and agreed to get the paint to the yard in time for the blasting.

Generate had been in touch with Kemp Sails. On Friday 3rd June, I left a message for Matt Atkins, the general manager. Matt phoned me back and I gave him the link to the test server to have a look at the expedition website that had just come on-stream. He consulted with Rob Kemp and they came back with the offer to sponsor the sails for the AGX. It was fantastic news. Matt told me the AGX was exactly the kind of project to promote Kemp within their prime market of cruising rather than racing sails.

Barrabas's new paint job was finished by mid-June. Her undersides were now beautifully smooth. I hand-painted a white bootstrap between the maroon antifoul and the gleaming bare metal of her sides.

Towards the end of June, the twin pressures of time and financial constraints were mounting. If I was going to make the departure date in October, I was going to have to forgo a lot of the work I wanted to do – no back-up generator, no watertight forward bulkhead, no new handrails welded on deck, no new running rigging organisers to take all lines back to the cockpit. Even without these items, I was going to hit the £100,000 bank debt limit I'd set. Although the bank had not specified a limit, it had intimated a reluctance to exceed this amount. My mood plummeted. Everything seemed to take on massive proportions, even the tiniest jobs. Through it all, I kept repeating to myself, '*I have to deal with this – nothing is a problem! It's all about attitude.*' I was becoming psychologically weakened, vulnerable to outside influences, the opinions of others who did not see the expedition from a similar perspective. People are generally well intentioned, but often blind to the point of view of others. The battle to stay true to myself became a constant and wearying skirmish. One incident occurred at the home of my ex-mother-in-law. In late August, Louise took the boys on a one-week holiday to Greece. The day after they left, I took up an invitation to go to her parents' house to 'talk things through'. Instead, my ex-mother-in-law launched an attack, accusing me of being a 'Walter Mitty' character. Walter Mitty fantasised, but never converted. I thought to myself, 'She's right – if I don't go!' It's ironic that I have to thank arguably my biggest detractor for providing a powerful spur through a misfired insult.

At the UKSA, I introduced myself to Paul Burnett, who taught the advanced engineering course. We discussed the problem I'd experienced with the blocked fuel line off Île d'Ouessant. Paul identified the line filter in the uplift pump as the probable reason why the engine was struggling at higher revs.

Water is heavier than diesel. In a diesel tank, a film of water can collect at the bottom either from condensation or water contamination in the fuel. A certain type of bacteria or 'diesel bug' thrives in this environment, proliferating to form a black sludge. If this sludge gets into a fuel system, it can block fuel lines, clog filters and incapacitate injectors. This sludge had caused the problem on *Barrabas*. I needed a more robust system to ensure that fuel reaching the injectors was clean. The Arctic phase was uppermost in my mind. *Barrabas* would probably be under engine for significant stretches because of light winds and drifting ice.

The system I'd designed en route back from France was to fit two Racor filters, each capable of filtering 500 litres per hour, the first situated between the main tank and a new 'day tank' and the second between the 'day tank' and the engine. A third filter, already on the engine, would make a final clean before fuel reached the injectors. An additional advantage was that a day tank increased my fuel capacity by 80 litres.

I was looking for an expert's opinion on the filter/day tank idea and Paul thought it excellent. Craig agreed that it sounded like a plan.

Back on *Barrabas*, I checked the small pump on the engine that pulls fuel from source and pushes it towards the injectors. Just as Paul had expected, there was a level teaspoon of black sludge in the filter.

I finally met Rob Kemp and Matt Atkins when they sailed to Cowes to compete in the Round-the-Island race.

'What did you have in mind for the sails?' Matt asked.

'You know my route, Cape Horn and the Arctic?'

Matt nodded.

'In a nutshell, the sails have got to be bulletproof, heavily reinforced at the tacks, clews and heads [the three points of any triangular-shaped sail] and reinforced reefing cringles.'

'So, all attachment points.'

'Yes. Also the mainsail should have four reefs instead of the usual three so I can use the fourth reef instead of a separate storm trysail.'

We agreed the design details and Rob and Matt went to work measuring up for several hours.

I had a number of transatlantic telephone conversations with John Curry in Vancouver, a former accountant who had bought Hydro-vane, originally a British company whose manufacturing base was still in England. Hydrovane was, in my opinion and in the opinion of others (including a few round-the-world yachtsmen), the best self-steering system in the world. John agreed to sponsor the AGX and the Hydrovane arrived at the UKSA for collection in early July, packed into seven wooden crates.

I took great care with the Hydrovane. Vertical and horizontal alignments had to be true, otherwise the resultant forces of wind and water acting on the vane and rudder would be unbalanced. A single lower bracket fixed on the underside of the sugar scoop and an 'A' bracket coming off the transom supported the shaft. The two stainless steel tubular bars of the 'A' frame were too long and needed trimming. With a hacksaw, it would have been an hour of sweat. I decided on a simpler approach. Craig introduced me to a self-employed welder named Michael Ferguson. Fergie (as everyone knew him) cut the stays to length. I asked him about other welding and metalwork that I needed done, not least boring out the thru-hulls to take the instrument transducers. He came to the yard that afternoon to rim them out.

A crucial piece of equipment arrived from Katadyn in Switzerland – the water-maker. I fitted the unit in the forward part of the hull, making use of two defunct thru-hull fittings, which had once been plumbed to a toilet.

By mid-July with so much still to do, my major worry was lack of time alone with *Barrabas* on the water. Perhaps the delivery trip from Montpellier would be the only sea trial I would have.

To make space for the day tank, I removed the old diesel stove heater. For heating, I fitted an Eberspacher system, running one of the hot-air outlets into the portside forward cabin locker to use as a drying cupboard. (On the voyage, the drying cupboard worked superbly – almost as effective as a domestic tumble dryer.)

The constant worry about money, combined with the long hours I was putting in on *Barrabas*, eventually took their toll and I went down with a severe bout of 'flu. Generate was working on promoting a new marketing initiative with Timberland and had entered my name as a contender for the inaugural Timberland scholarship. On Tuesday 19th July, I drove down to Timberland's HQ to meet the marketing team, struggling through the hour-long meeting with a thundering headache and a sore throat. Afterwards, I drove home and collapsed into bed with a soaring temperature.

Early on Wednesday morning, I was in the car again driving to Romsey in Hampshire to pick up the five new American Lifeline AGM batteries, which DMS Technologies had agreed to sponsor. These were powerful batteries, each of 210 amp/hour capacity, one for engine start and the other four to provide power to the rest of the boat – the house bank.

Still feeling the after-effects of the 'flu, I met Ray Field, who came to the boat with the new standing rigging. I had been in two minds about replacing it but confirmation that I had made the right decision came when we dropped the forestay and found severe wear at the masthead attachment. Ray figured that the forestay was close to parting. If it had failed at sea, the mast could have come down!

Ever since the art raffle, which had been modestly successful, Louise had been taking a greater interest in the project and had begun contacting the national and sailing media. She phoned me one afternoon in mid-July.

'I was talking to Andrew Bray . . .'

'Who's Andrew Bray?'

'Editor of *Yachting World*. He says he's just received a communication about someone called Graham Kendall. He's a New Zealander who's attempting the first vertical via the Northwest Passage!'

My world collapsed. I'd never heard of him or his attempt. I checked his website. He was currently in mid-Atlantic en route from New Zealand towards Canada. I looked at his website every day after that. His boat, *Australexpress*, was made of Kevlar, which seemed to me a dangerous proposition for close navigation in ice. I wondered how the Canadian authorities might view the risks.

Louise and I decided to take a short break in Dorset with the boys. We set off on Monday 25th July and spent an afternoon on Studland Beach until Benji soaked himself in the freezing sea and we had to go back to the B&B. The weather was awful, cold and overcast. On Tuesday, we all went to a small chocolate factory then on to Lulworth Castle. The weather deteriorated to constant rain, but through the gloom came some good news: I had won the Timberland scholarship and was being awarded £30,000! It had come just in time. My last bank statement showed I was down to my last £100. Without the scholarship, I would have been forced either to beg for more money from the bank, delay departure while I figured another way to raise funds, or abandon the expedition altogether.

By the end of July, I was through the bulk of the heavy work and, after more than two months ashore, I re-launched *Barrabas* on Saturday 31st July, sailing across the Solent and up Southampton Water to Shamrock Quay. A company of electronic engineers recommended by Tim were waiting to fit the navigation and communications systems.

While this work was going on, I re-covered the cuddy with exterior-grade clear polycarbonate sheets. Bernard's original covering had yellowed with UV exposure. I cut the new sheets to approximate sizes for the eight panels it would take to cover the frame, screwed the panels down, marked the outlines against the frames, trimmed the sheets and then moulded the bends and curves using a hot air gun.

Cowes Week is the biggest regatta in the world. The island was inundated with boats, sailors and spectators. I was pleased to be on the mainland, but Timberland reckoned Cowes Week (where the company had a stand) presented a good opportunity for a full press launch of the Alpha Global Expedition.

On Thursday 4th August, Louise and I went over to Cowes. The whole experience was surreal. The Alpha Global Expedition still seemed like no more than an 'idea', a formless dream. When we arrived in Cowes, the marketing manager, Niamh Lyon, whisked me off to the Timberland store and kitted me out with new clothing. Louise, to her delight, got a new pair of shoes. Timberland's PR agency had lined up a series of interviews – *Isle of Wight County Press*, Cowes Radio, ITV Meridian, *Yachting World*, Isle of Wight Radio and Solent TV.

At 4.00 pm, Niamh presented me with a 'giant' cheque for £30,000 in front of a large crowd. In my mind's eye, I could clearly see the lined face of a gypsy woman with a piercing blue gaze.

CHAPTER 8

Rules of Engagement

By mid-August, the end of the refit was in sight. Tim came down to *Barrabas* to install the software onto the purpose-made computer and my laptop that would act as a back-up. I stripped out the fore cabin and built in a workshop with timber supplied by Bob Hacker, who operated a small timber store at the quay. This space, where I could keep all my tools and spare parts, would be useful, not only from an organisational perspective but as an area where I could drill, saw, file and fix things without messing up other parts of the cabin. I fitted a small vice onto the workbench and finials for my toolboxes to keep them in place. Bob also lent me a book, *Two Against Cape Horn* by Hal Roth, a former winner of the Blue Water Medal. Whatever my trepidation, Roth's account of his time in the Cape Horn area did nothing to quell my fears.

Meanwhile, Graham Kendall had updated his website with news that caused a deluge of relief to flood through me. His entry for 26th August read:

> It is with a heavy heart that I have made the decision not to proceed further towards the Northwest Passage. The conditions are now too dangerous and I can't go against Mother Nature and common sense. The advice I have received from the Canadian coast guard and the ice experts in the Arctic is that the conditions in the passage are not favourable for this season.

My relief was in no way *schadenfreude*, but I had to acknowledge that Kendall's attempt at the 'vertical' had been generating some tension in me.

By the end of August, *Barrabas* was back at the Medina Yard. The new propeller shaft, made by a small marine engineering outfit in

Cowes and fitted in July, was vibrating badly. I dismantled the entire rudder and steering assembly to remove the shaft. At the workshop, we tested the shaft in a lathe. It was bent.

Fergie welded new block mounts at the base of the mast and fitted the storm bars that I'd designed to prevent seawater ripping the hatches off if *Barrabas* rolled in big seas.

During the early part of September, I snagged the boat, fixing a constant stream of niggly problems. Benji spent some time with me on board *Barrabas*, driving up and down the Hamble River. The sight of a small boy at the helm of a heavy steel boat seemed to amuse everyone who passed. By 8th September, the refit was finished except for the fitting of the new sails.

Permission from the Russian government to sail in their Arctic territorial waters along the Northern Sea Route (NSR – previously called the Northeast Passage) remained the major outstanding logistical issue. I wrote to the consular department at the Russian Embassy in London on 6th September. The polar section of the route presented an awesome challenge. NSR Administration had only ever allowed a handful of yachts to transit. I needed a visa, but I could only get it if I had special dispensation to be sailing in Russia's territorial waters. This dispensation would only be granted if various government departments agreed, including the Federal Security Bureau, Russia's internal security force, the new name for the old KGB.

One of the yachts that had previously received permission was Eric Brossier's French-flagged *Vagabond*, which made an eastward transit of the NSR in 2002.

I emailed Eric to get his advice on how best to proceed with the Russians. While these other yachts had set the precedent, the difficulty was going to be in persuading the Russian authorities to let me make my attempt single-handed, without an ice pilot on board. An ice pilot, an experienced seaman certified to navigate in ice, was a mandatory requirement for every vessel, regardless of size, sailing the NSR. But if I carried an ice pilot, I would effectively be sacrificing my single-handed status. According to the rules that I'd set for the Alpha Global Expedition, no one else could be with me on board while *Barrabas* was under way – no one.

Eric's response shocked me: '*Hi Adrian . . . we needed permission from Russian government to sail the NEP (Northeast Passage) in 2002. It took me three years to get it . . . Good luck, Eric Brossier . . .*'

This was an early warning of a saga that would escalate during my voyage towards the Bering Strait.

The unpredictable nature of the North Polar ice, its extent and drift, exposed any logistical planning to uncertainty. I exchanged correspondence with Lars Kaleschke at the University of Bremen's Institute of Environmental Physics. Lars wrote to me in September: '. . . *the sea ice coverage has a high inter-annual variability and the pattern is hard to predict if not impossible . . . global warming is on your side for your expedition . . . if the trend of the last nine years continues, you will have good chances . . . permission of the Russian administration could be the most uncertain factor . . .*'

The lateness of my application to the Russian government would prove a serious error.

With an unsettled feeling, Louise and I drove to London the next day, Wednesday 7th September, for the Timberland presentation at the Royal Geographic Society.

Barrabas was moored at Port Hamble Marina. On 12th September, I set off for Poole, where Matt and Rob, driving from the Kemp sail loft in Wareham, met me to fit the new sails. A sizeable crowd gathered on the quayside to watch the sails go up. A BBC film crew arrived in the afternoon and, with Matt on board, we took *Barrabas* out onto the water to try out the sails.

Bad weather kept me pinned down in Poole for the next few days. Martin Coldicott, whose children attended school with my boys, called to tell me that his brother-in-law, the BBC Radio 2 DJ Johnnie Walker, wanted to come and see the boat. They were staying at Johnnie's home nearby. The three of us spent a couple of hours on board then had lunch at a waterfront restaurant. I promised to take Johnnie sailing before I left on the expedition, weather permitting.

With work on *Barrabas* filling the week, I made sure I was at home each weekend to see the children. There wasn't much opportunity for exercise but I found time to put myself through a punishing route on the bike – 15 miles through hilly terrain, just to see how I fared. I was pleased with the outcome. Years of staying in shape had paid dividends with a reasonably high degree of residual endurance.

During the preceding few weeks, Louise had become increasingly involved with the expedition, finding supply sponsors and having fantastic success: Nivea, Ecover, Heinz, Cadbury, Mornflake, Clipper and Creative (MP3s) had all agreed to supply products. The Alpha Global Expedition seemed to be gaining momentum, an energy drawing support from both companies and individuals.

It was Thursday 20th September when Louise announced, 'I've made a decision.'

I was standing in the hallway of her house. 'Which is?'

She paused, gathered herself and said, 'I'm going to be the expedition manager.'

I was overwhelmed and hugely, massively relieved. I wanted to fling my arms around her, but instead I said, 'It'll be a lot of work.'

'Who else is going to do it? Someone has to manage the website, look after the charities, deal with sponsors and probably a host of other things we haven't thought of.'

'I agree. Thank you.' What more could I say?

'I have some rules.'

I frowned at her but stayed quiet.

'When it comes to PR, what I say goes. If there is water involved, you deal with it. In other words, you sail the boat, I'll do everything else. Agreed?'

'Agreed.'

'Right,' she said, 'the next job is to sort out a weapon and get a firearms licence.'

The risk of piracy attacks was a real danger to small boats passing close inshore along the coasts of West Africa and Brazil. I would be sailing through both these areas. I'd researched the incidence of pirate attacks on small boats while writing my novel *Cobra*. Yachts are soft targets: low freeboards and unarmed crews usually carrying valuables on board: money, jewellery, passports. Another risk would come from polar bears if *Barrabas* ever got stuck in ice.

'And we should announce a departure date.'

We decided on 18th October, Gabriel's birthday. It would have been our eighth wedding anniversary. Sir Chay Blyth had also departed from the River Hamble on the same date in 1970 at the start of his historic circumnavigation.

Between them, Rob Kemp and Louise arranged for *Barrabas* to sail past the Southampton Boat Show on Thursday 22nd September. I slipped my mooring at Port Hamble at 8.30 am and motored up Southampton Water towards the Red Funnel ferry terminal and Mayflower Park. Unbeknown to me, *Gipsy Moth IV*, the star of the show, was due to leave Mayflower Park on her round-the-world rally at 11.00 am. Not wishing David Green to think I was stealing the famous yacht's thunder, I asked Louise to give him a call to say as much and decided to hold station until after *Gipsy Moth IV* had sailed. At 11.30 am, looking resplendent, she passed me. It seemed incredible to me that since reading Chichester's book all those years before, his yacht and mine were now only feet apart, each about to embark on voyages around the world. A great welling of emotion rose up, prickling my skin and filling my eyes with tears. I watched her stern for a while and then turned *Barrabas* towards the show quays.

The announcer described my upcoming voyage. Spectators came onto the pontoon to have a look at *Barrabas*. Later that day, after I'd returned *Barrabas* to her mooring at Port Hamble, I went back to the show to spend the rest of the afternoon with Matt and Rob on the Kemp stand. Leaving with the throng at 7.00 pm was strange after the excitement of being watched and photographed by that same crowd earlier.

I was still waiting for two pieces of equipment from the United States. Ever since the harrowing disasters in the 1979 Fastnet race (15 fatalities) and the 1998 Sydney to Hobart race (six fatalities) when massively powerful weather systems wreaked havoc with the race fleets, discussion had ranged widely about the best way to stabilise a small boat in survival conditions. After months of research on the merits and disadvantages of deploying various types of drogue from the stern and parachute anchors from the bow, I settled on a Jordan Series Drogue (JSD). Designed by Donald Jordan, an aeronautical engineer and yachtsman, and developed in conjunction with the US Coastguard, independent research concluded that if all the boats in the '79 Fastnet and '98 Sydney–Hobart had been equipped with JSDs, the likelihood is that fewer lives would have been lost.

I contacted Don Jordan for his opinion on parachute anchors, first used by American fishermen after World War II. Surplus parachutes, deployed from the bows of the trawlers and coastal fishing boats, had the effect of slowing the boats in big seas. The problem was, the anchors 'snatched' when they inflated (with water), exerting huge loads on the attachment points.

Don Jordan sent me an email on Sunday 18th September: *I am now 90 and no longer answer questions. However, this is an emergency. YOU MUST carry the drogue on this wonderful adventure. The chute is a technical monstrosity. It has 30 times the drag of the drogue and acts like a mooring on the bottom. In a breaking wave strike, it would develop loads that no gear could stand. I wish you well. Don.*

As a result, Dave Pelissier of ACE Sailmakers in Maine was making a JSD for *Barrabas*, tailored specifically for her displacement.

I also wanted a second piece of critical survival gear and I was not going to leave until I had it – a solid, unsinkable lifeboat (in addition to the inflatable life raft already on *Barrabas*) small enough to stow on the foredeck, with oars, a collapsible sailing rig and watertight stowage compartments for emergency provisions and additional survival kit. After weeks of searching, I couldn't find anything in the UK. In America, David Hulbert had designed the Portland Pudgy. I contacted him. Development of the Portland Pudgy was at the end of the prototype stage and not yet in production. I explained my situation. David agreed to manufacture a one-off specifically for *Barrabas*.

But how were we going to get the lifeboat to England? Louise contacted DHL and the company offered not only to airfreight the survival craft from the US but to act as the expedition's official courier. Over the coming months, DHL would prove to be an invaluable sponsor, responding to rapidly changing situations with cheerful efficiency.

Louise came up with a sparkling idea – obvious really, but then all the best ideas are. As I was raising money for the Oxford Children's Hospital, could the hospital supply the medical kit? She put the idea to Janet Sprake, Head of Fundraising, who came up trumps. David Skinner, Head of Accident & Emergency medicine at Oxford's John Radcliffe Hospital, agreed to put the kit together, including prescription antibiotics and surgical equipment, and to be my shore-side medical liaison (David was also a keen sailor and kept his boat in Chichester). The offer included access to his full team, which ran a 24-hour rota and would be available to me if ever I needed advice or, worse, I needed to perform any surgical procedures on myself.

The final preparations were frenetic. On 1st October, my 45th birthday, Louise and I took time out and spent the day with the boys at Legoland. Fergie was busy fabricating stainless steel cages to house additional 20-litre fuel cans on *Barrabas*'s aft deck. I finally found an underwater collision repair kit from Alan Molyneaux, whose company supplied the Royal Navy. Barton Marine came on board as a supplier with new blocks for all the running rigging, and Martin Amy at Kelvin Hughes, the country's largest marine chart supplier, was busy collating my chart portfolio, including Russian charts sourced from the Russian Hydrographic Office in Moscow, covering the Northern Sea Route.

Sam Laidlaw called in early October. As former vice-president of Chevron Texaco Oil and now Centrica's chief executive, Sam's contacts included people in the high echelons of Russian business and heavyweight political figures in Moscow. He extended an open invitation – call if we needed any introductions. Despite my repeated letters, emails and calls to the Russian Embassy in Kensington Palace Gardens, I hadn't received any response. After Eric Brossier's comments, any expeditious route through the bureaucratic maze was welcome. I emailed Sam to say that we'd give the Russians a little more time but, more likely than not, I would take him up on his offer.

By the second week of October, Louise's garage was stacked with provisions: tinned fruit and meat, cooking oil, dried pasta, chocolate, vitamins and supplements, sauces and spices, porridge oats, rice, biscuits and ready mixed bread flour. Clipper had also supplied organic tea (bags), coffee and drinking chocolate. Running out of tea and coffee would be disastrous. I always drank prodigious amounts of the stuff but I can't drink either without milk. I bought 60 litres of long-life milk and 60 tins of Carnation evaporated milk. I began ferrying these supplies to Port Hamble, storing them around *Barrabas* in cupboards, lockers and beneath the cabin floorboards.

Time slipped away. Job lists seemed to grow ever longer. Louise and I were exhausted and, after a long discussion, we decided to defer departure to 28th October. Even with the 10-day postponement, it was still a race to get a tick against each item on my final checklist.

I visited Doug Florent at the Oxford Gun Club on Monday 10th October. Doug recommended a pump-action shotgun with a plastic stock to limit seawater damage. That afternoon, back at Louise's house, Brian Brewster, the Thames Valley Police Firearms Officer, stopped by to interview me and fill out the various documents I'd need for a firearms licence. While we were form-filling, the JSD arrived from Maine.

The next day, I was back on board *Barrabas*. Fergie had come over from the Isle of Wight to weld the fuel cages on the aft deck and the transom.

Sky News contacted Louise the following day, 12th October, after she'd issued a press release about the new start date. They wanted to shoot a pre-departure interview. I also agreed to pre-record an interview with BBC Radio Oxford.

1. *Barrabas*'s frames are laid.

2. Sir Francis Chichester whose circumnavigation in 1967 inspired me to sail around the world.

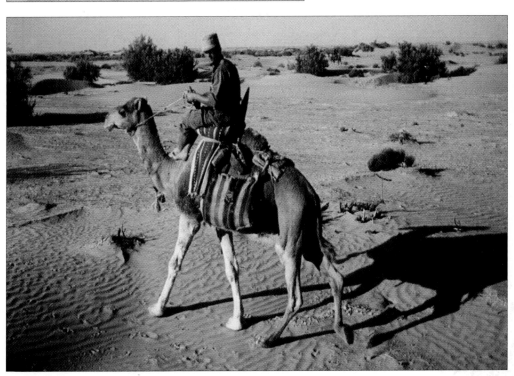

3. Bernard on patrol in the Algerian desert.

4. Our great friends, Christian and Tracy Foures, at their home in Normandy, France, 2003.

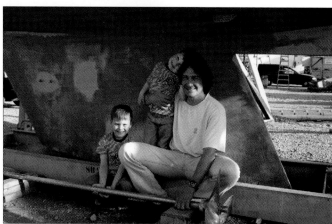

5. *Barrabas*'s refit gets underway at the Medina Yard in Cowes, Isle of Wight, June 2005.

6. Job done – *Barrabas*'s hull is as fair as new, July 2005. The bow etching of Neptune is clearly visible.

7. A final kiss for the boys

8. Louise who supported me throughout the voyage and managed the expedition brilliantly.

9. Sail past at the Southampton Boat Show, September 2005.

10. My parents with Benji in January 1999. My father died suddenly before I completed the voyage.

11. A last wave and I was eager to get to the start line, 28th October 2005.

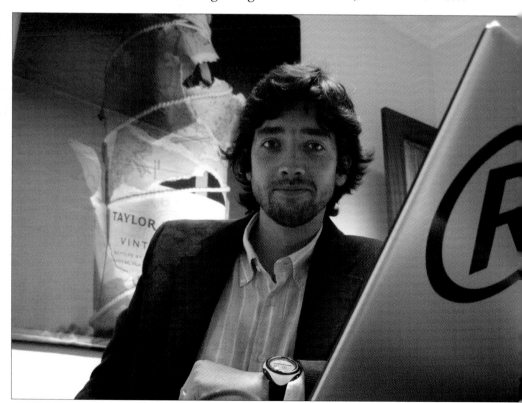

12. Ricardo Diniz provided invaluable routing advice from his base in Lisbon.

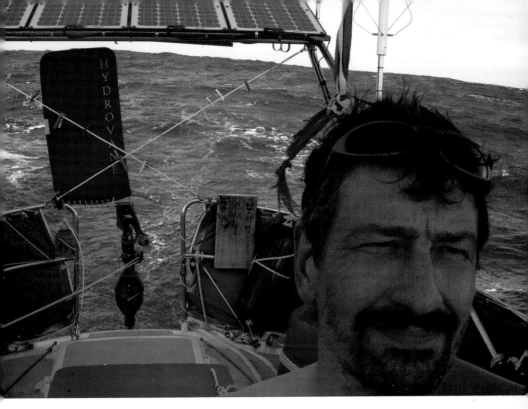

13. Sunshine at last after the storms in the Channel, November 2005.

14. Sailing under the asymmetric spinnaker close to the Canary Islands, November 2005.

15. Armed and ready. A suspected pirate boat was tracking *Barrabas* off the Brazilian coast, January 2006.

16. The first fish I caught with the spear gun, January 2006.

17. Approaching Oahu, May 2006.

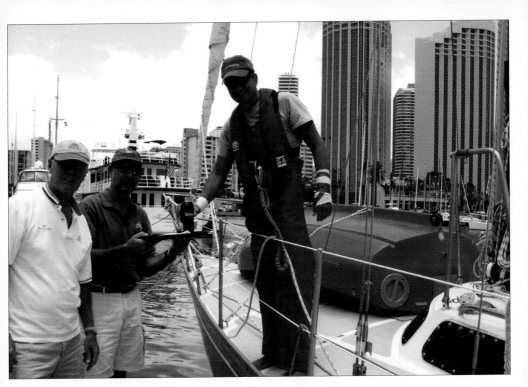

18. *Above* An ice cold Guinness from Michael Roth, Rear Commodore for Sail at the Waikiki Yatch Club. Ernie Woodruff looks on.

19. *Left* Media greeting in Oahu.

20. First step ashore after 193 days at sea.

21. Plotting position, July 2006.

22. Henk de Velde and me at the London Boat Show, January 2007.

23. In mid-winter, *Barrabas* was covered with snow and ice, March 2007.

24. Cam about to 'tattoo' *Barrabas* with an Inuit symbol, July 2007.

Tim Thornton gave me a series of tutorials on the computer on board *Barrabas*. Afterwards I went back to Louise's house, loaded up the car with more of the supplies stockpiled in her garage, then rushed back to *Barrabas* to meet up with Dick Everitt from *Practical Boat Owner* who was planning a big spread in the magazine.

Meanwhile, Louise was busy sourcing fifty 20-litre fuel cans to give me an extra 1,000-litre capacity. She eventually got them from Plastimo at trade price.

- On Saturday 15th October, the 'Pudgy' emergency dinghy was air-freighted to the UK from Maine and delivered to *Barrabas* at Port Hamble. I collected my charts and almanacs from Martin Amy at Kelvin Hughes in Southampton, then raced back to Port Hamble in time to meet the DHL lorry. Steve Walker, one of DHL's managers, the driver and I broke open the crate. The small lifeboat was bright orange and weighed 70 kg and, when we positioned it on *Barrabas*'s foredeck, it fitted perfectly! The final delivery came from Marlow Ropes and I spent the remainder of the afternoon replacing most of the running rigging.

On 18th October, I again wrote to the Russian Embassy in London, hoping for some indication that my application to sail the NSR had at least been submitted for consideration to the relevant departments in Moscow.

The UKSA had agreed to supply my fuel at cost. So, on Friday 21st October, Fergie brought his van from the island, collected the new fuel cans, took them back to the island, filled them and returned them to Port Hamble for loading. With *Barrabas* laden down with an extra tonne of fuel, I drove back to Oxford and met Louise at the BBC Radio Oxford studios for a live link-up with Johnnie Walker's 'Drive Time' show on BBC Radio 2. I was shown into a small studio room, hooked up to mikes and headphones, then left on my own. I was dirty from working on *Barrabas* all day. 'Wow,' I thought to myself, 'a year ago, the Alpha Global Expedition was just an idea in my head. Now I'm about to talk to eight million people!'

Louise was suffering from a severe bout of 'flu, the consequence, I surmised, of exhaustion and stress. She soldiered on, accompanying me to John Radcliffe Hospital the following day to pick up the medical kit from David Skinner. I sat with David in a treatment room for 20 minutes while he explained the contents: painkillers, motion sickness tablets, antibiotics, fracture casts, morphine, anaesthetics, tissue adhesive and surgical instruments. I thought of Vito Dumas on *Legh II* cutting into the rotting tissue of his arm with a knife. I made a silent vow to be very, very careful.

John Reed, the secretary of the World Sailing Speed Record Council (WSSRC), visited Louise and me on board.

It was Louise's idea to have my voyage monitored in some official capacity. I'd never heard of the WSSRC. Like Bernard Moitessier, I tended to baulk at officialdom and the WSSRC sounded exactly like the type of bureaucratic organisation I'd spent my life trying to avoid.

'So, John,' I said as he clambered aboard, 'what do I need to do to comply with your rules? For that matter, what are your rules?'

I was expecting him to produce a checklist and spend a couple of hours going over *Barrabas* while firing questions at me. At the very least, I was expecting to be asked to sign a declaration that my log-books would accurately reflect any and all events, actions and occurrences on the voyage. To me, one critical aspect of any verification procedure would be to record the number of hours on the engine (to check against the number of engine hours recorded at the end of the voyage and, if different, for it to then be incumbent on the sailor to satisfactorily explain that difference.) I was also expecting fuel samples to be taken for subsequent comparison with fuel samples taken after the voyage to determine whether additional fuel had been shipped during the passage.

John made a cursory examination of the cockpit and briefly looked at the winches to ensure they were manually operated and not electrically powered.

'Is that it?' I asked, containing my surprise with some difficulty.

'Yes.'

'Don't you want to see below?'

'Not necessary.' Then, with a totally straight face, he said, 'There's a fee for the WSSRC – £1,500. You can pay by cheque or cash.' He'd been on my boat for less than 10 minutes!

Louise and I looked at each other, then she laughed out loud. I was incredulous. Louise couldn't see his face. I could and I could tell he wasn't joking. I batted the issue aside. 'Let's forget about any fee for the moment. What exactly are your rules?'

John Reed talked for several minutes, then looked at me expectantly.

'So, if I've got this right,' I said, 'any form of assistance that includes going into port renders me no longer single-handed?'

'That's right. You can anchor, but you can't tie up to a structure connected to the land.'

'And if I hail a passing ship and they sling a pint of milk over the side which I then retrieve . . .'

'You're assisted and therefore no longer single-handed.'

'But if I have a problem with the engine, for example, and I need the engine to charge the batteries and I need the batteries to power navigation instruments and communications like the satellite phone for safety purposes, can I call an engineer and get the engineer to tell me how to fix the engine?'

'That's fine.'

'That's *not* assistance?'

'No.'

I was flummoxed.

'So, according to the WSSRC, Joshua Slocum and Sir Francis Chichester were not single-handed?'

'No.'

'Even though at all times while their vessels were under way, actually creating their tracks around the world and they were the only ones on board, you're telling me that they were not, in fact, single-handed?'

'That's correct.'

I sat back and thought for a moment. 'How long's the WSSRC been going?'

John puffed out his cheeks. 'We were established in 1972 to measure sailing speed over 500 metres, and now we're part of the International Sailing Federation.'

'So a pure sprint over a defined distance.'

John nodded, then went on to explain that their remit had expanded to include watercraft of various configurations, including windsurfers and eventually rules governing round-the-world races.

There had been no mention of the antipodal principle. When I asked him about it, he looked perplexed. I explained what antipodal points were and their relevance in shaping a vessel's track to a great circle.

'The first round-the-world yacht race was the Golden Globe in 1968. The antipodal rule was an absolute requirement. Chichester was on the judging panel – I think he may even have been the chairman of judges. Are you saying that the Vendée and other such round-the-world races don't comply to the antipodal rule?'

John shook his head. 'No, but those races are run according to our rules.'

'So, what about non-racing events like mine?'

'We reluctantly inherited those in 1988.'

'Reluctantly?'

'Well, they're difficult to monitor.'

'So how do you monitor them?'

'We just apply our rules.'

'But those are race rules.'

'Those are the rules.'

I was amazed. 'So, if I've got this right, the only way, according to your rules, that a single-handed circumnavigator can be a single-handed circumnavigator is if he or she sails non-stop. In doing so, there is no necessity to conform to the antipodal rule but they can take any type of assistance so long as it is not physical, in which case it doesn't count as assistance, even when that help might be the difference between a sailor being able to continue their voyage or having to abandon?'

I thought about all this for long hours afterwards. I noticed on the WSSRC website that Chichester was listed in their records, despite not conforming to their rules, as was Joshua Slocum. As a convenience, the WSSRC had Slocum's voyage on *Spray* listed as 'Boston to Boston' (one of their rules being that the voyage finish where it started), even though he left from Boston but returned to Newport, Rhode Island. (I wondered whether this *convenience* was to accommodate Slocum's inclusion on the basis that whatever anyone says, his voyage on *Spray* is accepted as being the first single-handed circumnavigation.) While the WSSRC had elected to ignore the antipodal requirement for round-the-world races because of practical constraints (why not just have two marks, antipodal to one another, which all competitors are required to hit and record?), the physical constraints to a circumnavigation route posed, for example, by landmasses did not, it appeared, merit consideration. Thus all circumnavigations via the Panama and Suez Canals were, under their rules, void.

No one had done what I proposed, and sailing in close ice situations would inevitably raise some awkward questions about use of the engine, towing, icebreaker support or even carriage through impenetrable ice to ensure the safety of vessel and crew (safety of life at sea being the overriding tenet of international maritime law). It seemed to me that to apply race rules to non-racing voyages, where the ethos was entirely different, was shabby thinking. To insist on rules that retrospectively voided the vast majority of recognised and generally accepted single-handed circumnavigations was akin, at best, to a badly tailored suit of clothes – ill-fitting – and, at worst, woefully inadequate. I also felt that to list record voyages, fastest and firsts, whether circumnavigations or otherwise, based on an ability or willingness to pay, could not possibly be right.

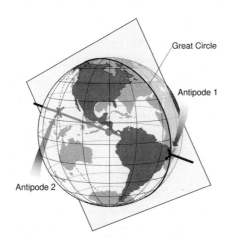

Great Circle

Antipode 1

Antipode 2

Any plane passing through the centre of the earth will define a Great Circle on its surface. Any two points diametrically opposed on a Great Circle are antipodal to one another.

Forget the WSSRC. I would set my own rules. I would start and finish at the same point; bisect every meridian of longitude; cross the equator twice in opposite directions; sail a minimum distance of 21,600 nautical miles and record at least one pair of antipodal points on my track. My attempt would be non-stop, but if for whatever reason that wasn't possible, I would also: stop in port on the proviso that it was absolutely necessary to do so for reasons of safety and primarily to avoid calling out rescue services and endangering the lives of other people; allow myself use of the engine if absolutely necessary for the safety of the vessel (manoeuvring in close ice situations); and allow myself to be towed, assisted by an icebreaker or transported in situations of impenetrable ice. Finally and crucially, I would be the only person on board while *Barrabas* created her track around the world.

I wrote these rules down. I read them aloud in front of a mirror, then looked myself in the eye. If I got through this, there was only one person I needed to satisfy.

★

With two days until departure, I conducted a final round of interviews. On the way from Oxfordshire to the Hamble, I collected my shotgun from the Oxford Gun Club. It had arrived that morning from Italy in tandem with my firearms licence from the Thames Valley Police. Despite repeated requests for an acknowledgement that my application to sail the NSR had been received at the Russian Embassy, I had still not heard back from the consular department.

I cannot remember too much of my last evening. Louise had booked the children and us into a B&B in Hamble. *Barrabas* was tugging gently at her mooring lines on the events quay at Hamble Port Marina. I stowed the gun and ammunition on board. There still seemed an infinite list of small jobs yet to complete but I dismissed them. I remembered once hearing someone say that if you waited until every last 't' was crossed, every 'i' dotted, you'd never leave.

We had supper at a pub in the village. The atmosphere was warm and congenial. An open fire crackled, casting dull orange light over thickly hewn wooden tables. The tinkle of conversation fell on me like warm rain but Louise and I were unusually silent. We both understood the magnitude of the voyage ahead but neither of us could quite grasp the reality of it.

I slept soundly enough. At 10.00 am, we were at the boat. Press and television crews arrived, filming and interviewing me for two hours. What I really wanted to do was hug my children and slip quietly away. Louise had collected a five-day weather forecast from the marina office – southwesterly winds at Force 7 (wind speeds of 28–33 knots). It would be choppy, but no more than 'uncomfortable'.

Matt Atkins then stepped on deck to crew for me until I reached the start line. I kissed Benjamin and Gabriel, pressed my cheek against the soft skin of their faces, closed my eyes and breathed their scent deeply. I reluctantly released each of them. Louise stepped towards me. Nothing needed to be said. I hugged her hard.

We slipped the lines and *Barrabas* turned her bow away from the pontoon, taken on the ebb tide, the low rumble of her diesel engine walking her sedately towards the river mouth.

A TV crew from SKY News buzzed around *Barrabas* in a rigid inflatable boat. Someone yelled at me for a comment. I shouted back, 'So far, so good – two miles down, 30,000 to go!' With the mainsail up and the headsail reefed, Matt clambered off onto the RIB. Moments later, *Barrabas*'s bow breached the start line, a line between

Calshot Spit buoy and Hillhead, and in that moment, 1.53.34 pm on Friday 28th October 2005, decades of dreaming, years of planning and months of preparation condensed and crystallised into performance. I was alone.

CHAPTER 9

Baptism by Fire

I eased *Barrabas* tentatively eastwards through the Solent, past the sea forts and through an anchorage area where ships rode at their anchor chains in the dwindling afternoon light. Hand steering, to prevent myself thinking about the children I had left behind and the months at sea ahead, I concentrated on weaving a zigzag course down the eastern side of the Isle of Wight. Close to the shipping lanes in which ferries plied between Portsmouth and France, I kept focused on tacking *Barrabas* into open water in a gathering southerly Force 6, eventually rounding Saint Catherine's Point on the south side of the Isle of Wight at 2.00 am. With the wind holding from the south, I put *Barrabas* onto a beam reach and set the autopilot.

Below deck, the night light over the chart table cast a dull red glow across the cabin while the bright lights of the island twinkled through the open companionway. I rested through the night, snatching a cat-nap now and then. By the murky dawn, the Isle of Wight had faded to a green-brown insinuation on the horizon. At 8.15 am, I ate my first meal – porridge and fresh coffee – and for the first time in my life felt seasick.

The weather forecast spelled an ominous deterioration through the day to Force 8 conditions. A pang of concern skittered through me. Yesterday's forecast had specified Force 7 at worst. I shortened sail in winds gusting to 35 knots.

Barrabas heeled over, her side deck flush with the surface. The air vent for the freshwater tanks was on the starboard side deck. Worried that seawater might find its way into my 400-litre water supply, I fitted a length of hose to the vent pipe and lashed it to the guardrail but I was soon to discover that my remedial action had come too late.

*Adrian: Saturday 29th October 2005

I know I keep thanking you for all you have done so far. It would have been extraordinarily lonely not to have had you there in an active capacity.
Whatever the eventual outcome, I am really proud to have come this far and your involvement means it is a shared experience rather than an episode that would otherwise have been locked in my head and invisible to others forever.

By early Sunday morning, even the most pessimistic forecast had not predicted conditions worsening to severe gale force 9 and, by late afternoon, storm force 10 winds were driving me too far north of west. I wasn't going to make it past Land's End.

If these conditions had been on the five-day forecast Louise had given me on Friday, I would have delayed the start. At 4.00 pm, I tacked to give myself sea room. Since my departure, I had gone 48 hours with little sleep. I thought about making for shelter but the south coast of England was a dangerous lee shore in the southerly winds. It was safer to stay in open water.

I heard ships on the short-range VHF radio requesting anchoring to ride out the weather. Throughout the night I tacked southeast then northwest, crabbing my way slowly, painfully, westwards and out of the Channel. The mainsheet parted, setting the boom free to thrash wildly from side to side. I caught the boom by turning the boat into the raging wind, lashing it down while I repaired the sheet.

And then I was swept off the deck – only by some miracle did I get back on board.

Adrian: Thursday 3rd November 2005

I'll stay with it and try to get clear of this weather. I've got today, tomorrow and maybe a bit of Saturday before another serious round of shit hits the fan. If I'm caught in that, I suspect it'll do me in – just for lack of sleep if nothing else! Other than that, I'm on top of the world.

*All emails from me are to Louise unless otherwise specified.

Lack of sleep was beginning to melt time. The aftershock of my close call with death had left me exhausted. By the end of the day, I'd had enough. Winds had moderated slightly but were still blowing at Force 8 from the southwest, pinning me down in the western approaches. The forecast indicated the weather moderating and a wind shift to the northwest and perhaps the opportunity to sneak clear of the Channel before another big depression rolled in from Iceland.

I thought about my options. Would the wind shift give me enough time to get out of here? Or would it be better, safer, to find an anchorage, catch up on sleep and tidy the boat while I waited for a better weather window? I decided to make for the Helford River (Cornwall). My decision did not elicit any emotion from me – this was the situation. I had assessed conditions and forecasts from the perspective of safety and practicality. I was neither upset at the delay nor relieved at the prospect of rest. If I did experience any type of reaction, it was relief at my detachment. I was reassured that, despite suffering fatigue from long hours of sleeplessness, my mind was functioning rationally and not emotionally.

Barrabas fretted at her mooring buoy. Close by, a collection of stone houses huddled together on the north bank of the Helford River.

I kept looking at the spot on the starboard side deck where I'd been standing when the wave swept me off the boat. I measured the distance between that spot and the aftermost part of the boat's structure: 1.83 metres, close to 2.5 metres if I included the full extent of my outstretched arm. The GPS had recorded an average boat speed at the time of 5.2 knots, equivalent to 2.6 metres per second. From the moment I hit the water, the boat would have travelled past me and out of reach in less than one second. One second!

I looked at my hands and flexed my fingers, then felt the pulses at my wrists and wondered at the fact that I was alive when I could so easily have been out there, floating face down in the sea.

A few small jobs had been left undone and I used my time in the Helford River to complete these: stocking the solid lifeboat mounted on the foredeck with food, a hand-held GPS and batteries, flares, manual water maker, a tarpaulin and parachute anchor. I surveyed the contents of the 'grab bag' stowed at the base of the companionway

steps and re-packed it with emergency medical supplies, water, signal-
ling mirror, more batteries, a handheld VHF radio, knives, torch, a
thermal survival aid and an SAS survival guide, waterproofed pencil
and paper and matches dunked in hot wax to keep them dry. The 'grab
bag' was a waterproof, plastic container with a screw top and a rope
handle. All boats at sea have one, or should have, and, if there is an
emergency where the crew has to take to the life raft, the bag is
'grabbed' on the way out by one of the crew.

Storm damage was relatively minor but I needed to reconstruct the
restraining bars for the fuel cans in the fore cabin and rewire the solar
panel array to bypass the solar charge regulator that had burnt out –
short-circuited by seawater. On deck, I replaced the headsail sheets,
rigged a new headsail furling line and replaced the boom breaker line
that had snapped when the main sheet had failed.

My main concern was water – seawater had contaminated all four
water tanks. I pumped them dry. A few litres of bottled water would
suffice until I was once again at sea and could operate the watermaker.

The newly installed Eberspacher diesel heater was not working. The
diagnostics programme indicated a fuel issue. I stripped the fuel supply
system working from the pump to the tank. With the standpipe out
and the valve open, I could not blow through. Figuring a blockage,
I fed a piece of wire up the standpipe – still no joy. I fed the wire
through the valve end. There seemed to be an obstruction. I disconnected the valve, shoved the wire through until it hit the obstruction, jiggled it about and to my amazement a small brass screw
popped out. It had orientated itself so the head was blocking the valve
in the open position. How had it got there? A mystery – a demonstration of the law of boats – *if it can, it will*. After an hour reassemb-
ling the system, I switched the heater on, waiting anxiously but with
rising euphoria as the cool air blowing onto my hand from the vent
became warmer and then hot.

On shore, Louise had support from David Skinner as medical
advisor and Tim Thornton to deal with technical issues. Ricardo
Diniz now joined her, although Ricardo was in Lisbon. Some months
later, Ian Johnstone-Bryden would join the team and go on to produce
a number of detailed reports about the expedition for his website,
Broadly Boats. For the first of these reports, Ian asked Ricardo to
describe how he had become involved.

As a keen sailor, I am aware of most projects that happen around the world. One day I got a Google alert about somebody trying to do something new. Well, there aren't many 'new' projects left these days! What could he possibly be doing? Less than 90 people have sailed around the world alone. And here was a guy from the UK about to go for it vertically!

The hardest part in any of my voyages has been the trials and tribulations before departure day. Getting to any start line takes a lot of cash, huge determination and dedicated consistency. I admire people who have the guts to get over that stage, let alone manage the bit at sea. After a few more moments reading the website, I could sense the amateur side to everything and had even more respect for the venture. Adrian was a relatively inexperienced sailor, a father of two with his ex-wife as expedition manager and a bunch of mates to advise him as he went along. I took my hat off to all of them, especially to the ex-wife! I wrote her a quick email suggesting she ignore all emotions for now and let the expedition get into the flow, as all these projects do so much sooner than one would expect. Funnily enough, Louise thought the mail was for Adrian but replied anyway. We kept in touch. I provided some advice in particular: meteorology.

I love the stuff. First thing I do when I wake up is look out of the window. Second thing I do is wonder how the waves are in relation to the wind speed and direction, both of which I figure out from a quick glance at the colour of the sky and cloud types. Meteorology came naturally to me as a kid. I grew up in a fishing village and wanted to know why certain days were good for fishing and surfing and others weren't. Listening to the old salty men of the sea helped fuel my passion towards this mysterious science.

I began providing more information, from suggestions to make their website more interesting to daily 'tips of the day' sent directly to Adrian's satellite phone. This must have been strange for Adrian. Suddenly, out of the blue and less than a week into his trip, a stranger from Portugal was almost co-managing his show. Above all, I just wanted to help in every way possible. I was not worried about Adrian or his boat. I knew he would get into the rhythm and the boat would take care of him. My major concern was the mother of two young boys and her mental stability managing all this. Louise is not a sailor. She has never been in this seat before.

On Monday 7th November, I dialled the number in Lisbon that Louise had emailed to me.

'Ricardo?'

'Yeah.'

'Adrian . . .'

'God . . . how're you doing? Ric, by the way.'

'Okay, Ric. Cold, wet, knackered, pissed off . . .'

'The usual then,' Ric laughed softly.

'There will be good days,' I said.

'There will be good days,' Ric affirmed.

'Louise has brought me up to speed on your involvement with the expedition. Great to have you on board!'

'Great to be on board.'

'I need to get out of here.'

'I've been looking. What weather system do you have?'

'MaxSea software. I can download weather reports through the sat phone. I've just pulled down one for the next six days.'

Ric had studied the weather. 'I figure the 9th.'

'Okay, I go with that.'

Adrian: Tuesday 8th November 2005

The weather window has arrived, bringing northwesterly winds which should get me towards Cape Finisterre on Spain's northwestern corner. I am anxious to be clear of Biscay with its notorious seaways. I leave from the Helford River at first light.

Louise: Tuesday 8th November 2005

You are very much in my thoughts as you spend your last night so close to home. So many people are behind you with this – feel that energy as you go on your way.

Stay warm, keep your safety harness on, drink three litres of water a day, sleep as much as you can, take your vitamins, eat well, write your diary, use the video cameras, enjoy your music and know that we three Flanagans will be counting the days till you come back safely. Speak to you soon.

By the time I was clear of land, the winds unexpectedly swung round from the northwest to the west and would drop into the southwest, impeding me again. Ricardo's detailed weather picture showed a new monster depression swinging in over Iceland.

Adrian: Thursday 10th November 2005

This is really ball-breaking. My weather shows a real mean bastard depression coming in and unless I make some south now I'll be hit with 40

*mile an hour winds again! My body rhythm has gone all to hell. I think I
managed some sleep last night and I kipped this afternoon.*

Friday 11th November in the Bay of Biscay turned into a bitch. The
weather built to yet another mindless fury. The boat took a real
pounding. At 3.00 pm, I decided to tack eastwards and wait until
evening by which time, according to Ric's information, I would get
northwest winds that would then push me towards the northwest
corner of Spain. I set the Hydrovane. It works by staying in the same
position relative to the prevailing wind – should the wind direction
change, the Hydrovane will follow it round and the boat will then
turn. At exactly 4.00 pm, I watched our course heading round from
150° (east of south towards France) to 210° (south southwest towards
Madeira) in 10 minutes. At last, the northwest winds! I raced south.

Adrian: Saturday 12th November 2005
*Ric is doing a great job – his reports are spot on. Aside from getting from A to
B, I need to be routed to avoid bad weather – I must nurture the boat – cannot
afford rigging breakages etc. Managed to get some sleep last night and had a
wash – first one since I left the Helford River but haven't managed to shave
yet! I daren't try in the heavy weather – I'd cut myself to pieces on the razor.
Both pairs of boots are wet inside. The pair I went over the side in absolutely
stink.*

I waited for the depression to hit and when it did, 45-knot winds kicked
up a mean, breaking sea. By the evening of the third day out from the
Helford River, I had been on the go for 30 sleepless hours. Sitting on
the banquette bracing myself with my feet against the folded sides of
the saloon table and nursing a mug of hot, sweet tea, I began to
hallucinate, seeing the cabin lights walking across the ceiling and
hearing voices too. I ate the leftovers of tuna spaghetti from the
previous day and tried to get some sleep before yet another night
from hell set in.

Adrian: Sunday 13th November 2005
*On those rare occasions when I have not been in survival conditions, I sit on
deck and think that here I am after all the thinking, planning and so on,
having turned an idea into reality. There is something incredibly creatively
rewarding in that.*

My latest weather file showed conditions worsening in Biscay but the situation looked calmer closer inshore. The north Spanish coast was 10 miles south. I gybed onto a southerly heading and sure enough, the seas became flatter, protected from the wind by the Spanish mainland. At 6.40 am, I gybed again onto a westerly heading to take me past Cape Finisterre and out of the jaws of hell that is Biscay in a storm.

I nosed round the headland, exposing *Barrabas* to the untamed Atlantic winds. The seas, herded remorselessly from the great open spaces of the ocean into the confined, rapidly shoaling continental shelf, built into lines of massive waves. I took the helm to guide *Barrabas* through the onslaught, angling her bows to the approaching waves. The water rushing past her keel was slewing her round. I had to apply tremendous pressure through the wheel onto the steering cables to hold her steady. As *Barrabas* slewed for the umpteenth time, a loud cracking sound ricocheted from somewhere below decks and the wheel suddenly went loose in my hands. One of the steering cables had parted! Rushing to the Hydrovane, I used the self-steering rudder to turn *Barrabas* through the wind and backed the sails, stopping her in the water. I had two spare cables, cut to length and fitted with turn-buckles. It took an hour to replace the failed cable and make the tension adjustments. I worried that only one spare cable might not be enough to get me round the world. Then, I had a small Eureka! moment. I could cannibalise the guard rails if I had to – four lines of 4 mm wire rope, two each side of the boat running through the stanchions from the after frame to the pulpit.

With the lights of the Spanish mainland twinkling in the darkness, we navigated along the coast. The depression moved eastwards. The wind moderated and swung round behind us and, at last, we had perfect sailing conditions to drive us south.

A school of dolphin came and danced with *Barrabas*. I watched them for a while but I was too tired to stay on deck any longer. For the last six days, I had only been able to mange catnaps. Conditions had been too dangerous to sleep for any decent length of time. I went below and crawled into my sleeping bag. I set the radar and got up every two hours to check the course and look out topsides for fishing nets marked by flashing yellow or white lights. On my second foray topside, I was within a mile of a trawler, but it moved off to the east.

It was getting warmer! Fresh from sleep and jubilant at our progress and the wonderful weather, I removed one of the two base layers I was wearing.

Adrian: Tuesday 15th November 2005
At last, a beautiful day's sailing – blue sky, fair wind, dolphins. Currently
following the Portuguese coastline, but tomorrow will head towards Madeira.
I managed to do the washing up this afternoon.

During the storms I was afraid, but I expect to be. Not to experience fear in
those conditions would be to underestimate the power of the sea to destroy on
a whim. Also, I had averaged probably no more than an hour of sleep a night,
so I was becoming seriously fatigued. However, my main concern was with
the massive hits Barrabas was taking. To be below and literally hurled across
the cabin because of the force of wave impacts again and again and again,
seemingly without end, began to make me wonder just how much more
punishment she could take. The steering cable exploding was just an example
of gear failure because of the stresses on the boat. There might so easily have
been show-stopping damage such as structural failure in the rig. I just needed
to get the hell out of there. Barrabas was magnificent. She took everything the
sea threw at her. Without hesitation, she would raise her proud bow for the
next punch. When waves were smashing over her deck, she seemed to quiver
as if to shake the water off. You can tell Bernard that my belief in the boat
was realised during that onslaught.

Louise: Tuesday 15th November 2005
I feel like a new woman since I know things are so much safer and better for
you now. Next weekend I am going to Lisbon to stay with Ricardo and his
wife, Lucia. I leave next Friday. Ricardo is bemused at our fondness for
Mateus Rosé! I am very, very excited! A Czech outdoor magazine contacted
me today for photos. News of your exploits has spread around the world! Boys
very well and asking about you – told them about the dolphins and they loved
it.

Ricardo: Website Report, Tuesday 15th November 2005
40.26 North 009.03 West
Portuguese waters
Just west of Adrian's position the bad weather was still producing gale force
winds. The sea state was so rough and confused that two of the new, super
advanced boats in the round-the-world Volvo Ocean Race suffered severe
structural damage and had to seek refuge in Portuguese ports.

Although no one had been injured in the Volvo Ocean Race, a tragedy
was to occur later that would be a chilling reminder of how close I had
come to death when I was swept from *Barrabas*'s deck.

Almost twelve months after my ordeal to get to the 40th parallel, the same unseasonably severe weather was to blight the start of the Velux Five Oceans Race, forcing four of the eight starters back to port in northern Spain to repair storm damage and wait out the weather, including Sir Robin Knox-Johnston on his Open 60, *Saga Insurance*.

For me, sitting on the deck of my brave little ship, feeling the sun on my skin, surrounded by a smooth and glittering sea with a gentle northeasterly breeze stoking our passage southwards, I was simply glad to have come through my first experience of single-handed open water sailing. It had been nothing less than baptism by fire.

Quite how far news of my voyage had spread around the world was impossible to gauge, but it did reach one man in Holland, Henk de Velde. A sailor and circumnavigator himself, I was surprised not to have heard about him, more so given the contents of his initial contact with Louise.

Henk de Velde: Wednesday 16th November 2005
Dear Louise,
Also my team is always very small. When I am on my way the other side of the team is one other person.

I did exactly the same voyage Adrian has planned, single-handed (expect some weeks with a Russian ice pilot) but not non-stop. I stopped in Argentina, Chile, Easter Island, Hawaii, Dutch Harbour, Provideniya, Tiksi, Murmansk, Tromsø, Holland – it took me 3½ years (including 10 months in Siberia) and 6 months repairing in Hawaii and waiting for the ice to go in the Bering Sea.

One thing: non-stop is almost impossible and I do not talk about ice but Adrian needs a Russian ice pilot (compulsory in Russian waters and the Russians consider the whole northern Arctic Sea north of Russia their territory). They will want him anyhow to clear in (probably Provideniya) and out (Murmansk).

Adrian must know that the way towards a goal is as important as the goal itself.

Henk de Velde was born on 12th January 1949. After a career in the merchant marine, he took to sailing, circumnavigating several times, first with his then wife, Gini, on a seven-year voyage between 1978 and 1985 then later as a single-hander. During a round-the-world voyage in 1992, his boat, a 60-foot catamaran, hit a submerged sea container. Henk was knocked unconscious and sustained skull fractures. In 1996, he sailed another catamaran, the 71-foot C1000, on another circumnavigation.

It was his sixth voyage that interested me. In 2001, aboard his steel monohull *Campina*, Henk set out to sail a vertical circumnavigation. Passing westwards through the Strait of Magellan and with a plan to sail Russia's Northern Sea Route, Henk did get permission from the Russian government to attempt the passage. Five yachts had previously received similar permissions: three Russian, one French (Eric Brossier's *Vagabond*) and one German. Henk's *Campina* was the sixth. The seventh yacht to get permission was the Irish boat *Northabout*. Other than *Campina*, all these boats were fully crewed, but the Russian government insisted that *Campina*, like all the others, take a Russian ice pilot on board.

I knew that to complete my voyage non-stop was improbable – storm damage or circumstances beyond my control might yet force me into port, but I was determined to maintain the single-handed aspect. I reaffirmed the vow I had made to myself at the outset: no one would be with me at any time while *Barrabas* was making way through the water. I still needed to secure permission from the Russian government and then convince them to allow my attempt on the NSR *without* an ice pilot.

I hadn't yet developed a routine, hampered by the amount of maintenance and problem-solving that had dogged me from the start. My only routine was my bowl of porridge each morning with brown sugar and evaporated milk, followed by two cups of freshly brewed coffee.

On a beautiful, warm day off the Portuguese coast with a perfect breeze for spinnaker sailing, I was stifling down below sorting out a battery problem. The batteries did not seem to be holding charge. I conducted exhaustive tests. In an ironic twist, I eventually traced a currency leak to the currency leak indicator!

Another problem occurred the following morning coinciding with the deteriorating weather, though this one was of my own making. I'd switched on the watermaker, but forgotten to open the outlet seacock to discharge the excess brine and relieve pressure in the system. The watermaker had blown out its valve. The trouble-shooting flow chart suggested that the pressure recalibration was a 'return to factory' job. I'd have to see what I could do myself.

Adrian: Saturday 19th November 2005

*Awful weather – very squally, winds gusting to 30 knots. Watermaker bust. I
collected rainwater in a bucket hung on the afterend of the boom so I'll be OK
for the next couple of days. Chichester, Knox-Johnston and the others didn't
have watermakers!*

*Think of me at about 10 tomorrow morning – I am going to be hit with
some serious weather that will go on all day. I have being trying to outrun it
today, but I'm afraid I'm going to get punched! I console myself with the
thought that sheer probability suggests that things have got to improve.*

A second message from Henk dissipated my nagging doubts over the
adequacy of my preparations.

Henk de Velde: Saturday 19th November 2005

Dear Louise,

*I just read the news on Adrian's voyage about electric repairs. Just to tell you
it's part of the game, I had to repair my broken boom in Iceland, I had to
repair my engine in Argentina and recheck it in Chile. I had to repair all
electrics on Hawaii. I had to repair sails in Dutch Harbour. I had to repair
the transmission in –40C in Tiksi. I had to repair my rudders in Murmansk.*

Give Adrian my best wishes. At heart I am with him.

I progressed slowly against the building seas and headwinds from the
southwest. An unstable patch of air just west of my position was
displaying all the characteristics of a hurricane in its early stages.
Ricardo was watching developments. *'We are monitoring this system
very closely. Although pretty certain that it will not build into a serious storm,
we want to keep Adrian moving towards the safest part of the cell, and that is
exactly what he is doing.'*

I bashed on through Sunday, head to wind, managing to hold my
course south of west. The batteries had made a full recovery. The
wind generator and solar panels were keeping the batteries at full
charge. It was one less problem for me to worry about as the storm
system enveloped us on its slow eastward track.

I considered how I was feeling. Fear had diminished, my respect
for the sea had not, but curiously being single-handed did not seem
strange or unnerving – on the contrary, my solitude felt natural.

Below decks, tied to the mast support post, Benji's green teddy bear
and Gabriel's red dog, two soft toys that the children had had as babies,

kept me company. Some part of my mind lingered constantly on the boys as if I had two hard drives running simultaneously in my head.

I was not yet in tune with the sea, though increasingly my feeling for the boat was instinctive. I went about the deck checking and re-checking the rigging. I still felt very much the interloper, spending so much of my energy fire-fighting, managing mini-crises and dealing with heavy weather instead of simply being part of the way of things.

By Sunday evening the storm had escalated, delivering 45-knot winds. My weather report showed one small area of red (the strongest winds) and I was right in the middle of it. Ricardo's reasoning was to get me west to the opposite side of the low-pressure cell and into better wind angles. That meant sailing directly into the centre of the low-pressure system, into stronger winds and bigger, more confused seas.

With *Barrabas* set, I went to work on the watermaker. I had less than two litres of drinking water on board. But I wasn't overly con-cerned at this point. I had plenty of tinned fruit (in juice) on board, 150 tins. Aside from the nutritional value of the fruit, I had stowed so much of it precisely for this reason – that if my water stock was depleted I had a fall back with the fruit juice and, because it was tinned, its extended shelf life meant that I would not be in any immediate danger. Plus, I had plenty of long-life and tinned milk as well.

The thread on the watermaker valve had been damaged by its forceful ejection. I filed the edges carefully, then screwed it back into the watermaker unit, trying to visualise how tightly it had been screwed down before so that I could get the pressure setting correct. It was guesswork but, after an hour pitching around in the confines of the fore cabin, I tried the watermaker again and after a few minutes beautiful, fresh drinking-quality water began dribbling from the end of the product tube. It was a huge relief. Now I could get on and sail the boat. I ran the watermaker for four hours until my two 10-litre jerry cans were full. For several minutes, I sat on the companionway steps looking at the water, occasionally leaning forwards to heft the cans. Never before had the vital necessity of water been so apparent to me.

Louise: Monday 21st November 2005

Can you fill me in on batteries, watermaker, state of mind, are you eating and taking vits? Are you okay?

I leave for Lisbon Friday and come home Monday. Big snow predicted this week. It is freezing here. The new website [which Ric had redesigned] has been incredibly well received. We now have a visitors' book . . . I am coping very well – the boys are not driving me half as crackers as I thought.

With the storm spent and northeast winds chasing me south towards Madeira, I emailed Louise.

Adrian: Tuesday 22nd November 2005

. . . after all the hoopla with batteries, watermaker, steering, weather and so on, finally I can give you that good message I've been waiting so long to send. All systems on board restored to normal working – makes you pretty self-reliant this single-handing business – electrician, rigger, sailor, navigator, washerwoman, cook, diesel mechanic.

Today the weather is perfect. I am sailing fast and straight on a direct line towards Madeira 200 miles away. I've taken some nasty bangs – deep bruise on the sole of my right foot, which makes putting weight on it a bit painful. I was thrown across the cabin twice in recent days and on both occasions hit my left forearm midway between wrist and elbow . . . I thought I had broken it – I felt nauseous for about 30 mins.

I am doing my first lot of laundry today – socks and base layer. I will hoist them up on a halyard to air dry. I'll also have a wash this afternoon and a shave.

I am eating pretty well – usually porridge and coffee for breakfast with a cooked meal mid-afternoon (high carb – pasta or rice with something). All this supplemented with tinned fruit, dried fruit and chocolate plus the vits etc.

Please give my boys a big hug and kiss. Green bear and red dog are my constant companions.

During a routine deck inspection, I noticed chafe on the foot of the headsail. There was no obvious cause. Just then, the sail luffed, its trailing edge flapping in the light breeze. As the foot of the sail agitated against the guard wire, the taping around the attachment of the guard wire to the pulpit unwrapped itself, exposing the split pin. The sharp end of the split pin had caused the damage. As I watched, the sail's action then flipped the tape, re-wrapping the pin, a trick of the wind. I would have to watch that to prevent serious chafe damage. I re-taped the attachment then repaired the sail, stitching the chafed edges together and patching both sides with adhesive sailcloth. As a precaution, I re-taped all the other guard wire attachments port and starboard, fore and aft.

★

Louise and I met Nikki and Paul during our honeymoon in 1997, at a Tuscan farmhouse where we were all staying. We'd been friends ever since. I knew they were following my voyage and a straightforward message from Nikki created a new awareness in me.

Nikki: Wednesday 23rd November 2005
We are so pleased to hear that you are making really good progress now, despite the setbacks. We are now in the throes of Christmas preparations (all that shopping again . . . Ugh!), but fortunately weather has been fantastic, cold, bright and crisp . . .

The infinity of space without walls, the absence of crush, the unconstrained vista where I could see the curvature of the earth – all these were now beginning to influence my perceptions. I was too recently into my trip to have gained a completely different perspective but too removed from normality not to be changed.

Christmas shopping? The idea seemed at once familiar yet distant, bizarre yet mundane. I later recognised this altered perception as a precognition, the first tremor, a forerunner to the seismic shift that would compel me to redefine my understanding of my world, from the inside to the outside.

I became increasingly reliant on Ricardo to take a longer-term view of the weather and develop strategies to route me safely across the wide swathes of ocean. To plan tactics to deal with immediate situations, I downloaded Maxsea weather files on a 24-hour basis. Towards the end of November, Ricardo sent a message telling me of a good wind corridor that would take me west of the Canary Islands, then west of the Cape Verde Islands towards the equator.

My father had taken up the challenge of engaging the Russian government, but we still didn't know which department to contact or, more specifically, who to call directly. I'd already been at sea for almost a month. Time was not on our side. I asked Louise to speak to Henk.

Henk de Velde: Thursday 24th November 2005
Louise,
If Mr Monko is still in his post then he is the only one to give permission. But it's also good to contact MSCO (Murmansk Shipping Company). They do the

routing of the ships including icebreakers and will give Adrian direction where to go or not!

Louise called Henk to get more details. My father had been in touch with the Foreign Office in London but, until Henk's message had arrived giving us a name, we had no idea of progress in Moscow. Was Nikolai Monko still in his post as head of Northern Sea Route Administration, and if so, had my application landed on his desk yet? If it had, how quickly was the application being processed? If approval came, I would need as much time as possible to then persuade Nikolai Monko, or whoever was now in charge of NSR Administration, to let me go without an ice pilot.

I spoke to Louise and she decided to chase things up with the Foreign Office. Although Dad had made headway, he was in South Africa while Louise, in England, had better access to British and Russian government personnel in London. Equally, I was apprehensive about overloading Louise but the very nature of Louise's role as expedition manager meant she was closer to the action.

Louise has a special ability to get people to listen and then act. That evening, I received a message, forwarded by Louise, while I ate a supper of spaghetti with tomato sauce and sausage, listening to Roy Orbison crooning in the background.

Laurie Brock: Russia Section, Foreign & Commonwealth Office, London, Thursday 24th November 2005

Hi Louise,
I have since found out that your ex-father-in-law has been speaking to Steve Hunt (Deputy Head of Russia Section). Steve is preparing a letter about your ex-husband's trip to send to the Russian Embassy here in London . . .

With the calmer conditions, the boat in order and my routine of inspections, checks and maintenance beginning to create a pattern of sorts, I began to relax. The books I had on board made an eclectic mix. I'd picked some off my shelves at home and some Louise and others had given me. From this limited library, I selected Campbell Armstrong's *Mambo*, which reminded me how much I enjoyed reading thrillers and how much I would like to spend my time writing them.

Louise: Friday 25th November 2005

*Well here I am in Lisbon! Already hit the shops and only came away with a
small gift for the boys. Ric picked me up from the airport . . . Lucia his wife
and baby Miguel have just come home after being away for the week so
haven't spent much time with her yet. Ric has shown me how he updates the
website every day . . . wow! I'll be at technical HQ for the next few days. So
glad I came.*

I contemplated the voyage ahead and thought about the experience
since leaving the River Hamble. The immense power of the sea could
have killed me already. Whatever the weather, I felt a constant awareness of that power ebbing through my consciousness. This was an
alien environment, dangerous and merciless. I wrote a poem sitting in
the cockpit while *Barrabas* sailed south towards the Canaries.

> Fall silent deep your thrashing might
> Crowd my mind full with fright
> My vessel's small upon your brow
> Your arms surround and grip us now
> My sails fill, my stem is proud
> We trespass here but speak aloud
> Our roll does echo your endless rhyme
> We share the night but day is mine
> We leave our wake but not a scar
> Instead a kiss upon your heart

CHAPTER 10

Enlightenment

Louise: Saturday 26th November 2005
Impressed by your progress! I am having a fabulous time here – eating, chilling, sitting behind my computer on your behalf – but that is my life now and I am enjoying it.

Louise was recharging but I suddenly felt incredibly tired. I was listless, unable to summon either the energy or enthusiasm for the smallest task, hardly bothering to stick my head above the companionway to make visual checks for shipping. The emotional drain of buying and refitting *Barrabas*, plus all the ancillary effort of finding sponsors and the wrench from the children, had finally caught up with me. The constant difficulties of the first two weeks of the voyage and little sleep had left me drained.

It would have been easy to submit to apathy but I forced myself to set about tidying the fore cabin and the aft deck. The pair of boots I was wearing when I went over the side still reeked. I soaked them in the galley sink in fresh water and laundry liquid.

Through this period of adjustment, a thought lifted my spirits. From the Helford River only a few days before, I was now between Madeira and the Canaries, heading towards Brazil, blown only by the wind. I was crossing an ocean. It seemed incredible, fantastic. But a deep depression in the west was beginning to move east towards me. The forecasters described the system as a tropical cyclone – exceptional for this time of year and latitude. It was going to be another howler. I reefed down as the winds built to 40 knots. *Barrabas* lifted her bows in the swell then came crashing down, shaking violently.

Louise: Sunday 27th November 2005
My few days here have just flown by – I can't believe I have to go home tomorrow. We went out for a very nice dinner last night with JP who is Ric's dad. JP used to work for BBC Radio in the UK for many years and now has a radio show in Portugal. (He is going to continue to plug you on his show.) They leave to go out for dinner at about 10 pm here. Haven't got to bed before 12.30 yet. Turned into a pumpkin the first night and still look like one!

At least Louise was having a good time (except for the pumpkin bit).

Louise had been in touch with Eric Brossier on board *Vagabond* somewhere in the high Arctic, asking his advice.

Eric Brossier: Sunday 27th November 2005
Hello Louise,
The most important thing is to have a Russian partner, an official company, who will ask the permission for you. Otherwise, it might be really difficult to get proper permission to sail the Northern Sea Route.
Good luck, Eric.

The second night of the storm was horrific, although I felt less worried because I was now confident of *Barrabas's* capabilities. She seemed stable as the centre of the depression passed over us. The wind tore the Windex (a small wind vane) from the mast top – a nuisance because I'd used it constantly as a visual aid to trim the boat. Sleep was impossible, so I settled on the starboard banquette below decks and began reading *Between a Rock and a Hard Place*, about the traumatic experience of a young climber, Aron Ralston, trapped by a falling boulder in the Canyonlands National Park in Utah in 2003. Close to death, he had cut through his elbow with a penknife to free himself.

Louise: Monday 28th November 2005
And how are you today? Heard on the TV that a tropical storm is approaching the Canaries – good thing you didn't hang around in Madeira!

You are doing so well – when I look at the map I can't believe how far you've gone.

Adrian: Monday 28th November 2005
Welcome back to Pear Tree Lodge. How are the boys? Had an awful night last night. Ricardo put me right through the eye of another depression. I had 40-knot winds all night. No sleep. The boat took a tremendous bashing again. This is the third time in three weeks he has routed me right through the centre of a depression. I am not very happy. The others may have been unavoidable but this one was completely avoidable. I could either have stopped and let it pass to the south of my position or turned west and run over the top of it. The problem is that heavy weather like that places huge stresses on the boat. The other problem is I get no sleep. So far because of this I've gone over 40 hrs with no sleep, which is debilitating. When the inside of the boat is trashed, cupboards ripped off the walls again, everything soaking wet and me damp, it's incredibly demoralising.

It is hot, but a clinging moist heat. I keep the ship's clock on UTC (your time). Local time does not really matter to me. My day is determined by the rising and setting of the sun, not a clock.

By the 'ship's clock', I meant the GPS timer, which I'd set to Coordinated Universal Time (UCT – the same as Greenwich Mean Time). But I also had a battery-powered clock that I kept on local time, though I hardly ever looked at it.

Louise: Monday 28th November 2005
I'm so sorry you've had a shitty couple of days – it will pass as you know. If you had waited . . . what was coming would have been worse. I have seen with my own eyes the software and methodology Ricardo uses to route you. He knows exactly what is out there and exactly what is coming. Trust me on this one. I know when the shit hits the fan it is horrid for you but there is always method in the madness when Ricardo is routing you. You just don't always understand the full method and only see the madness! Hang on in there.

The morning broke blue and bright, warmed by the African sun. The wind had dropped to 10 knots. I prepared the spinnaker – an involved process, especially single-handed. Effort has to be co-ordinated because control of the spinnaker occurs both at the mast and in the cockpit, so I had to execute economic manoeuvres and scuttle between foredeck and cockpit. The hoist was good and the spinnaker unfurled with a magnificent smack, blossoming like a giant flower of pinks, blues and turquoise.

Barrabas dug her shoulder in and jolted forward, slicing the water at eight knots. I didn't know it then, but we had weeks ahead of us before we would encounter another storm, south of Buenos Aires. I listened to Albinoni's concertos while the azure dimmed to indigo and myriad stars lit the night sky like fairy lights tossed onto tar. The two saloon banquettes doubled as my bunks and depending on the heel of the boat, I chose starboard or port, whichever was on the low side. A cooling draft blew in through the open central hatch drying the inside of the boat.

By next morning, I was refreshed. With daytime temperatures climbing to the mid-twenties, I had little need for clothing. I had a good rub down with baby wipes and wandered around the deck naked, enjoying the delicious unfettered sensation while the sun and breeze dried me. With *Barrabas* careening through the water and her deck bucking and rolling beneath my feet, I felt a surge of euphoria. I had never experienced freedom like this before, freedom spiced with the thrill of adventure.

Louise: Tuesday 29th November 2005
So pleased you're out of the poo again. Boys were so thrilled to see me and even more thrilled with their presents! Benji wrote a lovely piece about you at school with a great picture. It is now on the website and Benji is thrilled.

Barrabas has three keel bilges but only the forward and aft bilges are fitted with electric pumps. The forward bilge empties into the centre bilge, which I pump out manually. This was illogical so I rigged a pipe extension connecting the forward and aft bilges, which I could then discharge electrically. If I maintained a daily bilge inspection, I could avoid the centre bilge filling as an overflow and save myself the hassle of a manual pump-out. Bernard's minute attention to detail on *Barrabas* was impressive but I questioned the logic of the bilge arrangement.

Cupboard doors in the saloon and galley had broken loose during the storm. I re-fixed them but seawater had doused the galley cupboard hinges, corroding the brass. The hinges had seized. I oiled them in the hope that they would free up overnight.

That night, strange lights loomed beyond the horizon. Santo Antão, one of the Cape Verde islands, was the closest land to my position, 280 miles away to the south!

Ricardo: Wednesday 30th November 2005
Top 3 in the world for strange lights at sea is the area you are in now. I once sailed the pond with an old chap on his 16th crossing and he has seen strange lights in your area 3 times. If they do come and say hello tell them to visit my dad also – one of his major goals in life is to see and communicate with aliens.

I asked Louise for news from home, ordinary, everyday information. I was out here on the ocean while the world went about its business but, despite the freedom I felt, I still hungered for the trivia of home.

Louise: Thursday 1st December 2005
Carol Thatcher doing quite well in the jungle programme, George Best died when I was in Portugal, Tony Blair becoming less popular by the millisecond, Jeffrey Archer trying to get back in to politics and David Cameron saying it will never happen, Rod Stewart's girlfriend had a baby, Britons stranded in the Canaries after a deadly storm ripped through the Spanish resort!

With *Barrabas* sailing comfortably in the warm breeze, her course controlled inch-perfectly by the Hydrovane, I fetched the fishing rod, casting a lure on a wire trace with 50 metres of line trailing behind the boat, enough for the lure to sink a few feet beneath the surface and spin to attract fish.

Individual packets of ready-mixed flour in three shades – white, wholemeal and granary – should have made bread-making simple but my attempts at baking met with limited success. I eventually figured out the best mix and, on my third attempt, produced a good loaf. I cut three slices of the still-warm bread, coating each piece with a generous layer of Nutella chocolate spread, then settled on my bunk to finish Aron Ralston's book.

I'd had a few weird premonition-type experiences recently and another happened while I was reading. I put the book down, imagining Aron's location to be like the Spielberg film, *Temple of Doom*. When I resumed reading, Aron referred to the film on the very next page. It freaked me out a bit.

A line in his book embedded itself in my mind. '*Our purpose as spiritual beings is to follow our bliss, seek our passions and live our lives as inspirations to each other.'* I lay for some time thinking about that. It was the second tremor, nudging me closer to the realisation that the power to achieve, to do, to be as we want, is within each of us. The secret is in that realisation and then in the discipline of nurturing belief in ourselves. Through all of the criticism I had received from some sections of the media, friends, family and even strangers about the foolhardiness of the expedition, I saw that it was not just stubbornness that had compelled me. I had a belief in myself that others could not fathom, a silent, contained, hidden power that is everyone's to command but which few ever acknowledge. What was beyond my power at the moment was getting my application processed and approved to sail the NSR! The question of the Russian permissions hovered in my mind, bugging me, like the whine of a mosquito in the dark.

Louise: Friday 2nd December 2005
I haven't contacted Mr Monko yet but will write to him as his telephone numbers don't seem to be working. I will also chase the Foreign Office on their letter to Moscow. I will also call Sam Laidlaw and ask him to speak to the Murmansk guys.

Sam: Friday 2nd December 2005
Louise, I have a meeting on Tuesday with a very influential Russian and have told his staff in advance that I will be raising the subject. I will let you know the outcome. Best, Sam.

I didn't know the identity of the 'influential Russian' but, in concert with the efforts of the Foreign Office, this definitive action reassured me.

The wind corridor I was following towards the equator was taking me close to the Cape Verde islands off the west coast of Africa. On 3rd December, Ricardo posted a piece onto the website: *'For the next few days we will not be updating Adrian's position. All is okay and we know where he is, but we just don't want the pirates off the Cape Verdes to know too.'*

Adrian (to Ricardo): Saturday 3rd December 2005
Hi Ric . . . good plan about the pirates. Just before I left the UK, a small flotilla of yachts was being stalked in that area – they figured pirates so stayed tight together and used Iridium [satellite phone] to alert authorities . . .

I woke at 2.00 am (local time), covered only with the silk liner of my sleeping bag. The saloon hatch was open, peeling slices from the warm trade winds. *Barrabas* rolled beneath an ocean of stars. I watched through the open hatch. On deck, the moist, dusty smell of land scented the air. Santo Antão, the westernmost of the Cape Verde islands, lay due east of my position less than 80 miles away. I went on deck. Beneath the blanket of night, the sea seemed compressed. Cloud obscured the southern horizon, creating the effect of infinity and timelessness, while *Barrabas* cut her path of white luminescence.

I made a cup of tea sweetened with a spoonful of cane sugar and drank it with two slices of the delicious spongy bread I'd baked the previous day. Most of my fluid intake was in the form of tea. Perhaps I should have been monitoring how much I was drinking. A background headache was now reaching into its third day, maybe an early sign of dehydration or, more likely, the result of higher air pressure as we approached the tropics.

My fishing rod was in its holder and lashed to the railing on the aft deck. I checked the line. Fibres of fish tissue hung from the hook, the lure bitten through. A large fish had taken the bait then broken free. I replaced the lure and cast it back into the dark water more in hope than expectation. Later, after daybreak, I noticed the end of the rod straining. I tested the line for tension and with a brief spike of exhilaration felt an increase in drag. Slowly, I reeled in. Beneath the indigo veneer, a silvery dart zigzagged. The jackfish was about the size of a decent trout. At lunchtime, the fish – gutted and marinated in oil and lemon – sputtered in the pan. Its red meat blanched to chocolatey brown with the texture of soft chicken. I ate the fish with curried rice. It tasted wonderful.

In the afternoon, I patched two small tears in the spinnaker and stowed it on the foredeck, ready for immediate deployment if the wind dropped. On the afterdeck, I checked the fishing lure then cast it out into the ocean.

As well as email, I called Louise at least once a week as a way of simulating proximity to the children. Benji sounded sad and I could not really understand what Gabriel was saying but it was great just to hear their voices. They were about to go off to see the latest Harry Potter film. Louise reassured me that Benji wasn't sad, just into his Playstation, which I'd interrupted.

My left wrist had been aching and getting progressively worse. After a motorbike accident when I was at university, a fleet of Harley Street surgeons had deemed the injury inoperable, leaving me with a painful legacy, an 'unstable' wrist in which the scaphoid bone at the base of the thumb floats free, its binding ligaments severed. From time to time the scaphoid jammed, generating sharp pain. The discomfort I could deal with. The problem was the weakness and I found myself favouring my left wrist as I went about the daily jobs.

I caught another fish, bigger than the last at about four pounds. In the broiling mid-morning sun, I squatted on the afterdeck gutting and filleting the fish, clad only in a quick-dry towel wrapped around my waist like a sarong. *Barrabas* glided smoothly though the turquoise sea. In the steady northeast trades, sailing was easy. The constancy of wind strength and direction left me with little to do to trim the boat. Out of the shipping lanes, my time was my own. So far on the voyage I hadn't been bored. I often avoided tasks simply to bask in the sun or watch the sea and think. Sometimes I brought cushions into the cockpit. Shaded from the sun by a cover I'd rigged over the cuddy, I would lose myself in books punctuated with bouts of napping.

Below in the galley, I fried the fish in olive oil and garlic, then prepared a 'Cape Verde' fish curry (which I made up as I went along). After frying, I diced the fish, then poured in a jar of Nando's coconut curry sauce adding raisins, cane sugar, garlic purée, crushed pineapple, peanuts and crushed chilli. Setting the gas to low, the curry simmered away for fifteen minutes while I cooked plain white rice in the pressure cooker. I've eaten a lot of good curries in my time, but that one ranked in the top five.

By evening, the top of my bum was sore around the belt line. I checked in the mirror. A livid red line of sunburn stretched across my lower back.

Ricardo wanted me to bear away and make for 30° west longitude to enter the Doldrums. From my position that meant sailing southwest, putting the wind directly behind the boat on a dead run. The wind was getting to 12 knots, too much for the spinnaker. The mainsail threw a wind shadow on the headsail so I decided to gull-wing the sails by setting the spinnaker pole and sheeting the headsail through its outboard end. Then I let the boom carrying the mainsail out wide on the other side. The rig worked like a dream, generating 5 knots of boat speed in 10 to 12 knots of apparent wind. The gull-wing arrangement was as close as I could get to a 'trade wind rig' – two similarly sized headsails both flown from the forestay and each poled out on opposite sides of the boat.

Adrian: Tuesday 6th December 2005

My greatest emotion at the moment – amazingly, I don't have one. I have surprised myself by remaining completely 'normal' and not pitching between highs and lows as I was anticipating before I left. My mindset is 'just get on and do the job'. I don't feel emotionally deprived, psychologically vulnerable, mentally taxed, spiritually bereft or physically stressed (though I have been mentally taxed and physically stressed on this voyage already). I suspect all these things will come in time.

Taking advantage of the steady trade winds to get as much sleep as possible during the night, I was jolted awake at 3.00 am on 7th December by a thunderous crash. I was off my bunk and on deck in less than three seconds. Had we hit something? Had some part of the rig failed? I inspected the rigging using a torch but couldn't see anything wrong. There were no objects visible in the water and the ship's starboard hull looked okay (the side from which the noise had come).

Still worried, I went below to brew up and discovered the problem. One of the gimbal screws on the cooker had sheared. The cooker had collapsed down into its well sending the heavy pressure cooker and the kettle crashing to the galley floor. At least it was nothing serious! I fixed the cooker, had my tea and went back to sleep.

Some of the necessary regular jobs were so tedious that I developed a reward system to prevent myself ignoring them altogether. The worst categories were 1) jobs involving lifting floorboards – inspecting the batteries, wiring, bilges, transducers; 2) anything which meant having to reach into almost inaccessible recesses – cleaning the engine pan, checking fuel stored in the lazarette; 3) cleaning cupboards. Rewards were small but meaningful – chocolate, a cigarette, an extra spoonful of sugar in tea or coffee. For a really dirty job, I gave myself a really big prize like doing nothing for the rest of the day.

Now confident in my watermaker and with plenty of fresh water stowed, I gave myself a deck bath, my first of the voyage, washed my hair and had a shave. Here's how it usually goes: you get up in the morning, have a shower, go to work. While you're on the train or in the car or on the bus, you don't think about the shower you had. It's normal, you take it for granted. At least, that's always how it was with me. Until *that* deck bath. It felt so great! Cleansing, cooling, luxurious. My morale skyrocketed. I felt bright and shiny all day (inside as well as out). I'll never take a shower for granted again. Ever!

At night in the trade wind latitudes, I often heard thuds on deck. At first I wondered, 'What the hell is that?' When I went on deck, I found the cause and the casualties – flying fish colliding with *Barrabas*. It became routine in the morning to walk around the deck clearing the fallen. The most I ever found in a single morning was twelve. They are edible but full of small bones and unbelievably stinky. I wasn't tempted. Sailing across the Atlantic in the Clipper 2000 race, a flying fish had come through the open forward hatch one night and ended up lost among the folds of a sail stored in the sail locker. No one saw or heard it. Eventually, the stink became so overpowering, everything had to be emptied out of the forward compartment. The smell never left the boat. It put me off flying fish for life.

Adrian: Wednesday 7th December 2005
Stumbled upon a really outstanding breakfast variation. Made porridge the other day and had some cold plain rice left over. So mixed it all up and produced PORRICE – really good, sort of chewy. Have begun reading Ewan MacGregor and Charley Boorman's book about their motorcycle trip.

Louise: Wednesday 7th December 2005
X Factor still going – left in are good-looking chap Shane, Brenda, Journey South (the ex-plumber and electrician) and Andy, the ex-bin man. Carol Thatcher won 'I'm a Celebrity . . .' She is amazing. The nation saw her pull down her pants and pee next to her bed because she didn't want to go to the loo in the dark on the first night. When she parachuted in she was sick on herself.

It was becoming unbearably hot. The heat confined me below decks most of the time. I was not wearing clothes. Even going on deck for a pee (Carol Thatcher and I might have something in common after all) meant I was covered in sweat by the time I made it back below. I loved the evenings best with the air cooled and the sun blocked by the sails.

The tropical convergence zone or Doldrums is a transition area running along the equator. The spin of the earth causes reversal effects between the northern and southern hemispheres – the northeast trades of the northern hemisphere become the southeast trades of the southern hemisphere. The high surface temperature forces air to rise leaving a windless tunnel or fickle breezes. Thunderstorms are frequent. Beneath massed banks of cloud, the wind can scream furiously in a desperate quest to escape upwards.

A grey veil of rain advanced from the east. The wind picked up to 25 knots. Carrying full sail, *Barrabas* was overpowered. I had to reef the sails so, naked, I tried to furl the headsail but the furling line had jammed in the drum. I went to the foredeck to unjam the line while *Barrabas* buried her nose in the waves. Racing back to the cockpit, I got the headsail in, then rushed to the mast to shorten the mainsail. My course was due west, not where I wanted to go. I rolled out a little headsail, neutralised the Hydrovane, unlashed the wheel and put it hard over to port to get onto a more southerly heading. No response. I immediately thought, 'The steering's buggered again!' I lashed the wheel hard over to port and then went onto the sugar scoop and bent down low to look under the stern. Seawater soaked my head and shoulders. The rudder was amidships. I checked the steering mechanism below and saw the problem. The pin connecting the quadrant (cable wheel) to the rudderpost had sheared, disengaging the rudder. To make up a new pin would take 30 minutes, but if one had sheared, others would too. Better to fashion a more permanent solution, a key. It would take much longer and be more involved but I could take advantage of the Doldrums' intermittent winds and flat seas to get the job done.

The temperature below deck crept past 40°C. Sweat dripped off my nose like a leaking tap while I dismantled the steering system and removed the quadrant, 2½ feet in diameter and weighing 20 kg. Using an angle grinder, I cut a groove in the forward part of the rudderpost and a groove on the quadrant where the two opposed, each groove two inches long and a quarter-inch wide and deep. I cut the key from a small block of steel with a hacksaw. The stupefying heat limited work to ten-minute periods. It was a painstaking task. First, I was losing so much fluid in sweat that I needed to drink regularly. Second, the motion of the boat meant I had to brace myself using muscles in my legs, arms, back and neck. Third, the inverter kept cutting out because the angle-grinder was pulling more power than the inverter could deliver. On average, I was getting one minute's use of the grinder per 10 minutes. The job took up most of the day and by the end I felt as if I'd run a marathon, twice.

The result was not pretty, but it was functional. By 5.00 pm we were sailing again, albeit at two knots but going in the right direction.

By way of light entertainment, I started reading Jeremy Clarkson's latest book.

My passage through the Doldrums ended on Monday 12th December with the arrival of the southeast trade winds, though we were still in the northern hemisphere, 200 miles from the equator. With the wind now forward of the beam where previously it had been over the port quarter, I set the rig and Hydrovane for a close haul.

Life on board gradually distilled to bare essence: my space, physically restricted to 40 feet; my choices, limited by what I had in the cupboards; my options, confined to my own imagination. Contrarily, these reductions brought enrichment. The simplest tasks expanded to greater significance. The true value of existence became more apparent. For example, having a shave, not an activity usually capable of engendering euphoria, but a shave, when a rarity, produces a greater sense of cleanliness and when cleanliness is critical to the maintenance of health, given that I could not simply wander off to the nearest hospital should anything go wrong, the significance, value and enjoyment of it escalated. All this seemed further enhanced in the rarefied circumstance of near-total isolation. BBC Radio Oxford called on the satellite telephone at 8.30 am the following day, accentuating the contrast between my existence at sea and normal life at home. During the brief lead-in, I listened to the tail end of the sports bulletin and the local weather report. Here I was, close to the Atlantic equator, listening to Oxford United's latest football score!

With the stable weather and energy-vaporising heat, I was racing through my reading material. I started and finished Dan Brown's *The Da Vinci Code* – an excellent premise, the search for the Holy Grail, but what struck me were the similarities to the outline for a novel called *Sphinx*, which I'd written four years previously but hadn't finished, and *The Da Vinci Code* had sold over six million copies! I distracted myself by writing an email.

Adrian: Wednesday 14th December 2005
Reading a lot – so what have I got left? Authorized bio of T E Lawrence (. . . of Arabia), The Tibetan Book of Living and Dying *(philosophy),* No Second Chance *(thriller), an Umberto Eco novel –* The Island of the Night Before. *Then there's the* Oxford Dic of Ships and the Sea *(I'll do that cover to cover). I'll re-train myself on astronavigation. Plus the crosswords/word game books . . . then there are the instructions on the fire extinguishers, labels on the milk bottles and food tins, the computer help directory . . .*

Sam: Wednesday 14th December 2005

Louise, I spoke to my friend about permissions for the Arctic Sea transit. I am sure he will help although he did warn that it is risky and nearer the time, we should shout. Best, Sam.

Louise had emailed a copy of a letter written by the Russia Section at the Foreign Office to the Consular Department of the Russian Embassy in London. We now had definitive action from the British government. The identity of Sam's 'friend' remained veiled but at this stage it didn't matter.

I crossed the equator at 10.14 am on Saturday 17th December. My offering to the gods was modest – bread (stale) and a box of chocolate-filled squares (a breakfast cereal that I'd tried and didn't like much). I figured Neptune should have been pleased to see his portrait floating by, etched on *Barrabas*'s bows.

I had demarcated major milestones, each representing an approximate 25% progression to the Bering Strait: first, the Atlantic equator; second, Cape Horn; third, the Pacific equator and the fourth, the Bering Strait itself.

The weather generated ranges of cumulus clouds laden with moisture. Thunderclouds moved in around me. At one point, I counted eight mini-squalls going on. I was getting good at dodging them, but a big one ahead was going to get me. I decided to take a deck shower! As the rain came, I lathered up. The problem was that the wind beneath these clouds can pick up dramatically if only briefly. I was carrying full sail when the wind suddenly kicked up to 25 knots. The boat was overpowered, heeling over and pushing the side deck under water. I decided, mid-shower, to shorten sail. Soap streamed into my eyes, stinging like crazy. The wind strengthened, driving the rain horizontally. It was like taking a shower in a grit blaster. Shortening the mainsail involves working six separate lines between the mast and the cockpit: three reefing lines, the topping lift, the boom breaker and the mainsail halyard. So there I was, blinded, being hit by what felt like slow bullets, trying to keep my nether regions out of the firing line and execute the sail-shortening manoeuvre. By the time I was done, the rain had passed, leaving me still full of suds. I tied a rope around my waist, dived into the warm ocean and clambered out onto the sugar scoop at the back of the boat. Two cups of fresh water as a rinse and I was done. Then the full rigmarole with the lines in reverse to get the mainsail up again and we were off. Thus was my introduction to the southern hemisphere.

The next day, Sunday 18th December at 11.00 am, I smoked my last cigarette! My supply was limited by design, but naturally, as soon as the faintest urge for a smoke came, I went off and searched all the cupboards and compartments in the aftercabin just in case a packet had become dislodged and hidden itself away in some crevice. I didn't find any.

Louise had decided to take the boys to Mauritius for the Christmas holidays.

Louise: Sunday 18th December 2005

Benji's been unwell. High fever yesterday but slept it off (until 8.00 am) and he's much better today. We were out this morning and the boys bought their Christmas presents from you with the money you left them. Gabriel got a remote-control car and Benji a Star Wars game for his Game Boy – should keep him quiet on the plane on the way to and from Mauritius! They are thrilled at the extravagance. They got a few other bits as well as they had £35 each to spend (£20 from you and £15 from Father C). We came home and I cooked our usual Sunday roast – they are now absorbed with the car/game. A little later, we'll light a fire and watch The Polar Express. *Can you see Brazil?*

Adrian: Sunday 18th December 2005

No I can't see Brazil and I don't want to get much closer than I am now. Pirates are a big risk all the way down the South American coast, but particularly off Brazil. Remember a few years ago, a NZ yachtsman Sir Peter Blake was gunned down – that was in Brazil. Slightly different set of circumstances, but all the ingredients are available to create the risk: busy shipping lanes, ease of access to guns, a 'life is cheap' mentality imposed through brutal poverty blah blah blah. A few years ago a Swedish guy, single-handing, was making his way round the world stopping here and there. He was in the Caribbean and set off for South America. He has never been seen or heard of since. The yachting fraternity suspects pirates.

By the end of the month, I would have experienced my own close encounter with pirates. But for the moment, my mind was on other things – the Russian question was always there, of course, and, in addition to that, Rose Dale, a friend and Louise's neighbour, had given me a book, *The Tao of Pooh*, by American writer, Benjamin Hoff, which described the principles of Taoism through illustration with characters from *Winnie the Pooh* (a bit of a weird mechanism but there you go).

My personal philosophy, defined over many years, essentially mirrors Taoism: the recognition of an inner voice that always speaks the truth; awareness, inner quiet, adhering to the laws and forces of nature, living in the 'now' (which I've persistently failed to do), the concept of minimal effort (not laziness, though in my case, that was often true) – by not forcing a situation but instead letting what happens naturally happen naturally. I always knew that my ill-defined philosophy was informed by Eastern influence – natural enough, having spent so much of my youth in Hong Kong, Japan and Thailand. On some instinctive level, I understood these principles but it took a slim, childishly written book to crystallise them into a fuller understanding.

When I read *The Tao of Pooh*, the timing was coincidental but crucial. I was just beginning to sense, feel and appreciate the pulse, rhythm and heartbeat of the ocean and the natural world. I was receptive to the idea of change and growth and I felt myself integrate more fully into the energy around me, taken up in its arms and swept along in its flow.

The 'how' and 'why' of adventure is difficult to articulate. To me, it is a *sensing* within an individual, a particular mode of expression and a means of discovery that certain people seek out because of an overriding need to see for ourselves what lies beyond, rather than the mute acceptance of the experience of others. At the age of 18, my father had tried to convince me that I was not suited for medical school. My answer was emphatic. 'I may not be suitable, but I need to find that out for myself.' I stayed in med school for two years, then left. 'Wasted years,' my father told me afterwards, but I had answered a question to my satisfaction and in the process 'discovered' a truth. Had I not done so, the question would have remained, unanswered and unanswerable, for the rest of my life. It was the same with the Alpha Global Expedition – I had to do it. The thrill of it, the expectation of danger and even the hunger for it would reveal 'truths', answer questions like how would I cope? What would I find? I could never imagine or simulate this experience. I had to live it. As the days passed into weeks and months, it was becoming evident that the Alpha Global Expedition was delivering 'adventure' on a number of levels – physically of course, but also mentally and even spiritually. I was changing, maybe even evolving.

Louise and the boys flew to Mauritius for the Christmas holiday. I was happy for them but felt down, even slightly depressed, despite my recent 'enlightenment'. It was a combination of circumstances. First, Louise and the boys going away together reinforced my sense of isolation; second, my course would not take me clear of Recife in Brazil (where the continental landmass bulges into the Atlantic Ocean), which meant I would have to tack *Barrabas* eastwards; third, I was becoming increasingly worried that *Barrabas* would struggle to get round Cape Horn, sailing directly into the teeth of the prevailing west winds.

On the upside, I had written to Aron Ralston's publisher and Aron responded with a message just before Christmas.

Aron Ralston: Tuesday 20th December 2005

Adrian,

That's very cool that you're writing to me from the middle of the Atlantic! I'm writing to you from Aspen, Colorado, where it's snowing right now. I hope your expedition goes off with grand adventure and you handle it all with grace. Although the story will be better if you make some big mistakes along the way that nearly cost you everything but you find a way to make it happen anyhow (isn't that what adventure is all about?!)

I looked through your expedition website and it looks like you're well prepared and outfitted. That titanium stainless steel boat you've got looks hot!

Cheers, and obviously all the best wishes in the world for safe journeying and passage through the pack ice next year for you!

I hadn't told Aron nor reported on the website that I'd already made one seriously major mistake, which had almost cost me my life. The way a near-death experience forces a re-evaluation of all of a person's perspectives makes it intensely personal, particularly in the immediate aftermath of the event. I also felt that some sections of the media might have put a negative spin on the episode. Louise was the only one who knew.

CHAPTER II

Christmas, a Message from the Stars and Pirates

Adrian: Thursday 22nd December 2005

I hope you're settled into the hotel. Presumably you've now had an opportunity to infuse your circulatory system with pina coladas. At three degrees south, I had to tack to go 100 miles east and then tack back to prevent crashing into South America. Having one of the best sailing days so far – making a good line down the coast of Brazil. I am about 200 miles offshore. This wind should hold and then come round behind me and stay that way as far as Buenos Aires.

Louise: Thursday 22nd December 2005

Having a fabulous time. Gabriel in the pool floating with arm bands albeit in the shallow end but taking his feet off the bottom and he did that immediately! They are in their element. Everyone so friendly – food wonderful – archetypal Indian Ocean stuff – white sand, swaying coconut palms, turquoise seas. The manager is letting me use his secretary's computer for emails.

Don't forget to open your presents. Mine you will find boring until later in the trip. Matt's you will think is the best present you have ever received in your entire life – I know you . . . so let's see if I'm right!

I thought to myself, 'The best present Matt or anyone else could give me at the moment would be a pack of cigarettes . . .'

Ricardo had been out of touch for a while. Louise had warned me he would be away, though she wouldn't tell me why. They'd had an argument about it, Ricardo accusing her of undermining me psychologically by telling me that one of my 'support' structures would be temporarily unavailable. I understood his point, but he could not have known that Louise and I always communicated honestly – upfront, nothing hidden. That worked best for us. The thought had not occurred to me to be upset with Louise.

Ricardo: Friday 23rd December 2005

Forgive the long silence. Been so busy. What I am about to tell you is still confidential and will only be disclosed on the 27th. The Paris Dakar Rally is starting from Portugal this year and everyone is making a big fuss about it. I am not a rally driver (yet) so I thought I would ride on the back of this huge international event and go for the same destination by boat. A company we have been flirting with for 18 months took the bait and now we have put a project together in around 10 days. I had a cracking sail from south Portugal to base in Lisbon and enjoyed being alone at sea again. I have a solid fast 43 ft cruiser. Even has a fridge! I should take around 15 days to get down there, hopefully beating the cars! I want all this done and dusted by end of January. I depart Lisbon 31st December to the same start gun as the rally boys. Damn trade winds! The Saint Helena high is not where it usually sits, which is why you have these annoying head winds. Keep tacking on every shift. You are close to freedom. Ric.

From the start, I'd figured that it would take until the equator to shake out the boat. Now that I was in the southern hemisphere, time ran seamlessly and I felt that I was now 'into' the voyage, my disposition aided by the better weather since the Canaries' storm. Conditions were beautiful: a 12-knot southeast wind, blue sky and blue ocean. *Barrabas* was now pointing her bows towards the Falkland Islands.

Ricardo had warned of lights at sea – oil rigs, each protected by guard boats and ferries shuttling personnel between them.

Christmas Day. Louise telephoned. I spoke to the children – Father Christmas was due to make an appearance on the beach, arriving by speedboat. They were beside themselves with excitement.

The winds lightened, intensifying the heat. I hoisted the cruising chute, a lightweight sail, to try to maintain boat speed in the gentle breeze. Sweat ran in rivulets down my back and chest. The deck was too hot to stand on for long so I retreated below to send a plethora of emails. Old habits die hard. When it came to opening the presents, I followed a practised routine from childhood: look, smell, weigh, shake, rip off the coloured paper. A hot-water bottle and thermal socks from Louise and the boys (I felt real gratitude towards Louise later, when I used the hot-water bottle constantly in the Arctic). From Matt at Kemp Sails – lo and behold – a packet of Benson & Hedges, a mini bottle of champagne, Christmas pudding and an issue of *Maxim* magazine. I was jubilant, dancing around the cabin, yipping and hollering. I immediately sent an email to Matt . . .

May the blessings of a thousand angels fall upon you. What a totally inspired Xmas present . . . thank you. Louise emailed a couple of days before Xmas and said, 'Don't forget to open your presents, Matt has got you something you'll really enjoy . . .' so I wrote back and told her that the best present Matt or anyone else could give me right now would be a box of cigarettes! I ran out a couple of weeks ago (by design it has to be said, but nonetheless . . .). So when I opened the box . . . well, the choirs of heaven began to sing . . . and the high end (no pun intended) reading material . . . outstanding (again, no pun intended). The accompanying calendar now adorns the chart table . . .

Sky News called twice for live interviews. My parents in South Africa watched on TV while they ate their Christmas lunch.

I trailed the champagne from the back of the boat to cool it down but it had all the effect of a dunking in a warm bath (there was a fridge on *Barrabas* but I never used it because it pulled too much power from the batteries). The heat eroded my appetite, although I did get through a fruitcake and five mince pies.

Boxing Day was difficult and I knew it would be hard for Louise, remembering the deaths of Christian, Tracey and Alexandre on the first anniversary of the Asian tsunami.

I didn't know the exact time that they died, but I calculated that it must have been about 10 am where they were in Thailand. Taking account of time differences meant that was 2 am UCT. My position, at 33° west longitude, put me two hours behind UCT. It was just coming up to midnight, local time on Christmas Day (01.59 am UCT on 26th December), when I went on deck. Suddenly, I felt a powerful urge to look upwards. The sky was unblemished. The stars dazzled. As a child growing up in Thailand, I had watched the stars from the deck of the beach house in Pattaya. I knew the three stars in a line that constitute part of Orion's Belt as the Three Kings. Whenever I saw them now, I thought of Tracey, Christian and Alexandre. Directly above *Barrabas*, the Three Kings appeared to be mounted on top of the mast. At that exact moment, the brightest shooting star I had ever seen blazed across the heavens, moving from compass south to compass north. I checked the time. It was 2.04 am UCT. I heard splashing all around *Barrabas*. The night was very still – the wind light, the sea smooth. Dolphins were cavorting and diving. The dolphins played for 10 minutes, their bodies drilling torpedo wakes of green phosphorescence through the dark water. Then, as suddenly as they had come, they were gone.

I slept with the cruising chute still flying. I woke at dawn. The wind had strengthened. The cruising chute was flogging. I rushed on deck but, just as I prepared to drop the chute, it blew out, torn in two from head to foot. The loss of the chute was careless but not serious. I could improvise with the asymmetric spinnaker.

Louise: Tuesday 27th December 2005

Gabriel proclaims, 'I want to stay here forever!' Our routine is as follows: wake up between 7.15 and 8.15. Get ready and go for breakfast. We eat fruit: mango, watermelon, pineapple, papaya, all fresh off the tree. Bacon, eggs, waffles, pancakes, great fresh coffee, hot chocolate. Then I go and bag a sun bed by the edge of the pool for later (my god, I must be German). Boys go to kids club at 10. I go to my own private office they have given me and attend to emails etc. for about an hour or so. Then I go to the pool and read (magazine, book or Daily Mail, *which comes about every three days). Get boys at about one or two. Order poolside service – by a process of elimination from wading through the poolside menu we are down to a huge box of chips (great ones), virgin pina colada for Benji and me (sometimes mine's not so virginal) and freshly squeezed OJ for Gabe. We swim and play until four-ish then go for a walk down the beach – Gabriel wading up to his waist in the sea sans armbands. Then back to the room about 5.30 – 6.00 shower/bath, TV, colouring, toys and then dress up for dinner at 7.30. Huge buffet – different every night (Benji v adventurous). Last night we lay on a hammock outside our room and looked at the stars. Lights out at 10.30. Wake up next day and do it all again!*

Bright light loomed just below the horizon off my starboard bow. 3 am. I climbed halfway up the mast and glimpsed a white light. The boat was moving towards us fast. A beam swept through the darkness, a searchlight playing over the inky surface. The vessel closed to four miles then turned and maintained station off my starboard side following a parallel course. After 20 minutes, it fell back until it was lost over the horizon astern.

The radar was never on while I was outside designated shipping lanes and far enough offshore to avoid fishing boats or during daylight hours, unless mist or fog reduced visibility. I should have put it on once I'd seen the vessel just before dawn. I didn't and it still wasn't on at midday. I was below deck. Some intuition urged me to go topside and, as I stepped up into the cockpit, I got a hell of a shock! There was a boat right in front of me, 300 yards away. My body fizzed with a sudden rush of adrenalin. I guessed the other vessel weighed 100 tons. She was wallowing, engines off, no wake from her stern. Immediately, I thought 'gunboat' – one of the Brazilian navy boats that protect the oil rigs that Ric had mentioned (although I hadn't seen any rigs). She looked sleek, fast. The binoculars told a different story. Streaks of rust trailed down her sides, no markings. A fishing boat, then? There was no gear running out from her stern, no equipment on deck to evidence an offshore trawler. *Barrabas* was on a collision course. I unlashed the wheel and steered away. The boat was now very close, 150 yards. I could clearly see aerials and scanners bristling from the pilothouse but there was no sign of life on deck. Laundry flapped languidly in the hot air, strung between the pilothouse and the forward superstructure. Sea gypsies? Why would sea gypsies be 300 miles offshore? Or was it pirates?

Was this the same boat that had been tracking me earlier? Had they motored round so I would sail right past them, giving them the chance to eyeball the yacht by daylight? It was too much of a coincidence that I should appear to be tracked and shortly after, literally run into a boat 'parked' on the ocean. The aerials clinched it. If the boat was not a protection vessel or a commercial fishing vessel, why the degree of electronic sophistication?

I brought *Barrabas* to within 50 yards of the inert ship, close enough so that whoever was in the pilothouse could read the Alpha Global logo and expedition website address on the mainsail. I reasoned that a pirate vessel would be equipped with internet access. A check would confirm that I would be unlikely to have money or valuables on board. Maybe my thinking was far-fetched. Would a bunch of murderous pirates do research on an English website? Maybe not, but what alternative did I have?

As we passed, I looked back. An eerie sight – a dead ship on the high seas. That sixth sense, honed through 61 days alone on *Barrabas*, was unequivocal. This was a pirate vessel – menacing and deadly. The modus operandi of pirates in hotspots around the globe – the Malacca Strait, the Red Sea, Nigeria, Yemen, the Philippines, Brazil – was consistent when it came to attacks on small craft. Kill the crew, plunder the boat then sink it with the bodies on board, preferably in deep water, leaving no trace. I urged *Barrabas* to fly.

Within an hour, the vessel had disappeared below the horizon astern. I breathed easier. By 5.00 pm, I had covered 30 miles since my 'near collision'. On deck, fixing the starboard spray dodger, I noticed a ship astern. Through the binoculars, I recognised the distinctive profile of the vessel – it was the pirate boat. I watched her disappear westwards then switched on the radar and picked up the contact. There were no other boats around.

That night I didn't sleep. At 1.50 am, the bright loom of light reappeared in an identical position relative to *Barrabas* as the previous morning. I broke open the shotgun, loaded seven rounds in the magazine, chambered one and sat in the cockpit, the weapon resting across my knees while *Barrabas* barrelled along at six knots. An attack would most likely come before dawn. The radar's sweep picked out a contact off my starboard side, shadowing me as before. With the radar guard set to six miles, I stayed on watch. The radar alarm shattered the dawn at 4.30 am. The contact was at nine o'clock, range six miles. I maintained watch but made no further sightings. By daybreak, I had lost the contact. A large tanker came across my bows, range four miles. The pirate boat had peeled away, perhaps drawn to another target, perhaps deciding that *Barrabas* was not worth attacking.

Cape Horn posed the next danger. Despite the fact that I was still six weeks away, I felt the psychological barrier to entering this notorious stretch of water rise ever higher with each passing mile. A constant stream of depressions goes round Cape Horn, spinning clockwise. The winds at the depression's leading edge would be northwesterly backing to southwesterly as the depression tracked eastwards. I decided my strategy: sail on starboard tack (sailing with the wind coming over the starboard side of the boat) in the northwest winds, heave-to in the west winds then put the boat on port tack (wind coming over the port side of the boat) as the wind shifted to the southwest. Confirmation of my tactics came through in an email from Tim Thornton.

Tim: Wednesday 28th December 2005
A better bet is to time your rounding of the Horn. The depressions roll past pretty fast but with a day or so gap between them. Aim to make the last bit down to the Horn as a depression comes through and stay on starboard tack.

The wind will push you further south, but stay with it. Then tack on to port and you will be lifted, so as the depression passes you will be freed, and eventually find yourself reaching up towards Chile.

For now, conditions were good. The sailing was easy and *Barrabas* was making decent mileage through the days and nights. Occasionally, we passed through squall belts. My deck drills were by now so practised that I could heave-to, bend in a reef or shake one out, gybe round and have *Barrabas* sailing again in under three minutes. Usually, I waited 20 minutes between deciding on a sail change and executing the man-oeuvre unless circumstances were extreme. Half the time, the twenty-minute rule meant I took no action as conditions reverted back.

Louise: Friday 30th December 2005
We had a nice time out yesterday. We went to the nature reserve and went in an open top 4x4 on safari. Benji has got a sort of sick bug today and keeps throwing up but the nurse has given him some anti-throwing-up medicine – French stuff of course . . . they have a medicine for everything.

*Hope the pirates have F***** OFF and that you didn't have to deploy any weapons?!*

I don't think Louise had taken the pirate issue seriously and I was glad of that.

Adrian: Friday 30th December 2005
The pirates did not make an appearance last night – thank god.

Yesterday I was standing on the afterdeck taking some pictures. I noticed a shadow in the water following the boat. I put the camera down and lowered myself onto the sugar scoop to take a closer look. The shadow turned out to be a beautiful sailfish with a long, pointed snout. Close up, it was iridescent blue. The fish must have been three feet long. Unfortunately, I don't have tackle on board to fish for these (what great curry it would have made). I did think about the harpoon gun, but the fish must have read my thoughts. It seemed to look up at me, appeared to wink then fled to the depths.

New Year's Eve. Out there, in my peculiar and isolated time continuum, nature performed a spectacular fireworks display, the sun detonating as it touched the western water, hurling golden shafts through the clouds and spilling crimson into the northern sky. It seemed for all the world to be for my benefit alone. I celebrated New Year with a tot of Navy Rum, the first alcohol I'd touched for over two months. It nearly blew my head off!

I began the New Year, like so many millions, with a resolution – to keep the boat tidy and not allow small jobs to accumulate into an ugly pile. Apathy had leaked into my days, perhaps a consequence of the easy trade wind sailing and the searing heat. The easy option had been to relegate small, non-essential tasks to a worksheet that I would get round to at some point.

I started with the galley, stripping the cooker, scrubbing, cleaning and disinfecting every piece until it was gleaming, bleaching the sinks, clearing black gunk from the drainpipes and emptying and wiping out the cupboards.

Light winds in the afternoon meant I could make overdue repairs to the mainsail without compromising progress southwards. I took the sail down, running the slides off the mast track. The top three eyelets needed re-stitching and the webbing link connecting the top car to the sail had chafed badly. I made a new one. Running downwind with the boom fully extended brought the sail into contact with the shrouds. After more than two months at sea, agitation had caused areas of chafe, especially to the top batten sleeve. I covered the worn areas with adhesive-backed sailcloth, swung *Barrabas* round into wind and reset the main.

Dipping into a book of crossword puzzles and revising astro-navigation between chores became a tactic to conserve my limited reading material.

The brutal conditions we would encounter approaching the high southern latitudes were difficult to imagine. Big weather at 30° south showed on the weather files I downloaded but at our present latitude, just south of Rio de Janeiro, the sea state and wind were perfect. *Barrabas* hummed along, her sails goose-winged, the main tucked down at the third reef to avoid casting a wind shadow onto the headsail. I looked out to starboard, to the western horizon and imagined the land close by. A couple of days sailing in that direction and I could be in Rio. For a moment, the question flitted through my mind – should I go into port? What had been an idle thought took root and I found myself seriously considering the possibility. And then what? Call it a day? I realised how tired I was and how scared at the prospect of Cape Horn.

I thought about my 'coping' strategies. Feelings of vulnerability and unease permeated the voyage. Out on the ocean, an unnatural environment for man, I felt unsafe. This background noise was sometimes loud, sometimes barely audible, but constantly present. I missed people because of my isolation. I missed the familiarity of surroundings and routines because my environment demanded continual adaptation. I missed the children as if part of my soul had died. However, these apparently negative sensations had a hugely positive effect. They focused my attention onto just how good life could be if approached with an open and positive attitude, discarding regrets as useless baggage, and worries over the future as unproductive distraction. Attitude was all-important. The greater part of the challenge was psychological – how easy it would be to slip between the cracks and become depressed by missing the boys, home, comforts, by thinking about the costs and worrying about the consequences if it all went wrong. I didn't have any photographs of the children pinned to the bulkheads (but I did have some on the laptop) and I avoided dwelling on the past – disciplining myself to exist in the moment. But suddenly, I was weakened, tempted to end the voyage, and I found myself in a crisis of confidence. Could I carry on? Could I face the Horn? Seemingly out of nowhere, this crisis became almost overpowering. For the next 24 hours I battled the fatigue, the doubt and the fear until the crisis was past.

On Tuesday 3rd January, I marked my position – 100 miles east and 100 miles south of Rio de Janeiro. I altered course to take *Barrabas* closer inshore and better positioned to harness the half-knot currents running southwest down the Brazilian, Uruguay and Argentine coasts.

The dawn yielded to molten gold pouring across the absorbent sky. Massively stacked cumulus cloudbanks mushrooming upwards like silent, aerial explosions. Lightning moved overhead. I shut the main isolation switch in case of a lightning strike. For the remainder of the day the wind died, the sails flapping uselessly. By nightfall, the sea had stilled to oily flatness. The dark seemed more absolute than before. I lit a candle to provide a semblance of comfort while the lightning continued to bicker amongst the clouds.

An extensive front of dark cloud moved in from the west. The atmosphere changed. Sudden gusts swirled and rotated, the sails filling, then flogging, then backing, without the boat changing direction. I quickly furled the headsail. I did not have the deck lights on, which was a mistake because I couldn't see clearly. The wind picked up to 20 knots. *Barrabas* began to vibrate to the acoustic smack of sailcloth rapidly filling then deflating. I rushed topside. The head of the sail had unfurled, creating an inflated bag of material, which was flogging against the inner stay, 'bouncing' the forestay and vibrating the rig. The vibrations transmitted through the mast to the hull so the entire boat was shaking. The headsail had literally tied itself in knots around the forestay, the clew twisted around and over folds of sail material, locking itself in a half hitch. I tried winching the sail out but that made the knot tighter. Going forward, I flicked the spinnaker halyard around the forestay and pulled tight to deflate the bag and prevent the flogging, but the wind just ripped bags of sail out from beneath the twisted rope. I was naked, cold, tired and did not have a harness. I went below to put on oilskins and my lifejacket, thinking that the headsail had probably already sustained damage. The only option was to unfurl the headsail by hand. Screaming at the top of my lungs into the maelstrom, I stood on the pulpit and by sheer jaw-clenching effort unwound the sail. When the headsail was finally free, I sheeted out then re-furled. The whole process had taken two hours. A later inspection showed no damage, a testament to the quality of the sails and the first of several occasions when I silently thanked the sail-makers at Kemp.

I began reading Jeremy Wilson's *Lawrence of Arabia*, a Christmas present in 1989. I had been waiting for a suitable opportunity to read it. Now seemed like a good time.

The careless furl of the headsail was a precursor to a month of troubles. I decided to give the engine a run in neutral to get things working. It started on the second attempt but sounded unhealthy, with loud banging sounds coming from the area of the exhaust manifold. The casing became hot to the touch, leading me to suspect the cooling system. I checked the transparent, wire-reinforced seawater cooling tubes in the engine compartment and found discoloration. So the cooling water might have been partially impeded (there was water discharging from the exhaust). Another possibility was marine growth in the seawater intake on the outside of the hull, preventing full flow. I cut the engine, left it for five minutes, then restarted. It sounded better.

The engine ran for about 30 minutes, then began vibrating, then cut out. I couldn't believe it! The symptoms were exactly as I'd experienced collecting the boat from France. I left the engine off for 15 minutes then tried it again. It ran for three minutes, then phlegmatic coughing, vibrating and cut out.

I checked the fuel system but my belt and braces measures were working fine, delivering clean fuel to the engine. I agonised all night over the diagnosis. After drawing sketches and flow diagrams, I figured that it had to be the oil. When I checked the engine in the morning sure enough, all the oil (six litres) had bled out! The engine had been running with no oil. The chances of permanent damage were high. When I removed the oil filter, I discovered the problem. The O-ring seal from the previous filter had been left behind and had broken the seal on the new filter, allowing oil to trickle. I cursed myself for not going through a more thorough engine check before starting her up. I replaced the seal, put new oil in the engine, checked the fuel feed (just in case – working fine) started and prayed. She fired first time, sounded healthy and ran for several hours, recharging the batteries.

Just to be certain, I tied on and went over the side with a facemask, diving under the hull to have a look at the seawater intake to the engine. All clear.

For several days, I'd been fantasising about fresh fish. The line had been trailing but no takers. After 'morning chores' (cleaning out saloon cupboards) I pulled the line in to set a different lure; in fact, a series of lures I had bought in Spain during the delivery trip from France. These lures, designed to run close to the surface, might change my luck. Perhaps the previous lure had been too deep.

Splashes disturbed the surface all around *Barrabas*. Had I wandered in among a shoal of feeding fish? I went aft to monitor the line while we passed through the shoal. Still no takers. Back on the foredeck, I noticed shadows darting around the bow. A dozen sizable fish swam just ahead of the boat like miniature dolphins. I fetched the spear gun (Bernard's, he'd let me have it with the boat) and cocked the weapon onto the more powerful of its two settings. Lying prone on the foredeck with my head and shoulders protruding over the water, I could get the tip of the spear just above the surface. I took aim and fired. The spear ploughed a harmless furrow through the water two feet in front of my target. The anchor chain was digging into my ribs so I rolled onto my side and re-cocked the spear.

The fish were zigzagging fast. My shot had to be millimetre-perfect. I selected the target and watched it for a while, getting an idea of the swim pattern. I took aim at a point over the water while the fish was on a zig furthest out from the bow. At the point I judged the fish would turn on to the zag, I fired. Then all hell broke loose. The spear and the fish had merged too quickly for me to see and now the fish was thrashing on the surface in a pink froth. I could see the entry point of the spear just behind its head. I walked the fish back slowly to the aft deck, not sure how deeply the spear had penetrated, and lifted the fish. It was heavy, about four kg. The spear had exited though the gills.

I killed the fish and cut fillets, which I fried in olive oil then slow-cooked with peanuts, cashews, pepper and sweet chilli into a kind of fish satay.

I decided to ride the culinary wave – the fish satay was delicious – and attempted a sweet chocolate loaf. I ended up with something the weight and consistency of a house brick.

Louise called. She and the boys had flown home from Mauritius and just arrived back at the house. When I spoke to Benji, he told me he wanted me to come to his birthday party the following day, 6th January. I remembered what he'd said to Louise the year before. It was all I could do to stop myself from crying.

Adrian: Friday 6th January 2006

My darling Benji

It is your birthday today – you are seven years old! You have given me so much happiness and I am sorry that I am not with you today to share your birthday with you, but I am thinking about you (as I do every day).

Remember, you are my special, special boy. I have given Mummy some money so that you can go and choose a present for yourself. I love you, Daddy.

Despite the obvious contradictions, I liked to believe that the voyage of the Alpha Global Expedition would contribute to the boys' ultimate sense of belief in themselves. My chart portfolio included two world charts, one for Benji, and one for Gabriel. Each week I marked my position on the charts with annotations of what had happened during the previous seven days. I marked up Benji's chart on Sundays, Gabriel's on Mondays so that each would be unique.

We were by now 1,653 nautical miles south of the equator. *Barrabas* was like a furnace inside. The tropical sun beat down on her metal hull. With all the hatches and the companionway open, a draught eddied through the cabin. It was cooler below than on deck. I tied a torn teacloth around my head as a bandanna to catch the sweat before it ran into my eyes. Dehydration became an issue. I had Powerade powder on board, which I mixed with water to make up an electrolyte fluid. Every 30 minutes I drank a pint. Even lying on my bunk reading, making little or no movement, my skin stayed damp with sweat.

In 2003, when Louise and I had flown to New Zealand, toying with the idea of emigrating, we'd met Doug and Raewyn Pauling and become friends. On 8th January, I received a message from Doug:

Hello Adrian

I hope that you are well as you can be out there on the wide sea by yourself! We think about you often and I really feel privileged to be able to send you an email direct.

Over the New Year period I had more than one glass on your behalf, some of them while talking to my sailing friends about your journey. There is a group here in Auckland who watch your progress with interest and we all keep tabs on the website. None of them have done the solo thing but they all have ocean-going experience and can share your feelings.

It was amazing. Here was a 60-year-old man saying he felt privileged to be able to write to me direct! The truth was that I felt privileged that someone in New Zealand (or anywhere else for that matter) would take the trouble to be interested in what I was doing.

I downloaded new weather files. The good conditions looked set to continue, but my anxieties about Cape Horn began to dominate my thoughts.

CHAPTER 12

The Big Storm

Barrabas was sailing beautifully. The weather and conditions, bar the odd squally day, had until the last few days been consistent, warm and sunny. On 12th January, *Barrabas* found her 'slot' (as I call it) – the sweet spot that is so difficult to attain, the play between wind, water and rudder relative to the sails. It was the first time that *Barrabas* was truly in that groove and I knew it because she felt different. The wind was just aft of the beam and we may have had the benefit of a half-knot current. She was cruising at six knots with a double-reefed main, gliding effortlessly through the water. There was no bounce, no challenge from the water against her hull, no sandpapery resistance. The co-dependent forces at play to maintain the boat in the slot were too complex and too fickle to maintain for long but while *Barrabas* was perfectly tuned, it seemed as if the sea itself was grease and she was simply sliding downhill.

Although *Barrabas* had briefly slipped into her slot, conditions then changed with near-windless periods interspersed with sudden blows of 25 knots. When the wind blew, we made good speed southwest. If the daily runs of the previous week continued, we might be rounding Cape Horn by the end of the first week in February. The southern hemisphere summer runs through December, January and February, with a significant variation in storm frequency during the different seasons, a 10 per cent storm frequency in summer against 40 per cent during winter. I marked our position. We were at 34°53′ south, exactly the latitude of Buenos Aires, 500 miles away to the west.

In July 2005, while I was fitting out *Barrabas* at Medina Yard, my father had telephoned. He'd seen Roz Savage being interviewed on the local TV news. Roz was a rower, preparing to attempt a trans-Atlantic. I emailed a message of good luck to Roz. She sent me one back, having looked at my website, and we arranged to meet up a few weeks later, after Cowes Week. The tropical storm off the Canaries that had lashed *Barrabas* as we passed the islands in late November 2005 had disrupted the start of her race. She eventually got away on 30th November, but worse was to come when the guy who was supposed to be sending her weather information went AWOL. I'd offered to help by providing weather data and I'd been sending her weather forecasts twice a week since. By mid-January, she was halfway across the Atlantic.

Roz: Thursday 12th January 2006
And as Adrian predicteth, so it came to pass . . . thanks for the weather info. You must have some friends in high places – ever since you started providing my weather, it's been nigh on perfect, so thank you very much!

My 'friends' were the Gridded Binary Data (GRIB) weather files, a format capable of packing a huge amount of information into a small electronic packet that had proved so accurate for me and, so it seemed, for Roz. I could request and download the files and then view them ready geo-referenced through the MaxSea software. My habit was to request wind speed, direction and wave heights. Of the various display options, I preferred 'wind bubbles', a bubble etched with an arrow to show wind direction with a figure contained within the bubble indicating wind speed in knots. My GPS communicated with the computer to show my position within the weather file so I could see exactly what was happening around me at any time for the period I had requested. GRIB, developed by NOAA (National Oceanographic and Atmospheric Administration), part of the defence department of the US government, collated data from satellites, weather buoys and balloons, which were then fed into a complex computer model to predict weather.

Later, as I approached Cape Horn, Ric agreed to take over supplying Roz with weather information. He was also using GRIB files and while his part in my voyage had moved to a more strategic role in route planning, his GRIB reports would give Roz the immediate information she needed. She would eventually make it to Antigua on 13th March after 103 days at sea.

Friday January 13th started badly, a threatening ensemble of steel sky and leaden sea. From our latitude of 36° south, close to the Roaring Forties (the area between latitudes 40° to 50° south, where the wind is consistently strong, *roaring* predominantly westwards), I could expect bad weather from here to Cape Horn and then northwards, *if* we got round, to a similar latitude on the Pacific side.

Louise: Saturday 14th January 2006
Had a great time at the Boat Show yesterday. Visited all our sponsors exhibiting, walked around handing out leaflets, met Andrew Bray and had coffee with John Curry and his wife, hung out with Matt and Rob and Toby (they are fab). In this month's Practical Boat Owner *you have a triple-page colour spread and in* Sailing Today, *most of page 9.*

I sent an email to the Murmansk Shipping Company about a week ago and still haven't had a reply from them. I will keep persevering. The Russian Embassy hasn't even responded to the letter from the Foreign Office.

'Great!' I thought. Were we ever going to hear from the Russians?

The weather, like my frustration, built through Saturday and by Sunday morning *Barrabas* was running downwind with one reef in the mainsail. Ric had advised me to expect winds of 18 to 20 knots. My own weather file indicated something similar but these GRIB reports, despite their accuracy in predicting wind direction, consistently under-estimated wind speeds. Experience had taught me to add 5 to 10 knots to predicted wind speeds greater than 20. At 30 knots of wind, I would have normally shortened the mainsail to the third reef but, because we were running, the apparent wind on the sail was less, so I kept the main slightly fuller at the second reef.

The seas began to heap. I kept checking the state of the weather from below decks while the Hydrovane held *Barrabas* on her course. At 8 am, I prepared the cockpit lines to shorten sail. Too quickly, the wind escalated, whistling then shrieking and finally screaming. The seas, goaded by the winds, turned from ugly to monstrous, great walls of water rampaging up behind *Barrabas*'s stern. Very soon, in the dimmed lighting of this boiling theatre, their crests began to tumble over in great grinding cauldrons of hissing spume. The noise was intimidating, seeping into my skin and climbing up to invade my mind, replacing control with chaos.

Barrabas was committed to her course. It was too late to heave-to and stop the boat to shorten sail. To heave-to in these seas would mean exposing the boat's side to the potential devastation of 25-foot breaking waves, risking a capsize or, worse, a complete rollover.

I checked the wind instruments – 42 to 45 knots constant. All too frequently, the readout registered 48, 49, 50 knots. As waves passed beneath the hull and gripped the keel, *Barrabas* slewed to windward. The sudden decrease in the angle of the wind-strike on the sail pulled *Barrabas*'s nose further into the wind, heading her up. The power of the pull began to override the Hydrovane's ability to steer the boat back on course and I had no option but to take the wheel and hand steer. I did so for hour after gruelling hour, watching behind as giant waves stormed past in a relentless sequence and thinking about Vito Dumas and Bernard Moitessier running before the seas. It was certainly the right tactic for *Barrabas*. She was similar in size and displacement to Moitessier's *Joshua*.

Sometimes there was not enough space or time between waves to line *Barrabas* up correctly to take the next one on her port quarter. Physical and mental fatigue began to bite and I began to mistime my turns.

Water cascading across the deck loosened the spinnaker, bagged and lashed, at the base of the mast. The wind whipped some of the sailcloth free. It blew over the side and as soon as the sailcloth touched the surface, the water gripped it and pulled it free of its sock so that it was streaming behind *Barrabas* and acting like a drogue, slowing her down. There was no way I could pull the spinnaker back on board. The control lines for the sock had become snagged around the mast. I pulled a knife from my pocket and, clipping onto a strong point on the transom, I leaned far out over the aft deck and cut the spinnaker free.

The force I had to exert on the wheel as the water whipped the boat round, exacerbated by the fact that *Barrabas* was carrying far too much mainsail, required the total of my strength. I knew that the steering system would not take that degree of punishment for too long. I prayed for a break in the weather, a lull, just enough time for me to heave-to and reduce sail. No lull came. After six exhausting hours, I felt a slight release in the wheel beneath my fingers. I doubt another helmsman would have noticed it, but I had become so attuned to *Barrabas*, to the way her heartbeat, that when the first strands of her steering cable parted, I felt it as keenly as an earthquake. I gripped the wheel harder. The slight bucking came again and then the wheel went free, all tension gone as the cable failed.

I knew at once that the boat was in serious danger. She was out of control. A wave pushed us skywards and, even as I sensed her nose heading up, I was unclipping my lifeline to go below and secure the companionway to prevent a massive flooding in case she rolled. Most boats, if rolled, will right themselves. If they lose the keel, they will still float. But *Barrabas* was made of steel – she would not float. If water swamped her while she was inverted in a full capsize, the weight of it would quickly exceed the weight of the keel. It would be her death knell. She would not come up again. The storm covers were over the hatches, but I had to get the companionway closed.

I quickly called Louise. It was late morning in England. I explained the situation and gave her my co-ordinates. I asked her to be on standby. If I hadn't called her back within one hour, she was to alert Falmouth Coastguard and relay my co-ordinates. Falmouth would then liaise with the Argentine coastguard.

Barrabas had headed up and turned beam on to the seas. If a capsize was coming, now would be the time. I had to get back up on deck and drop the mainsail. Now, side on to the wind, the sail was thrashing and in 50 knots of wind, the flogging was unbelievably violent. In the few minutes that it took me to get to the mast, clip on my lifeline, release the halyard and drop the mainsail, the severe flogging was enough to damage or even destroy most sails. Rob Kemp and Matt Atkins knew that *Barrabas* would experience frequent, extreme conditions and that the sails needed to be able to meet those demands. Incredibly, when I inspected the sails later there was no damage at all. For the second time in a few short days, I whispered my thanks to them for their craftsmanship.

With the mainsail down and lashed, the wind took hold of the five square metres of headsail I had been flying to stabilise the bow. *Barrabas* pointed back downwind and the Hydrovane took over. Because the Hydrovane is completely independent of the ship's rudder, a steering failure does not render the Hydrovane useless, as it would most other self-steering systems that operate by controlling the ship's rudder.

Two hours later, I had replaced the failed steering cable. By morning, the winds had calmed to 16 knots.

The force of water over the deck had also ripped away some of the Treadmaster anti-slip decking. The wind generator had broken, with repercussions on my fuel reserves for battery charging. Without the wind generator, I would have to run the engine more often to keep the batteries charged. The inverter, which converts the ship's batteries' 12 volts to 240 volts, shorted out, which meant I could no longer use any power tools. I did have a small back-up inverter of 300-watt capacity to charge the cameras and provide emergency lighting. Two 20-litre jerry cans had torn out from their mounts in the aft cabin, leaking 15 litres of diesel into the bilges. The shackles securing the tack of the mainsail to the gooseneck had failed but with the mainsail reefed down, there was no longer any load on the tack. I could repair that later.

A bad wrench to my right shoulder left me barely able to lift my arm. I diagnosed damage to the shoulder joint capsule. Luckily, the centre of a high-pressure system due to pass over would give me a few days of calm and time for my shoulder to mend.

My relationship with the sea changed. I respected it more but, curiously, feared it less. *Barrabas*'s reassuring strength and my developing seamanship skills had coped. Faced with the sea's wrath, fear was a wasted emotion because it altered nothing. This was a time of change in the voyage, both in my perceptions and in the character of the ocean. It was bigger, more ominous and less quiescent. I wondered whether this was my mind playing tricks as we closed on Cape Horn. My relationship with Louise was about to deteriorate as well.

Falmouth Coastguard called on the sat phone at 10 am on Monday morning, the day following the storm, triggering a bout of anger that I directed at Louise. Despite calling her back within the hour as I'd promised during the storm, she had already alerted Falmouth Coastguard. They were calling to check if everything was okay with me.

Falmouth Coastguard controls the international registry of EPIRBs (emergency position indicating radio beacons). Any distress signal activated anywhere on the world's seas is picked up by Falmouth. Knowing the GPS location of the signal, Falmouth will then alert the nearest MRCC (Maritime Rescue and Co-ordination Centre), which in turn puts a rescue plan into play. Before leaving the UK, I had notified Falmouth of my plans and we agreed that in any perilous situation Louise would alert them on my instruction so they would at least be prepared if the situation escalated. I was adamant that any alert would be a last resort, taken only if I was literally stepping up into the life raft (if I was 'stepping up' it meant the boat was sinking). There is an ongoing argument whether private boats engaged in non-commercial activity should rely on rescue services. Adventure demands total self-reliance. I decided that any alert would be in extremis only. My instruction to Louise had been to prepare her, not for her to act.

At 10.15 am, Louise called – I told her I did not appreciate her acting unilaterally. We both shouted at one another. I said I did not want to talk any more and put the phone down but not before I told her that I had come to hate the voyage. It was the first time my psychological containment had really cracked. I wondered later whether some instinctive sense before the storm had led me into that crisis of confidence when I was close to Rio de Janeiro.

My spirits lifted when a school of dolphins visited the next day while I was replacing a failed reefing block at the mast base (damaged by the spinnaker lines under tension). When I went below and switched on the computer, there was a message waiting.

Louise: Tuesday 17th January 2006

I hope you are not still angry – I did what I thought best to protect you, and our team are in agreement that I took the right course of action. Being furious with me will not help anything. My priority is to help keep you as safe as possible – I am and have been all along totally committed to that and needless to say I am mightily relieved that the situation resolved itself.

Are you really hating it all as much as you told me? That concerns me greatly.

I felt foolish, humbled. How could I be so bloody selfish, as if starting out on the Alpha Global Expedition wasn't selfish enough. I cursed myself out loud. Louise was looking after our children, worried sick about me, and that situation was liable to become significantly more dangerous, at least until I was sailing northwards in the Pacific away from Cape Horn. Falmouth Coastguard had not been in the least put out when I spoke to them and had told me that Louise's actions had been correct. I thought for a long time about why I had become so angry, which led back to the concept of the need for self-reliance. I think now that Louise's call to Falmouth Coastguard had taken a measure of control of the situation away from me, making me answerable to third parties. My self-reliance had been ruptured and, with it, some of my confidence had gone. I called her back, tried to explain and apologised.

Perhaps it was the tension of the storm, frustration that the Russians were not responding or having been at sea for almost three months.

Maybe it was the looming threat of Cape Horn. Whatever the cause, from that point on, I began to feel restless.

Ricardo: Wednesday 18th January 2006
The southern oceans have begun their pounding. Let's guide you in nice and safe and with plenty of back-ups in the next few weeks.

I went on deck to change sail. Winds had dropped, slowing *Barrabas* to a crawl. I was at the mast. A noise of rushing air impinged on the sound that had become so familiar, the slosh and ride of water against the hull. I turned quickly. To my astonishment and amazement, a whale, perhaps 20 feet in length, floated on the surface, watching me. I didn't know what type of whale it was but, judging by its unblemished back, it was young. The whale circled around *Barrabas* in a figure of eight pattern, gliding under the bow, turning onto its back to show a white belly (I didn't think whales could do that). Then it was gone. My spirit soared. It was a wondrous experience.

The following day, just as I passed into the Roaring Forties, I saw whale spouts a mile away off the starboard beam.

Sam: Friday 20th January 2006
Louise,
The person I spoke to who runs Sovcomflot, the Russian state shipping company, has made the passage twice with an icebreaker. Whilst in principle he would be prepared to help with permissions, he strongly recommends against it as a very hazardous endeavour. In addition to the ice, the winds can be very tricky. They recently had to abandon and evacuate a 15,000-ton tanker crushed in the ice. Not what you want to hear I know but better to be honest. I hope Adrian is doing OK, we are all thinking of him – his progress and determination are really inspiring. Love, Sam.

The note from Sam was encouraging. The influential Russian Sam had mentioned before turned out to be Sergey Frank, who, aside from heading Sovcomflot, was also a former transport minister in President Putin's cabinet. He could probably exert some influence, particularly as Nikolai Monko's department (by now we had learned that Nikolai Monko was still in his post at Northern Sea Route Administration) formed part of the transport ministry. However, there appeared to be some misunderstanding of my intention. Ships, ice-strengthened and led in convoys by an icebreaker, made transits through the pack ice. I was not planning a passage through ice in wintertime. If I was going to get through the NSR, it would only be possible in ice-free waters and that meant in high summer. I needed to clarify my timings and the anticipated conditions. The polar aspect of my voyage was the essential heart of the circumnavigation attempt. I wrote an explanatory note to Sam, which included the following paragraph.

. . . *Whilst at all times of year the Arctic – Russian and Canadian – is hardly an environment to trifle with, there are extreme differences compared with winter. Summer air temperature on the coast is +2° C as against –50° C in winter. The edge of the permanent ice is (usually) way off the north Russian coast. The extent of seasonal ice melt and growth depends on prevailing weather conditions. The problem is that inter-annual variability in these conditions means predicting ice conditions is impossible. My plan, whilst challenging, is not reckless. I will approach the Bering Strait in mid-July. Meanwhile, my shore-side weather and routing team will have been monitoring the ice-melt pattern and the rate of the receding ice limit since early June. They will also have been monitoring wind patterns to determine the likelihood of a southerly wind. Historical data comparisons will generate a 'probability' scenario. In other words, because of the inter-annual variations in weather factors, I will only be able to determine the feasibility of a passage through the NSR when I get there in mid-July and the summer ice melt is well under way . . .*

The air temperature was beginning to fall and for the first time since I'd been in the southern hemisphere, I was wearing a thermal base layer. Since the storm, Louise had been concerned about me, worried that my resilience was weakening. She was right, but my lapse in telling her that I'd come to hate the voyage was careless and not entirely true.

Adrian: Sunday 22nd January 2006
Please disregard my comment about not enjoying this experience so far – the fact is that some of it is good, some indifferent and some bad – like life! I miss the children of course. It's just that when there is a bad scene going on like I've had all week, it colours the memory and the whole ball of wax seems shitty . . . on a good day, the bad bits fade and the feeling is that the whole trip has been good. So please don't worry – I am fine, psychologically strong, resolved and determined as ever.

A thunderstorm roiled overhead, hurling forks of lightning seawards. For the second time, I had to disconnect the boat's electrical system. By some majestic contrivance, nature seemed to have picked up on the deteriorating situation between Louise and me.

Ricardo's venture to Dakar had gone well – he'd arrived at the same time as the cars. More recently, he'd been looking at the possibility of entering the Velux 5 Oceans race due to start in October, which had left Louise feeling more vulnerable.

Louise: Monday 23rd January 2006

I'm glad things with you morale-wise aren't as bad as they have started to sound over some weeks, although I don't know if you're just saying everything is OK to keep me calm/quiet? I have felt very destabilised with all of this since I went on holiday and then got back to no Ricardo and that row which should never have happened. I have felt also increasingly distanced from you. I had a long chat with Ricardo today and I am feeling much more confident now that a) I will have someone to talk to who really understands b) that you will have the support you need c) that the website will be back the way I like it i.e. updated constantly with items about your conditions/where you are in the world etc. By the way – Ricardo has now abandoned all plans for the 5 oceans . . .

Adrian: Monday 23rd January 2006

I have felt distanced from you as well, but I think having been away for coming on three months it's hardly surprising. Anyway, I'm just going to have to learn to deal with things better at my end. You know the storm etc are stressful episodes but I'm not sitting here a quivering wreck. I just get on with the job. It is true that I am very anxious about going round Cape Horn. There's also this ongoing saga of the Russians.

I am quite serious about my state of morale – I am fine really. I can tell you, when I am sailing north along the Chilean coast back towards the warmth and the sun with Cape Horn in the bag, I'll be on top of the world (even though I will be at the bottom of it!).

I was still nervous about going round the Horn. Could *Barrabas* really do it? Could I? I had my doubts, but I didn't want to alarm Louise. I had upset her enough.

I went to the foredeck and unlashed the Pudgy, lifting the dinghy onto its side and leaning it against the guardrails to uncover the forward hatch. I could see the hatch cover was bent out of shape. Its forward left-hand corner was lifting and not making a seal with the deck-mounted base. A lot of seawater was streaming through the gap when seas broke over the deck. I placed a block of wood under the forward right-hand corner and stood on the opposite corner to bend it back. I then wedged a bit of metal under the handle on the inside to tighten the seal and stuffed a piece of rolled up T-shirt material beneath the lip of the hatch to absorb water before it could find its way in.

Since entering the Roaring Forties, the weather had changed, adopting a peculiar pattern. I put it down to our proximity to South America's eastern seaboard and the thermal effects of the landmass on the west wind sweeping across the continent, from the Pacific Ocean into the Atlantic. The 24-hour cycle had become characterised by a complete absence of wind at night with blows of 20 knots during the day. I could almost set my watch by it – the winds dying at 6 pm and reappearing at 8 am the following day.

After a month without a cigarette, I was feeling proud of myself. That night, as I was lying in my bunk and rolling to the motion of the sea, my mind drifted, conjuring up memories, a kaleidoscope of images. In 1982 at the age of 22, I'd spent a year travelling around Sri Lanka, taking in a side trip to India to have a look at Tiger Hall, my father's boyhood home just outside Hyderabad. I'd already studied medicine for two years in London and was due to go to Sandhurst the following year. I'd used the time in between to go travelling on my own. It had been a wonderful trip, buzzing around the place on a 250cc motorbike. Suddenly, I could see it! The image was so clear it might have been the previous day. I was squatting by the side of the road, clad in sarong, many bangles and long hair, passing the time of day with some local builders when one of the men offered me a cigarette called a bidi. It was like smoking shredded tractor tyre. After coughing and spluttering, one of the other builders offered me something else, in a yellow box. Curious, I took the box from him – tea cigarettes. Tea! It's a dried leaf! It was another Eureka! moment. By candlelight, I dissected a tea bag. Then I found the thinnest paper I had on board (a writing pad). With great care, I rolled a cigarette. The first drag was a bit papery, like a whiff of smoke from a freshly lit fire on a chilly night. Then the herb burned beautifully and I smoked the reefer-like creation. I learned later that Augustine Courtauld, a rich man's son who joined Gino Watkins's Greenland Expedition in 1930, became stranded on the ice-cap through the long polar winter. Three weeks before he was relieved, he ran out of pipe tobacco and tried smoking tea. He didn't like it much. After my initial try, I decided I didn't like it much either.

CHAPTER 13

100 *Days*

During his circumnavigation of Antarctica from 1972 to 1973, David Lewis devised a system of lines and pulleys to control *Ice Bird*'s tiller from inside the cabin. My repair of the steering quadrant was holding well, but the steering cables would always be vulnerable in big seas. I had the emergency tiller but I needed a way of controlling it from the cockpit so I spent the day designing and implementing a system similar to the one that David Lewis had rigged. I put two eyebolts through the end of the tiller, then tied two 5 mm lines to the bolts, led each line through small blocks shackled to the fuel cages either side of the afterdeck, then led them back across the aft cabin coach house to a second block. Having made the crossover, I attached more blocks to lead the lines to the cockpit sides, up the framework of the cuddy then down by the wheel. The crossover of the lines meant that when I pulled on the starboard line, the tiller went left turning the boat to the right. To try the system out, I neutralised the Hydrovane and steered manually, tugging on the lines and sending *Barrabas* on a mad zig-zag over the water while I got used to the very different feel of the tiller.

Ricardo: Wednesday 25th January 2006
Your days of no wind are over and you will get a rude awakening today as a front goes over bringing with it 30-knot winds at least . . . variable light

winds will change to a distinct NW 15Kn then rapidly back to south and
southwest by 8 am. Good that you are close inshore as you will miss the worst
of it.

As January drew to a close and *Barrabas* sailed further south, the
weather worsened with winds regularly gusting to 40 knots. Wind
direction became less predictable as low-pressure systems whipped
around the bottom of South America. For much of the time I was
headed with the wind coming from the southwest, precisely the
direction in which I wanted to go. I was only able to make south by
going eastwards and west by going northwards. I developed a strategy
to bring *Barrabas* round and heave-to, first on port tack, then on
starboard and by forereaching (the slow travel that a boat which is
hove-to makes through the water), judge the more favourable course.
By heaving-to, I would not be giving up too much ground while waiting for better winds.

I read and re-read the Admiralty pilot for the South Atlantic region.
Admiralty pilots are books published by the UK Hydrographic Office,
giving sailing directions for most of the coastal areas in the world,
describing recommended routes and detailing geographical and
navigational information. To enter the Cape Horn area through Le
Maire Strait between Isla de los Estados and Tierra del Fuego was not
an option. Tides through the Strait were fearsome and *Barrabas* did not
have the speed to make it through on one turn of the tide. Dangerous
overfalls (areas of very rough water) extended 18 miles eastwards from
the western tip of Isla de los Estados. I would have to give the overfalls a wide berth, which meant adding 100 miles to the Cape Horn
passage.

Every boat has its Achilles heel – for *Barrabas* it was her steering
system. She was a robust boat, heavily constructed, and beautifully
welded. Most of her deck equipment and below-decks workings were
handmade to the same careful and detailed specifications as the rest of
her hull and rig. The traditional steering system, a cable-controlled
quadrant, did not exhibit any obvious design deficiencies and, although
the rudder was heavy, much of the mechanical force acting on the
rudder was taken by its skeg mounting. But the steering cables were
just too thin. To save loading the steering cables, I used the emergency
tiller lines whenever I needed to *lash* the rudder to complement the
Hydrovane. Despite my cosseting, the steering failed again on Monday

30th January. But this time, neither the cables nor the quadrant were at fault. The steering wheel itself had seized.

The spindle connecting the steering wheel through the binnacle to the chain and cable assembly had seized in its nylon bearings. To get to the spindle, I had to remove the compass from the top of the binnacle. It was a finicky job and without the assembly instructions, I wasn't sure if I was taking the compass apart in the correct sequence. Several of the screws had also seized. I felt my frustration beginning to build. With *Barrabas* bucking on the heaving seas, the job was even more difficult. The screwdriver kept slipping. I gashed my finger. I accidentally broke the compass. It would cost £500 to replace. By this time, my frustration turned to anger and I hurled the broken compass over the side and into the water. I felt like a kid chucking toys out of its pram, but at least I could now see the spindle. With the advent of GPS, a ship's compass is no longer the vital piece of equipment it once was. In addition to the ship's GPS unit, I had three handheld back-up units, so I wasn't concerned about finding my way.

A toothed cog on the spindle took the steering chain, similar to the chain assembly on a bicycle, although the chain segments were much larger at one inch wide. Four through-bolts prevented the cog rotating independently on the spindle. What I was about to encounter was another example of the 'law of boats' – *if it can, it will*. The head of one of the bolts had sheared off flush with the smooth steel surface of the cog. To get the nylon bearings out, I had to remove the spindle and, to get that out, I had to free the cog. I unscrewed three of the four bolts securing the cog. I would have to drill out the fourth screw. Stainless steel is much harder than mild steel. Drilling into it is difficult. My access to the bolt was limited and awkward through the eight-inch opening at the top of the binnacle and the spindle was positioned six inches down into the binnacle. With the movement of the boat, I could only drill in short bursts (I had a cordless drill and the 300-volt inverter was sufficient to charge the batteries). With the tip of a bit even minutely engaged in its excavated hole, the slightest sideways movement of the drill snapped the bit clean in two. I tried every conceivable method to hold the drill steady, but in the end, nothing worked except to sacrifice one bit after another. The whole operation took 15 hours and cost me most of my small bits, about 20 in all. In the meantime, *Barrabas* sailed on, the rudder held firmly by the tiller pulley system.

At nightfall, the recalcitrant bolt remained impaled in the spindle.

The holes I'd drilled around the bolt looked like the petals of a flower. Winds gusted to 35 knots, making any further work impossible. The seas built to a 12-foot swell with a lot of spray coming across the deck. I shortened the mainsail to set *Barrabas* up for the night.

Conditions provided a good simulation of the Horn, sailing into oncoming winds on rough seas. At 11 am, I went onto port tack under a deep-reefed main and the storm jib hanked onto the inner forestay, with a plan to tack every six hours and monitor my position to get a good idea of how I would fair in the Cape Horn westerlies.

Partly because of my preoccupation with the repair at the binnacle, which I still had to finish, and my messing around with the sail plan, but mostly because of the continuing dissonance between Louise and me, I had not sent any updates for several days. She finally broke the silence, her annoyance tangible..

Louise: Tuesday 31st January 2006
That was my communiqué was it . . . a copy of what you sent Ricardo anyway? How about filling me in on things like the question I've asked several times – did you deploy that drogue in the end, like what wildlife have you seen since the whale, like what is your daily routine, like what are you eating/reading, like have you come to any deep and meaningful conclusions about life?

I abandoned my 'head to wind' experiment. By 2.00 am on 1st February, I found myself becalmed once again. Close hauled in winds of 18 knots or more, *Barrabas* could make 10° to 15° on either tack, but in lesser winds, she ended up sailing not much better than a line perpendicular to the target. In very light winds, she would actually lose ground. The conclusion was inescapable: I would have to heave-to in winds below 18 knots.

A message from Louise reminded me that Saturday 5th February would mark my 100th day at sea. She also attached another message, posted on the website:

Paul Mead: Tuesday 31st January 2006
I'm a very modest yachtsman from the east coast where I sail my production built Jaguar 25 out of a place called Pin Mill near Ipswich. I've been chasing a dream for the last 30 years (I'm actually 44) to sail the Atlantic single-handed . . . I've taken a keen interest in Adrian's voyage and found it very inspiring. It's so nice to come across an expedition that is based from the

grass roots. The B&Qs of this world are great boats with great skippers but out of reach and touch to most people's imagination. I feel Adrian is carrying the baton out there for the common man and he has my vote over and above any multi-million pound expedition.

I read this message several times. It was important to me on a number of levels. It illustrated how one person's actions could inspire another to step outside the box of constraints that were accepted as normality and enrich his or her own life.

I wanted to re-awaken that golden age of adventure sailing, a time before professionalism (and commercialisation) took over, inspired as I was by Joshua Slocum, Vito Dumas and the single-handed sailors of the post-war period.

The process of adventure is complex, individual and impossible to fully articulate but sewn through with common threads: thrill, dare, challenge, need, discovery, unpredictability. What pattern any one person weaves from these threads is what makes adventure so irresistible. For the Alpha Global Expedition to satisfy me fully, I needed uniqueness. Many sailors had crossed the Atlantic, the Pacific, the Arctic, the Southern Ocean, but no one had ever stitched all those together into a vertical circumnavigation. The key to uniqueness lay in the Arctic. No one had ever sailed this icy wilderness alone, whether through Russian or Canadian waters, as part of a circumnavigation. No one had even entered the Northern Sea Route alone in a sailing yacht. To do this, I needed Louise, and her own adventure in all of this would unfold in a way neither she nor I could ever have imagined.

This message from Paul Mead was the third tremor in a series of tremors that would ultimately coalesce to shift me towards something much more fundamental, much more real and much more valuable. Yes, I wanted to imbue my adventure with a unique quality and provide myself with a unique experience but subliminally, the emphasis was changing. I had started out on a record attempt where adventure was a by-product. But there had been a gradual transition towards the predominance of the adventure with the record aspect of my voyage becoming less important. With this shift, I could relax more and I began to truly enjoy the voyage and, because of that enjoyment, I was able to realise so much more from my journey. The crisis of confidence I'd suffered off Brazil was past.

Dad: Wednesday 1st February 2006
Dear Adrian,
Received the following email from David Scott-Cowper yesterday. Not very
encouraging but I suppose realistic.

Hello Gerald
I have been following Adrian's progress with interest down the North and
South Atlantic. With regard to undertaking the Northern Sea Route, the
Russians, up to date, appear to have been insisting that a Russian pilot
accompanies the crew on the vessel sailing this route. The three sailing boats
that have done it have all had fluent-speaking Russians on board and those
people had experience of the route. The first sailing boat to pass successfully
along this way was the German yacht, Dagmar Aaen, *under the command*
of Arved Fuchs. I know that he spent approximately 10 years devoting his life
to obtain this achievement. The second was a boat called Vagabond, *under*
the command of Eric Brossier and he too spent many years trying to obtain
permission and again had to have a Russian pilot on board. The other sailing
boat was Northabout, *an Irish contingent, again a Russian pilot and fluent-*
speaking Russian had to be on board. All of these three boats had crews
ranging from six to ten people. There was also a Dutch yacht attempting the
passage and unfortunately he had to be rescued as his vessel received damage
from the ice and I think it cost his sponsors quite heavily in salvage fees.
   For my part, I tried to obtain permission in the early 1990s and
reconnoitred the North East Passage on a Russian icebreaker in 1990 in the
hope that I could obtain contacts for granting permission. When again I tried
in the years 2000 and 2002, the insistence was that a Russian pilot had to
accompany me on board.

Although we'd never met, David had phoned me before I left England
to wish me luck and offer advice. A truly remarkable man, David was
the first single-handed yachtsman to circumnavigate both west to east
(1980) and east to west (1982) via Cape Horn in his 41–foot yacht, *Ocean
Bound*. He was also the first sailor to complete a single-handed
'powered' vertical circumnavigate in a motorised surface craft, *Mabel
E Holland*, a converted lifeboat. During this powered voyage, David
became the first seaman to transit Canada's Northwest Passage
solo (although it took him four seasons to do it). My father was right.
The message from David was discouraging but I wasn't David. I
felt *destined*. Permission would come. My belief was absolute. But
like two counter-currents, my anxiety about the permission remained

(mainly because we hadn't heard anything from the Russians), despite my deep belief that it would come through in the end.

Peculiar wind patterns continued to dog me – becalmed at night, but now daytime winds were gusting to 35 knots. For the second time, a whale visited us, this time a pilot whale, about 15 feet in length, which took up station 20 metres off my port quarter and accompanied *Barrabas* and me through most of the afternoon of 1st February.

I woke to a beautiful day. The wind had unexpectedly come round to the northwest during the night. I trimmed the boat for downwind sailing and dropped the storm jib. While *Barrabas* bounded southwards, I went back to work on the binnacle, eventually getting the broken screw out, fixing the bearing and putting the steering system back together.

Ricardo had been 'researching' Cape Horn, including talking to local fishermen and a Brazilian sailing friend who had experience of the area.

Ricardo: Friday 3rd February 2006
If you were at the Horn today you would have a downwind sail all the way around. The perfect windows do exist.

Downwind around Cape Horn going westwards! 'Yeah, right,' I thought. It did happen, sure but I'd be down there for weeks. What I needed was 10 days of downwind conditions. Then I had another thought. 'In your dreams!' My nervousness about Cape Horn was heading towards fever pitch.

In anticipation of my 100 days at sea, Louise sent out a press release.

This Sunday (5th February 2006), Adrian will have been at sea for 100 days and covered approximately 7,500 nautical miles. During that time, he has coped with dreadful weather, starting from the very first week when wind and bad sea conditions forced him to retreat for several days. He has survived winds of up to 50 knots and 35 ft waves. He has lost his spinnaker, ripped his cruising chute irreparably, been unable to rescue his fouled water, fixed his watermaker, sorted out electrical problems, mopped up gallons of spilt fuel and dangled himself under the boat on numerous occasions to fix the rudder. He's stripped the engine down after that failed, lost the use of his wind generator and dealt with steering failure (about four times now). He has also sailed with dolphins, tuna, sail fish, albatross and whales, caught his own fish suppers, finished most of his books, basked in the sun, invented new recipes, been tailed by pirates, had extra-terrestrial experiences and crossed the equator. And we're only a quarter of the way into this!

A quarter of the way through! And I'd been washed off the boat, which Louise and I had decided to keep to ourselves for the time being! It was amazing to me that I had travelled so far. But just thinking about the fact that I would have to do the same distance three times over again was exhausting.

Just after midnight on Saturday 4th February, the wind went to the northeast. I set full sail to get *Barrabas* creaming along. She was sailing beautifully. True wind was touching 20 knots and though by no means extreme, caution suggested that I ought to bend in one reef but I wanted to make hay while the wind blew in the right direction. My strategy to sail conservatively and avoid any unnecessary stress to the rig was for the moment abandoned. The tail end of the southern hemisphere summer meant the onset of worsening weather around Cape Horn wasn't far away. I had to get through as quickly as I could.

Winds built through the early morning and by 6.50 am, the anemometer was recording gusts of 25 knots. Time to reef down. Occasionally, *Barrabas* refused to sail or manoeuvre as I directed. Whether we had an opposing current that Saturday, I don't know, but *Barrabas* would not tack. I tried gybing. She refused to come round with the boom in board. The only way I could get her to swing her stern through the wind was to let the boom out wide, build boat speed then spin the wheel hard over to turn her and hope I could get the boom in fast enough before the wind smashed it across the deck. As she came round, I pumped at the main sheet to bring the boom back in board, but I wasn't quick enough. The boom slammed across and, although it was not a major slam, the gooseneck attachment smashed. I must have taken *Barrabas* through hundreds of gybes – a familiar, practised routine. I was annoyed. The repair would take time, costing us valuable ground.

To replace the gooseneck, I needed to disengage the boom from the mast. I thought about the best way to do this without taking the sail off the boom and, with the boom weighing over 80 kg, I also wanted to avoid any heavy lifting. After thinking about the problem for several minutes, I decided on a plan. First, I dropped the mainsail and lashed it down onto the boom. Then I untied the main halyard from the head of the sail and tied it around the end of the boom nearest the mast. I did the same thing at the afterend of the boom, using the topping lift.

Using a block and tackle either side and halfway along the boom secured to the deck and the main sheet under tension, I created a bilateral downward pull to counter the upward pull of the halyard and the topping lift. Now I had to devise a method of pulling the boom backwards to disengage it from the mast and create a sufficient gap in which to work to replace the gooseneck. I did this by rigging the storm jib sheets from the forward end of the boom through blocks fixed (at the same height) to the afterdeck frame just below the solar panels and then down to the winches. By winching the jib sheets, I pulled the boom backwards and critically, the up-hauls and down-hauls kept it level. With a new gooseneck fitted, I eased the jib sheets and re-engaged the boom. It slid home perfectly.

A press photographer following my voyage through the website sent an email to Louise:

Rob Wheal: Saturday 4th February 2006
It seems Adrian is well equipped to deal with pretty much anything the journey throws at him. I was just intrigued as to why he would have 15 drill bits of the right size on board. I imagine Barrabas to be some sort of Tardis,* because Adrian always seems to have the equipment on hand to do the job, whereas I frequently end up doing three trips to Homebase to buy stuff I forgot the last time. Good planning I guess.

Ellen MacArthur had said (not to me, I read it somewhere before I left) when she was asked about spares, 'Take two of everything.'

I did put a great deal of planning into the spares and tools I carried. Clearly it's better to have the right kit in the first place but sometimes improvisation is the only option. One French racer in a Vendée Globe race could not start his engine. He needed it to charge the batteries. Without power, he would lose navigation and communication. Unable to hand-crank the engine, he set up a system of lines and pulleys (not dissimilar in principle to the tiller steering I had copied from David Lewis) connected at one end to the engine crank and, at the other, to the aft-end of the boom that was set out wide. He then gybed the boat. As the boom crashed across, the lines transmitted a ferocious rotational force to the engine crank and up she started, thus saving his race.

---

*Dr Who is a BBC children's programme in which Dr Who, a time lord, travels the cosmos in a Tardis, a small phone box-like contraption that is much bigger inside than outside and contains every tool imaginable.

Ricardo: Saturday 4th February 2006
Confirm big blow for Sunday morning with low centred over Falklands. NW 40kn. Reach or even go downwind towards the Falkland Islands. You will be able to turn back to a SW course before midnight. Until Tuesday night stable 30kn from the north.

The Falkland Islands lay 225 miles south-southeast. I planned to pass to the west of the islands. At 7.00 pm, I crossed latitude 50° south, moving into the 'Raging Fifties' and across the official 'start line' of my attempt to round Cape Horn. For the moment, the wind was blowing from the southwest at 34 knots giving me a bumpy, rolling ride because, even though I was sailing head to wind, the seas were more on the beam. Several big breakers crashed over the cockpit and afterdeck.

I stayed awake until the clock tripped over into Sunday. I had been at sea for 100 days!

I was fine, bar the odd knock. My left wrist was causing me some concern. It ached constantly. I had started strapping the wrist for support.

My diet became heavily carbohydrate-based as the temperature dropped: rice, pasta and bread with a variety of sauces created from the various condiments in the larder. I tended to eat a lot of the same thing, then get bored and go on to something else.

I slept as much as I could and with one near miss so far, I was more alert near the shipping lanes. Otherwise, I tried to keep to a regular light/dark, day/night pattern.

I missed my children, warm pubs, hot baths and crisp bed sheets. As I sailed on, I came to appreciate just how small our world is – I had been a third of the way around it on a small boat going at walking pace in 100 days. The earth's vulnerability struck me – like a human body, every function depended on another. A failure in one would lead to the collapse of the whole.

My tension mounted with every mile south towards the Horn. It must have been very clear to Louise. Despite us both celebrating my 100 days at sea, we had not recovered from our argument.

Louise: Sunday 5th February 2006
Up till the time the boys and I went to Mauritius, we seemed to be pretty connected, with you wanting to be involved in what we were up to. Since we got back (I don't know if it's just your power situation so there's less time to write) I am feeling totally unconnected to you. It is difficult when I spend a

*huge majority of my time doing things on your behalf and just generally
thinking and worrying about you. It is a very unsettling feeling – probably
difficult for you to understand. I know it's you doing the dangerous, scary
stuff but that doesn't cancel out my issues and insecurities and things I am
coping with just because my feet are dry. Today you are a quarter of the way
through this and believe me it seems like you've been gone ages – the prospect
of the same again three times over feeling the way I do today seems very
daunting. Maybe I should be keeping this all to myself but as you know that's
never been my way!*

During the long windless patches, *Barrabas* drifted north on the Falklands current as if she was tethered by a great elastic band, progressing
south then being pulled back, stretching out the time it would take us
to get to Cape Horn. Every mile south had to be massaged from the
wind and coaxed from a reluctant sea. The percentage of usable north,
east or west winds seemed unlikely to get me to Cape Horn before the
end of February.

I worried about Louise and knew her well enough to understand
that the loss of equilibrium between us would gnaw at her. Cocooned
on *Barrabas*, I could distract myself much more easily.

Adrian: Monday 6th February 2006
*I appreciate everything you are doing – I know it is difficult for you at times. I
am a bit stressed but will be fine once Cape Horn is under my belt . . . the
last three weeks since the big storm have been frustrating – becalmed half the
time and in storms the other half. Trying to get to Cape Horn is like someone
telling you that in 10 days you have to go 15 rounds with Mike Tyson (and, by
the way, you will be blindfolded and have your hands tied) and there is
nothing you can do about it – it would make you understandably
apprehensive. With the wind generator packing in, life for me is very
uncomfortable – I have to conserve power which means no heating or regular
comms.*

I gave a live-link interview to Anne Diamond at BBC Radio Oxford.
Louise was in the studio, though we did not manage to talk to one
another.

Louise: Tuesday 7th February 2006
*Thanks for the email. It is difficult for both of us. I will be as relieved as you
when you're round the Horn so let's focus on that for the moment . . . Benji*

has been home this week with a virus going round – over 100 children at school are off. He had a high temp on Sunday but is over that and now has a cold and is just generally below par.

You and I were being interviewed live simultaneously yesterday! Anne Diamond is headline news. She is currently starring on Celebrity Fit (fat)! Club *and it has been discovered that she cheated by having a gastric band op before starting the show. The other celebs are furious and she is front-page gossip everywhere. I sent her a supportive email of course. This all happened yesterday morning as she was interviewing you!*

This was good news – whenever Louise sent me trivia, it was a sure sign of recovery. Either she had forgiven me or decided to let the whole matter pass.

CHAPTER 14

Cape Horn

Sea mist descended. It was cold. The Falkland Islands were now abeam to the east. We had entered the Cape Horn region.

For the last few days, I had been using the gas burner to heat the inside of the cabin and strung a washing line over the cooker to hang and dry socks and gloves.

Ricardo: Thursday 9th February 2006

Between Friday night and all of Saturday you should have 30kn northerlies and perhaps 40kn as the front passes over Saturday/Sunday. It is summer down there so it will not be more than that. Wind is denser down there and the cold will make it all seem worse than it is. You have seen a lot worse and I am OK with what is coming.

My GRIBs indicated worse conditions. Ricardo had composed a piece for the website, which I only saw later. In it he'd written, '. . . *not that far west of the legendary island of Cape Horn there is a patch of Pacific Ocean with no wind at all. The patch is as wide as London to Moscow! But a low-pressure system is already affecting the area and Sunday will see gale-force winds and large seas blasting through the small gap between the two continents. Cape Horn is not going to be friendly and Adrian will be right in the middle of it . . .*'

★

Isla de los Estados was now just 74 miles south of my position. Past the island, the Cape Horn current ripped along, sometimes reaching nine knots close inshore, sufficient to overpower a small engine. Only by venturing deep into the Southern Ocean could we avoid it and create a better angle to climb north towards the Pacific.

Water, driven by wind and current through the narrow gap between South America and Antarctica, heaped into confused seas spiked with dangerous cross-breaking waves. *Barrabas* took big hits broadside. Three times, rushing crests struck her port side just forward of the midpoint, slewing her round, twisting her hull with loud, groaning noises. The Hydrovane held course as *Barrabas* ploughed on under deep-reefed main and storm jib.

Ricardo and I communicated as frequently as possible, sometimes exchanging several emails a day. I could have no definitive plan to get round Cape Horn. Conditions were too unpredictable. While my general strategy was to heave-to in the westerlies and play the veering winds to our advantage as the depressions tracked eastwards, immediate actions would be determined by the information I received on board, information fed to me by Ricardo and what my senses were telling me.

The depression was deepening. Winds to storm force 10 (48–55 knots) were imminent and expected to last for three days! I decided to back off and wait in deep water, protected by the continental land mass, avoiding Burdwood Bank east of my position over which the shallower water might gather up into monstrous seas.

The vicious low cell tore through Cape Horn on Sunday 12th February while I held station, hove-to 100 miles north in lighter winds. I ordered up a five-day GRIB of the Cape Horn area, studied the data intently, then went on deck to make checks – running rigging, standing rigging, cuddy, emergency tiller, guardrail wire tension, life raft, dinghy lashings, hatch storm covers. The Hydrovane was vibrating – the bolts securing the gear to the transom needed tightening – all other checks were clear.

In the murky twilight, I saw the distant lights of a ship on my forward horizon. I absently watched the lights migrating west, towards Argentina. Was it a fishing boat or a cruise ship? The relative safety of a larger vessel compared to my small yacht seemed to compound my vulnerability and with that, my tension ratcheted up a notch at the prospect of facing Cape Horn alone.

Adrian: Monday 13th February 2006

I have looked at the weather for the next week for the Horn and whilst not ideal, I'm going for it now! I could wait a week or two and find that no good window materialises. Cape Horn is not going to lie down for me. There is nothing hysterical in the coming week's weather but the situation is so volatile down here things can change without warning. I know that if I delayed it would be because of my psychological fear.

Back in England, Louise and Gabriel had both come down with 'flu, so now all three of them were ill and confined to the house. It seemed that Cape Horn was going to be rough on everyone.

Louise: Monday 13th February 2006

As long as you are comfortable with your decision then that is the most important thing. I will be thinking of you. Shouldn't have ventured out today but I did. We went to your house to pick up the mail and then on to Tesco to shop (cupboard bare). As I was coming down the escalators from the café, Gabriel had a change of heart about following me so I turned round to go up (on the down escalator!) lost my footing, bashed my leg on the escalator and smacked my temple and eye on the Perspex side panel. Very nice couple picked me up and the man went to the top to retrieve Gabriel. I have a black eye! I have cursed you a few times this week for not being here to share the load while we all feel so shitty. Hopefully by the end of this week we'll all be feeling better. Hope you're feeling strong about tomorrow . . .

Ricardo: Monday 13th February 2006

No clear window this week that is long enough for you to get through in comfort. There are a few nice moments with 10kn at the Horn tomorrow and then Thursday but neither are long enough to get you around before the next low hits. Patience, but I would back a decision to go for it if you feel comfortable with that.

Josh Hall has sailed alone around the world three times. I am working with him on a global ocean race and he is a good friend. He is a guru of the sailing world and a sailor to look up to. He says what you are doing is very special, he admires you and sends you best wishes. He also said that to get around the Horn will be life-changing and that the good modern solo sailor has '. . . good movies, good porn, good wine and a sense of humour . . .' So there you have it!

There was no wine on board, no movies and no porn (how did that happen?) and as for a sense of humour, mine was still intact, although I found 'anger' to be a good coping mechanism – if I shouted and screamed at the wind and waves, fear receded like an ebbing tide.

Louise forwarded a message from Bernard De Castro. *'Je suis la route de Adrian jour après jour, le Cap Horne n'est pas loin! Je lui souhaite courage et détermination pour la suite.'* ('I am following Adrian's route day by day, Cape Horn is not far away! I wish him courage and determination for what lies ahead.')

Strip all else away and the essential heart of adventure becomes clear – the unknown. Take that final step into the unknown and a traveller becomes an adventurer.

In 1936, Captain Warwick M. Tompkins sailed his 85-foot schooner, *Wander Bird*, with a crew of ten, including his wife and two children, from Gloucester, Massachusetts, to San Francisco. The track of the *Wander Bird* took her westwards around Cape Horn, and of that challenge, he wrote:

A man who loves the sea and ships can aspire to no more searching test than a Horn passage. It is the last word in the lexicon of sailormen. There Nature has arranged trials and tribulations so ingeniously that in the van of all synonyms for sea cruelty and hardship is the ironbound name of Cape Horn. Winds blow elsewhere at times as strongly as they do south of fifty. Seas elsewhere may pyramid as high, break as heavily. There may be places equally remote and as bleakly lonely. Currents in other regions may be as adverse. These foes the sailorman may encounter separately or in pairs here and there, aye, encounter and best, but always in his heart he will wonder if he could face all combined. If he glories in the unequal contest of human muscles and artifices with the ocean, if the sea shouts an insistent challenge, he can never be truly content until he has voyaged from Fifty South in the Atlantic to Fifty South in the Pacific in his own command. This is the ultimate test, given to very few to know.

Barrabas and I had travelled from England to this place, the coccyx at the base of the Andean spine. Our travels together were at an end. From here on, we would be adventurers together.

The legend of Cape Horn had beguiled me since childhood. In 1520, when Ferdinand Magellan passed through the strait that now bears his name, hundreds of campfires dotted the hillsides to the south. He called the land Tierra del Fuego, Land of Fire, believing it be a vast continent. More than fifty years later, in September 1578, Francis Drake sailed through the strait aboard the *Golden Hind*. On the Pacific side, a storm blew his ship far to the south. Open water led him to suspect that a clear water route might exist linking the Atlantic and Pacific oceans.

Acting on Drake's presumption, a Dutch merchant, Jacob Le Maire, and navigator Willem Schouten persuaded the elders of the Dutch town of Hoorn to finance an expedition to explore the possibility. They sailed in May 1615 with two ships, *Eendracht* and *Hoorn*. The *Hoorn* was destroyed by fire while she was beached for cleaning on the Patagonian coast, but in January 1616 the *Eendracht* passed through the narrow strait between Isla de los Estados and the mainland (now called the Le Maire Strait). The explorers sighted a high peak that they believed marked the southernmost point of the land. They named the peak Kaap Hoorn after their sponsoring town. The English later anglicised the name to Cape Horn.

The clipper ships, whose sailing times Chichester sought to better, passed east around Cape Horn carrying cargoes of wool and grain from Australia to Europe. The opening of the Panama Canal in 1914 and the US transcontinental railroads killed the Cape Horn sea trade. The last commercial vessel to ply the Cape Horn route was the steamship *Pamir* in 1949, en route from Australia to Finland.

This is a savage place. The Southern Ocean rolls ceaselessly around the planet goaded by westerly winds, which without land to decay them, regularly build to hurricane strength. At the Drake Passage, which separates Tierra del Fuego from Antarctica, the 2,000-mile-wide Southern Ocean is forced through a 600-mile-wide gap, sucking water in from the Pacific side and spilling out on the Atlantic side. The sea maddens into a frenzy. Currents rip around the headlands. Winds are funnelled by the high mountains of the Andes and the Antarctic Peninsula, colliding over the waters of the Drake Passage. On the South American side of the passage, depths are relatively shallow. The seabed on the Antarctic side is more than six miles deep. This dramatically sloping bed has the effect of spinning the water channelling through, adding to turbulence. To sail round Cape Horn eastwards, from the Pacific to the Atlantic, with the wind behind and the currents favourable, is challenge enough. To go westwards, against winds and currents, is arguably crazy. Of all the millions of square miles of water that cover the earth's surface, it is this stretch around Cape Horn that has earned the reputation as the most treacherous of all. It is, quite simply, the Everest of the seas.

On the island of Cape Horn there is a navigation light. The Chilean navy maintain a station there. There is also a memorial, the silhouette of an albatross. It is there to commemorate the 10,000 mariners who have been killed trying to better the Horn.

It was time to go. We sailed southeast in the early morning of St Valentine's Day, on a course to clear the eastern end of Isla de los Estados with its dangerous overfalls. The sky changed quickly from light, broken cloud to a purple darkness. At the outer margin of the overfalls, the log showed speed through the water of 6.2 knots. The GPS displayed speed over the ground at 3.4 knots. The Cape Horn current was running at 2.8 knots.

By 7.00 pm, we were past Isla de los Estados and south of the island. The wind, which had been flukey, shredded by the island's high peaks, came round to the northwest. Close-hauled, *Barrabas* was on a good heading, southwest. The latest weather data, which I'd downloaded at 4.00 pm, indicated the northwest winds holding through Friday, the perfect wind to get me to the Diego Ramirez islands. In the late afternoon, I picked out Vancouver peak on Isla de los Estados. The mountains of Tierra del Fuego silently watched our progress.

With the wind shifting to the west during the night, I hove-to and monitored our drift. Too fast! We were moving east at two knots, borne along on the Antarctic current that drives the Southern Ocean ever eastwards. The strategy that I had deliberated over was not going to work. I gybed *Barrabas* and headed south to take us towards the latitude of the Diego Ramirez islands, still 150 miles away to the south-west. Through the night of 15th February, the winds then moved to the north as I slept for a few hours. I woke, sensing a difference in the attitude of the boat. Something about her motion through the water generated an excitement in me. I stumbled from my bunk and peered at the GPS. I wanted and needed our course to be 260°, just south of west to put us on a line directly towards the Diego Ramirez islands. I blinked. I could scarcely believe the figures on the small screen. COG 2-6-0 (Course Over Ground 260°). Bloody fantastic!

I trimmed and re-trimmed the rig for three hours – shaking reefs out, putting reefs in and altering the sail combinations until I was squeezing every drop of speed out of the elements. The northwest wind, forecast to hold until Sunday midday, might yet give me my prize – if not, I faced the prospect of being beaten back, unable to match the onslaught of wind and current from the west. The Cape spat squalls at us – letting me know that she could defeat me at any time.

I thought and re-thought our strategy – stay high or go south, meet the blows coming in the next 24 hours or dodge them and waste valuable time – tactics, tactics, tactics. But for the moment we were heading west and eating the miles. Incredible surges of emotion swept through me, from the rock-bottom despair of drifting east to the euphoria of sailing due west . . . to sail Cape Horn solo, against wind and current, what a dream that would be . . .

At 9.00 pm, a squall front came over. Our northwest winds disappeared, to be replaced with headwinds from the southwest. I hove-to, drifting north and east at three knots. Was this a permanent wind change or a temporary consequence? My euphoria transformed once more to despair, watching in desolation as the precious westing we had made slipped away.

Two hours later, another squall passed over, flipping the winds back over to the northeast. We were sailing again, due west! I tended *Barrabas* constantly, steering either side of due west to wring out every yard – it was grinding work. Every yard westward was like a small nugget of gold in the pan.

Reality defied the forecasts. Through Thursday 17th February, the wind huffed then stilled, speeding us on, then teasingly slowing *Barrabas*. Sometimes we stalled, drifting back. By late evening, *Barrabas* sat becalmed, the rigging flogging and groaning. I switched the computer on.

Louise: Friday 17th February 2006

UK won silver in the Winter Olympics yesterday, a girl called Shelley Rudman from Wiltshire in the bob. She only took it up four years ago! I am keeping everything crossed that luck with the wind stays with you. Took the boys to see Narnia yesterday, although Gabriel fell asleep in the best bit – the battle scene at the end. Sun is shining today and I think spring is on its way . . . slowly – birds pulling worms out of the lawn, a few crocuses and snowdrops here and there. Cheers me up no end. Can't say I have been very happy for some time. I have found this all much, much harder than I thought. Looking forward to sitting in a warm pub with you when this is all over and dissecting it all, knowing it is behind us both. A good long chat face to face would be great now.

Adrian: Friday 17th February 2006
*What's up – chat about what . . . this was always going to be hard . . . if
you have things to get off your chest, tell me – it will help.*

Louise: Friday 17th February 2006
*Nothing specific I want to get off my chest – just general things making me
feel down. Selfish really – I don't really have anything to moan about. Yes,
this did give me a new focus, which on balance has been positive, but it has
also brought with it a host of other things to make me feel even more worried,
paranoid and insecure than I already do! One day when you're past the Horn
and in clear seas and sunny skies and I'm feeling shit, I'll probably commit it
to email, but not now. Once you're past the Horn I'll probably feel tons better
anyway!*

Barometric pressure was falling. The wind arrived at 10.00 pm, but
from the southwest, not the northwesterly I'd expected. Although Ric
was giving me weather information, I had come to rely on the GRIB
data from my own MaxSea programme. Now that reliance was compromised. The superb accuracy of the preceding months was gone.
The weather patterns at Cape Horn were too complex for a com-
putational model to translate accurately. I set *Barrabas* to a close-haul
with the headsail deep-reefed but the mainsail full to keep her bows
pointing up on our preferred course just south of due west. As night
settled in, the solitary rock of Horn Island lay 50 miles northwest. I
didn't want to risk being caught over-canvassed in the dark so I reefed
down and then went to my bunk. Sleep came easily. When I woke at
1.00 am, we were sailing southeast on 142°. The wind had spun round
through the hours of darkness. I raced on deck, gybed the boat, set full
sail and eased the boom wide. We were running downwind around
the Horn!

I sat at the chart table. In the three days since coming round Isla de
los Estados, we had sailed close-hauled tight to the wind, reached with
the wind abeam and run, with the wind behind. We had braced squalls
with 40-knot gusts and been set adrift to ride the Antarctic current in
despair without enough breeze to ruffle smoke. I wrote caustically in
the log:

Log: Saturday 18th February 2006, 1.43 am.
56.38south, 66.19west, COG 270, SOG 4.2, Wind E 12, BP 997(↓)
. . . the only scenario left to complete the set is a real blow . . .

To the west, the worst storm of the Cape Horn summer of 2006 gathered its strength. I would not have long to wait.

Low grey cloud, pregnant with rain, blocked us to the west. *Barrabas* was delicately poised, a soft wind from the east was pushing her gently towards the Pacific. The grey cloud, incongruous among its fluffy white neighbours, was coming towards us, propelled by an opposing wind at higher altitude. Suddenly, the air exploded. The wind-speed indicator cycled through numbers, 42 knots, 45 knots. I started the drill to reduce sail, hair whipping around my face. I eased the vang (a line from the underside of the boom to the bottom of the mast) and tensioned the topping lift (a line from the after end of the boom to the mast top) to lift the boom and make it easier to get the mainsail down. Just then, the shackle connecting the halyard to the head of the mainsail failed. The sail thrashed wildly. I tore at the sailcloth, pulling it down onto the boom. The halyard had dropped down inside the mast, only stopping at the masthead because of the knot in its end.

I furled the headsail. *Barrabas* settled beam on to the seas under bare mast (lying ahull). The pendulum motion of the boat was too great for me to climb to the top of the mast to retrieve the halyard. Lying ahull would give me time to think.

My immediate thought was to use the topping lift as a substitute halyard, but that would mean lowering the heavy boom onto the cuddy, then bracing it somehow to stop it sliding off and crashing down to the side deck. In those winds, the main shortened to fourth reef would suffice. Instead, I decided on a makeshift rig. The seas would build quickly. The main halyard would have to wait. The spare halyards were stowed in the aftcabin. I fetched a block, grabbed a spare halyard, then went back to the mast. I let the rope spill from my hands, then with one end between my teeth, I climbed the mast steps to the level of the lower spreaders, about halfway up. Wrapping one leg around the mast to hold myself, I shackled the block to a mast step, ran the halyard through the block and climbed back down to the deck. *Barrabas* bucked wildly – with no mainsail up she was unstable. I tied the end of the halyard to the head of the mainsail then pulled down on the other limb of the halyard for the hoist. *Barrabas* immediately settled. The wind had shifted. It was now screaming out of the west.

What were my options? Gybe and go north – not enough sea room. Run before the storm going east towards the Atlantic and lose ground

– what then? Could I make up the lost ground? Would I? West, straight into wind, was impossible. I had to go south.

The storm raged all day and into the evening. The seas had now built to 25 feet. A general rule of thumb: a breaking wave, equivalent in height to the beam of a vessel, has the power to roll that vessel over. *Barrabas*'s beam was 11 feet. I set the Hydrovane and lashed the wheel hard over to windward to create some angle between the side of the boat and the oncoming waves. This attitude would avoid direct beam-on wave strikes and keep *Barrabas* on her fastest point of sail as a defence to save our precious westing. The seas developed into cresting walls of water over 100 metres long. The question was no longer *if* we would take a dangerous strike, but *when*. I calculated the risk. *Barrabas* had strength, weight and relative speed on her side. If we ran east-wards with the wind behind, the deteriorating weather and increasing storm frequency heralding the end of summer might never let us back in.

It was then that the head blocked, regurgitating effluent into the bilges. The manual bilge pump was out of action. The outlet for the electric pumps on the port side was underwater with the heel of the boat. I had done my screaming in the wind, raging at the weather just as the weather was raging at me. I stood below decks, clinging to the companionway. 'Great,' I thought. 'I'm in a bloody washing machine with four gallons of sewage!' I smiled as the wind tore about us. Braced below decks, I could hear the fuses of the bombs – the sizzling rush of breaking water, then the massive impact of the strike. Each time, the boat stopped dead, her rigging shaking, bulkheads groaning as the hull twisted. I was already exhausted even though I'd managed some sleep only 15 hours before.

The capsize came at 4.00 pm just as I was throwing some food waste over the side. The storm boiled around us. I pulled the companionway hatch open and took two steps up the companionway, poking my head and shoulders into the maelstrom. Bracing against the extreme heel of the boat, I readied myself to chuck the waste downwind, over the port side. Long, breaking crests raked the ocean, leaving great, flattened swathes of white. The boiling foam of spent waves crashed and tum-bled. I clutched the bucket of rubbish, ready to hurl its contents out. Then a sizzling sound behind me, menacingly low at first, then amplifying quickly. I yanked myself round, protected from the wind by the side of the cuddy, but all I could see through it was a wall of white, crushed water. The wave covered the deck, the cuddy, filled the cockpit, churning. It was slow enough for me to know what was happening, but too quick for me to move. *Barrabas* heeled, and then kept going, further and further with a heart-stopping momentum. My chest compressed against the side of the companionway hatch. For an instant, looking through the clear sheeting of the cuddy was like looking though a face mask underwater. All was still. The tip of the lower spreader touched the surface of the sea. *Barrabas* was neither floating nor sinking, just suspended sideways on the ocean's surface. Below me, the instrument panel above the chart table on the ship's port side had become the new floor directly beneath my feet. Icy water cascaded off my shoulders, around my waist, between my legs, and poured onto the panel. It's difficult to say how much water hit the chart table but half the panel was submerged – at least 20 gallons. I looked down in horror. If we recovered from this, I thought for sure I'd lose most of the electrics – cabin lights, bilge pumps, watermaker, deck and running lights, and maybe even the radar and GPS as the seawater went to work corroding the terminals behind the switch panel. Already, I could hear the sizzle and pop of electrical circuits shorting out.

Barrabas's keel, filled with four tons of ballast, pulled her slowly back upright. The spreader lifted from the water, the sail caught wind and smacked taut, creamed water gushed from her deck, running through the scuppers like a hundred open taps.

I slammed the companionway hatch shut. The seawater inside had mixed with spilled sewage and was sloshing over the cabin floor.

Seawater had shorted the computer's voltage converter and now acrid white fumes from an electrical fire began spilling from the cubby-hole housing. I used a cloth to douse the flames. The storm was building. Sleep was impossible. I was too on edge, too scared. Every bone-jarring impact seemed to sound the boat's death knell, but she just kept going. Through the long, dark night, I braced myself below decks. Occasionally, I poked my head up above the companionway but all I could see was blackness streaked with the dull grey spume of broken waves. The noise was deafening. The rolling seas groaned a deep bass. The wind shrieked a high-pitched whine. This was the sound of fury and it terrified me.

Ricardo: Saturday 18th February 2006

You are in the top half of a low but Sunday/Monday as she moves east you will get southerlies, south westerlies, south easterlies. Make the most of them.

It will all go quite light as you progress NW and into the eye of a high
pressure. You will be on the east side of the system so will enjoy glorious
conditions. All is clear at least 1,000 miles to the west of you so you will be OK
and get around just fine now. I think you will have a really nice few days.
Monday afternoon you will have a red carpet from Horn to trade winds. Get
all sail up and and just fly out of there and north as fast as you can with the
great conditions at hand.

'Yeah, really!' I spoke to the back-up laptop. With the voltage-
converter blown, the main computer was out of action. The mess on
the floor had mostly seeped back into the bilges. It was Saturday
evening. I hadn't slept for 20 hours. Sunday was another country.

The storm raged through the night, driving us further south, the
northwest winds spiking to 50 knots and never falling below 40. Even
with minimal sail, *Barrabas* heeled so far over that her port side deck
skimmed beneath the surface. I stayed below decks – to keep warm, to
stay safe. The latest forecasts indicated that conditions would continue
like this for at least another 24 hours. I was exhausted and battered.
Could I cope with more of this?

'Get a bloody grip!' I said out loud. 'Of course you bloody can!' I
went to the chart table. 'See that?' I said, pointing to the barometer. I
squinted up at the needle. 'See what it says – one zero zero two – hear
that, 1002 and rising. That means high pressure is on the way. You
know what you should be worrying about, eh? Getting bloody sun-
burnt. Of course you'll f****** make it!'

I felt slightly better after that, but not for long.

Log: Saturday 18th February 2006, 9.45 pm.
57.06south, 66.31west, COG 205, SOG2.0-3.02, Wind NW 40+, BP 1002 (↑)
This is the worst weather I have encountered on the voyage so far by
some considerable margin. The seas are big and dangerous. The wind
has a fierce power to it. The combination is potentially lethal.

The further south we went, the longer we would remain in the path of
the depressions. Drifting ice was another danger, more so the further
south we went, but heaving-to in those big, steep, breaking seas
presented an even greater risk than moving.

The seas continued to pummel *Barrabas*, hurling more big hits
against her starboard side, but she absorbed the blows. Like a sparring
boxer, she ducked and weaved, presenting her side obliquely to draw

power from the waves. The Hydrovane held course and the sails were set.

At dawn on Sunday, I spent three hours pumping the bilges by hand – a mix of oil, petrol, seawater and sewage – into an empty fuel can. The joint of the flexible hose on the manual pump leaked so I clamped that with one hand while pumping with the other, eventually removing over 100 litres, which I tipped down the galley sink. The spill had turned the cabin floor into an ice rink. In the pitching seas, every movement needed planning. The consequences of a slip or fall, a broken leg or worse and my chances of getting through this would evaporate.

I talked aloud, for hour after hour. Sometimes I shouted, sometimes I screamed. I had to control the panic chasing around my guts like some mad, cornered animal desperately seeking any means of escape. I spoke about every mistake I'd ever made, every regret that ate away at my core like rats in the dark. I went up on deck and clipped my lifeline to a strong point in the cockpit while the wind and the spume flogged my face. If the worst happened and *Barrabas* capsized and sank, I was out of rescue range. Death was close. Which breaking wave would be my executioner? I waited, like a man on the gallows.

The realisation when it came was startling in its clarity. I was afraid of fear itself. I started to laugh.

'Is that it,' I yelled at the sky. 'Is that all?' Maybe fear had loosened my grip on sanity. Or maybe my fear, like smoke in the wind, had been shredded and was gone. I realised with a deep sense of shock that I was actually *enjoying* this. An image floated across my mind – a train carriage with hundreds of commuters packed together like sardines in a tin, going to some place they didn't want to go, to do something they didn't want to do, existing but not living. 'No!' I shouted until stars spangled my eyes and my throat hurt and my voice was hoarse. I went below, still grinning like an idiot. My focus stayed on the glass – barometric pressure was slowly creeping up, 1003, 1004, 1005 . . . the wind still tore through the rigging, but without the intensity of earlier, as though the heart had gone from nature's fight. Even from below deck, I sensed the depletion.

That great British morale-booster, a cup of hot (and in my case, very sweet) tea was not available. The gas cylinder, housed beneath the cockpit seat, was empty and too inaccessible to change over in these conditions.

Barrabas had managed to stay west of south, but only by the narrowest margin. Now, with the air pressure rising, the wind began backing round from northwest to west, forcing our course off to 180°, due south and then progressively to east of south.

I gybed *Barrabas* several times during the afternoon to see if we could make a course west of north with the wind coming over the boat's port side but each time the compass slid away to the east, forcing me to gybe back.

Despite the uncertainty of the forecasts, they indicated a definitive wind shift at midnight, with perhaps 48 hours of favourable winds to get me past the longitude of Cape Horn itself and clear – it was make or break!

A sudden squall pushed the winds to 46 knots – a temporary aberration in what had become a clear pattern of change. *Barrabas* battled on, shaking and vibrating. Wind-churned water found every weakness to penetrate the inside. Everything was wet: my bunk, sleeping bag, clothes and, once wet, they stayed wet. I glanced at the glass – 1008.

Finally, at 11.30 pm, our course dropped into the east as the wind went to the west – this had to be it! I gybed round, bringing the wind over the port side, setting *Barrabas* as close to the wind as she could go. The storm had forced us 200 miles south, into the iceberg belt and serious danger. We had to get back north but our heading had to be the right side of north, west *not* east. Then the compass began to slide towards north – 350°, 351°. My eyes were riveted to the display. 352°, 353°. I could barely breathe. I yelled at the top of my lungs, 'Please hold! Don't go anymore! Stay west!'

The GPS compass heading stopped its slide at 354°, six degrees west of north.

Log: Sunday 19th February 2006, 11.47 pm
57.29 south, 66.25 west, COG 355, SOG 3.5, Wind W 30, BP 1008 (=)
. . . this is it – we either break the Horn with this window or we ourselves get broken.

I stayed watching the compass and periodically checked topside until 3.00 am on Monday 20th February. With little more to do but wait for the winds to back round more and improve our heading, I collapsed, fully clothed, into my damp sleeping bag. I had gone without sleep for 50 hours.

As I slipped quickly into the oblivion, I could not know that one of

the greatest physical challenges of my life awaited me at dawn and that
the red carpet Ricardo had promised would unroll before me in a way
that I would never have dared dream.

At daybreak, with the storm spent, I stood on deck in the cold early
light. To take advantage of the favourable weather window that had
emerged in the night, *Barrabas* needed to fly full sail to make north and
out of the path of the storm-stuffed low-pressure systems flooding in
from the west. To do that, I had to go to the mast-top to retrieve the
halyard. The wind was gusting at 30 knots. The sea was running with a
20-foot swell, the aftermath of the storm. As I stood on the pitching
deck and watched the horrific pendulum motion of the mast, I realised
I had another mountain to climb.

I attached two straps to the D-ring of my safety harness. Each strap
was fitted with a carabiner at its other end to clip to the mast steps as I
ascended in case I slipped or fell. Clutching the mast, I stared up.
Although not particularly high as masts go, it seemed to tower above
me to an impossible height. It was a psychological game. Just climb,
don't look down, don't think about the movement of the ship, just
hold on, don't think about the consequences of a fall. I raised myself
up, standing on the granny bars, then reached up and gripped the steps
at full stretch. Right foot on the mast winch, left foot in the lowest
step, leg bent at the knee. I breathed deeply then heaved myself up,
half a metre with each step.

I made it to the top, resting frequently. The physical effort of just
holding on was exhausting and, the higher I climbed, the greater the arc
of the mast's pendulum motion. Wearing half-fingered gloves, my
fingertips became numb with cold. Finally, above the upper spreaders,
I heaved myself up 10 more steps, resting between each. When I judged
the knotted end of the halyard within reach, I grabbed it with one hand,
clamped it between my teeth then clung to the mast with both arms.

Thirty minutes later, bruised and drenched in sweat, I stepped back
onto the deck. My knees buckled and I fell forward among the rigging,
feeling the reassuring strength of *Barrabas* waiting patiently for me to
get up.

Log: Monday 20th February 2006, 7.40 am
57.05 south, 66.13 west, COG 344, SOG 3.2, Wind W 18, BP 1014(↑)
It has been so hard. I have invested every ounce of my strength, every

drop of my emotional reservoir, every shred of my psychological resilience, every calorie of my spirit. Barrabas has been utterly magnificent. She has taken the punishment. Time and again she has been dealt keel-shuddering blows. Most times they stop her dead in her tracks. But she brings her bow round and surges on. She is so brave, so courageous. She has spared nothing to keep me safe. I weep in gratitude to her as I write this. I could not have asked more of her. She has the heart of a lioness. And still she fights on.

Through the day, the wind continued to lighten and the glass kept rising. At long, long last, *Barrabas* was flying. At 5.53 pm local time, she crossed westwards over longitude 67°.15′ west, the longitude of Cape Horn. We were on the Pacific side.

The Diego Ramirez islands, my target when I had entered the Cape Horn area, now lay 45 miles west northwest. At 4.30 am on Tuesday 21st February, I came on deck and sighted the islands – black, jagged

teeth in the steely maw of the ocean. A single whitewashed house, a
weather station, was perched precariously on the largest island of the
group, San Bartolomé. I called on Channel 16 and spoke briefly with
the weatherman but he could add nothing to the fantastic news I had
just received from Ricardo.

The high-pressure system over Cape Horn was blocking the depression to the west, giving me fair conditions until Saturday! The prospect
of 50-knot winds on Wednesday, Ricardo's previous interpretation, had
now receded. If the high pressure stayed static, as Ricardo reckoned,
then *Barrabas* would be pushed downwind all the way to latitude 50°
south on the Pacific side, the official finish of our rounding of Cape
Horn.

After my brief conversation with the weather station, I slept again
for four hours. By evening, the winds were in the east. *Barrabas*, under
full sail, sped along at seven knots, her boom splayed out on one side,
her headsail poled out on the other. We sailed on over the following
two days, the air temperature becoming noticeably warmer, my breath
no longer clouding and my feet no longer feeling like ice blocks. For
now, Cape Horn smiled as we sailed beneath blue skies. Albatrosses
wheeled in fanciful free flight. On my northern horizon, sun-polished
ice peaks towered heavenwards and the sea was a mauve cushion laced
with white. It was a scene of staggering beauty.

With the prospect of running almost literally downhill out of Cape
Horn, I had time think of other things. The Russian government had
acknowledged my application to sail the NSR but, as expected, Northern Sea Route Administration, Nikolai Monko's department, was insisting that I have an ice pilot on board. I thought through the options
and called my father in South Africa.

'I've got an idea,' I said.

'What's that?'

'Put the ice pilot on an escort vessel.'

'Who's going to arrange it?'

'Don't worry about it just now. Suggest the idea. If they go for it,
then we can think about the practicalities.' The biggest practicality was
money. I couldn't pay for an escort vessel. I imagined the cost would
be prohibitive – fuel, fees, crew wages, not to mention the cost of the
ice pilot at around US$5,000. 'Here's my thinking,' I said. 'If we can get
them to agree in principle, then if ice conditions are good by the time I
get there, they'll be more minded to let me go solo – no ice pilot, no
escort vessel.'

As we rolled along the red carpet, the Hydrovane threw up a problem. By this time, I had personified some of the gear on board and the strongest character to emerge, essentially a helmsman who didn't need food or sleep, was Harry (the Hydrovane). I spoke to him whenever I was on deck and occasionally yelled up from below, 'What the hell are you doing, Harry!' 'Well done, Harry!' 'You're behaving like a prick, Harry!'

With the main shortened to second reef, *Barrabas* was still turning into the wind, the sails flogging as they depowered. At first light on Saturday 25th February, I put a third reef in the main, then a fourth, all the while shouting at Harry for being so bloody lazy. Still *Barrabas* turned her bows into the wind. I went to check the Hydrovane. The screw linking the vane to the pendulum that moves the rudder shaft had sheared, effectively disengaging the vane from the rudder. I apologised to Harry profusely. With a 30-foot swell and 30-knot winds, I tried to get the sheared bolt out, but it was jammed in too tightly. I removed the linkage piece, clamped it in the vice (a bit of good thinking buying that vice!) and got it out. Then I put the whole thing back together with a new screw.

I charted our position. We were 279 miles south of latitude 50° but, happy to be under the psychological barrier of 300 miles, I rewarded myself with a hot-water footbath in the cockpit. Meanwhile, my socks were drying out in the oven – baking on low heat. That worked very well and raised my morale for the rest of the day!

Cape Horn was never going to let me past without spitting in my eye – and spit she had, with ferocity and with venom, challenging *Barrabas* and me to the very limits of our endurance. Then she gave us reprieve and showed us her kinder face, a face of startling beauty. At 3.18 am on Tuesday 28th February (2218 UCT, Monday 27th February) *Barrabas* breached latitude 50° south in the Pacific Ocean. We had officially completed our west-about rounding of the Horn!

I came to Cape Horn with hope and fear. Now I was leaving exhilarated and with memories of an experience that would endure for my lifetime.

I quickly sent an email to Louise, asleep in her bed, and then collapsed into my own bunk. The next morning Louise called, in tears and full of pride. No comprehensive record of Cape Horn roundings exists (as far as I am aware). The Cape Horners' Association listed me as the seventh single-handed sailor to round the Horn westwards, less than the number of astronauts who have walked on the moon.

www.alphaglobalex.com
Guest Book: Tuesday 28th February 2006
Adrian, WELL DONE! Huge congratulations. I am delighted for you
achieving this lifetime ambition. I remember you talking about this at
Stonyhurst. All the best, Roger.

CHAPTER 15

The Russian Front

Could I really get permission from the Russian government to sail their Arctic waters and become the first single-handed yachtsman ever to do so? This question came to dominate my passage across the Pacific Ocean.

More immediately, sleep became imperative. Although the Chilean coast was close, 200 miles to the east, I had enough sea room to manoeuvre even closer in as we sailed on northwards, putting distance between Cape Horn and myself. The air, still heavy with moisture, kept the inside of the boat damp. I didn't mind. *Barrabas* could ride the Humboldt Current running along the coast to speed us towards the southeast trade winds, which would sweep us on into the tropics. The thought of warmth and light after the long weeks of greyness added to my relief at being through Cape Horn.

I got to thinking about solitude. Since childhood, being alone had never bothered me. I was happy in my own company. Four months of solitude since leaving England did not pose the difficulties for me that it might to others. Through the isolation, I felt the closeness of the people following the expedition's progress, especially Louise and Ricardo, who had lived almost each moment. I felt responsible to them and that sense of responsibility created the illusion of our being together. I had the advantage of satellite communications. I only had to pick up the phone and within seconds I could be talking to anyone I chose. That simple knowledge was sufficient to dispel any feelings of loneliness.

Louise, whose jubilation at the successful rounding of Cape Horn was greater than mine, had slipped into despondency. I called her on 1st March. She and Ricardo had fallen out again. I felt that Ricardo's most important role was in his support of Louise, not me. If that crumbled away, she would feel more isolated than I did. The problem was Louise's concept of herself. Her lack of self-belief generated a tendency for over-reliance on other people, yet she had huge resilience. Louise was, in many ways, a conundrum. I knew she would bounce back. Management of the expedition would, I hoped, peel away the doubts she harboured about her own abilities and, from there, the indomitable, confident and able woman that I knew was hidden beneath would emerge.

As a way of bringing closure to the Cape Horn phase of the voyage and as a mechanism to hide from my worry about Louise, I wrote a poem.

Cape Horners' Tale
Cape Horners both, proud to be
Sailing on a tranquil sea
Calm's reward for where we've been
Rest a while from what we've seen
On deck braced, screamed at waves
Towering high in monstrous caves
On our shoulders, clouds pressed hard
Fractured water, piercing shards
Seas try to tear my ship apart
Break her back, but not her heart
From down in deep she raised her bow
Shrugged her shrouds, I don't know how
While Cape Horn slept, we stole on past
Our first time here and now our last
Cape Horners both forever will be
My courageous boat, *Barrabas* and me.

Now that I was past Cape Horn, I looked in more detail at making an antipodal point. I studied the charts. Any point I selected had to be antipodal to one I'd already passed in the Atlantic. Because of my proposed route through the Arctic, points antipodal to that part of the route were not available (they all fell on the Antarctic continental landmass). The selected point would have to be somewhere in the Pacific. I settled on one southwest of Japan (at 24° north, 143° east) diametrically opposed on the earth's surface to a position I'd passed off the coast of Brazil (24° south, 37° west). The problem was that my selected point was in tropical storm country. The season ran from May to September and, if my assumed timings were anywhere near accurate, I would be there in June! But the other options were worse. To go to a point south of the equator would mean having to navigate the labyrinth of the South Sea Islands and risk getting caught in the hurricane season around New Zealand and the eastern coast of Australia.

As *Barrabas* sailed further from Cape Horn, I set about compiling a 'wish list' of spares and replacement parts. To my amazement (and great relief), none of the electrical circuits had been damaged following the switch panel's dousing with seawater during the capsize at Cape Horn. The computer's voltage converter and the electronic control head for the heating system remained the only two casualties. I hadn't decided whether to take a supply drop, but Louise could begin to get the items together. Aside from the converter and the heating-control unit, I also needed a new dynamo for the wind generator as an auxiliary battery charger. A resupply would mean sacrificing the 'unsupported' status of the voyage, but this consequence no longer held much significance for me.

The high-pressure system over the southern Pacific had shifted east. Depressions queuing up behind were now rampaging though Drake's Passage to Cape Horn where I'd been only a few days before.

Colonel Mario Montejo, Commander of the Chilean Coastguard, who had been in regular contact with me, apologised for a late response to one of my position reports. He'd been dealing with an incident involving one of the boats in the Volvo race, which had entered Cape Horn eastwards just as I made my exit.

Ricardo: Thursday 2nd March 2006

The mother of all lows is about to blast Cape Horn with 10m waves and 70 knots of wind. The Volvo Ocean Race boats are in trouble . . . you are clear of all of this and will only take some large seas from the southwest although no bigger than 5m. My GRIBs show NW, W, SW winds for the next few days. My advice is that you sail on the course that gets you max boat speed, even if that takes you a bit closer to land in the next 24 hrs or so. The low will

not hit you but the further north you are the better. New SW winds will be
with you between Sunday and Monday. Around Monday, try to get further
northwest as this will set you up better for the next 20 days or so. No point
beating though, just try to edge your way west of north when possible.

Boy, was I pleased to be out of there!

Then came Friday 3rd March. I climbed onto the afterdeck frame to get the serial number of the wind generator so Ampair, the manufacturer, would know exactly the model I needed. *Barrabas* lurched. I slipped. As I fell back, I grabbed the frame with my right arm fully extended. My right wrist separated. Perhaps not quite a full dislocation but the bones 'stepped up'. My wrist looked horribly deformed. I knew from dislocating my shoulder that I only had a very short time before muscle spasms would make it difficult to get the bones back in place. I stepped down onto the deck, leaned forwards and closed the fingers of my right hand around the grab rail running along the top of the aftcabin coach-house. I then leaned back, arm straight, tractioning the wrist. A low clunk came as the bones realigned themselves. Any pressure through the palm caused excruciating pain. Now I had two knackered wrists! Soft tissue injuries always take longer to mend than broken bones. For a single-handed sailor, the problem of injury or illness compounds because there is no one else to keep the boat tramping along. For most of the remainder of the voyage, both wrists had to be tightly strapped for support.

Meanwhile, my father was having limited success with the Russians. Sam's contact at Sovcomflot had nominated Andrey Kechashin in its Moscow office to liaise with the authorities on my behalf. Sam, who I had put in touch with my father, had passed this information on.

Dad: Friday 3rd March 2006

I have sent the hard copy of the application form and manual to Louise to send to you. The frustrating thing about dealing with the Russians is that every time I ask them to comment on the application, they send me another manual. I then revise the application inserting any new bumph from the latest manual and so it goes on. Unfortunately, it is not a precise clearly laid out format.

I have now sent Andrey Kechashin of Sovcomflot in Moscow a copy of the application and asked him to try and nail down Nikolai Monko. Specifically, he should ask Monko to define precisely what additional information they require, and that things like pollution insurance and bilge storage capacity etc. may be necessary for 20,000-ton ships but are not relevant to a small yacht. Let's see what happens now.

Anyway, I think 150 days at sea including west about the Horn is in itself a huge achievement and something of which you can and will forever be proud.

Barrabas was slamming badly as the wind built from the northwest, but making five to six knots with the help of the Humboldt Current. Being inside a boat bashing into head winds is like being in a series of minor car crashes. The boat shudders and vibrates. Anything not lashed down or properly stowed gets thrown about the cabin (including me if I'm not holding on). I reefed the sails to give her a more comfortable, slam-free ride at the cost of having to bear away and reduce speed. The Chilean coast loomed 100 miles away off my starboard side. The winds would have to drop deep to the west to get me away from land. I decided on a limit. I couldn't stray any further east than longitude 75° west, which lay 15 miles away on my starboard side. Any closer than that and I would be in the danger zone on a lee shore with insufficient searoom to manoeuvre. If the winds had not shifted to get us away by then, my only option would be to heave-to and wait.

Cape Horn still clutched at us, the rolling depressions blanketing the sky in thick, grey cloud. I compensated for this by extending my chocolate allowance until we crossed latitude 40° south. Then, I promised myself, I would go onto a fruit diet! I waited anxiously, watching the winds and hoping for a shift as we drew dangerously near to the treacherous Chilean coast hidden beneath my eastern horizon.

> **Log: Sunday 5th March 2006, 4.30 pm**
> *41.57 south, 75.33 west, COG 340, SOG 4.8, Wind WSW 20, BP 1019 (↑)*
> *Alleluia! The wind went deep to the west southwest at 1.30 pm! I picked up speed, and we were able to go on to 340°! The objective is to make as much north as possible and get some west to create more sea room.*

Ricardo: Sunday 5th March 2006
Wow, that's a bit close to land! Well, down in Ushuaia is a Volvo 70 that almost sank and a top Open 60 that lost its rig. Well done for still being in one piece!

The wind shift had come just in time. I set full sail and went to bed. I woke 10 hours later to a beautiful 'blue' morning – blue sky, blue sea. *Barrabas* had done well during the night. We were now only 53 miles from latitude 40° south and pulling steadily westwards and away from land. I plotted a course for our next target – Hawaii. If I did decide to take a resupply, Hawaii was the logical option. From there, my antipodal point was a downwind sail of 3,000 miles in the trade winds. That evening *Barrabas* crossed northwards over latitude 40° south, the psychological line spelling an end to the Cape Horn phase of the voyage and the beginning of the Hawaiian leg. I recorded the moment:

> **Log: Monday 6th March 2006, 7.45 pm**
> *39.59 south, 76.18 west, COG 340, SOG 5.0, Wind WNW 22, BP 1022 (↓)*
> . . . *Yippee! I am officially out of the shit zone!!!*

The weather settled into a more predictable, stable pattern, a forerunner to the southeast trade winds. I set the sails and the Hydrovane, then busied myself tidying the boat. I fixed the manual bilge pump, a difficult job because of the awkward access. I found myself wandering about in flip-flops and sleeping without the washboard in place at the head of the companionway. T-shirts and shorts replaced base layers and mid-layers.

Drawing level with the Chilean capital city, Santiago, I rewarded myself by stripping down the sink drainage in the galley, clearing handfuls of stinking, black sludge – the legacy of dumping effluent down the sink after the Cape Horn capsize. The work was cleansing in a metaphorical sense, wiping away the residues of fear that had shadowed me for weeks.

A whale (type unknown) came alongside, then dived under the boat, nudging the keel, causing the boat to heel over. I didn't believe it was aggressive behaviour and nice to think *Barrabas* had a new friend. I was more concerned that the whale might damage the self-steering rudder.

Heading north on 10th March and gradually widening the gap between *Barrabas* and Chile turned into the best day of the voyage so far: a perfect temperature, a warm 12-knot breeze coming over the port quarter, blue skies studded with high cloud, sparkling indigo water. *Barrabas* was reaching at six knots, but hardly heeling. The serenity, the space, the singsong of the sea, made it a day to savour.

The Pacific Ocean had a very different character to the Atlantic. It felt bigger and somehow fresher. The ride of the swell was smoother, less short and choppy. For the moment, I was happy and so was *Barrabas*.

On Saturday 11th March, I sat at the chart table plotting our position. I glanced across the South American continent to the Atlantic side. At the same latitude, the date read 13th January. I arrived at Isla de los Estados on February 14th, one whole month later. We had made it here from the same latitude as Isla de los Estados on the western side in 15 days – twice as fast!

The wind shifted more deeply to the southwest, bringing our course round to 295°, close to the islands of the Juan Fernandez archipelago. I trimmed Harry, altering course to 310°, and eased the boom. High above, the Milky Way dazzled so brightly it looked like a stage set.

The following day I cooked a wonderful meal of sardines, tomato sauce and spaghetti (ironic that my favourite meal should be tinned fish) and then slept. My charts of the area were small-scale. The thickness of a pencil line equated to 10 miles. I knew we had to be getting close to the archipelago. In the early evening, I went up on deck. There, looming on the western horizon, was the mountainous silhouette of Juan Fernandez Island. This was the island where in 1704 Alexander Selkirk, a crew member on the privateer *Cinque Ports*, marooned himself following a violent confrontation with the ship's master (he actually asked to get off the ship). Four years later, Woodes Rogers, circumnavigating on an expedition of plunder, picked him up. Quickly recognising Selkirk as an outstanding seaman, Woodes Rogers awarded him command of the ship. In England, Daniel Defoe heard the story and based his novel *Robinson Crusoe* on Selkirk's adventures.

Unlike Selkirk, I had clothes, although most of my stock, save for a pair of underpants and two T-shirts, festered in a bin lashed in the aft cabin. To save water and tedium, I decided to wash one item a day. The heated drying cupboard no longer worked. The oven proved a good alternative. I cooked less in the rising heat and the savings in gas went on 'baking' my laundry to bone dryness.

I spoke to Louise the next afternoon. Benji was poorly again. Maybe he was like me – a warm weather person (why the hell was I going to the Arctic?). The news reinforced the one aspect that I had come to loathe about the voyage: missing my boys.

We discussed the Russian question. My father, despite his efforts, had been going round in circles. Time was becoming an issue. I encouraged her to take over the whole process without specifically saying so.

While I took a deck bath with warm water, my first for eight weeks, I mulled the situation over. My father had done what he could. He perhaps did not have the same emotional investment in the outcome as Louise, and I felt Louise would bring more energy to finding a solution. But I was anxious not to leave my father feeling slighted in any way.

Louise's response was typically proactive. She immediately wrote a letter to Tony Blair at 10 Downing Street and then called John Bercow, our local MP, at the House of Commons. He could get an inside track to the higher echelons within the Foreign Office.

I don't believe in coincidence as some kind of arbitrary occurrence. Cause and effect can transpose to the metaphysical – that's my belief. Many proverbs testify to some ill-understood machination that contrives to bring about some wished-for event – for example, 'Where there's a will, there's a way', 'Be careful what you wish for'.

In fulfilment of this bizarre effect, Louise received a call from Ian Johnstone-Bryden on 13th March. Fully versed in my progress via the expedition website, Ian planned to write articles for his own boating and shipping news website. He wanted additional information. During their conversation, Louise outlined the difficulties in penetrating the Russian administration. A one-time computer 'researcher' and former government employee with a web of contacts within the military and intelligence communities, Ian offered to help. Two days later, Louise received an email:

Ian Johnstone-Bryden: Wednesday 15th March 2006

I have spoken with the Russian IMO (International Maritime Organisation) representative. Nice chap, enthusiastic and prepared to take your case forward, although how fast or how successful he will be we have yet to see. His name is Igor Ponomarev. He is expecting an email from you following my conversation with him 20 minutes ago. He is in the right part of government, if not the same department. I did check and he is not FSB (at least as far as SIS is aware).

I am also due to speak with William Hague later today. He is a very nice chap and has lots of vigour. As Shadow Foreign Sec it's in his brief but he also has some personal contacts in Russia that may be useful.

The Federal Security Bureau, Russia's internal security apparatus, was the old KGB re-branded for democratic Western palates.

The winds continued to drop into the south and eventually flipped southeast. On the same day as Louise achieved her breakthrough on the Russian front, *Barrabas* hooked onto the Pacific trades.

After long consideration, I decided to take a supply drop off Honolulu – principally for spare parts for the wind generator, computer and heating system.

For the next few weeks, my daily position plots would describe a more or less straight line to the Hawaiian Islands. The plan at this stage was straightforward. I would sail past Honolulu. A boat ferrying the items shipped out from England by DHL would come alongside, transfer the items and on I would go, without stopping.

The next day at 4.32pm, the log tripped over to 12,500 nautical miles. We had sailed more than half the distance around the circumference of the earth and, for the moment, it seemed that everything was going well.

Louise: Thursday 16th March 2006

I have now spoken to the Russian Gov Rep for the IMO in London, he sounds great and is going to try and help. Ian has spoken to William Hague and written to Prince Philip's office. I have contacted Blair and John Bercow . . . so let's see what happens.

Tim Thornton, always available at the end of a phone to give me technical advice (to deal with my temperamental back-up laptops), emailed me with another piece of great news. We had been discussing the best way to get ice maps. Tim's contacts through his work on the Galileo project, the European rival to America's Global Positioning Satellite network, had come through with a means of providing me with near real-time satellite imagery of the Arctic ice. Unless the ice cleared completely (unlikely), ice maps as an aid to navigation were, in my opinion, essential. Tim had spoken to Richard Proud, who was also subcontracted to the Galileo project. He, in turn, had contacted Simon Chesworth at MDA Geospatial Services, a Canadian company operating the Radarsat I and Radarsat II earth orbiting (EO) satellites.

Tim to Richard: Thursday 16th March 2006

A friend of mine is heading up the Pacific to go across the top of Russia or Canada in a sailing boat (preferably Russia, but he is still trying to get permission). Can you think of any good high-res EO imagery that will help him with icing? We can download here and give him the info he needs. Obviously a short time from satellite pass to image availability is pretty important.

Richard to Simon: Thursday 16th March 2006
If you guys happen to be making routine acquisitions in the above area of interest, would you be interested in sponsoring him and supplying some imagery or ice maps?

Simon to Richard: Thursday 16th March 2006
We are not making routine acquisitions over Russia – only Canada. However, if we can get some publicity out of this, then I think I can persuade a few people that we can help provide imagery.

Great news for two reasons – satellite imagery would give me 'eyes' on the ground and if the Russians knew this facility was available to me, the impression of a well-organised expedition could only be reinforced. Taken together with the enhanced safety of having detailed ice maps to aid navigation, the argument for a solo transit became powerfully persuasive.

A castle built on the beach. It looks strong, with ramparts, bastions, towers. The tide rolls in lapping at the walls. The structure begins to collapse, layers peeled away, falling and flattening in the water, losing all shape and definition. Up until mid-March, I was quietly satisfied with my emotional and psychological resilience, surprised even. Now, like a sandcastle, I felt myself slowly crumbling. I missed my sons. The prospect of enduring a similar period, five months, perhaps longer, before I saw them again became harder to bear. My conviction was great, but I felt vulnerable in the underbelly to morbid introspection. Benji, a strong, healthy, happy boy, had frequently been ill since my departure. Was he pining? Was I? Gabriel, younger, less aware and less emotionally developed, seemed fine. My guilt at leaving the boys never really left me at any time during the entire voyage. Guilt, like jealousy, is a canker, which can grow, corrupt and eventually crush. I realised too that I felt guilty about something else, something to do with Louise. I had to think hard to understand it.

Our telephone exchanges had become increasingly technical, impersonal. Louise did her thing, I did mine and somewhere in between, the umbilical link carried only data – weather, position, conditions, updates – and always short and sharp because of cost. The emotional support we sought from one another had vanished.

I telephoned Louise. We had a long chat, nothing technical, stopping and spending time with each other.

Louise: Monday 20th March 2006

It was great to chat 'normally' last night. I know it was expensive but I think once a month or so we need to have a good chat like that. Good for both of us!

Got a call from Tony Blair's office this morning to say they are looking at my correspondence and will get back to me.

Igor Ponomarev, the permanent representative of the Russian Federation to the International Maritime Organization and chairman of the Maritime Safety Committee, had been as good as his word. Louise called me.

'You're not going to believe this!'

'Try me.'

'I've just put the phone down to Igor. He's had a long talk with Nikolai Monko . . .'

'Does Monko know about the AGX?'

'110 per cent. He said it was uppermost in his mind!'

I sat stunned. It had taken so long to get through to the right person and now that we had, it seemed scarcely believable.

'That's great,' I said. 'Look, you'd better send a note to Sam filling him in.'

'Already done. I did it straight away. Sent it to your father as well. There's more.'

'What?'

'Monko told Igor he would do everything in his power to get you through the Russian Arctic!'

'Wow.'

'And Monko said he can see that potentially there's some very good publicity for them, positive British–Russian relations, co-operation, all that.'

'What about the idea of the escort vessel?'

'Yep. Monko knows about that. He's prepared to talk about it, but this bit's a little confusing.'

'How?'

'Well, unless I misunderstood Igor, Monko's insisting on at least a Russian speaker on board and an inspection. An inspection would mean stopping in port. I asked Igor if he could get back to Monko and ask whether it'd be possible to have the inspection at sea and for a costing on an escort rather than an ice pilot.'

'That's bloody fantastic.'

'Good, eh!'

'I knew you were the right girl for the job!'

I went on deck. A mauve wash coloured the skyscape. The clouds seemed oversized. Through squinted eyes, I looked at the hugeness of the space and the clouds scattered about the horizon and I could imagine a futuristic city silhouette of close-knit tower blocks and domes. I hoped the Russian developments were more concrete.

An email from Sam the following day confirmed the solid progress.

Sam: Wednesday 22nd March 2006

Louise

I hesitate to mention this but Sergey Frank, CEO of Sovcomflot, says he is 90 per cent certain that he will be successful in securing the necessary permissions. It is not clear yet whether this is with or without a pilot but Sergey is a keen sailor and understands the point and the promotional possibilities.

This was movement! The combined approaches from within both British and Russian government circles and Russian commerce now seemed almost certain to yield results. To allow *Barrabas* to go through short-handed would not be new, given that in 2003 and 2004, *Campina*, Henk's boat, had entered the Northern Sea Route with a two-man crew – himself and Boris, his ice pilot. Could Nikolai Monko be persuaded to go one further and let me try it on my own?

Henk de Velde: Friday 24th March 2006

Great news. As long as you don't have a Russian NO there is a YES.

By which I guessed Henk meant that until the Russians categorically refused me permission to sail the NSR single-handed, the door was still ajar and I might yet slip through.

CHAPTER 16

Tuning In

Before we were married, Louise, knowing about my fascination with T. E. Lawrence, had taken me to see his grave in the village churchyard near his home in the southwest of England.

Gradually, I was working my way through *Lawrence of Arabia*, Jeremy Wilson's authorised biography of Lawrence. Here was a man selected by fate for greatness and subsequently marooned by an inability to accommodate the burden. Some aspects of his character seemed immediately familiar: the frequent need for quiet and solitude, the peace gained by focusing on the simplest of things, the essential desire to live with bareness, the need to play with words and write (and a sense of inadequacy born as a consequence). Lawrence would undoubtedly have understood my need for this voyage, without hesitation or requiring explanation – as an adventure, an expedition, a mission, a test, a road, a circle, a need, a fulfilment of sorts. What a thing it would be to have five minutes of his company! I promised myself to make a 'pilgrimage' one day to Cloud's Hill, his house in Dorset.

I had always wanted to see Hawaii too, although it looked like I would only get a glimpse of Honolulu from the sea. Here, Louise was helping me again. The resupply items were being delivered to her house. DHL had agreed to airfreight the package to Honolulu. To take the plan forward, Louise had contacted a few yacht clubs on Oahu.

Ivan Chan Wa, Commodore of the Waikiki Yacht Club, had responded immediately – no problem bringing the stuff out to me and for good measure, they would chuck in fresh fruit or 'whatever he may need'.

I wanted to show Louise my appreciation. I called Nikki (incredible that from the middle of the Pacific Ocean, I could talk to Nikki in rural Suffolk by dialling a few numbers!). Could she arrange a delivery of flowers for Louise on Sunday, Mother's Day?

As in the Atlantic, the constancy of the trade winds meant I had little to do to sail *Barrabas*. She happily ploughed on, recording daily mileages from 100 to 120. Occasional mood swings in the weather might involve bending in a reef or shaking one out but otherwise I could relax, giving my damaged right wrist a chance to mend.

I made twice-daily tours around deck at dawn and dusk, armed with my spear gun, peering over the sides for any fish that believed they had found the protection of the mother ship but which to me might look good in a curry.

I saw no sign of human habitation on the planet – not a single aircraft or the lights of a faraway ship. The last ship I'd seen had been six weeks before, on February 12th, before Cape Horn. My total isolation emphasised the enormity of the Pacific Ocean and whereas I'd previously felt the world to be small, its size now ballooned in my imagination. This place was vast, limited only by the horizon beyond which the massive expanse of the ocean fell away and continued on, out of sight.

I was back to glorious nakedness, like a character from *Lord of the Flies* who'd escaped the book, grown to adulthood in the intervening years and materialised on a boat somewhere in the South Pacific.

Monotony crept into my diet and, although eating generally disinterested me in the heat, I developed a craving for sweet, stodgy food, so my breakfast now consisted of coffee and '*Barrabas* Pancake' – oil, flour, oats, sugar (lots) and evaporated milk blended together and deep-fried. I ate it with a coating of condensed milk.

On the chart table, an ever-evolving list of jobs rolled, like the Pacific swell, from one page to another. Each time I struck one job off, I added another to the bottom.

The stench of diesel seeped from the lazarette. This large stowage compartment at the back of the boat, measuring the width of the ship, three feet long and four feet deep, occupying the space from the underside of the deck to the bare inside of the hull, was filled with 20-litre jerry cans. Two of them had leaked, punctured by constant agitation against the end threads of through-bolts securing the Hydro-vane to the transom. All 17 cans had to come out. I wiped the lazarette clean and fixed rubber pads over the ends of the bolts before re-stowing the fuel.

The port main winch seized. I took my time servicing it, sitting in the sunshine, enjoying the breeze, naked and nut brown. I had no spare parts for the winches (some Tardis) and worried that a spring might have failed. I discovered that solidified dirt and hardened grease on the spindle were stopping the free rotation of the gear cogs. I cleaned every part and put the whole thing back together but no dice – it remained stubbornly seized. I stripped the starboard winch to check rotation, cleaning and re-greasing it in the process, then repeated the procedure on the port-side winch. The parts were small and intricate so, to remember the sequence, I put each part into a numbered plastic bag as I took it off, beginning with 1 and ending with 17. Reassembly was by components in each bag in the reverse order.

The gaps between jobs (or during jobs – the winches were broken into several 'shifts') I filled with reading or napping, more usually both. For the moment, Yann Martell's *Life of Pi* was on the reading menu.

Health-wise, I was in good shape. My loss of appetite resulted in an almost visible shedding of surplus flesh put on in the colder climate of the deep south, although a nasty mouth ulcer developed at the front of my lower gum – not much to see but it hurt like hell. Vitamin depletion, perhaps. I started taking a range of Viridian supplements.

Nikki had arranged for a single orchid. I said to Nikki not to get a big bunch of flowers because Louise and the boys were off to Dubai to visit Karen, an old school friend, and she would not get the opportun-ity to enjoy them. The orchid was a great idea. Louise was thrilled. She called to tell me. Benji said he wished I was going with them, and so did I! After the miserable English winter, the sun would be good for the children and revitalise Louise.

I had a nightmare session with the laptop, not for the first time. The email programme kept tying itself in knots. I was starting to develop a Pavlovian-type reaction to the sight and thought of using the laptop but, instead of salivating, I felt my blood pressure rising. Very few people had direct access to me via email, mainly to prevent viral con-tamination. Asking people not to send large emails seemed to get the same response as asking them, please, to bite their hands off! Someone (better to remain nameless) had dumped a 48 kb message. Fifty dollars later, because the line kept dropping part-way through transmission, the computer got itself all tangled up again. The only remedy – a rushed call back to Louise before they set off for the airport to ask her to access the server on the internet and get rid of the message.

Two jobs remained outstanding before I could get down to some serious lounging about. The first was a slow leak from the fuel day tank that was staining the hot air inside the cabin with the sickly smell of diesel. I repaired it by draining the tank then applying a two-part epoxy. The second involved the watermaker holding tank. To avoid a vacuum inside the tank preventing the flow of seawater to the water-maker, air had to get in. The problem came when the tank filled then overflowed. The excess then found its way to the bilges. To pump the bilges drew heavily on the batteries and mildew thrived in the hot, wet environment of the fore cabin sole. I sealed the water-in and water-out hoses in the tank with a quickset two-part epoxy and introduced an air bleed pipe, four feet of narrow-bore tubing, sealed at its point of entry into the tank. I tied the end of the air tube to the bulkhead, high above the waterline.

The next day, after the epoxy had fully cured, I checked my work while the watermaker was running. No leaks!

Small improvements like that made an enormous difference to my life on board, as did a sense of personal cleanliness. I gave myself a hair-cut on deck in case hair in the bilges clogged the pumps. The result was not bad, at least from the front.

Twitching, I fired up the laptop. It worked. A message arrived from Louise:

Louise: Friday 31st March 2006
Having a lovely time. Spending mornings by the pool after a hearty buffet breakfast then out with Karen in the afternoon to a mall where they have huge kids' play zones more like funfairs. Karen and I went to a BBQ last night and Rosie her house-cleaner came and babysat at Karen's new lovely flat and we all spent the night here. Off to the hotel for big brunch this morning. Boys' behaviour not great! Maybe it's because they are acting up for Karen, but hopefully it will pass when they get used to it here. Ric says you have fab sailing conditions for at least the next 30 days!

Sliding the laptop to one side, I glanced at the GPS. We had 3,300 miles to go to Hawaii. I looked at the chart. The Galapagos Islands were presently the closest land mass just over 1,200 miles to the

northeast. I was about as far from land as it was possible to be anywhere on the planet.

Louise and I had reconnected and that equilibrium fed through to
other areas. I slept more deeply and met jobs with greater enthusiasm.
I took greater pleasure in the seascape around me and enjoyed my
time more fully.

The idea of supermarkets, cars, television and the threads of ordinary life had receded. Looking out over the vast expanses of the ocean,
my solitude, living on *Barrabas* – these things seemed normal, natural.
Roof tiles, shops, Wellington boots, mud, crowds – these things
seemed no more than the memories of a long-ago visit to a strange
place.

Was this just a trick of time? Of course. When I stepped on land
again, everything would be as familiar as though I had never been
away. And yet, out there . . . something else, something . . . elemental.

I was changing. A slow graduation, so slow I had not noticed. I no
longer sailed *Barrabas* with constant reference to instruments. She
spoke to me in her soft voice. I often woke at night and went on deck
to trim the sails or adjust the Hydrovane without any tangible reason
to do so – no wind fluctuations, no alteration in the sea state. I began
to know by instinct what was coming. I was fusing and merging with
the natural world around me. My rhythm no longer beat to a different
drum. I breathed with the sea.

That night I drifted off to sleep while the earpieces of the MP3 player
delivered Robbie Williams to somewhere inside my auditory cortex. A
small vibration brought me awake. *Barrabas* seemed to be 'tugging'. I
stared through the open hatch. Against the stars, the spinnaker pole's
up-haul twanged like the strummed string of a guitar. On deck, the
night air plucked at me with cool, refreshing fingers. I tightened the
up-haul. The headsail ceased its luffing and *Barrabas* settled back to an
even pull through the water. I went below and slept, dreaming of
cucumber and tomato sandwiches and ice-cold Coke.

Bright sunshine was streaming into the cabin when I woke. I sensed
the boat was fine. She had kept on while I slept. I looked around my
small living space. It would be a photo finish as to which was the
bigger – my space or a prison cell. The fore and aft cabins were full of
fuel, stores, sails and accumulating garbage in white bin sacks. I lived in

the central section comprising the saloon and chart table with the head
on the port side and the galley on the starboard side. For the moment,
I was on the port side, the low side of the boat. Either way, my bed
measured 21" wide and 78" long. Two layers of 3" deep foam cushions
laid end to end provided mattressing. The saloon table stood between
the banquettes, its leaves folded to give me access to the fore cabin.
The companionway steps, between the chart table and the galley, led
up to the cockpit.

The inside of the boat was by now crisply dry. Below deck, the
temperature climbed to 40°C under the tropical sun. To escape the
heat, I constructed a crude sunshade from the ruined cruising chute.
Beneath this turquoise tent, the whole of the cockpit area was in
shade. I furnished it with cushions taken from the saloon, laid out on
the cockpit seating, providing myself an alternative place to read or
eat.

Slowly, the winds moved east, tentative flicks at first as the southeast trades gave way to their northeast counterparts. To get a better
angle, I gybed the sails, re-rigging the spinnaker pole on the starboard
side. Both my wrists still ached. Planning tasks became essential to
avoid further injury. I was only halfway through the voyage, at best.
How were my wrists going to hold out until the end?

From deliberation and long habit, routine divided up my days:
breakfast, morning chores (two hours), coffee, reading, lunch (occasionally), studying astro-navigation, nap, practice with the sextant,
reading, bed. Like a child, I needed the structure and predictability of
a set timetable. During the afternoons, I was usually in the 'tent'.

Years before, while I was a bachelor living in London, I'd taken myself off to night school to study the theoretical side of astro-navigation.
Now I had the opportunity to put it into practice. The challenge to
master the art (and science) of astro-navigation provided me with
mental stimulation in addition to reading and it would take me closer
to Chichester, Knox-Johnston and the other pioneering single-handed
sailors who'd had no other means of navigation except the use of a
sextant.

Once I'd refreshed myself on the academic principles, I moved on
to familiarising myself with the Almanac and reduction tables (com-
putations used to interpret sextant readings and extrapolate meaningful positions). I then had to adjust the sextant, using the moon for side
and index errors (a sextant measures angles of planetary bodies relative

to the earth – a sextant's mirrors need to be correctly calibrated). I was then ready to practise 'pulling down' planets, the sun, the moon and stars.

A school of dolphin appeared one afternoon. I tapped out a simple numerical sequence on the side of the boat with a winch handle. They stayed for what seemed the mandatory 10 minutes, splashing around the bows, looking at me as if I was as simple-minded as the elementary language echoed through the water. One dolphin did seem intrigued, staying on for a further few minutes, chippering and squealing.

Louise: Wednesday 5th April 2006

We are all really brown – in fact Benji looks like a local! We went to Wild Wadi, a water park which was great and of course, the boys loved it.

Had an email today from Douglas Alexander, the Overseas Minister from the Foreign and Commonwealth Office! He is talking to the Russians too!

I took my first-ever noon sun sight and calculated my latitude at 04°.55.2' south. By comparison, the GPS showed 05°.14'. So fair to say then that I was out 'by a mile' – 18.8 nautical miles to be exact. However, for a first, self-taught effort, I was reasonably pleased. The next day, I plotted my first sun-run-sun. The sun sight gave me a decent fix but the noon sight was wrong, 40 nautical miles out. Practise with the sextant would put that right!

A big bank of nimbostratus brought northeast winds, the first sustained northeasterlies since Cape Horn. We were closing on the equator, now just 240 miles away.

Louise: Sunday 9th April 2006

Tomorrow is our last day and then back to cold and reality. Two weeks more of school holidays so I will have to think of things to do to occupy the boys. One sure-fire appointment is at the cinema as Ice Age 2 has come out at home. I am going to have to spend quite a bit of time getting your shipment together. I take it all to DHL on the 21st. I have managed to really switch off from the AGX on this holiday, but I will be ready to do battle when I get home.

We crossed the equator for the second time at 1.57 am on Tuesday 11th April (0957 UCT) and, as though to mark our completion of the southern hemisphere phase of the voyage, the equator manifested itself as a white line! The line, two feet wide, ran arrow straight across the ocean, east to west as far as I could see in either direction, like a freshly painted road marking or an aircraft's vapour trail blazed across an azure sky. Was this the convergence between the equatorial and counter-equatorial currents? I doubted it. Algae of some kind? Unlikely. Spillage or discharge from a ship? I never did figure it out.

One spike pierced the benign constancy that had come to mark the passage of my days – the fragility of the email system. Aside from communicating with Louise, I requested and received weather information by email. What should have been a simple procedure for sending and retrieving emails usually became an hour-long battle, reprogramming and rebooting and, more often than not, long (and expensive) conversations with Tim on the satellite phone. I shouted at the computer, frothed at the mouth and bloody nearly ripped out its electrical mooring lines to hurl it into the purple wastes of the ocean.

When I'd calmed down, I put the situation into context. Chichester, Knox-Johnston and Blyth got on without email, much less satellite telephones. Knox-Johnston's radio packed up after a couple of months and everyone thought the worst until he pitched up off New Zealand! As for weather, if I needed it, Ricardo was a phone call away armed with precise, satellite-derived data. None of the other three benefited from GPS either!

My GPS was working. I plotted my position. 2, 400 miles to Hawaii. To make myself feel better, I called Louise.

'My sitting room looks like a bloody warehouse!'

I asked, 'How big is this package going to be?'

'A pallet.'

'A pallet?' I wondered where I would stow everything.

'You've got the new cruising chute in there from Kemp.'

'I guess.'

'I've just had a conversation with Michael Roth.'

Ivan Chan Wa was Commodore, Michael, Rear-Commodore for Sail at the Waikiki Yacht Club. He seemed to have taken personal responsibility for me.

'And?'

Louise was giggling. 'I asked him, "Will you be able to get a boat to take this stuff out to Adrian?" "Yes," he said. "No problem and I'll put on a couple of lays." I was shocked, so I told him, "Michael, what you do is your business, but I don't really think it's appropriate that you tell me that. I may not be Adrian's wife, but I am his ex-wife. And further-more," I said, "anybody else on *Barrabas* will cancel out the single-handed nature of his voyage!" '

'What did he say?'

'He told me I was his kind of woman, but that by lays he meant leis – you know, the traditional Hawaiian flower garlands.'

I was approaching the central Pacific shipping lanes. At 4.38 am (local time) on 18th April, I went on deck to check my horizons. There, on my starboard bow, were the lights of a passing ship – the first sign of human life I'd seen for 65 days! I sat watching the lights until they disappeared, feeling a peculiar mix of emotions. My complete isolation had brought me to the point where I existed in my own realm of the ocean – just me, the dolphins, the wahoo, the seabirds. The ship, like a trespasser, had infringed upon that governance. At the same time, I was reassured by the proximity of other people mainly because I knew, for the moment, that I was safe. If something happened now to *Barrabas*, help was close at hand.

In the latter part of April, something changed. The weather turned ugly. The seas heaped to massive 40-foot swells. The wind screamed hysterically. Day after day, the elements writhed in fury. The con-stancy of wind and water that had been my norm, blurred and van-ished. No rational explanation offered itself. The instincts on which I had come to rely abandoned me, as if mere instinct could not decipher the complexity of what was happening.

Ricardo could see the cloud formations above me on satellite images and wanted to know conditions on the ground. I told him. Ricardo, I could tell, was at a loss but he contrived an explanation – the con-fluence between the southeast and northeast trade winds together with the fallout from a massive low-pressure system to my north.

The Hawaiian Islands were by now 2,000 miles away. On such a long voyage 2,000 miles seems like nothing at all. If I could hold a 100-mile-a-day average, I would see Hawaii in early May. But 2,000 miles is the same distance as London to Nova Scotia on the other side of the Atlantic Ocean! Or as far as Lisbon to the Azores and back!

In a curious coincidence mirroring what happened at Cape Horn, the toilet refused to flush, although this time there was no sewage slopping over the floor. The toilet worked on a vacuum principle – close the lid, pump out the effluent and the resulting vacuum sucked seawater in from outside. *Barrabas*'s underbelly was alive with marine growth, gooseneck barnacles, a marine forest in miniature – the barnacles must have blocked the intake. Racing sailors rely on the simpler 'bucket and chuck it' principle (to save the weight of having a toilet on board and the time it takes to fix when, inevitably, it breaks or blocks). Ricardo said he did the same. I had been at sea for 180 days. Weight was not an issue for me and I had plenty of time to sort out problems. More importantly, having use of a 'bathroom' was one of the few activities I could maintain in order to simulate at least a semblance of normality. The bucket and chuck it method would never work for me.

The unexplained weather phenomenon we were going through did register in Hawaii – they called it 'unseasonable storms'. Forty-eight million gallons of sewage washed down into the harbour at Waikiki, exactly where I was heading. Michael Roth had given Louise co-ordinates, which she passed on to me, a waypoint at Diamond Head buoy offshore from Honolulu, where I was to make the rendezvous with the supply boat from the Waikiki Yacht Club.

I woke at daybreak. I could tell by the boat's motion and the rush of water past the hull that the wind was 16–18 knots and we were making five knots through the water. The sky through the battened Perspex hatch was blue. At last, a decent day! Suddenly, an almighty bang reverberated around the starboard side. Green water cascaded over the deck obliterating blue sky. I had closed all the hatches and the companionway as a precaution against spray strafing the deck. *Barrabas* lurched. An organisation tray containing nuts, bolts, screws, torch, knife, MP3 and a collection of other odds and ends flew off the saloon table, over my head and hit the ceiling, which was now horizontal from the saloon table. *Barrabas* had just taken her second capsize.

Then she screamed.

A year before, Benji had run into the path of a car. The car swerved, missing him by inches. In that instant, everything stopped – breathing, heart, movement. Life, for the brief time it took for the car to go past, floated in a kind of adrenalin-soaked animation. So it was when *Barrabas* screamed. All other sound muted, just the solo high-pitched, grinding, tearing of steel as *Barrabas* slowly righted herself. I rushed on deck. The sails remained tautly shaped by the wind – no telltale chinks of daylight coming through rents or tears. The shrouds, I counted all twelve, were rigid. The mast stood proud, erect. I could not see any damage. I searched, but could find nothing.

★

As I broiled on deck, a school of wahoo sought shelter beneath *Barrabas*'s hull. I spotted them by chance five or six feet below the surface, the sun's rays glinting turquoise and green off their backs. Bits of stale pumpernickel excited their cursory interest, then they disappeared forward into shadow. The abundant gooseneck barnacles seemed much more appetising. I found an out-of-date can of fruit, spilled the peach segments into the sea and polished the ring-pull top. Four feet of fishing twine knotted through the ring-pull and my lure was ready. Beside me, the spear gun was armed. The ring-pull skimmed and twisted in the roughened wake, catching and reflecting sunlight. This proved a greater temptation than stale pumpernickel and slowly the wahoo emerged from beneath the stern, expertly slowing to let *Barrabas* pass over. They surfaced like miniature, iridescent submarines, nosing the can top. I reeled the ring-pull in until the fish were only inches from the back of the boat. Spear gun in hand and standing on the sugar scoop, I fired and missed. Their patience exhausted, the wahoo dived to their cruising altitude, accelerated and disappeared once more into their shadowed sanctuary.

On the same day I was harmlessly firing at fish, Louise turned forty-six. I dialled her number.

'*Barrabas* calling,' I said in the manner of a Eurovision Song Contest judge when Louise picked up.

'They're wonderful . . .' Nikki had come to the rescue once again. A huge bouquet had just arrived on Louise's doorstep.

'Picked 'em myself, swam across two oceans . . .'

'Seriously, thank you. I've just put them in water. How are you doing?'

'Okay. I spoke to Ricardo. I'll go over the top of Hawaii and approach Oahu from the north. That way I won't have to beat into wind. Ric reckons the northeast trades will funnel between the islands so if I go over the top I can approach Oahu downwind.'

'Well, everything's ready for you.'

'Thanks. I do have one problem.'

'What?'

'I've got no charts for the islands.'

'You'll manage.'

Louise's total belief in my ability to get *Barrabas* to where I wanted to go was heartening.

'Well, I'll call Michael and get his view – local knowledge and all that. You doing anything this evening?'

'Some of the girls are coming round.'

The idea of people 'coming round' seemed odd to me. Today, 1st May, was my 186th day at sea. I had not seen another person in all that time. The prospect of talking to people on the resupply boat made me apprehensive.

My advance towards Hawaii had come to be dogged by stalling wind, a legacy from the bizarre weather patterns since crossing north over the equator. The following day I was on deck. Beneath a steely sky heavy with the promise of rain, *Barrabas* bobbed on a mirror-flat sea. In the thinning light of evening, occasional zephyrs stroked the surface and ruffled the hot air. Mug of tea in hand, I stood on the aft deck looking sternwards to the south. Some inexplicable sixth sense compelled me to continue staring in that direction. A wave was coming, although the horizon showed only the gentle curvature of the earth. Nevertheless, I knew a wave was coming. For 20 minutes, I maintained my vigil. Nothing happened. I did not feel alarm. This was not an area noted for rogue waves. I was far from land and in deep water. A tsunami only presents danger when the massive energy of the surge strikes the continental shelf.

I called Ricardo. There was no answer so I left a message and then called Michael.

'Aloha, Adrian,' Michael said. We talked for a short while then I asked him his advice about approaches to Oahu. 'The seas south of the big island are among the roughest in the world. Give that area a wide berth . . .'

'The big island?'

'Hawaii Island, we call it the "Big Island".'

'How far south?'

'Where are you at the moment?'

I gave him my position, about 270 miles from Hilo, the main town on Hawaii's east coast.

'Or pass east of the big island then come south through the Molokai channel between Molokai and Oahu. That's the general rule here, come in from the north, leave to the south.'

'Sounds good to me.'

We said our goodbyes with the promise I would call as I neared Diamond Head. I reckoned to get there on Monday 8th May.

A distant beep announced the arrival of a text message on the satellite phone. Ricardo must have assumed I wanted weather information. His text read:

Feel free to call now if you wish. Expect the same as today for the next 20 hours or so. Now wind will arrive from southeast and back east and northeast, max 15 kn. Tsunami warning false alarm. (04/05 00:00 UCT).

I re-read the message several times, just to make sure I had understood it correctly. I immediately called Ricardo.

'I didn't know anything about a tsunami!'

'Your message said you thought a wave was coming?'

'That was just a feeling!'

'Wow, man – you're really tuned in!'

'When was the tsunami alert issued?'

Ricardo consulted notes and gave me a time in UCT. I converted the time difference. An earthquake in the region of Tonga 3,000 miles south had initiated the alert at exactly the time I had sensed its presence the previous day.

Still feeling dazed from the improbable coincidence, I wandered around the deck making a casual inspection of the rigging and deck gear. Perhaps we are all linked to the natural world in some fundamental but indefinable way. Perhaps our abilities to 'tune in' are at a rudimentary stage of development and in our broader evolution, this ability will evolve over generations into some higher language. Vague thoughts of butterflies' wings setting off hurricanes on the other side of the world floated in my mind as I fingered the starboard lower shrouds. They seemed loose. I kneeled to hand-tighten the bottle screws, but how could the shrouds be *this* loose?

I went aloft to inspect the rig and found a catastrophic rigging failure. A through-mast bolt holds the tangs supporting the fore and aft lower shrouds. On the port side, the tang seemed fine but on the starboard side, the bolt had pulled down tearing a three-inch gash through the wall of the mast. In a big blow, the mast would almost certainly come down!

How could I have missed this? When did it happen? It must have been the capsize – the 'scream'.

I jumped back on deck, dropped the mainsail and reefed the headsail to ease the load on the mast, although I needed to strike a balance because reducing sail area would progressively increase the pendulum motion of the boat, creating a different type of stress on the rigging.

I flopped into the cockpit, my pulse racing as much from the shock and realisation that my world had changed as from the panicky rush to shorten sail. Hawaii was no longer a sail-by. I had to go into port.

'Shit!' I shouted. Two immediate problems: one of additional, unforeseen expense, and the other, a crucial delay in my schedule, upsetting my delicate equilibrium. Could the knock-on effects jeopardise my chances of getting to the Bering Strait on time?

To relieve the damaged area from excessive loading, I quickly rigged two halyards around the lower spreaders in figures of eight to avoid fouling the mainsail track, tensioning each line with a block and tackle fixed to the toe-rail. As if to test both my resolve and the makeshift repair, the wind escalated to 26 knots. An electrical storm moved in overhead. Lightning illuminated the sky like giant bombs detonating in the clouds. *Barrabas* began to pitch wildly.

'It's a bloody conspiracy to bring the mast down,' I said to Louise, expecting any second to hear the twanging of parting lines and the mast crashing into the sea.

'There's a reason for everything,' Louise said calmly. I had noticed a progressive change in her disposition and philosophy as the voyage had unfolded. Now she was deploying calm and rationality against my volatility, a straight reversal of our relationship during seven years of marriage. As was usually the case now, I began to settle into a more comfortable acceptance of the hand fate had dealt. 'You can fix the mast but also get the batteries checked over, sort the computer properly, wash your clothes, have a rest, see a wonderful place and you know what . . .'

'What?' I said.

'Have a bloody great, beautiful steak, French fries and a crisp salad all washed down with ice-cold beer.'

'Um . . . beer,' I thought. 'What I wouldn't give for an ice-cold Guinness!'

CHAPTER 17

Honolulu

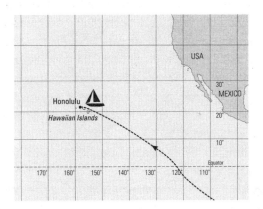

The 'Big Island' hid beneath a great ball of mist and haze as I passed round its eastern and northern flanks. In the northeast trades, I was now on a lee shore as I passed westwards over the next island in the chain, Maui. As a precaution, I called the US Coastguard, explained the situation and agreed to maintain a four-hourly reporting schedule. If the mast and engine failed, I would need a tow into port.

The cliffs on the northern side of Molokai, the next island westwards, are among the highest in the world. From three miles offshore, I looked at these great walls of granite disappearing skywards, their towering tops lost in low cloud. The sight fascinated me but the sooner I was past them and in the channel between Molokai and Oahu, the happier I would be.

Ricardo was right. The winds accelerated between the islands, kicking the waters of the Molokai Channel into a moody, choppy confusion. Circular currents neutralised the Hydrovane's attempts to hold course so I hand-steered *Barrabas* through the night of Sunday 7th May. At dawn, the lights of Oahu's coastal settlements gave way to a raw and breathtaking landscape: a mountainous, volcanic spine drifting to a flattened coastal plain thickly covered with rich vegetation.

Diamond Head, a volcanic crater edging seawards from the southern shore, shimmered under a morning sun already suffusing the air with heat. Buildings nestling in the crooks of its limbs emerged as I neared the land. Houses set among palm-fringed gardens close to the beach began to reveal themselves in detail. Moving cars winked in the sunlight. As *Barrabas* rounded Diamond Head, the great sweep of Waikiki's crescent beach backed by layers of skyscrapers stretched away towards Pearl Harbor. I stood on deck, still steering *Barrabas* under reduced headsail, and marvelled. Approaching land from the air is exciting but from the sea, the experience is more intense, the smell and sound enriching the sight. Here, in the middle of the largest ocean on earth, stood a full-blown, money-fuelled city set in a lush, tropical landscape. I had found Atlantis!

At 11.00 am, I called Michael. Ten minutes later, while I guided *Barrabas* around the red-painted buoy at Diamond Head, a small cruiser bounced over the water towards us. I waved. Three men waved back: Ivan Chan Wa, Michael and a British member of the Waikiki Yacht Club, Ernie Woodruff, brought along as 'translator'.

'Aloha!' one of the men shouted.

I guessed by his voice that it was Michael.

'Good to be here!'

The boat buzzed around me for a few minutes taking pictures, then nosed closer in.

Michael was shouting across the gap. 'There're some reefs by the beach, so follow me in but stay right behind.'

'Okay,' I said. I had the headsail up but I'd dropped the mainsail and turned the engine on.

Michael cupped his hands around his mouth. 'What'd you like to drink when we get in?'

I didn't have to think for long. 'An ice-cold Guinness if you got one!' I yelled back.

Michael waved, gunned his engine and moved ahead of me.

I motor-sailed behind the little cruiser across the Honolulu water-front, a stunning fusion of sea, sand, palm trees, high-rises and dramatic volcanic backdrops. As I entered the channel into the Ala Wai yacht basin, the Ala Moana Park slid by on my left: manicured lawns, trees, shrubs and flowers. I drank in the sight, the liquid green whetting my parched imagination. I was struck by the sheer beauty of the place. Even the name of the city was appropriate. In the Hawaiian language, Honolulu means *place of shelter*.

Sails furled and engine gently gurgling, I nosed *Barrabas* to her mooring on a hammerhead pontoon behind an American yacht, *Astor*. In the stillness of the basin, the heat pressed down. Sweat trickled down my back. I took off my heavy weather salopettes. People on the pontoon made off my lines. I cut the engine. After six and a half months (193 days) at sea, *Barrabas* was at rest.

The yacht club had contacted US Customs and they were also on the pontoon to clear me in. Until the formalities were complete, I had to remain on board. The escort launch had parked up elsewhere. I saw a tall, bearded figure amble along the pontoon carrying a tray.

'Aloha, Adrian,' Michael said when he reached *Barrabas*'s side. 'Welcome to Honolulu. Here's something to cool you down!' A can of ice-cold Guinness beaded with condensation sat on the tray. I began to salivate. The Hawaiian press had gathered on the quayside, notified and briefed by the club's PR manager, Bobbie Jennings, who had been in constant touch with Louise during the preceding weeks. Cameras rolled, shutters clicked, microphones pointed. I drank the Guinness and talked, my words tripping out in an unstoppable flood. The leis that had caused Louise so much confusion appeared from somewhere and were draped around my neck as well as a special lei of woven tea leaves, a particular honour for *Barrabas*, which I hung over her bow as is the tradition.

Finally, the moment of setting foot on dry land arrived and with it a mixture of conflicting emotion: relief, satisfaction, pleasure, hesitancy. Together, *Barrabas* and I had sailed the first single-handed non-stop passage between the UK and Hawaii. Now it was time for me to leave my ship, if only temporarily. The prospect of our separation was strangely daunting as if, by stepping ashore, the umbilical link between me and *Barrabas* would be broken, leaving me more alone on shore surrounded by people than I had been on my own for months at sea. I realised in that instant just how connected I had become to her, how much I cared for her, how much I loved her.

When I had read about Chichester's epic circumnavigation, a secret ambition had embedded itself in my psyche. Sir Francis had sailed over 15,000 miles between Australia and the UK on his homeward leg, at the time the longest single-handed passage ever made. I ducked below decks. My log showed we'd travelled 18,045 miles from England. I had gone further than Chichester. I kissed *Barrabas* and stepped ashore surrounded by a brace of well-wishers and press.

The Waikiki Yacht Club is in the heart of the Waikiki downtown area. The clubhouse itself is an idyll of urban tropical splendour: a long, low building open to the marina and overlooked by towering sentinels of glass and steel with vanguards of gently swaying palms. Bobbie Jennings, in her sixties, clutched my arm as we made our way towards the clubhouse along the pontoons, fearing that I might pitch head-first into the water. Surprisingly, I was steady on my feet, but her arm through mine was comforting. We sat at a table. I was being garrulous and foolish, but I didn't care. They looked at me as if I was a space cadet and let me talk. Lunch arrived: New York steak, fries, chicken mayo and papaya salad and ice-cold beer! Food had never tasted so good.

That first evening ashore, Ernie drove me to a mountaintop lookout before descending to Kailua where the beach, fringed with fir and palm, would compete with any in the world. Dinner followed at a beachside restaurant. I couldn't resist a second steak washed down with cold Budweiser! To be there, seeing people, hearing the hubbub of conversation, smelling the scents of land and feeling the firmness all around instilled a fresh sense of pleasure and appreciation after the months of isolation at sea.

Barrabas was losing half a knot of boat speed because of the drag created by marine growth on her undersides. The next day I met Les Vasconelles, a diver for a company specialising in scraping the undersides of boats. He was fully booked but agreed to do the work there and then. He already knew my story! Afterwards, Les refused to take any payment, telling me he wanted to be part of the expedition and this was how he would like to be involved. Les surfaced to show me the size of the gooseneck barnacles. Some of them, growing in clusters, measured six inches.

'You got somethin' fouled on the prop,' he said, pushing his mask up onto his forehead.

'What d'you think it is?'

'Dunno. Could be fishing twine. I'll go take another look,' and with that, the mask came down and he disappeared. A few minutes later, he surfaced again. 'Seems solid.' He handed me a piece of material cut from around the shaft. I turned the piece over, shaking my head with incomprehension.

'I reckon it's twine, got wrapped round and melted with the friction,' Les offered.

That seemed like a plausible explanation. The material was grey and had been molten at one time; now it was set in rucks like a tiny piece of lava.

'Can you cut the rest of it off?' I asked.

'No problemo,' Les said and he was gone again.

I heard the scraping and cutting while I pottered about inside the boat. Eventually, I heard Les haul himself onto the pontoon and went to join him. He had a collection of bits of grey plastic. 'Got most of it off. Reckon your shaft's a bit loose though.'

I thanked Les and thought no more about it.

The consignment of replacement parts and additional supplies was in Ernie's warehouse from which he ran his quilting company. Michael arrived in a pick-up and together we delivered the various packages to the yacht club. I spent the rest of the day opening and disseminating everything that Louise had put together – the target list had been filled 100 per cent, plus some additional cold-climate clothing items.

At lunchtime, Rick, a yacht club member who operated Blue Diamond Welding, inspected the mast damage. We could make repairs with *Barrabas* afloat. To get access to his equipment, *Barrabas* needed to move to the work dock where the hoist could lift Rick's equipment to the level of the lower spreaders. I cast off at 6.00 pm with Ernie on hand to help.

I set to work wiring in the new wind generator and the new heating-control unit. A tricky piece of work involved replacing and rewiring the voltage-converter unit that powered the ship's computer.

Articles appeared in Tuesday's press following the television news coverage of the evening before. The club secretary told me that a number of people had come down to the club wanting to see *Barrabas*, including visitors from England. Unfortunately, they were barred entry for security reasons. When I went to a local store to pick up copies of the *Honolulu Advertiser*, the checkout lady recognised me and became very excited!

Dan Toye, an itinerant marine electrician, charged up the boat's battery bank and put the batteries through a thorough health check. He used a galvanic meter to test for currency leaks. The all-clear came as a relief.

I took the mainsail to North Sails Hawaii for minor repairs. There, Jim Maselli wasted no time in getting to work, immediately appreciating the need for urgency. More than 7000 miles lay between me and the Arctic ice sailing via my chosen antipodal point southeast of Japan. Time was not on my side. Both Dan and Jim were members of the club.

Rick's crew fixed the mast by welding two 3-inch-square, ¼-inch-thick stainless steel plates to the damaged areas and made a new through-bolt, slightly longer than the original to account for the additional thickness of the new plates. Despite the repair, I decided I had to modify my sailing strategy by reefing the sails at lower wind thresholds than previously. The consequence of slower boat speed would, I figured, be balanced by the reduced drag of the cleanly scraped hull.

I wondered around the sprawling shopping mall just across the road from the yacht club gates. Presents for the boys needed to be light-weight and unbreakable for airfreight. I settled on Hawaiian shirts and for Louise, a handmade necklace of delicate shells and a shoulder bag decorated with a Hawaiian palm print pattern.

Michael drove me to Costco to restock on vital commodities like tinned milk, then, together with Ernie, I had lunch with Ed Reinhart, another club member, at his house at Koko Head. The setting was sub-lime, part-way up the side of an extinct volcano with a pool terrace out front and a sweeping view of the bay and Honolulu beyond. The conversation centred largely on philosophy and self-knowledge – he was interested to know how long periods of isolation had affected me. I think I disappointed him.

The following evening after dark, while I was refitting the shrouds and putting on the repaired mainsail in the orange glow of the work dock floodlights, Ed arrived carrying two bags.

'Bought these for ya!' Ed hoisted the bags on deck. The bags were marked with the Borders bookstore logo. 'Thought after yesterday's talk you could do with some more reading material.'

I made coffee and we chatted for a short while in the cool of the evening. On Monday 15th May, I loaded all the fuel onto the boat then went out to dinner with Michael and his family at his mountaintop home. Being a sailor, Michael needed no explanation of antipodal points, and when I explained my selected position was southeast of Japan, the information met with a pursing of the lips.

'They've just had a big hit.'

'Typhoon?' I asked.

'Yep.'

I felt dread. Although it was the beginning of the hurricane season in the north Pacific, my ETA at the antipodal point, 3,200 miles due west, was 20th June – four weeks. Historical data suggested that the majority of typhoons spun away from Japan and tracked northeast over open water, exactly the course I would be following once I reached the antipodal point and made the turn for the Bering Strait. With the damage to the mast and the delay in Honolulu, the chances of meeting with a typhoon escalated dramatically.

On Wednesday 17th May, Elizabeth, DHL manager in Honolulu, came to the marina in the morning to collect the box of mini-DV tapes (I had shot 20 hours of video footage since leaving England) and the gifts I had bought to send back to Louise. Before packing the tapes, I recorded a message for the children. At 1.30 pm after a (healthy?) lunch of hamburger, fries and Coke on board with Ernie, I slipped my mooring. After six months alone, it felt strange to find myself once again on the wide ocean with only *Barrabas* as company.

As the mountains of Oahu and the high-rises of Honolulu faded into the mists of low cloud, sadness descended at leaving a group of new friends who by their help had now become an integral part of the Alpha Global story. Ivan's efforts to locate the right people to carry out the work on *Barrabas*, Michael's generosity with his time, Bobbie's enthusiasm and Ernie's inexhaustible good nature had all combined to enrich my adventure.

Through all the drama of discovering the damage to the mast, the last-minute change of plan to enter port and the excitement of seeing Honolulu, I had pushed the Russian dilemma to the back of my mind, helped along by the knowledge that Igor Ponomarev was on the case.

Just before I left Honolulu, Nikolai Monko wrote to Louise stressing again that an inspection of the yacht was necessary and quoting various rules and regulations suggesting that the presence of an ice pilot on board was mandatory to assist with communications, navigation and search and rescue, should that become necessary. Nonetheless, the guidelines for shipping through the Northern Sea Route constantly referred to ships above 300 tonnes. This apparent contradiction still left us with some room to manoeuvre. Louise decided to insinuate herself into this narrow gap by writing directly to Roman Abramovich in London.

While *Barrabas* headed west in the balmy trades, Louise sent me an update on the Volvo Ocean Race fleet, now crunching into 15-foot seas and 30-knot winds 1,300 miles from Land's End. Conditions like that can be uncomfortable, but when racing a light displacement boat at the extreme limits of its performance reaching surfing speeds of 20 knots, conditions quickly become lethal. A Dutch crewman on ABN AMRO TWO was swept overboard. The yacht immediately mounted a search and rescue effort. Thirty-two–year-old Hans Horrevoets was located and lifted aboard. However, despite the efforts of fellow crewmembers to resuscitate him under the direction of medical advisors from Derriford Hospital in Plymouth, Horrevoets failed to regain consciousness and died. He was married with a young son. The tragedy brought home just how close I had come to death in similar circumstances. Louise added a caveat to her message: KEEP YOUR SAFETY HARNESS ON PLEASE!

Ernie Woodruff: Honolulu, Thursday 18th May 2006

Hi Louise,

Well it was sad to see Adrian leave. In a few short days, we had become good friends. However, it was also exciting to see him motoring out down the channel to the open sea. We raced around Magic Island to see him pass the last channel buoys and unfurl his jib. Barrabas was underway on a quiet sea with a steady breeze. He tells me that he will come back with you and the boys. I can say on behalf of Ivan and Michael that we will look forward to meeting you. You have done a sterling job in support of this challenge, and as ever, these things never work without the right team around you. Keep up the good work and stay in touch. Let Adrian know that we watched him out and he and the boat looked good.

CHAPTER 18

Magic Number

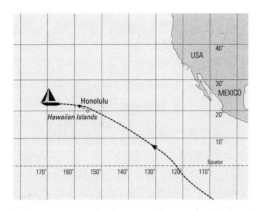

I lost myself in reading, beginning with Gerald Seymour's *Traitor's Kiss*. The reading helped time pass. I forgot the closeness of land and once again established my shipboard routine.

In Honolulu, I flushed and refilled the water tanks. The discharge was stagnant but not the bacterial soup I had been expecting. My water strategy from now was to take from the tanks and replenish using the watermaker to keep it fresh. Now being able to fill the kettle from the sink, clean with fresh water and, if I ran the engine, wash in hot water added huge comfort to my life on board. The new wind generator powering the batteries day and night meant I could use the watermaker more frequently.

During my shopping foray in Honolulu, I also bought a comb-through haircutter in Walmart. I tried it out on deck. When I checked in the mirror, I had inadvertently given myself a 'flat-top' cut – not bad. Feeling pretty pleased with myself, I finished *Traitor's Kiss* and started on Michael Connelly's *Lincoln Lawyer*.

My usual habit when dealing with delicate situations is not to rush. Ever since receiving the communiqué from Nikolai Monko, I had been turning the problem of the Russian permissions over in my mind. I decided to write to him directly and to copy the letter to the various people who had become involved. These included the Russian ambassador in London, the British ambassador in Moscow, Margaret Beckett

(then the British Foreign Secretary), Tony Blair, Igor Ponomarev, Sam
Laidlaw and Sergey Frank, the purpose being to apply subtle pressure.
It was important to give Monko options. I concluded the letter . . .

*. . . I do not wish to take unnecessary risk in making a transit of the NSR
and will only proceed if ice conditions are very favourable; the boat is strong
and well equipped; if it is possible to lay on a Russian escort vessel then
requirements for an ice pilot can be satisfied and safety measures ensured. I
trust you will appreciate the unique nature of my endeavour and consider it
worthy of making exceptions to the usual procedures governing vessels making
a transit of the NSR . . .*

While in Walmart, I made a second purchase, two small gold earrings,
one for me, the other for *Barrabas*. On rounding the Horn, a sailor is
entitled to wear a gold ring through the ear (or, if it's your preference,
through the nipple). The direction round the Horn determines which
ear. The ear (or nipple) closest to land gets the ring, in my case then,
the right ear. The confusion with latter-day fashion trends is that a ring
through the right ear signifies gayness in men, but since there was little
prospect of my being propositioned, this did not concern me.

In her press release following my successful doubling of the Horn,
Louise wrote . . . *'As for wearing an earring, I think Adrian will probably
pass!'* She knows me well, but clearly not that well. I had my ear
pierced in Honolulu. With difficulty, I fitted the ring having worn a
stud while the piercing healed (easier to rotate to keep the channel
clear). The other privileges bestowed on Cape Horners are the right to
piss to windward (presumably to avoid the streams of other pissers)
and to rest one foot on the table while making the loyal toast (providing the table is in the wardroom of a British warship). So, hooped and
bestowed, I drank a toast with one foot on the saloon table (seeing as
Barrabas was flying a British ensign and carried a weapon and live
ammunition, I decided she qualified for the occasion as a British warship) then went on deck to piss to windward.

The timing of my letter to Nikolai Monko coincided with the
indefatigable efforts of Ian Johnstone-Bryden. He had spoken with
Admiral Sir Jonathon Band's PA. She asked for an email confirming
the detail and promised to try to find a route to the Russian Navy at
high level. Ian also spoke to an old friend of his on HMS *Warrior* who
was on loan to CINCFLEET (Commander in Chief). Ian's contact
knew the personnel in the Royal Navy team who had rescued seven

Russian sailors trapped for three days in an AS28 mini submarine off the coast of the Kamchatka Peninsula in August 2005, after fishing nets ensnared the sub 190 metres below the surface.

The British six-man team led by Commander Ian Riches flew to Petropavlovsk from Prestwick Airport and managed to free the submarine after a tense six-hour operation using a Scorpio 45 ROV (Remotely Operated Vehicle) to cut through the nets. The Russian crew only had a few hours of oxygen left.

An internal message would go from them to the Admiral's office with their Russian contacts' details.

On the same day, 23rd May, Louise received a phone call from John A. Mann II in Moscow who handled public affairs for Millhouse, one of Roman Abramovich's companies. Roman Abramovich had tasked him with helping us out. A fluent Russian speaker, John promised to call Monko directly.

Ian Johnstone-Bryden: Tuesday 23rd May 2006

Hi Louise,

All of us, now thousands and maybe millions, following Adrian are immensely proud of his achievement. I am very pleased to have been a tiny help and pleased to see the threads coming together with the Russians.

The FCO lobbying from our embassy in Moscow will positively complement your direct communication with Monko and the very interesting approach from the Russian personalities. The latter will probably clinch things in the end because in Russia one hand washes the other and always has.

I am greatly encouraged that you will now have the help of the 1st Sea Lord. The Russian Navy owes the RN a favour or two for the rescue of the submariners and the Russian Navy still has precedence over civil Russian Agencies. They are also in a position to provide an escort vessel. I do not know which part of the RN will make the approach but Sir Jonathon Band is as high as you can go in RN ranks.

When you next email Adrian, you should bring him up to speed because I doubt he appreciates just how many people are working to help him achieve his dream.

Ian was right. Louise was on the ground working through the daily correspondence and shaping developments while I received the occasional précis, once removed from the action. I was amazed at how Louise had managed to generate the momentum she had, but not surprised. Her tremendous capacity to get on and do things without prevarication combined with her natural enthusiasm made her unstoppable.

Hurricane lamps had been on my final departure list but somehow slipped off my radar and never made it on board. Louise had included two lamps in the Honolulu consignment. The lamps cast a soft, buttery glow as night fell over the ocean. The light flickered over the cabin – warm, cosy, homely.

During every moment at sea, danger was my neighbour and fear was my shadow. I worried constantly about the threats around me: would I collide with a submerged container and hole the hull; would I stray into a whale-breeding ground and excite an attack; would a storm bring breaking waves and knock the boat down or worse, roll her over? Any mariner who does not fear the sea invites disaster. Now there was the additional concern about the rig – could it hold, could it take the sustained pressure of another 12,000 miles? To live with fear is a grinding, exhausting business. I listened perpetually to *Barrabas*, even as I slept, for any unfamiliar sound. I felt the movement of the boat, sensing impending change from myriad signals: the altered rush of water against her sides, her changed attitude, variation in her roll. What I was listening for was danger – had my neighbour come to call? If the worst happened, could I launch the life rafts in time, grab the panic bag, retrieve the emergency beacon and activate it properly? In Honolulu, I bought three sheathed hunting knives, items also overlooked on my final list. I wore the biggest of the three on a belt. Another I lashed to the outside of the cockpit cuddy (starboard side) and the third to the stanchion bars at the mast. These blades had a single purpose – to cut the bindings of the inflatable lift raft stowed on deck amidships and the hard dinghy lashed to the foredeck. The knives gave me comfort – they would save precious seconds in the desperate panic of abandoning *Barrabas*.

Conditions since leaving Honolulu continued to be near perfect with the wind astern at 12 knots, the sea a deep and glittering blue, the sun warm on my back.

Admiral Sir Jon Band's Flag Captain had talked the Russian situation over with the naval attaché in Moscow, who advised against a formal navy-to-navy approach. He believed this might encourage some searching questions about the Royal Navy's connections with the Alpha Global Expedition. This concern was in view of the very sensitive military installations along the NSR and the deteriorating political situation between Washington, London and Moscow. However, the

Flag Captain asked the commercial section at the embassy what they were doing to sort the situation, requesting that they keep him informed of progress so that he could report to the First Sea Lord.

Ian's opinion was that things had moved forward a notch. The combined efforts of the various threads in play might ultimately achieve a result.

Louise: Friday 26th May 2006

John (Mann) spoke to Monko who says he is simply not able to bend the rules for you even if he wanted to. They haven't had an accident since 1983 and are proud of that record! However, Monko did say that it might be possible to have an ice pilot on a separate boat at a cost. I have asked John to find out how much. He is getting back to me on Tuesday. He will also address the inspection issue with Monko although now that you are not going for non-stop it is a little hard to justify why an inspection would be a problem.

To me, this was a breakthrough. This concession towards an escort vessel implied a de facto agreement to let me try the NSR. Just as the breakthrough came, the wind died.

I called Louise to thank and congratulate her on progress so far.

'And guess what,' she said after telling me first that Benjamin was losing all his milk teeth. 'Yesterday, I took the boys to a craft fair and afterwards to see an open garden in Brill and who should be there directing people in to the car park – Sam Laidlaw!'

'You're kidding.' Brill was a hilltop village close to where we both lived.

'No kidding. Turns out it's his parents-in-law's place. Anyway, we had a good chat and he wants me to put him in touch with John Mann. Apparently, Sam knows Roman's two senior lieutenants and wants to chat it over with John.'

I stayed silent for a moment assimilating the coincidence. Or was it? With his recent move to Centrica as chief executive, he had dealings with the Russians. British Gas, wholly owned by Centrica, buys 30 per cent of its supplies from Russia; not surprising then that Sam would know all the big players in the Russian energy market.

Our conversation returned to the children. I knew Benji had been getting occasional headaches. 'How's Benji? I know it's futile but I worry like hell about that sort of thing, makes me feel very guilty for being out here.'

'Benji's fine. The headaches have gone, but there's a new issue.

Gabriel fell in the garden and hurt his arm. I did all the rotating and checking. I'm sure it isn't broken but I called David Skinner who said if he's complaining tomorrow I should take him in just in case it's a green stick.'

'God! How's he now?'

'Dosed up with Calpol and he seems fine, just a bit sore.'

While I was at the chart table, I logged my position – 2,400 miles to the antipodal point (AP). If I could cover 100 miles per day, I would reach the AP on 21st June, one day behind schedule. I could live with that but I still felt pressured, more so than at any other time during the voyage. The thumbscrew was the clock – seconds dribbling inexorably into the void. The wind had disappeared five days before, a full 50 per cent of the time since leaving Honolulu and with each breathless minute, my window for making the Bering Strait and the Arctic shrank. I had anticipated a fast run towards the AP, flying a spinnaker most of the way with boat speeds of five to six knots pretty much a foregone conclusion. The routing charts indicated a less than one per cent chance of westerly winds, but that is what I was experiencing. It was depressing and frustrating. The slower the boat travelled, the faster marine growth would colonise the hull in these tropical waters. Boat speed would erode, increasing time to target and closing my window even more. I tried to remain positive, cleaning the boat, checking the rig, servicing the engine, practising emergency evacuation procedures, planning ahead and corresponding. But mostly I read – escapism that ate time. I had just finished a book on psychocybernetics – first published in 1960, the year of my birth – by an American plastic surgeon, Maxwell Maltz MD. He died in 1975. Maltz was way ahead of his time in his evaluation of the self and what it means to be productive and happy as opposed to stressed. It was apposite reading. I reminded myself constantly that the lack of wind was not some celestial conspiracy to thwart my goal but nature working to nature's laws in which a lone yachtsman on a small boat was an irrelevance. I accepted (grudgingly) that I was at the mercy of some greater power and my mind bent to the Taoist belief that I must be as water and flow easily around obstructions rather than try too hard to roll them aside. But flow as I might, my eye was still drawn to the clock and the sweep of the hands around its face, leaking time.

I decided to head further south to find more stable wind. Perhaps I was floating too high on the top of the trade wind belt. Ricardo agreed

in a text message . . . *'Go further south to 19° north. More wind there . . .'*
(30/05 21.29 UCT)

Louise: Tuesday 30th May 2006
Gabriel was still in a certain amount of pain this morning so I took him to the hospital. He has a green stick fracture to the radial head. So it's a sling for a few days and then no contact sports (??!!) for three weeks, he will be fine for sports day at the end of term though. I am taking him back tomorrow for a check. So that's how I've spent my morning, he is having a quiet time at home today and then back to school tomorrow.

Put Sam in touch with John Mann. Spoke to Damian at the Foreign Office. They are also going to write a formal letter requesting assistance for you to their counterparts in Russia and setting target dates for chasing if they haven't heard.

Damian Thwaites, a senior staffer at the Russia Desk of the Foreign Office, had spearheaded the dialogue with the Russian authorities in London, particularly with the First Minister at the Russian Embassy in London, Andrey Chupin.

Adrian: Wednesday 31st May 2006
I'm very upset about Gabo's arm – I feel useless out here (I am useless out here!) Heavy guilt feelings going on now.

Louise: Wednesday 31st May 2006
Don't feel guilty, these things happen – they are boys after all! I took Gabe back to the JR and he is feeling much better. He doesn't even want to wear the sling but I am insisting that he does at school this week if for no other reason than the other children don't knock him. The doctor said it should be fully healed in 2–3 weeks.

So with that, I rummaged through my library with the 'stay positive' message from Max Maltz still ringing in my head. While *Barrabas* found her way south towards latitude 19° north, I lay in my bunk and got lost in Afghanistan reading: Khaled Housseini's *The Kite Runner*.

On a small boat, anxiety comes from either the brutish assault of heavy weather or the mind-numbing frustration of windless conditions. The pleasure is milked from somewhere between these extremes. The light winds continued through the first days of June. *Barrabas* crawled along at two knots. The sound of slatting sails grated on my nerves. I sat there, locked down in my still, oceanic prison with no means of escape.

I slept doused in sweat but woke at dawn. We had just passed 19° north. The wind, as though contained behind an invisible wall began to blow. True wind touched 22 knots. Apparent wind on the sails showed 15 knots, my new threshold for bending in the first reef but the wind had to be consistent. It kept dropping off to 12 knots. *Barrabas* skewered the water under full sail.

At 6.25 pm local time, we crossed the International Date Line – 24 hours disappeared. I would get them back when I re-crossed the date line sailing northeast towards the Bering Strait. First, I needed to make the AP and then get onto a northeasterly heading.

Louise: Friday 2nd June 2006

I love my presents – I am wearing my necklace as I type this. What a lovely treat. The boys were very excited when they got their letters and shirts.

I have been watching the tapes using my video camera on the TV. Boys and I watched your message to us. Yes . . . I cried. The boys thought you were actually talking to them and were kissing the screen. I am now working through and cataloguing each tape.

A few more miles south then I gybed the main, putting the boat onto starboard tack. My plan was to recover northing back up to 19° north and then goosewing again onto a heading of 260°, thereby describing a gentle zigzag course. Running dead downwind created too much roll. Offsetting the stern a little to the following swell smoothed the ride. We hummed along at seven knots. Dense banks of low cloud channelled the wind. Gradually, *Barrabas* clawed back some of the lost time. The trick was to strike the right balance between making the miles without stressing the rig. I loosened the lower shrouds so that the intermediates and cap (upper) shrouds took most of the strain.

If my problems with windless conditions were frustrating, a shocking reminder of the vagaries of life on land arrived in an email from Louise.

Louise: Monday 5th June 2006

Nikki just rang me and told me two weeks ago they were burgled while she was alone with the children at night. They came into her bedroom and took all her jewellery. She is devastated.

Nikki and Paul lived in rural Suffolk. The idea of strangers poking around in the dark while the children slept was appalling, the more so to me cocooned in *Barrabas* with nobody else around for hundreds of miles. I went on deck savouring the peace and serenity of my environment. The message from Nikki reminded me that this time, this experience, was limited. I had to enjoy it.

The combined anxieties of deadlines, typhoons, the ongoing Russian saga and my imagined delicacy of the rig ganged up on me. For the first time on the voyage, I became ill. Simultaneously, a nasty sty developed on my eye, a huge boil erupted on my backside and on 6th June, just as the log tripped over to 20,000 miles, I went down with stomach cramps. My health has always been robust, probably helped by regular exercise since the age of eight – rugby, running, gym work and latterly cycling kept me in reasonably good shape. At 5 foot 9 inches and broad-shouldered, my weight rarely went above 160 lbs. Injuries, yes – I now kept both wrists permanently strapped and I was ever conscious of my right shoulder – but I had not been ill, until now. Fever pushed beads of sweat out of my skin, weakness pervaded my body, lethargy set in so that even raising a book to read required concerted effort.

I figured the stomach bug had come from drinking the tank water. From now on, I would divert the watermaker output direct to clean 10-litre jerry cans and use the tank water only for washing, filling the kettle and as emergency reserve.

My days became long. Most of the time I lay naked on my bunk, a quick-dry towel spread beneath me to absorb the sweat running in rivulets down my face, neck and chest. With the steady trades bowling us along, we continued gaining back lost time. Clear of any shipping lanes and landmasses, *Barrabas* was free to sail on with little for me to do on deck. The title of the book I was reading pretty well summed up the state of my existence, *The Agony and the Ecstasy*, though of much greater interest was the story of Michelangelo it described. Beautifully written as a biographic novel by Irving Stone, Michelangelo's life fascinated me. I knew something of the trials and tribulations he had endured during his life, but as with T. E. Lawrence, my knowledge of Michelangelo was sketchy.

Both these men were victors and victims of their time. They sought and struggled towards their own concept of perfection, often ridiculed through the jealousies of lesser men. Each was possessed of a kind of rage that fermented within, then burst forth and found expression in their respective pursuit of fulfilment.

They shared a respect for the beneficent face of authority, but were openly, if foolishly, irreverent of that other side: establishment's capacity for deceit. Michelangelo particularly had an enormous re-source for compassion, tempered by a dismissive intolerance of what he considered the lacklustre, the impotent, the mediocre and the im-pure as pertained to art.

Each was in his way possessed by an inability to compromise on principle, driven to displease the appeasers and the disciples of con-vention. Both incurred the exasperation of those many with neither the wit nor vision to see beyond the low walls of their own limitations and unable to understand the greater needs, sensitivities and drive of those earmarked by destiny.

If I took out any reference to greatness, I could certainly identify with the foibles of these two men. As days passed, I rolled between moments of joy and incredulity that I had managed to come as far as I had on *Barrabas*. It seemed inconceivable that I was out in the ocean alone. But like a drug high, the euphoria dumped me down into the troughs of despair – had I bitten off more than I could chew? Could I deliver on the promise? Could I finally fulfil myself in the only way I had dreamed since childhood?

I knew I was on a fever-fuelled rollercoaster made reckless in the absence of tempering advice from other people. I could have reached for the medical kit and dosed up on broad-spectrum antibiotics, but equally I knew that I would emerge stronger if I let the fever work itself out.

Louise, by some weird form of telepathy, seemed to sense my sudden zeal.

Louise: Wednesday 7th June 2006

I know you are apprehensive about the Arctic. Since you rounded the Horn west-about solo . . . YOU CAN DO ANYTHING. I believe in your ability 1,000 per cent whatever obstacles are thrown your way.

Boys really enjoyed the cricket last night so we will make that a regular thing. I will buy Benji his own bat as he shows a real interest. He says that cricket is his favourite followed by golf then footie then rugby.

Only four more tapes to watch. Your tapes are even better than Coronation Street *(boys hooked now!) or* Big Brother *(on again and addicted). I am loving every second and am not ever fast-forwarding.*

Sam Laidlaw had been in touch with Eugene Shvidler at Roman Abramovich's office to reinforce Louise's request for assistance. At the same time, Damian Thwaites asked the British Consul-General in Moscow to intercede with the Russian Ministry of Foreign Affairs. She in turn met with Sergey Krutikov, chief of UK–Russia bilateral relations. Krutikov promised to begin consultations immediately. Damian himself would follow up with Andrey Chupin.

While all this was going on, England beat Uruguay 1–0 in their opening game of the World Cup. I stayed horizontal, seeing off Michelangelo and racing through Campbell Armstrong's Jig trilogy, *Jig, Jigsaw* and *Heat*.

In the area of the Pacific we were sailing, submarine mountain ranges disturbed surface water flow, particularly when an aggressive wind whipped across the top. I made a navigational error going south of Wake Island. The waves were steep and breaking over the mountain ridges and summits, coming at me from different angles. Twice, cross-seas caught *Barrabas* in a pincer movement – one wave breaking against her port quarter and the other against her starboard side, slewing her round then tipping her dangerously over to one side. Everything loose in the cabin went flying. After eight days of good winds with daily mileages in excess of 100, a massive low-pressure system a thousand miles north began stealing the wind, leaving me with dribbles.

I noticed that the wind generator was rocking. Its mounting pole extended nine feet above the deck to allow clearance for the propeller. The mounting pole was in two parts screwed together at the mid-point. I had to take the wind gen down. This involved clambering up onto the after frame supporting the solar panels – precarious, particularly while the boat was rolling, and awkward given the weight of the wind gen. Nonetheless, I managed it, unscrewed the pole, introduced a quick-setting epoxy into the tread and reassembled the pole.

A cruise ship passed close by, two miles off my starboard side, presumably en route to Honolulu. It gave me quite a shock. I had gone on deck for some air to escape the stifling cabin and there it was, this oasis of bright lights. I thought about the passengers on board sitting down to three-course dinners, taking hot showers, sleeping in beds. The luxuries of everyday life had receded to distant figments. I was missing trees again and flowers and riding a bicycle and seeing the way the sun can glint off a girl's hair and the smell of cut grass and the hubbub of conversation in a crowded room . . .

David Skinner: Tuesday 13th June 2006
Sounds like a gastro problem from dodgy water together with rundown secondary to this and sty etc. Could take penicillin for eye but key is good water.

My reporting of the fever elicited a large response from various people around the world. One in particular came from Bob Kahn MD in Pacific Palisades, California. A yacht racer with over 100,000 sea miles, Bob had also been medical adviser to Brad van Lieu, a competitor in the 1998 and 2002 Around Alone races. Bob's advice was . . . *'Re: eye sty . . . it is a bacterial infection . . . suggest if you have it, antibiotics and hot water soaks, do not squeeze! Re abdominal symptoms . . . no solid food . . . liquids only till improves.'* I had not eaten solid food for four days.

Our friend Rose Dale took an alternative approach. She wrote to Louise . . . *'Has Adrian got any Marmite – sorts out a sty pretty quickly!'*

I detest only a few things and Marmite is one of them.

Adrian: Thursday 15th June 2006
What am I supposed to do with the Marmite (if I had any, which I don't. I place it in the same category of appeal as raw sewage) – shove it in my eye? Thank Rose anyway.

Louise called to tell me that Gabriel swept the board at his sports day! I wrote back.

Adrian: Sunday 16th June 2006
Hi . . . so pleased about Gabo . . . here's something you can read to him . . .

'My darling Gabo

Mummy telephoned me on my boat and told me that you did very well at sports day and that you won three races and came second in the other one. I am so proud of you Gabriel. I wish I had been at school to see you, but next

year I will be there shouting and cheering. You make me very happy. I love
you, Daddy.'

I still have stomach cramps and fever. I woke this morning and the towel I
lie on was completely soaked. It's beginning to get on my wick!

I am 600 miles from the AP, so 6 days 'til I make my turn for the Bering
Strait providing wind stays.

According to Ricardo's assessment, the wind would hold and then, once I made the turn, curve around pushing me towards the Bering Strait for a while. He also reported an 'all clear' on typhoons, but the Caribbean had just seen its first hurricane of the season.

The abdominal pain persisted. Every time I stood up, sweat erupted. I decided not to mention it any more to Louise. If it did not clear up on its own pretty soon, I would have to take antibiotics. Heavy cloud and squalls moved in all around us. When a shower came over, I went on deck and managed to wash my hair. It was pretty darn cold but at least I was clean.

I was somewhere in the northeastern Pacific, southeast of Japan – precisely where, I could not be certain because I was now navigating with the sextant. My GPS was alive and well (as were the three hand-held back-up units), but for want of some neural stimulation and to put theory into practice, I decided to navigate a 1,000-mile passage and then check my derived position against the GPS. Aside from the elemental enjoyment of navigating by means of the sun, there was the more serious consideration of acquiring a skill that might one day be critical. Once, when I was crew on a yacht sailing the English Channel en route to France, the ship's GPS failed. Two of the crew were carrying personal hand-held GPS units. Both failed. Luckily, we were close enough to the French coast to identify landmarks against the chart and navigate to a safe harbour. But what if . . . no one on board knew which way up to hold a sextant!

The great pioneering sailing soloists – Slocum, Dumas, Chichester, Knox-Johnston, Moitessier and Blyth among others, my role models – did not have electronic navigation aids. Navigating by the sun, moon and stars compromises precision by comparison with GPS but that electronic sheath of insulation had kept me from fully appreciating the glorious contrivance of the universe to lead sailors across the feature-less sea.

During the exercise, we reached another huge milestone. At 5.00 am local time on 19th June, the log clicked to 21,600 nautical miles – a magic number. We had sailed the distance equivalent to the circumference of the earth!

That night as I turned in, the stomach pains were severe. I slept long and late. The next milestone followed that morning. At 8.40 am local time, we reached the antipodal point at position 24°.11′ north 143°.22′ east (I used the GPS for confirmation). *Barrabas* had hauled back all the ground lost through the earlier calms. Down came the spinnaker pole and the goose-winged sail arrangement. I put *Barrabas* onto starboard tack, course 027°, close-hauling for the first time since Cape Horn in a 12-knot east-northeast breeze. This singular event marked the end of one phase and the beginning of another. We were heading north towards the Arctic.

CHAPTER 19

Bearing Up

Typhoons (translated from Chinese to mean 'great wind') can develop suddenly and move with ferocious velocity. My immediate objective was to get to latitude 30° north. For the moment, only the warm zephyrs of the dragon's breath propelled us along.

The Jordan Series Drogue was my main defence against a typhoon – 300 feet of 1½-inch braided line stitched with 160 mini-drogues each of 8-inch diameter. The drogue, deployed aft, would bring *Barrabas*'s stern to wind, reducing the risk of capsize, or worse, a full rollover through 360°. It would also slow the boat (carrying no sail or just a handkerchief of headsail). The multiple mini-drogues, variously deployed through all the phases of a moving wave, would create an elastic effect like a giant bungee. A larger, single drogue collapsing and inflating with the passage of a wave could exert sudden and massive shock loading.

Rogue waves and tsunamis posed other dangers. The spawning grounds for these monsters were the Izu-Ogasawara and Japan trenches running along Japan's eastern seaboard, submarine cracks in the earth's crust 10 miles beneath *Barrabas*'s keel. Living in Yokohama as a child, I remembered the frequency of earth tremors as these tectonic plates jarred and slid against one another. A teacher's instruction to get under our desks as the classroom vibrated was almost as routine as basic arithmetic or playing marbles in the wire-meshed recreation compound.

A high-pressure system around us stilled the air. For now, the dragon slept.

Moving beyond the range of the northeast trades, the winds would become much more variable, particularly the 600-mile-wide band of the 'horse latitudes' between 30° and 40° north. Horse-carrying ships, plagued by the frequent calms and soaring summer temperatures at these latitudes, often ran low on water, insufficient to sustain crew and livestock. The horses went over the side or into the pot.

On the same day as I made my turn for the Arctic, Benji was watching England draw 2–2 with Sweden in the World Cup.

I waited for civil twilight. I had pre-computed where to find Jupiter and picked it up on the sextant when I couldn't see it with the naked eye. It was exciting, and my first planet sighting. I took and reduced the sight and applied it to that day's sun-run-sun. Running fixes are a bit woolly. I narrowed our position by running the Jupiter plotline back to my second sun sight's transposed plotline. The result compared quite favourably with the GPS.

The high-pressure system shepherding us continued delivering very light winds at four to seven knots. I was back to excruciatingly slow progress. The previous batch of stalling winds before reaching the AP had forced me to re-evaluate my schedule, to make the AP by the end of June. By recouping the losses and hitting the AP on 20th June, I allowed myself the delusion of a 10-day cushion. I worked hard to keep *Barrabas* moving, constantly gybing the sails. After yet another gybe of the goosewinged sails, which meant dropping the poled out headsail and re-rigging the spinnaker pole on the other side, sweat was steaming off me. The practised drill, 10 minutes' hard effort on deck, resulted in the loss of a litre of sweat! Just as I finished, I heard the Iridium text message alert.

Ricardo: Saturday 24th June 2006

TYPHOON WARNING!!!: something is brewing only 200 miles north-west of you. Not yet official, but it could cause unstable, unexpected wind shifts, and weird seas. Keep course over ground 060°.

I had to get back east, to a waypoint at the junction of 150° east longitude and latitude 30° north. The thought of a typhoon gathering so close filled me with dread, colliding as it did with memories of the

Cape Horn storm. A broach or worse, another capsize, and the mast might snap.

A round of thumping headaches alerted me to the danger of dehydration. The fever still raged on. When had I last eaten? Days ago, six or seven. I began reading David Cowper's book *Northwest Passage Solo*, describing the hazards and dangers of Canada's Arctic corridor. It made salutary reading and a convincing argument in support of my decision to opt for the Northern Sea Route instead. It took David four seasons over three years to get through the Northwest Passage from east to west.

For the moment though, my focus centred on the typhoon risk. Ricardo's next text gave me some reassurance.

Ricardo: Sunday 25th June 2006

Typhoon not yet official on the Japan Meteo site but conditions are in place for something to happen soon . . . you will not be hit directly but it may cause irrational wind shifts and weird seas.

Instead of dwelling on what might happen, I distracted myself by concentrating on my sextant navigation exercise. My final derived position after 1,048 nautical miles put me 2.8 miles north of actual and approximately 1.5 miles west of actual. So, all in all, not a bad result!

Aside from the typhoon threat, my other concern was negotiating the Aleutian Islands, the passes between the islands made treacherous by powerful rip tides streaming through the narrow gaps. The massive depths of the Aleutian Trench on the southern side of the chain suddenly shoaled up to the islands, creating the potential for huge seas. It was another forbidding ordeal in store. My plan was to stay well out to the west and track along the Russian/USA boundary to avoid the narrow passes.

Aside from dealing with the damn fever, typhoon threats, growing anxiety about the Aleutian Islands and the frustrations of no wind, I kept up a continual dialogue with Louise about developments with the Russians. The diplomatic machine ground ponderously along. The Alpha Global Expedition was hardly a priority in the greater scheme of Anglo–Russian bilateral relations, but to me, it was the centre of my universe and the lack of news made me think that nothing was happening.

'I'll write to everyone. Well, to you and you can copy it out,' I said to Louise.

'What'll you write?'

'Ask some questions, get Mr Monko to start thinking about the practicalities of my actually making the transit.'

'I'm onto everybody all the time, hammering away. They're probably all sick of me by now.'

'We'll keep bashing on.'

'The problem I'm going to have is raising money for the escort.'

'We can worry about that when everything's in place.'

'What are your questions?'

'First, has Monko definitively agreed to an ice pilot on an escort boat? Second, because time is tight, can we forgo the inspection, and third, from where to where along the NSR do I need to be escorted?'

'I think you'll have to go in for an inspection. You stopped in Honolulu, so it doesn't matter now.'

'True, but worth asking if only to save time.'

I also wanted to start moving forward with the question of where an escort vessel would come from: Russian Navy, Russian Coast Guard or more likely a charter of a commercial fishing boat or coastal trader. I wrote the letter, emailed it to Louise and she dispatched it onwards.

When it landed on John Mann's desk in Moscow, he called Nikolai Monko. The answer to the first question was a definitive 'yes'. The escort would accompany me from Chukotka in Siberia to the Straits of Novaya Zemlya. As for the nature of the escort, Nikolai Monko referred John to a Mr Zuev, an experienced mariner who he had instructed to put together a proposal for the escort. This latest development was encouraging. But John's take was . . . *'He [Zuev] is taking his time about it but I will call him again and try to speed him up . . .'*

In the meantime, Ian had followed up on his initiative with the Royal Navy.

Ian Johnstone-Bryden: Tuesday 27th June 2006

I have spoken with the RN today and agreed a form of email which I have sent this morning marked priority that can be forwarded to the Defence Team in Moscow by Jon Band's Flag Captain.

Reading the correspondence, I think you are very close to a breakthrough with the Russians. It is now a question of whether it will come through in time.

I have asked that the Defence Team come up with suitable Russian Navy

and Coastguard contacts that FCO should be able to talk to or provide for you
to pass on to your contacts in Moscow to follow through on.

It is always very frustrating trying to work out where things are going and
where to apply pressure but the RN reps will either talk directly to the
Russians or provide the Embassy commercials with the information and
encourage them to follow through. As Monko appears to have warmed to the
concept of an escort vessel etc, all approaches should prove complementary.
My feeling is that you are now pushing on a slowly opening door.

What we did not know and could not ask was whether Roman
Abramovich or Sergey Frank had taken any direct action with their
personal contacts within the Russian administration and particularly
within the Politburo itself.

I had thought that music would be an indispensable part of my days
and nights, but it turned out to be less so than I'd imagined. First, my
concern about power consumption – the amplifier drank electricity –
made me cautious. More than that, the sea sang its own song; its
tempo, pitch and volume as varied and infinite as the potential for any
composer with a handful of notes to arrange.

By the end of June, I began feeling chilly at night as we climbed
north above 30° north and east past 150° east longitude. The threat
from typhoons receded as *Barrabas* scampered away from danger. For
the first time in weeks, I slept with the lightweight sleeping bag open
as a cover. As I gazed through the open hatch at the stars pin-holing
the black vault of the night sky, listening to Albinoni's Adagios, I was
thinking about the ice. The Arctic ice mass would be beginning to
break up at its coastal extremities. The Centre for Marine and Atmospheric Research at the University of Hamburg predicted the ice
receding to an historic minimum during the oncoming summer of
2006.

Andrey Kechashin at Sovcomflot in Moscow had also been in touch
with Nikolai Monko. Northern Sea Route Administration was for the
moment insisting that I put into port, probably Provideniya, for an
inspection. Their ice forecast for the summer optimistically mirrored
Hamburg's view. They reckoned the Vil'kitskiy Strait, the critical point
of the transit, would clear of ice. It was early days, but we needed to
sort out an escort boat and quickly. If I got the green light, how would
we pay for it? We would need as much time as possible to find
funding.

On Friday 30th June, I started wearing clothes again, just a T-shirt

and baggy cotton trousers. A depression closed from the west bringing
24-knot winds. I set *Barrabas* to run downwind along its eastern side.
She bolted away, getting up to nine knots, fast for her and good for
me. I checked back through my log – 10 days since I had eaten solid
food. The muscles of my stomach, chest and shoulder now stood out
in sharp relief and my face was gaunt. Sir Chay Blyth had lost his
appetite completely during his circumnavigation in 1970/71 and had to
force food down. I figured I had better do the same so I made lunch of
sardine spaghetti! When I'd eaten, I felt sick and a thunderous headache began rampaging around inside my head.

  While England prepared to play Portugal in the World Cup quarter-
finals, John Mann had been onto Mr Zuev. Early enquiries highlighted
the difficulties of finding a suitable escort vessel. Zuev had reviewed
several options, concluding that a tugboat offered the best solution. As
for the cost, Zuev hoped to get back to John by the middle of the following week.

John Mann: Friday 30th June 2006
*That's the latest information I have. I explained to Zuev that people are
getting nervous, with just a few short weeks until Adrian's arrival. He asked
me to pass along the message not to worry as he's confident everything can be
resolved in time.*

I sure hoped so!
  During the preceding weeks, a debate had been going on in the
sailing media about the precise requirements of a 'true' circumnavigation. The first 'human-powered' circumnavigation was coming
to a head with question marks against the routes of some of those
making claims. One self-styled 'authority' asked me to comment. The
requirements seemed obvious to me (though my interpretation of
certain aspects fell foul of the official rules that I had chosen to disregard
anyway). In my opinion, the track of a true circumnavigation had to
contain at least one pair of antipodal points. I was pleased to get a
message (forwarded by Louise) from Sir Francis Chichester's son, Giles,
a member of the European Parliament and an experienced yachtsman.

Giles Chichester MEP: Friday 30th June 2006
*My father was a very good and particular navigator. He placed great store on
having passed through two antipodal points during his 1966–67
circumnavigation. So good for Adrian in being similarly proud of doing it.*

Running before the seas with the boom out wide and the mainsail tacked down at the fourth reef, akin to a storm trysail, the boat was still heading up into wind. I had to drop the mainsail. A preventer line stopped the boom from swinging inboard if the boat accidentally gybed. Attached to the aft end of the boom, the preventer ran to a block on the foredeck then back to the cockpit. To drop the main, I needed to centre the boom then heave-to. I had the boom halfway in when a wave crashed up behind in the pitch black. I could only see the luminescent froth as the crest broke a few feet astern. The rush of water beneath the hull gripped the skeg and the keel and with a mighty flick spun the boat through 120°, putting the wind in front of the small area of mainsail. Then the preventer failed.

Time slowed to flow like molasses, sensations and awareness focused to sharp points, thought processes became magically lucid and accelerated. The boom was crashing inboard at alarming speed. I desperately worked the main sheet in the cockpit. I managed to duck as the boom flew across the cockpit – I sensed it more than saw it. Its flight caused the main sheet to slacken. On *Barrabas*, the main sheet controlling the boom runs through a block attached to the traveller on deck and up to another block attached to the underside of the boom. The line relays between the two blocks eight times through sheaves set within the blocks, both ends of the line emerging from the lower of the two blocks. This arrangement set up a ratio of forces so that I could haul the boom inboard, even with the full mainsail flying under tremendous load. The eight runs of line momentarily transformed from a regimented series into a viper's nest of tangled rope. I let go of the sheet, which then caught around my right shoulder. As the boom went over and the sheet began to tighten, it gripped my right arm and shoulder, bodily lifting me from the cockpit and smashing me back against the cockpit coaming. My shoulder kept going, up, out and away. At the precise moment when my shoulder reached maximum stretch and where dislocation was the inevitable next step, the boom stopped with a loud whipping crack as the main sheet became taut. If I had not taken the sheet in as much as I had, it might have ripped my shoulder clean out of its socket. It was a severe, excruciating wrench. For the next two days, I couldn't lift my right arm more than a few inches away from my body.

To make matters worse, I called Louise. England had lost their World Cup quarter-final to Portugal on penalties! (Ricardo was delighted.)

I collapsed into my bunk, cold, miserable and in pain. As ever, I found refuge in a book, this time *Shadow of the Wind* by Carlos Ruiz Zafón, and then finally slept until 5.30 am.

In the dim, misty morning, I came on deck to adjust the Hydrovane. To my astonishment, a huge tanker lumbered past less than one mile astern! I had been on deck 10 minutes before but never saw the ship! I called on the VHF.

'Did you see me on radar?'

'Yes, but only just. You were a very small contact.'

'Easy to miss?'

'Very easy to miss.'

Great, I thought, I'm in a steel boat with a 50-foot steel mast acting as a bloody great radar reflector and these guys have difficulty seeing me!

The wind continued blowing relentlessly at 28 knots. I rigged the storm jib and tied off the headsail furling drum to take the tension off the tricing line.

The latest GRIB showed the west wind curling north and spiralling into a revolving low-pressure system, the centre passing directly overhead with wind speeds accelerating to 37 knots. From experience, I knew these wind speeds would be conservative. Another low-pressure system sat northeast of my position. A narrow high-pressure ridge ran between the two lows. If the depressions collided . . .

I telephoned Louise, gave my position and asked her to call the British Meteorological Office and get them to have a look. Weather bombs are the most severe of all winter storms, characterised as intense low-pressure systems with a central pressure that falls 24 millibars or more in a 24-hour period. Something similar had caused the 1979 Fastnet disaster. That race took place in August and here I was in the northern hemisphere summer. The 1998 Sydney to Hobart race catastrophe came about by three low-pressure systems colliding. I didn't like the look of the forecast.

I checked the drogue. I hated to phone Louise with this kind of thing, but with Ricardo away racing in the tall ships race, I had little choice. Louise said she was going to call him also.

Ricardo: Monday 3rd July 2006

I am in Weymouth getting cleaned up and ready for the tall ships. All ok. Sorry to hear about your shoulder.

You should be in light airs now. That is because you are in between lows. 500 miles to the west of you there is a vicious little 997 brewing and she is heading directly for you. Expect variable wind directions since the centre of the system will be going over you. Max wind speed 40kn. I also think the seas will be really confused and quite large at times between now and Wednesday.

I comforted myself by baking a loaf of bread and eating two slices with my homemade anchovy paste (anchovies, mayonnaise and chilli sauce mixed).

The wind bounced around, never staying in the same place for long. Since making the turn at the AP, the unreliability of the weather, our stop-start progress, the nasty depressions and the pain in my shoulder drove my sense of humour away. God, I hated this voyage! Maybe I was delusional, but I got the distinct feeling *Barrabas* had had enough too.

Heavy rain pounded against the coach house, reducing visibility to half a mile. I switched on the radar. A distinct contact lay three miles off my port side. Despite repeated attempts to raise the ship on VHF Channel 16, there was no response.

The grinding wind did not stop. The sky turned a low malevolent purple. The reduced visibility added to the risk. I gave up calling the ship and manoeuvred past.

A ray of light in my otherwise dark world came in an email with the latest update from Northern Sea Route Administration.

Andrey Kechashin: Wednesday 5th July 2006
Reply received today from Mr. Nikolai Monko:
'Dear Andrey Mikhailovich, good day.
The authorization for the yacht guiding through the seaways of NSR could be granted provided the following terms and conditions are fulfilled:
1. The yacht should be escorted. An ice pilot will be on board the escort vessel.
2. The inspection of the yacht could be carried out at sea by the ice pilot and the master of the escort vessel.
3. The agreement with Murmansk Shipping Company for yacht guiding through the seaways of NSR should be signed.
4. Navigation through the NSR to be carried out in ice-free waters.'

Had banging on about attempting the NSR *only* if the passage was clear of ice given Mr Monko assurance? I liked to think so. The Murmansk Shipping Company controlled the icebreaker fleet operating in the western part of the NSR where I would be most likely to encounter problems. I knew that an agreement with MSCo was mandatory. The idea of an inspection at sea would save time.

Great news – the stage was set for me to become the first yachtsman to enter Russia's Arctic waters single-handed. However, my immediate concern was still with the approaching depression. It had formed into a tightly packed ball of isobars. Ricardo's description of the system as a 'vicious little 997' was partially right: vicious, yes, but little, no. This thing was 800 miles across, wider than the length of the UK from John O'Groats to Land's End!

Winds climbed to 35 knots, heaping the sea into a lumpy, rucked carpet. I prepared the boat for the onslaught: storm covers over the hatches, deck inspected, repair on the mast checked, cabin stowed, bread made, JSD ready for deployment, storm jib rigged for a quick hoist. I felt like an expectant father counting down the hours: two down, eight to go!

Everywhere, water dripped in, from the windows and hatches, the companionway, through-deck fittings leaking into the headlining and the water finding its way out through the sides. There was one leak over the chart table. I stuffed clothes around the windows and along the sides of the headlining.

During the night while I tried to relax (impossible) reading John le Carré's *Absolute Friends*, a loud knocking started up from the starboard side deck. I grabbed my oilskins and rushed on deck, squatting and listening. The knocking came again. I edged towards it. The anchoring anode was rolling back and forth, clattering into the toe-rail. Phew! I tied it down and retreated below.

The threatening storm dissipated and fractured before reaching *Barrabas* as we desperately scuttled northeastwards, but the winds continued blowing between 30 and 40 knots, piling the seas into hillocks of cresting water. Some kind of wave strike was inevitable, but I couldn't stand watch 24 hours.

It came at 5.00 am on Saturday the 8th July, a massive wave strike on the starboard side. Everything on the saloon table flew off, even a broad, flat-bottomed tray with sides lower than the finials on the table. *Barrabas* heeled to 70°. Water cascaded through the chinks and cracks at the edges of the closed companionway hatch. Not again! I tore out of my sleeping bag to get to the chart table. Water sloshed as high as the radar screen, computer screen, radio, keyboard and switch panel.

I dried everything off quickly and inspected the computer compartment beneath the hinged chart table. It seemed to be dry. I needed a weather GRIB. The computer worked, dispatching my email request into the ether. I waited a few minutes, then went into email and dialled out to see if the new GRIB had arrived. An error-screen appeared. When I rebooted, a message popped up telling me there was no signal. The computer then went to sleep, and that's as far as I got. Water must have got into the machine somewhere. The computer never recovered. I went to the back-up laptop.

I reproached myself (harshly and loudly). After my experience at Cape Horn, I had organised a defence against just such an event but I hadn't put it into place. In Honolulu, I'd bought a transparent plastic shower curtain (Walmart $5.99) and hooks that I'd screwed into the cabin headlining around the companionway hatch to hang the shower curtain. The arrangement of hooks created folds in the curtain to catch incoming water, which then slid harmlessly to the cabin floor.

Somehow, the mainsail's leech line had run through. The leech (trailing edge) was flapping like a maddened wing transmitting vibrations through the whole boat: mast, deck and hull. *Barrabas* weighed in at 15 tonnes. The forces were huge and although Kemp had constructed extremely strong sails, much more of this and damage to the sailcloth might be critical. However, I could sense the wind easing so instead of dropping the main and killing boat speed, I snuffed the flogging by moving the mainsheet right up to the windward side of the traveller to put a twist into the sail and then tightened the fourth reefing pennant to tension the leech.

The Bering Strait beckoned, 1,523 miles to the north. I called Louise. She and the boys were off to a fête in the neighbouring village of Cuddington. We had all gone along the previous year. The thought of being at an English village fête in the summertime filled me with joy. I tried not to dwell on the weeks and months still ahead. The distance and time seemed unendurable. Instead, I suspended myself in the present, moment by moment.

The wind quietened. At last, I managed a decent sleep, climbing into my sleeping bag at 7.00 pm and not emerging until 8.00 am the following morning.

A combination of changing factors kept me pinned down in a black mood: the loss of the main computer, no word from Zuev despite his repeated promises of finding an escort vessel, and now the Russians were insisting I had a valid visa (how the hell was I supposed to get a visa?). The effort to stay cool became increasingly difficult as the seconds turned to minutes turned to hours turned to days of lost time. As a 'treat', I put on the cabin heating.

Occasionally, just when I needed it most, some fillip would arrive through the post.

Campbell Armstrong: Sunday 9th July 2006

I read your reports and enjoy them enormously – I'm having a vicarious adventure, so it seems, and your descriptions of the sea, and your own fortitude, solitude and resolve are wonderful to read. The sea is sometimes cast as a demon, other times a benign but utterly unpredictable ally, or even a spiteful bully you need to beware of. I imagine the long nights, the emptiness of ocean, the vastness of sky – and you, sailing on and on. I wish you well and safe voyage, safe return.

To give myself a solid target to aim for, I set a deadline of August 10th, exactly one month away, to be on station at the Bering Strait. A distance of 2,300 nautical miles separated Provideniya from Novaya Zemyla across the length of Russia's Northern Sea Route. If I could travel at an average speed of three knots for twenty hours within each 24-hour period, with four hours stationary for sleep, we'd cover 60 miles per day. I needed 38 days, say 40 days, with two days' grace to travel the 2,300 miles. Forty days from August 10th took me to September 19th. The re-freeze would begin around September 16th.

A grand total of 1,800 miles separated us from Provideniya, and 31 days to do it, an average of 58 miles VMG (velocity made good) per day. Since turning at the antipodal point, the daily VMG averaged out at 63 miles. So, despite the seemingly slow speed and apparent abundance of time, the reality based on performance was touch and go as to whether I could make it.

Barrabas had slogged through 23,000 miles. Maintenance became of a more pressing necessity. I went to the top of the mast to string 'halyard preventers' between the mast steps and the shrouds to stop the main halyard from wrapping round the steps. I also inspected the rigging aloft and noticed severe chafing to the headsail halyard on its sheave. I dropped the headsail with *Barrabas* hove-to, cut off 18 inches, retied the halyard with a bowline and then re-hoisted the headsail.

Louise: Monday 10th July 2006

I am sure as every day passes you are feeling more and more apprehensive about your Arctic approach. Hopefully our issues can be resolved by the end of this week and we will know how to proceed. You have lots of people behind you now. You are not alone and as I keep saying . . . every day out there is a day closer to home.

After five days of battling storm fronts, nature finally gave me a break. The trail of these fronts left the wind blowing from the northeast, precisely the direction I needed to be sailing, so for the moment *Barrabas* made no appreciable gains towards the Bering Strait. Over the next 36 hours, the winds came round to the southwest, allowing us to continue our slow crawl towards the ice zone. Already, two layers of thermals, gloves, woolly hat and thick socks insulated me from the cold. My lightweight sleeping bag would soon have to give way to the heavy-duty one. If temperatures got seriously unpleasant, I could always put one sleeping bag inside the other to create a 'mega' bag.

My right shoulder remained sore but serviceable. I had damaged the last surgical repair while showing off in France two years previously.

''Av you ever been rolleur blading?' Christian asked.

'Non.' Emphatic.

'Non! Mon Dieu! You must.'

Christian (an excellent all-round sportsman) decided now was the time. Down we trooped to the boardwalk along Deauville beach. The scene was classic: two pretty French girls, me overconfident. The next thing I knew, my legs were in the air, my backside on the deck, my fall broken (just) by my right elbow, the force of which had tried to push my shoulder joint up through my skull. I felt the surgical fix tear, knew I had turned green. All thoughts of pretty girls (French or otherwise) were washed away as waves of nausea swept through me. I never had the damage looked at and I realised at the outset of the Alpha Global that this weakness needed protecting. After going over the side and snagging the shoulder twice in the main sheet during accidental gybes, I felt grateful my arm still constituted part of my body.

I started the engine and watched the amp meter. The charge indicator needle stayed motionless. What now? I scrabbled to lift the floorboard at the base of the companionway steps to expose the four house batteries and the melange of cables writhing over their tops. I found the problem. The positive lead had disconnected from the battery terminal. With the engine humming in neutral, I waited until the batteries had sucked up charge. If we were going into the ice, close-quarter manoeuvring would have to be under engine. Now was as good a time as any to check the drive.

Up in the cockpit, I eased the throttle forward to engage. I knew immediately that we had a very serious problem. Horrendous clanking reverberated from the propeller shaft – metal on metal. I left the drive turning for 30 seconds, listening intently to make a diagnosis.

'F***!'

I slipped the engine back to neutral. What the hell had happened? How could it have happened?

I'd replaced the propeller shaft during the summer refit and paid particular attention to the engine and drive, anticipating the high mechanical demands of navigating in ice. The propeller shaft trans-mitted through the hull via a stern tube, part of the hull construction. Cutlass bearings supported the shaft in the stern tube at the inboard and outboard ends, holding it firm. The cutlass bearings prevented lateral movements and assisted the shaft to spin true. I got up from my seat in the cockpit and went below to examine the bit of mushed nylon Les had given me in Honolulu.

The curve of where it fitted round the prop shaft was clear, the inside surface discernibly one piece and not a lot of fused strands, its grey colour the same as the cutlass bearings. It wasn't fishing line but part of the cutlass bearing that had worked its way out along the shaft and been mangled by the propeller, no longer able to support the shaft. I had effectively lost use of the engine. How much of the bearing re-mained? Did it matter anyway? I had no idea and no way of knowing until the boat came out of the water. The route to Provideniya was now blocked. I had to find somewhere to take *Barrabas* and get her out of the water. But where?

CHAPTER 20

Louise for President!

The fickle winds and my conservative sailing tactics had put us nearly 800 miles behind schedule. Now I had to deal with the problem cutlass bearing! I pored over the charts, calculator in hand. The conclusion was inescapable. The prospects of getting to the Bering Strait in time to have a sensible crack at the Northern Sea Route were receding fast.

I could not help but lower my head into my hands. With an effort, I overcame the rising mist of tears. I fought for control – this was no time for emotion. *Barrabas* was hurt. It was true that her hurt was my hurt, but I had to be pragmatic, assess the problem in the context of the rapidly shrinking time-window and find a solution.

The fix was straightforward, but *Barrabas* had to come out of the water. With no aft support for the prop shaft, it might have bent, in which case it would need straightening or a new shaft fabricated.

Should I go into a Russian or an Alaskan port? After consulting my various pilotage books, I decided to put into Nome, self-styled 'metropolis' of northwestern Alaska . . .' There was no language barrier, parts were likely to be more available and customs procedures less involved.

The settlements dotting the western and northern Alaskan coasts are remote, but Nome is the largest of them with a population of 3,000. With an action plan outlined, I called Louise.

I quickly reassessed my timings. If I could make it to Nome by 10th August, get the boat out, repaired and back in the water by the 14th, make the short passage across the Bering Strait to be on station at the eastern entrance to the Northern Sea Route by August 15th, it might still be possible – just.

I fired off a series of emails to Louise. The Americans still used the imperial measuring system while *Barrabas*, being French, was metric. I figured it would be easier to have replacement bearings sent out from the UK. They could be waiting for me on the ground instead of me sourcing parts, saving valuable time.

Adrian: Tuesday 11th July 2006
We have to know what is going on in Russia – I know you can only call John and he can only try and call Zuev. I need new cutlass bearings sent from the UK (I don't have spares because I didn't plan on stopping and getting hauled out, plus having replaced the cutlass bearings and the prop shaft, I didn't expect this kind of problem!).

I'm trying (and generally succeeding) in being positive about this – I (or more correctly Barrabas*) has a serious problem – potentially a showstopper – I have a solution: haul out, inspect, replace . . . but we must know what is happening in order to plan and prepare . . .*

Louise contacted Vetus in Holland. Vetus led her to Denis Rawle at Exalto UK, their British distributor. Denis was happy to oblige. The bearings came in three external diameter sizes.

Adrian: Tuesday 11th July 2006
Here's the rub – I need two of them, one for the inboard end and one for the outboard end. The outboard one is definitely buggered. The inboard one may be but I won't know until I pull it out, which can only happen with the boat out of the water. Because we don't know the exterior diameter, I will need to have 3 of each x 2 i.e. 6 bearings of which 2 will be the correct size. Put it to Denis that I will return the 4 unused ones and see if he goes for this!

In the dim light and windless conditions, the solar panels and wind generator were fighting a losing battle to keep the batteries charged. I turned the engine on again. Thirty minutes later when I shut it off and went to close the seawater intake, I found the service alternator lying in the engine well. Its base plate had sheared, fatigued to destruction by the relentless vibration. More expletives coloured the air.

'Bollocks! What the FRIGGING hell else can go wrong!?'

The second, engine-mounted alternator charged the engine-cranking battery. I could still use the engine to charge all the batteries by connecting the engine-cranking battery to the house bank using jumper cables. Another job for Nome – fabricate a new base plate. I could not go into the Arctic without a back-up alternator.

Despondency knocked at the door. I had to stay focused, pragmatic. The seriousness of the shaft problem lay in the solution rather than the problem itself. Would I find suitable facilities in Nome to lift *Barrabas* out, straighten the shaft if necessary and fabricate a new alternator base plate?

Louise, charged with these questions, wasted no time. She found out that the Nome harbourmaster was a woman called Joy Baker.

Louise: Wednesday 12th July 2006

'Dear Joy

Adrian has some problems with his boat and we are trying to decide how best to proceed as it will definitely involve taking Barrabas *out of the water. We were wondering what the feasibility of him getting things fixed in Nome was, so I pose the following questions:*

1) Is there a lift-out facility in the port?

2) A marine stainless steel fabricator needs to be identified.

3) He needs to check the shaft for true alignment.

4) If the shaft is bent, straighten it.'

Joy L. Baker: Wednesday 12th July 2006

There are limited options in this community so it really depends on the weight of the vessel. There is a large 75-ton crane that is tied up on a construction project (more than likely not available since they'd have to set you down within reach of the crane and that would interfere in the construction). There are a few smaller lifts like a 40-ton rubber-tyred crane. Both are owned privately so you'd have to make arrangements personally. I am not aware of any local stainless steel fabricators. That would most likely have to be done out of Anchorage or even Seattle.

Barrabas nudged past the northernmost North Pacific shipping lanes in poor visibility and deteriorating weather. By dawn, winds were back to

35 knots kicking up 20-foot seas. This was rapidly becoming a familiar cycle of bullshit, calm, bullshit, calm.

Through this whirlwind of mishap and leaking time, a thought took root somewhere deep in my subconscious which, over the following few days, pushed itself to the surface like a deeply embedded thorn.

'I think it may be the only option,' I said to Louise. I'd outlined my thoughts in an email and she'd rung me back. She was crying.

'Are you absolutely certain?'

'There are too many unknowns and not enough time. Anyway, nothing is certain.'

'This is so difficult for you.'

'Difficult for you too,' I said. Louise had lived and breathed the expedition, picking me up when I was down, handling the press, maintaining the website, investing her energies in keeping the show on the road, finding sponsors, coaxing politicians, diplomats, billionaires and captains of industry. Had it all come to this?

'If you break the AGX in two, winter the boat in Alaska . . .'

'I know, I know. There are a lot of considerations – cost, not to mention having to psyche myself up again, leave the children . . .'

'I meant, you, what about you? How will you feel?'

The truth was that I felt okay about the decision. 'I'm okay. Sure, in fact. I can't control circumstances out here. There's no point in fighting what cannot be changed.' I resorted to my favourite expression. 'It is what it is.'

'Really?'

'What about you?' I knew she was exhausted. Amidst the tears, I could hear relief.

'Whatever you decide.'

'We'll crack on, but we know where we go if time runs out.'

The decision, if that's what it came to, exhausted me. I went to my bunk, wrapped in the heavy-duty Arctic sleeping bag for the first time, and slept solidly for eight hours.

Adrian: Saturday 15th July 2006
Message for John Mann . . .
'*Hello John*
I will put into Nome, Alaska, to effect repairs. As for the escort vessel, my difficulty is this: without a good idea of the associated costs, I cannot

determine feasibility and it is rapidly coming close to being impossibly late to raise the requisite funds.

I reckon that I have until August 20th to be on station at the eastern entrance to the NSR. If I can get to Nome by August 10th, repair the boat, then it is only a short passage across the Bering Strait to rendezvous with the escort.

Money and the extremely limited time in which to find it are likely to be the showstoppers unless we get some information very, very soon.'

My schedule kept revising itself to accommodate the changing situation, deadlines shifting forwards, mission creep, like a gambler hoping the next spin of the wheel would go his way.

John Mann: Monday 17th July 2006
Good news. I just talked to Zuev. He has received a list of available boats with NSR navigation certification from one of the ports he'd been talking to. He's going to go through it, pick one, and then determine the costs involved. He wants to meet with me tomorrow afternoon to present whatever it is he works up. So, some progress at last.

My mood turned as foul as the weather. The mainsail was shaking itself to pieces. Laziness or lethargy – I had not sorted out the leech line. *Barrabas* pitched and rolled on the uneven sea.

*Log: **Wednesday 19th July 2006**, 8.00 pm.*
It's like Cape Horn here, a relentless succession of lows with 30 to 40 knot winds, which blast the hell out of you for three days and then not a damn breath of wind for four or five days. It's totally ghastly. I think people must be insane to want to pay for this kind of thing. Sitting here writing this, I reckon I ought to be committed to a lunatic asylum for being out here on my own for 10 months!

The wind died overnight. By morning, the sea was like oil. For the first time, I thanked whatever gods were lurking for the calms. I took the mainsail off the boom and stuffed it down the companionway to sort out the leech line. The job took five hours. I had asked Louise to include a roll of sheathed wire in the consignment to Honolulu without any specific purpose in mind. I threaded the wire through the narrow leech line channel, then tied the leech cord to the end of the wire and pulled it through. Doing this along the length of the sail's luff (leading edge) was fine because the channel was in sections, broken where the reefing cringles were located. The leech was trickier because the channel was continuous and unbroken along its entire length. I hooked up the sail, from the anchor chain locker to the aftermost part of the aft cabin, to make the leech channel taut. I could only get the wire about halfway along. There were a few frayed patches, so I worked the wire to these and pulled the leech line through in sections. It was quite a job then getting the sail back on deck and rigged – one small mercy of no wind!

John Mann: Friday 21st July 2006 (14.21 Moscow)
Zuev ducked out on me on Tuesday because he thought the trip was off. I can only assume Monko told him so.

Zuev was also apparently out of town again the past couple of days, which explains why he hasn't answered his mobile. Monko said that he had the same information that I did – that Zuev had found a boat and was coming up with the business plan side of things (i.e. pricing). He also said he'd go talk to Zuev to speed things along. I will give him a call in a little bit as well.

John Mann: Friday 21st July 2006 (15:41 Moscow)
Talked to Zuev. Another reason he hadn't gotten in touch with me is that the people he'd been in touch with wanted $15K a day. He understood the insanity of that (and I'm not sure what kind of boat he was looking at). He said he'll be back in the office Monday and will make some more calls. I guess I'm going to need to call him every day to keep him on track!

$15,000 per day! Yeah, right! I assessed the reality. Any boat in the Arctic would be carrying cargo of some description. Ice-strengthening implied a vessel of at least 100 foot in length with a crew of ten. Wages, fuel, insurance – it might add up. Equally, there was probably an element in the figure of, 'Rich guy, private yacht, screw him!' It was hard to know.

Well, whatever happened, we were heading for Nome. Back in England, Roger dug up an excerpt from one of Michael Palin's television series when he had travelled through the town.

Nome is a very whacky town, taking pride in bizarre statistics such as the fact that it is 75 miles away from the nearest tree. It lies on the southwest coast of the 200-mile-long Seward Peninsula, named after George Seward, the

American Secretary of State who bought Alaska from the Russians in 1867 for 7.2 million dollars. (Even though this worked out at roughly two cents an acre it was not a popular purchase and the territory was referred to at the time as 'Walrussia' and 'Seward's Ice Box'.) We are quartered at a seafront hotel called the Nugget Inn on Front Street next to the Lucky Swede Gift Shop.

There were in fact three Swedes who, in 1898, struck lucky in nearby Anvil Creek and started a classic gold rush, which in two years turned a stretch of Arctic desert into a city of 20,000. There are different versions of why it was called Nome, all of them suitably eccentric. One Harry de Windt, who passed through in 1902 and described the gold-mad town as 'a kind of squalid Monte Carlo', claims that it derives from the Indian word 'No-me' meaning 'I don't know', which was the answer given to early white traders when they asked the natives where they were. The most popular explanation is that Nome came about as a misreading of a naval chart on which a surveyor had noted a nearby cape with the query 'Name?'

This piece of levity was welcome and a message from Henk put my troubles into context.

Henk de Velde: Saturday 22nd July 2006
A voyage including going over the top, like Adrian is doing now, is the most demanding. For example, look at the problems on my voyage in 2001–2004. First: expelled from Russia. Second: engine problems in Argentina – I lost six weeks. Third: struck by lightning north of Hawaii – I had to return to Honolulu and by the time it was repaired I was too late to go north so I lost six months. Fourth: wintering 10 months in Tiksi, Siberia because of too much ice. Fifth: rudders bent in very heavy ice and I had to get help from an icebreaker etc. All together it took me 3½ years. So you see, Adrian is not doing bad at all.

With the northern shipping lanes behind me, I relaxed my deck watches. I was below decks, in the head (on it actually) and came up on deck to check conditions To my astonishment a small ship rolled stationary in the water less than a quarter of a mile off my port side! I tried to raise the ship on VHF radio, but surprise, surprise, no response. It looked like a local coaster. Maybe the thought of going into port, or the cold, made me less vigilant. The combination of boredom, tiredness and a desire to stay warm propelled me into my sleeping bag at every opportunity. On Sunday 23rd July, I lay there, 3.00 pm, thinking, 'What a way to spend a Sunday – no pre-lunch pint of ale in the pub, roast beef and Yorkshire pud, a walk in the woods in the afternoon and newspapers in the evening after the children are in bed!'

Louise wanted details of the cutlass bearing measurements. Without a set of callipers (mine rusted through and now slept with the fishes), I remembered I had a second pair of dividers. Using pliers, I squared the tips, then put each leg into the vice and bent them inwards. I then put the dividers around the shaft, closed the points then drew the dividers up. The prop shaft pushed the points apart by the extent of its diameter and I read the distance between the points against a scale. It gave me an accurate measurement of 40 mm.

The Foreign Office had come up with a possible solution to the vexing question of a visa. The British Embassy would issue a letter of Consular Guarantee in lieu of a visa, effectively assuming responsibility for me. To lend weight to the idea, they first wanted Northern Sea Route Administration to issue an official permission. Chickens and eggs flitted though my mind. Would NSR Administration issue the official permission without my having a visa or something in its stead?

At the request of the Foreign Office in London, John Makin, the British Consul in Moscow, called on Nikolai Monko. The two men met to discuss the intricacies of my proposed transit. Nikolai Monko had offered himself as a direct point of contact with the British authorities from now on. Any concessions would, I guessed, be consequent to this meeting. It was a big step forward.

John Mann: Monday 24th July 2006
I spoke to Zuev today and he's got more people on board in the Far East identifying a suitable escort boat. He's thinking fishing boat now. We are scheduled to finally meet tomorrow afternoon.

The Aleutian Trench runs south of the Aleutian Island chain and plunges to depths of 9,000 metres, its north face rising to shoal depths around the islands themselves in the space of less than 60 miles. The waters driven by winds from the southwest towards the islands could, without too much provocation, chuck up into massive seas. The narrow gaps between the islands provide the only outlet. The Japanese yachtsman Kenichi Horie, after making an east to west transit of the Northwest Passage in 1974, rolled twice south of the Aleutians and limped badly damaged into Hawaii. David Scott Cowper weathered tremendous, confused seas in Unimack Pass en route towards Australia after his transit of the Northwest Passage under power in his converted lifeboat, *Mabel E Holland*. I had to approach with caution. To give myself the best chance, I decided to pass the islands through the widest point available, between the westernmost of the Aleutians, Attu Island (US), and Ostrov Medynn (Russia). Stalemate Bank complicated the issue. Lying west of Attu Island, the water over Stalemate Bank shallowed to a mere 30 metres. To avoid the bank, I would have to stray into Russian territorial waters. The angle of approach presented an immediate problem.

The great promontory of Poluostrov-Kamchatka dangles from the mass of the Russian mainland like an accusatory finger pointing at Japan (it was off this promontory that the Royal Navy team rescued the trapped Russian submariners). The promontory deflects low-pressure systems eastwards then northeastwards. Get caught in the lee of Poluostrov-Kamchatka and I could find myself with little or no wind. Go too far east and I would have to beat back to get on line. Neither the charts nor pilotage gave the gap between these two islands a name, so I called it Stalemate Pass. Positioning was crucial – 100 miles to the pass. Winds were light. I set the mainsail at the second reef with barely any headsail flying to hold *Barrabas*'s bows high to the wind but with minimal boat speed. Like a leopard hunkered down in the long grass stealthily inching forwards, I had to keep *Barrabas* steady for 36 hours until the wind came round to the southwest to take us through the pass on a downwind run.

At 3.30 am on 25th July the radar alarm woke me. I went on deck. In the darkness, I saw lights dead ahead and closing, white over white, green to the left, red to the right. How many bloody ships were there out here? I was looking directly at the bows of this one! I rushed below and issued a security alert. The radioman answered and altered course to starboard, as I requested. He passed within quarter of a mile of me and I recognised the vessel as the same one I had almost run into a few days before. The ship must have passed me unseen and picked up cargo. This time she was sitting low in the water.

Before entering Russian territory, I advised the Maritime Rescue Coordination Centre (MRCC) at Vladivostok. Despite the fact that their phone wasn't working and the email address listed in the Admiralty list of signals kept bouncing back to me, the message got through. Equally bizarrely, MRCC Vladivostok couldn't contact me. Instead, they informed the United States Coastguard (USCG) at Juneau, who then called *Barrabas*. I spoke with Lt. Mara Miller, who had 'googled' *Barrabas* and so knew all about us.

Together, Lt. Miller and I tried to decipher the email in broken English that Vladivostok had sent Juneau. The words 'shot', 'range' and the phrase '30-mile restricted limit' led me to suspect a firing range on Ostrov Medynn. Unfairly perhaps, the idea of some rookie Russian artilleryman eyeing *Barrabas* through binoculars and declaring enthusiastically while he loaded his shells that a yacht has been set up as target practice, sprang to mind. The ever-courteous Lt. Miller agreed to converse with Vladivostok and find out more. A couple of hours later, she called back to tell me that no, it was not a firing range but a protected area reservation (presumably environmental) extending 30 miles offshore from Ostrov Medynn. With that bump ironed out, the winds swung round to the southwest as forecast and we began the run through the pass, our course over the ground shifting between 0° and 37°.

At close to midnight on Tuesday 25th July, a bout of food poisoning hit me. I now habitually checked the sell-by dates on all my food. My dinner of spaghetti with basil pesto, salmon and sardines was all in date. Everything had smelt okay before I cooked it. I eventually managed to get back to sleep at 6.00 am, only to be woken again by the four-mile radar warning alarm with a contact dead on the bow. I managed to raise the ship on the radio and then proceeded to have a long chat with the radio officer, who was interested to know all about the expedition. The ship was the *Long Beach*, registered in Panama with a Filipino crew.

At 1.30 pm, we crossed northwards past latitude 54° north, marking a successful transit over the Aleutian Trench and through the Aleutian Islands/Komandorskiye Ostrova chain. My apprehension about making the transit ranked high among the most nerve-racking points of the voyage, rivalling even my trepidation about Cape Horn! I also breached the psychological barrier of less than 1,000 nautical miles to Nome and shortly afterwards crossed back west over the International Date Line, recovering the 24 hours I had lost earlier.

John Mann: Wednesday 26th July 2006
Here's a rundown of my first face-to-face meeting with Artur Mikhailovich Zuev.

I was expecting a frail, small elderly man given how he sounds on the phone. Instead, I was greeted outside his office by a large, jovial, potbellied gentleman of 78 years. His card says he works for a firm called Inter-regional Transportation Company or MTK for short. It appears to me that he does not work full time at this point, but is nevertheless a very respected man in the organisation and in shipping circles having spent 20 years on the Northern Sea Route. Also present at our meeting was Yevgeny Viktorvich Zvonov, his assistant and one-time seafaring engineer.

When we sat down, he informed me that he was in touch with yet another group of his contacts out in the Far East and that they were once again searching for a suitable escort boat after the last group came back with the exorbitant price I mentioned before. He explained that one problem was that the NSR is less used today than during the Soviet period and a lot of the ice-class boats that might have been able to make the trip are now in disrepair.

It was at this point that Zuev recommended sending Zvonov out to the Far East – either Petropavlovsk-Kamchatsky in Kamchatka or Nakhodka in Primorsk. They believe that they could settle this whole problem in a matter of days if they had someone on the ground, given that the nine-hour time difference makes communication during work hours difficult. I calculated that with the airfare of $1,000, five days of hotel around $500, five days of per diem (their request) around $600, plus other expenses, we could be looking at $2,500 in costs.

After our meeting, I was treated to lunch with four shots of vodka (if you call that a treat . . . it basically killed my afternoon productivity), I explained that a) the expedition is working on a shoestring budget and b) I didn't have any authorisation from Governor Abramovich to get involved financially. As such, I explained that I could not promise that the option they presented would be accepted. I promised to pass along word to the expedition team, but nothing more.

Yesterday evening, I conferred with a colleague of mine who has spent a lot of time in Chukotka and who himself has carried out several land and sea expeditions of various types. My question to him was if, perhaps, he had any maritime contacts in Chukotka that might provide us with an alternative to Zuev. He informed me that most of the traffic on the NSR is west to east and that it will be very difficult to find someone going the other direction. Perhaps this is one of the challenges Zuev has faced, though he hasn't mentioned it specifically.

In short, I'm now not quite sure what the best course of action is. We're finally getting to that period where time is short and I don't feel much progress from Zuev's side. At the same time, he's the one Mr Monko has put on the case so I'm hesitant to circumvent him given that we need Monko to

grant passage. I'm also worried how much Zuev would achieve if we don't
take his solution. It's catch-22 in several dimensions.

So that's where things stand. I'll await word from you before I contact
Zvonov (Zuev's put himself in the hospital for a few days) with our reaction.

Adrian (to John): Thursday 27th July 2006
Hi John,
Thanks for the summation of your meeting with Zuev. As for being on a
shoestring budget, I have to tell you that I am now wearing flip-flops,
shoestrings having long since disappeared.

I am 850 miles from Nome, Alaska, and should be able to be on station to
RV with an escort by mid-August.

Every stage of the voyage presented a new set of challenges. The
Pacific Ocean is very deep. The Bering Sea, north of the Aleutian
Islands, is shallow. Towards Nome, the seabed progressively shoals
to less than 30 metres depth. A series of contour lines on the charts
showed these progressions. My task now was to make sure we crossed
these steps in light winds to avoid the vicious surface chop that even
moderate winds could generate.

The wind was blowing at 30 knots, the seas throwing *Barrabas*
around mercilessly. I tried holding her port quarter to the seas but the
cross-wave pattern made this impossible. For the first time in a long
while, blue sky showed through tears in the cloud. Barometric pressure started rising. Maybe the air pressure was responsible for the
thumping headache behind my eyes. I cooked and ate curry and
stitched up the underarm seams on both sides of my mid-layer, which
was beginning to fall to pieces.

The confused wave pattern rocked the boat from side to side, and
with the wind screeching in the rigging and everything creaking and
groaning, tension came. The locker contents paraded around in their
confined spaces, impatiently knocking as if clamouring to be free. The
tension settled in my shoulders, roosting there. With every precipitous
roll, muscles tightened and tension worked its way more deeply in,
sapping and exhausting. I felt the weight of the strain beneath my eyes
and in the heaviness in my limbs. I felt it in the hollow space excavated
deep in the pit of my stomach. I set the boat to cope as best she could,
then sat and waited for the fury to abate. When it did, the tension,
with nothing left to feed on, crept silently out and away like an
uninvited ghost and the exhaustion turned to sleep.

A white and red light hovered below the cloud base far behind the stern. Perhaps it was a plane or a helicopter too far away for me to detect movement. I switched on the VHF to Channel 16 and put on a masthead light. The light remained for several hours, immobile in the sky, too low to be a satellite, too high to be the masthead lights of a ship. The light stayed stuck to the sky, immutable like an unblinking eye. Suddenly, it vanished. Gone, switched off. I have no explanation!

I spent the morning doing housework – disinfecting the heads and galley sinks, wiping the floors and generally tidying. Low grey clouds scudding to the east brought a chill wind. I didn't much like the look of them and shortened sail as a precaution.

The day had begun bright and blue but by mid-afternoon the light had dimmed to a steely grey. The low clouds moved over us. The seas became steeper. By 4.00 pm, we were in 40-knot winds. Waves built to sheer-faced 25-foot monsters, stampeding before the wind like a hunted herd, crests tumbling. I sat up in the cockpit and whilst my trusty Hydrovane steered *Barrabas*, wave action was slewing the boat so wildly that the headsail was backing. I kept the Hydrovane working while I faced backwards watching the seas, making steering corrections to take the more aggressive waves stern-on. The wind then shifted quite suddenly. It was not long before the seas crossed with breaking waves, colliding almost at right angles to one another. After 25,000 miles, I had not experienced such confused water.

Three large waves rode up behind *Barrabas* forming themselves into a crescent. I adjusted the steering to take the centre wave. My angle was just off. The foaming water got hold of the keel and slewed *Barrabas* viciously to port. At that moment, the left-hand wave broke and smashed into *Barrabas*'s port quarter. The water's grip was murderous. I braced myself in the cockpit and watched in fascinated horror as green water threw *Barrabas* over, rushing over the afterdeck. The massive forces were too much for the rudder cables and the wheel spun freely as they parted. The water tore through the starboard dodger as if it was made of wet tissue. *Barrabas* spun through 180°, sails flogging as she turned head to wind.

I immediately fitted the emergency tiller, control lines already rigged and run through blocks to the cockpit so that I could control the rudder by pulling down on the starboard and port lines. There I stayed, beneath the protective cuddy for the next two hours until the storm blew past. Finally, I put *Barrabas* onto a beam reach, port tack as the wind continued to veer and moderate through the night, shaking out reefs to give me more power.

I was grateful for the calm that followed. The Honolulu consignment contained 5 mm-gauge steering cables to replace the narrower 4 mm cables fitted, the additional strength more able to absorb knocks taken by the rudder from ice. I spent most of the day on Monday fitting these thicker cables, saving time on the ground in Nome. Four hundred and seventy-five miles now separated us from the settlement. It seemed like infinity.

John Mann: Monday 31st July 2006

I spoke to Nikolai Monko today. He said the only remaining documentation he needs is:

A) Certification on the technical condition of the escort ship.

B) Your visa, if you've got it (I know you had something in the works on this) just in case you have to make landfall.

These are the only documents left to worry about for the NSR approval process.

Now for the unpleasant news. We've got a bit of a hold-up as Zuev went into the hospital for minor elective surgery last week and his assistant Zvonov took ill over the weekend. I've put Monko on the case in resolving the issue but it'll be tomorrow before I find out what comes next.

Bloody hell! This whole process seemed to be giving with one hand and taking with the other. How long would Zuev be in hospital? Did he have cirrhosis of the liver? At least I could deal with the visa issue.

'You're almost there!' Louise said. Excitement registered clearly in her voice.

'D'you mean almost there with the Russians or almost in Nome?'

'Both!'

'Well, we can't do anything about Zuev's medical condition, but can you ask Damian at the FCO to get onto Mr Monko and let him know that the British Embassy in Moscow will issue a Consular Guarantee in lieu of a visa?'

'I've already done that.'

I raised my eyes to the cabin headlining and thought to myself, 'This woman should be running the bloody country!'

*

A deep throbbing filled the air around *Barrabas* like a continuous roll of fast-approaching thunder. The reverberations thumped around my head. I rushed on deck just as a huge USCG C-130 Hercules screamed overhead at less than 500 feet. I ducked below decks flicking the VHF to Channel 16.

'US coastguard aircraft, this is sailing yacht *Barrabas*, do you copy?' I watched though the window as the great bird banked round to the north.

A low hiss of static, then, 'This is United States Coastguard aircraft, please identify yourself.'

'This is British sailing yacht *Barrabas*.' I spelled out B A R R A B A S. The radioman repeated the spelling.

'How many crew on board. Please spell your name, sir. Callsign.'

'Mike Hotel Delta Victor Three.'

'Your last port of call, Captain?'

'Honolulu.'

'And where're you headed?'

'Nome.' I figured they knew who I was from Lt. Miller.

The aircraft hurtled passed once more, then climbed away to the south.

We chatted while the C-130 ranged in wide circles around us.

'Anything we can do for you, sir?'

I wondered what an aircraft moving at 300 mph could do for a sailing boat moving at walking pace. 'Any female, blonde crew you could parachute down here would be welcome.'

The radioman laughed. 'No can do, sir.'

'Very well, I'll make do.'

'Have a good day, sir.'

I watched the C-130 diminish to a speck then blink out in the low scudding cloud.

I found three more books, ones that Michael Roth had given me, hidden in the 'nuts and raisins' cupboard. I couldn't believe my luck. To celebrate, I gave myself a baby wipe bath in front of the heater outlet in the saloon. (I also wanted to test the heater. I had sat on the burner unit by accident whilst working on the steering cables.)

My mood remained buoyant all day because of the books and the flypast. USCG knew my position, knew my intentions. Lt. Miller had agreed to call ahead to Nome and alert the customs and border control officer, Bob Gentz. I felt safe – whatever happened now, I'd be okay. The realisation made me acutely aware of how vulnerable I felt at sea, how that vulnerability shadowed me every second, the pressing weight of it. As darkness fell, the distinctive sounds of whales' blowholes came from somewhere close by.

I spent most of the following day, Wednesday 2nd August, reading Tom Robbins's *Villa Incognito*. Part of my seeking solace in fiction was to quell the inevitable jitters about crossing the 200-metre contour line. We edged across at 10.00 pm. From now until we reached Nome, the increasingly shallow water presented a constant threat.

Barrabas made steady progress towards Saint Lawrence Island. Mercifully, the forecast indicated fine weather. With winds blowing from the southwest, I decided to pass south of the island to avoid the wind shadow cast by its mountainous spine.

So taken was I with Tom Robbins, I immediately launched into the second of his books, *Fierce Invalids Home from Hot Climates*, silently thanking Michael for introducing me to this great writer.

Ricardo sent two satellite ice images lifted from the University of Bremen's Department of Environmental Physics website, in my opinion the best of the internet sites displaying this type of imagery (Eric Brossier also used this resource during his 2002 NSR transit in *Vagabond*). The pictures showed the ice receding to an almost unbelievable extent. This year was looking even better than 2005, when the ice had cleared completely from the Russian Arctic coast. I could not have dreamed of better conditions. Yet for an entire week, I had heard nothing further on the search for an appropriate escort vessel. The news from Ricardo plunged me into a monumental psychological battle between elation and despair. Could I get the repairs done in time? Would the repairs hold? Could the Russians find an escort vessel? Would the escort vessel be prohibitively expensive? Did we have enough time or not? Ice conditions looked like being the best (for my purposes) in recorded history. The tug-of-war between anxiety and ecstasy was evenly poised. It could go either way. We were getting down to the wire.

The great, hummocked mass of Saint Lawrence Island slid by, invisible beneath my northern horizon. At 9.45 am on Sunday 6th August we passed westwards over the 30-metre contour line. Taking advantage of the light southwesterlies, we ran dead downwind towards Nome, exactly 100 miles away.

By evening the following day, Alaska's mountainous coast loomed beneath blue-streaked skies warmed by a soft sunset. I sat up on deck, the radiance of the sun gradually dimming from gold to orange to pink. Detail etched on the rugged rock faces faded with the light. Nome huddled beneath the mountains 20 miles away. I hove-to for the night, drifting gently eastwards. Despite my worries about how I was going to get *Barrabas* out of the water, excitement at making landfall flickered through me. This was frontier country. Nome would be a startling contrast to the glitz and wealth of Waikiki.

CHAPTER 21

No Place Like Nome

I made it to within a couple of miles of the harbour entrance, but with no charts and no engine to manoeuvre into port, I put a call in to Joy Baker. A local fishing boat, *Juliana III*, came out and towed me into the sanctuary of Nome's small, protected harbour. At 11.00 am on Tuesday 8th August, I tied up alongside the harbour wall, throwing my lines to a baseball-capped, heavily bearded figure who spoke in a slow drawl. Like a number of people I was to meet over the following days, George Fullwood had sought the isolation and anonymity of the wild wastes of the Alaskan tundra two decades previously in the hunt for gold. Now he worked for Crowley Marine Services, whose 90-ton crane sat close by with its mighty boom reaching skywards above *Barrabas*'s mast. My heart sang. Could this be the answer to the question of how I was going to get *Barrabas* out of the water?

Bob Gentz arrived to check my papers. Joy Baker came down to say 'Hi' and introduced me to Tim Shields, Crowley Marine's terminal manager.

I clambered ashore after 84 days at sea, this time slightly less steady on my feet than I had been in Honolulu. Bob Gentz was a big man. He stood in front of me, feet apart, both thumbs tucked in behind his belt buckle, navy blue uniform crisply ironed and adorned with a number of gold shields.

'We got ourselves a problem.'

I had made the mistake of calling him 'Bob'. 'What's the problem, sir?' I asked.

'Well,' he said, head crooked to one side, 'seems like you're an illegal alien.'

I couldn't help but think of the mysterious red and white light I'd seen hovering in the sky. A spaceship from another galaxy maybe?

'How so?'

'You got no visa.'

'I'm British. Do I need a visa?' I feigned ignorance.

'Yessiree.'

I was half expecting Bob to spit a dollop of chewing tobacco into the dirt.

'Well, there's a problem with the boat. I had to come in.' Quickly, I explained what I was doing, the Russians, where I was going.

'I checked you out,' Bob said proudly. Presumably, this followed the notification from Lt. Miller that I was on my way in. He knew about Honolulu. 'You got emergency parole in Hawaii, right?'

'Right.'

'Parole for emergency visits is limited to one a year.'

I thought quickly. 'What period does a parole normally cover?'

'Thirty days.'

'I was in Hawaii for nine days, so might it be argued that I still have 21 days left?'

Bob thought about this for a while then said, 'Don't leave. I'll be back, probably tomorrow.'

'Do you mean I have to stay on the boat?' I was fantasising about fried egg sandwiches. I needed to get to a supermarket.

'Don't leave town.'

The roads from Nome led nowhere. Air and sea offered the only routes in or out. 'Don't worry, officer. I can't leave, not that I want to of course. The boat's engine's out of action and I can't fly out because I've got no money.' Bob drove off leaving a cloud of dust hanging in the air.

I strolled with Tim to his office, a 19th-century clapboard house up the road. He had heard most of what I'd said to Bob.

'Can we use the crane to hoist the boat?'

'What she weigh?'

'Fifteen tonnes.'

'No problemo.'

Relief washed over me. I slumped back in my chair amidst piles of paper and files. 'That's great.' I smiled broadly.

''cept one thing.'

'What?'

'Rick's away on a job. Rick operates the crane.'

'When's he coming back?'

'Dunno. Company business. Two days, a week.' Tim shrugged.

'I can't wait that long.'

'Dan could do it.'

'Who's Dan?'

'My brother. Works for Crowley up in Kotzebue.'

'Where's Kotzebue?'

Tim got up and stabbed at a map hanging on the wall. 'Half-hour plane ride north.'

'Can he do it?'

'Sure, but you'll have to pay the fare, here and back.'

How much could it be? 'Okay, let's do it,' I said.

Tim reached for the phone while I wandered around the rest of the house looking at pictures of Crowley Marine tugs hanging in frames and some softball trophies won by the local boys' team, which Crowley sponsored.

'Yo! Adrian,' Tim called. I went back to his office. 'Thursday afternoon.'

Dale Whitney was more difficult to find. I trudged along the airport road out of town to a small settlement of dilapidated huts on the opposite bank of the river. Everyone knew everyone in this town. George had given me directions. The rusting domes of two Nissen huts concealed the front door of Dale Whitney's house. I knocked. The door opened. A small octogenarian (83 as it turned out) dressed in the thickest and oldest pair of woollen long johns I had ever seen stood framed in his doorway. A welder and steelworker, Dale Whitney had lived in Nome for 30 years. His hair was white, sticking up in places. Gold-rimmed glasses sat lopsided on the end of his nose. He looked like Father Christmas on his day off. Halfway through my explanation of who I was and what I wanted, Dale ushered me inside. He lived with an army of cats. I finished my explanation.

'So,' I said. 'Would you be able to have a look at the prop shaft, see if it's bent and if it is, straighten it?'

'How long you here for?' Dale asked

'A few days.'

'Get George to bring the shaft round.'

I thanked Dale and left, stepping around trays of cat litter and discarded boxes of Corn Dogs.

The next day I slept through until noon. Bob Gentz collected me at the boat and we went over to his office to do the 'paperwork'.

'Okay,' Bob sighed, heaving himself into his swivel chair. 'We'll give you parole, extend your waiver for a visa over from Honolulu.'

'That's great,' I said.

'Normally there's a charge, but we're gonna waive that too.'

It seemed like I had a new friend. 'Well, thank you, sir,' I said, just to be sure it stayed that way.

On Thursday evening, Dan fired up the crane's massive diesel engine. With a spreader bar hanging from the crane's hook, we figured there should be sufficient lateral distance to hold the cables and straps suspended from the spreader bar away from the rigging. (We were going to crane the boat out of the water with the mast and rigging in situ, a 'first' for everyone involved.)

I'd rigged two lines, running beneath the hull, fore and aft of the keel. With 50-foot-long steel cables hanging down and guy lines attached to hold them off the rigging, the boom of the crane swung out to position the spreader bar directly above the mast. Forty-foot straps hung from the cables on one side. We tied my pre-rigged lines to the free ends of the straps and pulled them under *Barrabas* and up the other side, attaching their ends to the suspended cables on that side with giant shackles.

The hoist was slow and even, and as *Barrabas* cleared the dockside we turned her through 90° using guys tied to the deck cleats. With the gentlest of motions, Dan lowered *Barrabas* onto wooded blocks just enough to 'ground' her without placing excessive loading on the keel. Dan then locked the boom so that *Barrabas* was held firmly, securely suspended.

Another yacht entered the small harbour, tying up in the spot *Barrabas* had just vacated. Her owner and sole crewmember came ashore to spectate proceedings. With *Barrabas* settled, I then met Jerry, a retired ex-NASA scientist from San Francisco. Later he showed me round his boat, *Arctic Wolf*.

During the tour, I noticed quite a number of heating outlets. Jerry expanded on his various warmth-generating systems. The one part (or two, depending on how you look at it) of my anatomy that stubbornly refused to get warm when the temperature dropped much below 5°C was my feet. After Cape Horn, I was lying in my bunk (with cold feet) fantasising about electrically heated socks . . .

With barely controlled hand and arm gesticulations, bobbing head movements and rapid-fire speech, Jerry rummaged in an eye-level locker. He ripped out items of clothing, tossing them over his shoulder. They floated down and settled like giant, multi-coloured snow-flakes. With an exclamation of delight, he turned, holding what looked like a regular fleece-lined jacket. What set it apart from the rest of the blizzard was the electric cable issuing thin and snake-like from its lining.

'This is what I do,' Jerry said, his excitement hampering his efforts to don the jacket. Then, finding the end of the cable, he shoved it into a nearby 12-volt socket. 'In 20 minutes, I'm toast!'

I was delighted at the display, but didn't mention that in English being toast was not a desirable state.

With tongue part-way into cheek, I asked, 'You don't happen to have heated socks?'

'Oh, sure!' Jerry cried, arms spreading wide. 'And pants and gloves too!'

I was speechless. Here was my fantasy come true, the end of cold feet. 'I could really use a pair of these,' I said holding up the socks.

Jerry fired up his laptop, hooked into the local WiFi network and found the website for the magical manufacturer of heated clothing – www.gerbing.com.

With George's help, I disengaged the steering quadrant, removed the heavy steel rudder, loosened the coupling and slid the prop shaft out. It was immediately obvious what had happened. The cutlass bearings had melted with the friction of the spinning shaft. The bearings were seawater-cooled and lubricated. Had I, at some time before arrival in Honolulu, run the engine in gear without opening the cooling valve? It was academic now.

George drove me to Dale Whitney's place with the shaft tied down and blocked in the back of his flatbed truck. We left the shaft with Dale then drove to the airport to take delivery of the new cutlass bearings that Louise had sent via DHL to Nome. Back in Dale's huge workshop beneath the domed roof of one of the Nissen huts, we put the shaft in a lathe. The shaft was out of alignment by 30 thousandths of an inch.

Dale (who held a Masters degree in engineering) reckoned it was as good as new.

I celebrated this piece of good news (not to mention saving the cost of replacing the shaft) with an enormous T-bone steak cooked in pepper and honey.

I called Louise the next day. 'The cutlass bearings are slightly too large diameter.'

'I've found someone in Anchorage who can make the alternator thingy, maybe he can help you. His name's Gary Feaster and his company's called Greatland Welding and Machine.'

'Fantastic – have you got an email address?' I scribbled it down on a cigarette packet.

'And I've been onto Jeff Gerbing . . .' Louise said.

'Jeff Gerbing?'

'The heated suit man!'

'Of course. And?'

'He's going to give you the full monty – jacket, salopettes, socks, gloves, the works.'

I was elated. I then called Gary. Could he fabricate a new base plate? No problem, he said, just send me the bits to copy. And the cutlass bearings? Shave off 1/16th of an inch? Send them too. I hitched a ride out to the airport and express-couriered the broken base plate and cutless bearings to Greatland Welding and Machine in Anchorage.

Rick Kostiew arrived back in Nome on Monday 14th August. Originally from Boston, Massachusetts, Rick was another stowaway, running from the crime and urban sprawl of one of America's most violent cities. In his fifties, his shock of white hair and distinctive Bostonian brogue made him instantly recognisable by day or night. At first shy, adopting a serious expression as he looked over *Barrabas* suspended in the straps slung from his beloved crane, Rick and I soon developed a strong rapport. It was not long before a smile split his lean face and the wisecracks started flowing.

'You wanna clean out the stern toob,' Rick said.

'You got a tool for that?'

Rick nodded towards the warehouse just across the street from *Barrabas*, Crowley's workshop. 'I got every type of tool you could imagine and then some. I got a tool for pokin', pushin', widenin', narrowin', cuttin', smoothin', you name it, I got it.'

'I've got a tool for poking too, but that's about it.'

Rick chuckled, shuffling his feet. 'I bet you don't done too much o' that out there,' and still chuckling to himself went off to the 'shop' to fetch the reaming tool and flex extension to bring power out to *Barrabas*.

My mobile phone rang. Louise's number flashed on the small screen. I pressed the phone to my ear. Someone in the Russian government had decided that a letter of Consular Guarantee from the British Embassy in Moscow was insufficient. They insisted I have a valid visa. She'd been onto Marie Forsyth, Consul at the British embassy in Washington DC. This was the plan: the British Embassy in Washington would wait for the official permissions from Moscow to arrive at the Russian Embassy in Washington. Once done, a British Embassy car would drive my passport to their Russian counterparts. The Russians would issue the visa (and take the payment for it) and then return the passport to me via DHL. Marie needed my passport, visa application, payment for the visa and a DHL return pouch for the Russians to use.

I put the package together, including a US postal order for the precise amount of the visa, and went to the airport to courier the package to DHL in Anchorage for onward carriage to Marie in Washington.

I had already been in Nome for longer than I planned, but then I had not expected the Russians to refuse the Consular Guarantee. My timings were slipping again. I was hoping for a three-day turnaround, but with no news of any progress on the escort vessel, a three-day turnaround on the visa would probably be unimportant. I could not leave Nome until the escort and its costs had been finalised.

While I was busy filling forms at the airport courier desk, the attendant said, 'Oh! Got a package for you right here,' and she hefted up a box. The new alternator base plate and milled down cutlass bearings from Gary.

On the morning of Thursday 17th August, everything changed. The visa issue suddenly thrust itself forward as the crucial factor. The Iridium rang.

'You're not going to believe this!' Louise was breathless.

'What's happened?'

'They're letting you go! It's amazing. No escort, no ice pilot, no nothing.'

'What!' Had my ears deceived me? 'What d'you mean?'

'John sent me an email. I've forwarded it on to you. Mr Monko received instructions, orders to *make it happen*, get you through the NSR, solo!'

'I don't bloody believe this. Really?'

'Really!'

I fired up the laptop, waiting impatiently while the hard drive whirred and clicked. I rang out and pulled down the email.

John Mann: Thursday 17th August 2006

Well, it looks like your persistence has paid off, as well as the strategy of attacking on all fronts. Basically, as I understand it from conversations with Zuev yesterday and Monko today, the situation is as follows:

Monko received orders from the Ministry of Foreign Affairs to 'make this happen'.

Adrian will need to receive permission from the Federal Security Service (FSB to be present in high-security border areas). This is a regular process. I am to contact a Mr Igor Vasilievich Chomai tomorrow to find out what he needs to grant this permission, but according to Monko, he is predisposed to granting it (apparently, he also has orders to do so).

Monko wants all the contact information for Adrian to pass on to the people out in Chukotka and everyone else involved. Due to the good ice conditions, Alpha Global will be allowed to continue without the previously discussed escort boat.

He did add a caveat that, if by the time Adrian gets to Pevek (on Chukotka's northern coast) the situation has deteriorated at all, then the escort option might have to be revisited. If that is the case, then Monko's people would provide some sort of escort. No details on what that might be, but hopefully we won't have to cross that bridge.

Wow! How had this come about? Who had said what to whom? Ian's view was unequivocal. No one *ordered* the FSB to do anything. The Directorate of Internal Security was a law unto itself, even in so-called 'modern' Russia. Only the President's office could issue such a directive and President Vladimir Putin, being a former chief of the KGB, well . . .

I reeled at the likelihood that the Alpha Global Expedition, the boyhood dream of an anonymous Englishman managed by his equally anonymous ex-wife from a village in rural Buckinghamshire, had percolated up to one of the most powerful political offices in the world.

The Russian Embassy in Washington DC would surely receive the necessary paperwork imminently. Maybe all the paperwork was already there. Louise alerted Marie Forsyth in Washington of this latest development.

Time began slipping by more quickly. Each time I looked at the clock, two hours had mysteriously disappeared. The new cutlass bearings fitted snugly into the stern tube housings, the prop shaft was back in place and coupled to the gearbox. The heavy rudder was back on.

While I waited for my passport and visa, I scraped the last of the barnacles off the boat then washed the hull down with thinner. I had noticed tins of antifoul in the shop. Crowley no longer maintained their boats in Nome so the antifoul was surplus. Rick let me have some and he laid on rollers, paint trays and masking tape.

John Mann: Friday 18th August 2006

I found out today that Adrian needs to stop in Provideniya (and maybe Murmansk) to say hello (and goodbye) to the Russian border guards.

When I spoke to the FSB border service today, they informed me that the only document they need to grant permission for Adrian's transit is a letter from the regulatory agency involved, which in this case is the good Mr Monko! I've already dropped a note to Monko asking him to write that letter. Below is the instruction from Monko:

Ministry of Transport, Russian Federation
Federal Agency for Sea and River Transport
17.08.2006

To: O.N. Yanenko, Captain of the Sea Trade Port of Provideniya
I.A.Boreev, Captain-Inspector of State Port Control of the Port of Provideniya

I entrust you to conduct an inspection of the yacht *Barrabas* at the port of Provideniya in accordance with the shipowner's schedule.

The yacht should travel in clear water along a coastal route through the Northern Sea Route under the instructions of the Sea Operations Staff, and in case of ice, with an accompanying boat with ice pilot on board.

Upon receipt of permission from the RO UFSB RF for DVO (Regional Office of the Federal Security Service Directorate for the Far

East Region) and the existence of an insurance policy, issue Permit
No. 37/06.

Respectfully,
Head of the Department for Icebreaker Facilitation and Hydrography
Northern Sea Route Administration

N. A. Monko.

As the days ticked themselves off the calendar, my frustration built.
What was happening now? I was back on that familiar seesaw, bouncing up and down between euphoria and despair. My expectation of
fast action from the Russian authorities following the stunning news
from John had fizzled whilst people tried to figure out who should
write which letter to whom. I had to go now!

'Be patient,' Louise cautioned. 'We've come this far. It won't be
long.'

I busied myself with the logistics of the NSR transit. So late in the
season, I might not have the luxury of sailing the entire route along
Russia's Arctic coast. In light winds or headwinds, *Barrabas* had to keep
moving forward. The consequences of becoming iced-in during the re-
freeze did not bear thinking about. *Barrabas* had to be carrying enough
fuel to motor the entire length of the NSR if necessary. I assessed my
fuel stocks: 1,000 litres. With fuel for heating and fuel consumption at
three litres per hour (running the engine at higher revs) factored in, I
needed 2,500 litres. As a contingency, Louise had already sourced and
ordered a further 50 x 5-gallon fuel cans. George drove me to Icy View
north of town to pick them up in his flatbed.

I had lined up my 100 fuel cans, 50 old and 50 new, in regimental
array on the floor of the shop.

'What kind of fuel you got in there?' Rick asked.

'Regular stuff from the UK. Some from Honolulu.'

'You need winter grade. That stuff'll turn to wax at 0°.'

'Would this work – I decant 50 per cent of the fuel from 50 of the full
cans to the 50 new ones so they're all half full . . .'

'Yeah, yeah, yeah. We fill with winter grade, waxing point −60°, and
the mix should give you a waxing point somewhere around −20°.'
Rick was fiddling about with test tubes and pipettes, adding various
chemicals and measuring colour changes against a chart to ensure this
would work.

I decanted the fuel, then George filled the tank on the back of the flatbed with winter grade diesel and drove up and down the lines of fuel cans, topping them off.

On Wednesday August 23rd, Rick lifted *Barrabas* back into the water. Getting the fuel on board occupied me for most of the next day. The combined weight, two tonnes, could raise the boat's centre of gravity, destabilising her. To keep the boat stable, I distributed the fuel as low down as possible, securing the cans with ratcheted webbing straps. With the operation complete, red fuel cans carpeted practically every inch of floor space on board. The starboard bunk, around the chart table, the toilet and the galley were the only fuel-free areas below decks.

John Mann: Thursday 24th August 2006

Got up early today to see what I could get done on this visa issue. I talked to my contact in the FSB and he's not yet received the letter from Monko's people. So I contacted Monko's assistant and he said he is unfamiliar with this specific issue. Furthermore, he's unable to issue such a letter himself until Monko returns next week. All together, I appear to be caught in a roundabout without an exit.

Nikolai Monko had gone on holiday! Louise and I had talked about the likelihood of wintering *Barrabas* in Nome repeatedly since first mooting the idea six weeks before. I was tantalisingly close – one letter from the FSB. I could sense John's bewilderment and frustration mounting in parallel with my own.

'Look, what's the worst that could happen?' I said to Louise. 'I'm a lone yachtsman on a sailing boat moving at walking pace – hardly a threat to Russian national security.'

'You mean just go?'

'Yes. Mr Monko's issued the order, he's under orders, so if I just go now without this FSB letter . . .'

'You'll end up in some Siberian gulag.'

'Can you put it to the Foreign Office?'

Shane Jones: Russia Desk, Foreign & Commonwealth Office, Friday 25th August 2006

I would draw your attention to an incident last week in which, according to the Russian authorities, a Japanese fisherman strayed unauthorised into Russian territorial waters and was shot dead.

You will appreciate the FCO's concern to ensure that the arrangements
required by the Russian authorities are in place before Adrian sets off to
transit the NSR.

Maybe it would be better to wait! Nikolai Monko was still not back in
his office. John rang round furiously, pulling in every contact he could
think of and talking to every department in the Ministry of Transport's
Sea Division, eventually ending up at the Security Department of the
River and Sea Agency. They made enquiries and reported to John that
the request for FSB clearance should come from the Russian Foreign
Ministry and not Nikolai Monko!

Louise copied all the correspondence from the Foreign Office, John,
British Embassy staff in Moscow and Washington DC, Sovcomflot and
Ian's ongoing efforts with the Royal Navy to Sam Laidlaw. Perhaps
one directed thrust might create a domino effect through the diplomatic inertia. The Russian ambassador to the United States occupied
the most sensitive and powerful office among the overseas diplomatic
corps of the Russian government. Sam knew the ambassador personally. On 31st August, he wrote directly to His Excellency, Yuri V
Yushakov.

John Mann: Thursday 31st August 2006
I spoke to Neil Abbot at the UK Embassy in Moscow . . . and copied him in
on some of the emails circulating around. I asked if he could effect the request
to the FSB through the Foreign Ministry, which he said he'd work on today.

That's where we stand at the moment. So, now we're again waiting on the
results of the UK Embassy's efforts before we can move forward.

My days in Nome soon fell into a familiar routine. In the mornings, I
downloaded the latest batch of emails and fired off replies. Then I
walked to the supermarket to provision for the day, mainly because
I enjoyed the exercise. After an article appeared in the local newspaper, *The Nome Nugget*, people regularly stopped me in the street
asking about the latest developments with the 'Russkis'. En route to
or from the supermarket I detoured to the library, logging on to
www.seaice.de to check the ice. Back on board *Barrabas*, I continually
tinkered with the engine and the rigging, sometimes wandering up to
the hardware store for bits and pieces to keep the boat in a constant
state of readiness.

John Mann: Monday 4th September 2006

There is apparently some ice forming in Vil'kitskiy Strait so there could be problems passing through . . .

I spoke to Neil Abbott at the embassy. There's all kinds of activity on both the FSB letter and visa fronts but no results at present.

On Wednesday 6th September, a storm blew in from the west bringing 50-mile-an-hour winds. Whatever happened, the storm would keep me pinned down in Nome for 48 hours.

I found Rick in the shop.

'If I have to leave *Barrabas* here for the winter, what d'you think would be the best way?' I had mentioned the possibility to Rick already, so he'd had time to think about options.

'Come have a look out back.'

Rick led the way to a storage area behind the warehouse. A row of cradles the size of sea containers lined the back wall of a larger warehouse across the street. Each one held a massive gas cylinder. 'Lift out the cylinder and lower the boat down.'

I studied a cradle. 'Not enough height for the keel and I don't think it's wide enough.'

'You got the measurements?'

'No.'

'So get the measurements.'

'I can tell by eye.'

'Or,' Rick said, 'get two containers and put the boat between them.'

'Too much weight on the keel.'

'Or, dig a hole and lower the boat down so she's sitting on the ground . . .'

'Deep enough so there's no weight on the keel!'

I went to talk to Tim about the possibility of wintering the boat in Nome. I wanted to put the idea in play as a contingency. The ice edge appeared stationary. The window for 2006 looked like it might be closing. By late evening, I fell into another exhausted sleep.

The mobile phone's chirruping woke me. I scrabbled for my watch – 6.30 am.

'They're letting you through!' Louise exclaimed.

'Good morning,' I said blearily before her words registered.

'The Russians are letting you go!'

I bolted upright. 'What?'

'John can't understand it and neither can I. But who cares?'

'That's great,' I said but my voice lacked enthusiasm. 'Big problem though. The ice has stopped receding and new ice is growing at Vil'kitskiy Strait. You saw John's email. The western side is blocked.'

Two emails from John later in the day confirmed Louise's news.

John Mann: Thursday 7th September 2006 (15:08 Moscow)
Update: Just spoke to Monko. He says go to Provideniya. I wish I knew for the love of all that's holy why they couldn't have decided this earlier . . .

John Mann: Thursday 7th September 2006 (17:54 Moscow)
Dear god, could this get any more confusing?

OK, I spoke to Andrey Kechashin at Sovcomflot. He said he spoke to the border guard service and that everything can be done at Provideniya. His understanding is that the FSB's border guard service can grant the permit there on the spot. Apparently, it's a normal procedure when you've got boats transiting. Well, this flies in the face of everything we've been told.

So much for the letter of authority from the FSB, but did I need a visa or not? I called John.

Apparently not, according to Monko.

Something did not stack up. 'I don't know . . .' Instinct was telling me that without a visa, the Russian authorities would either turn me away from Provideniya or worse, arrest me and impound the boat.

'I gotta tell you that I've had it from three sources now that new ice is forming,' John said.

'I know, John. I think it's too late . . .'

Damian Thwaites: Russia Desk, Foreign & Commonwealth Office, Friday 8th September 2006
Our Consul-General at the British Embassy in Moscow, Jessica Hand, called on Vyecheslav Pavlovskiy, Director, Consular Division of the Russian Ministry of Foreign Affairs (MFA), on 7 September to discuss the consular requirements relating to the expedition.

She informed him that Nikolai Monko, Director, Federal Agency for Maritime and River Transpor, has advised Adrian that he does not require a visa and that he should proceed to Provideniya . . . Pavlovskiy made it abundantly clear to our Consul-General that Adrian would require a visa.

I should also add that Simon Smith, Director, Russia, South Caucasus and Central Asia Directorate in the Foreign & Commonwealth Office, has raised the issue of both visa and permission to transit directly with Andrey Chupin,

Deputy Head of Mission at the Russian Embassy in London, requesting him
to make representations to his colleagues in Moscow, on both counts.

More confusion. I walked to the library on Front Street to check the
ice. A massive floe of ice blocked the western side of the Vil'kitskiy
Strait. It had grown, north winds bringing down even more ice. I
leaned back in my chair and stared at the library's Artex ceiling. Nome
to Provideniya, three days, allow two days for the inspection, then 18
days to Vil'kitskiy. I did not bother finishing my thought. It was too
late. *Barrabas* would have to over-winter in Nome.

I trudged back to the harbour. The storm had passed but left a
residue of low, grey cloud. I wandered about below decks, talking
aloud to *Barrabas*, explaining the situation. I had to leave her. She
would be safe. Rick was here.

The phone trilled an unwelcome intrusion. I smiled at Louise's
rapid-fire enthusiasm. 'How are you?'

'Well . . .'

'I've got something to tell you . . .'

'The ice . . .'

'Me first,' she insisted. 'Sam just called. He's just spoken to a guy
called Gulshko at the Russian Embassy in Washington. All the papers
are at the embassy, MFA permission, the authorisation letter from the
FSB. He can issue the visa now. You'll be out of there tomorrow.'

'Louise, I need to tell you about the ice.'

I spent the day preparing *Barrabas* for her long winter hibernation,
taking the sails off the rig and bagging them for storage in the
warehouse, clearing the deck lines, oiling and stowing the blocks and
then the back-breaking task of getting the 100 fuel cans off the boat and
into the warehouse. I worked on silently, until darkness and exhaustion defeated me.

Eric Brossier: Sunday 17th September 2006
Hard to stop, but congratulations for having permission to sail single-handed!
Good luck for the next part of the trip.

Rick used the crane to lift the mast from *Barrabas*. In pouring rain, I
tidied the lines and shrouds and then wrapped the mast with industrial
shrink-wrap and covered it with tarpaulin. Rick then spent several

hours digging out *Barrabas*'s 'pit' on an area of ground to the side of the Crowley warehouse, excavating a trench, 25 feet in length, three feet wide and seven feet deep.

With the mast suspended from the crane, we 'walked' it to the Crowley oil storage depot and laid it on palettes, distributing its weight as evenly as possible.

With tyres positioned around the trench, Rick carefully and expertly hoisted *Barrabas* from the water and lowered her gently into her winter home. The underside of her hull sat snugly on the tyres, her keel, skeg and rudder six inches clear of the bottom of the trench.

I packed the delicate electronic equipment and charts into boxes and stowed them in the attic of the Crowley office.

Cam Kristensen, one of Rick's team, carved traditional Eskimo snow goggles as gifts for the boys. I bought Rick 200 cigarettes as a gesture. George drove me to the airport.

As I stared down through the small oval of Perspex locked in my own world of colliding emotions, I realised I had come to know a certain truth. John Ruskin captured its essence when he wrote, *'There is no wealth but life – life, including all its powers of love, of joy and of admiration.'*

Barrabas and I had come far together, we had shared pivotal moments, weathered danger, rejoiced in the elemental beauty of the sea, taken care of one another and journeyed the hard road. I was anxious at leaving her but I knew that the people of Nome, that small and remarkable place, would care for her until I returned.

PART II
Over the Top

CHAPTER 22

Home and Away

The Atlantic Ocean spread endlessly beneath the aircraft's wings. The idea that I had traversed those spaces in a 40-foot boat was almost incomprehensible. Yet at sea, nothing had seemed more normal than sailing along day after day. Then, thoughts of driving to the supermarket, attending school plays, watching the evening news or flying on a plane had seemed bizarre.

'Excuse me, sir. We have chicken or lamb today.' The pretty flight attendant smiled at me offering the lunch menu. The first-class section was half-full, the seat next to mine empty. A United Airlines representative had met me at Washington DC's Dulles airport when I stepped off the plane from Chicago and whisked me to the executive lounge. 'Your wife called us, sir. My, what a voyage you have been on . . . we are happy to upgrade you for the transatlantic flight.'

Six weeks in Nome had isolated me from the reality that after 11 months, I would have to postpone my voyage to the following year after the spring thaw. Separated from *Barrabas*, back in the world of modernity – coffee shops, designer clothes and no longer cocooned – depression tugged at me for an hour or two while I waited for a connecting flight from Anchorage. Travelling to Seattle and Chicago, where I had to stay the night (my first sleep in a proper bed since leaving England), the reality took hold.

In the days of the Cold War, the idea of a lone, Western yachtsman venturing into Russian Arctic territory would have been unthinkable. Today, it remained politically and militarily sensitive. Permission to attempt the passage single-handed was a huge breakthrough, a first, and I had to hold on to that to keep my motivation alive.

I glimpsed my sons' faces through the half-glazed doors of the arrivals hall – eager, expectant faces etched with excitement. I remembered all those years before, the arrivals hall at Kai Tak, when the expectant faces had been those of my parents. Time had flipped the roles. I stood for a moment behind the doors, watching them and seeing the fathomless beauty that is only visible to a parent. Other passengers trundled past. All those miles, all that distance, all my thoughts. Now here they were, made flesh, like a miracle, two miracles. They were sitting on the floor at the end of a human corridor in front of Louise. Would time and distance have created space between us? Might some deep strand connecting me to my children been severed? I pushed the door. Gabriel saw me first and was up and running. I genuflected to receive his little, airborne body. I squeezed my eyes tightly shut, but tears seeped out anyway. Benjamin, older, more self-conscious, walked towards us. When he got to me, he opened his arms and wrapped them around my shoulders, his face to one side against mine, and in some minute but tangible way seemed to melt into me.

Louise and I hugged and almost together we said it seemed only a day or two since I had left. She persuaded a taxi driver meeting somebody off the flight to take some pictures and then we were out into the cold night and driving towards Buckinghamshire along familiar, unchanged roads. I sat in the back of the car with the children, no distance between us, no severed connections.

I turned 46 on 1st October. Louise threw a party in a marquee set up on the driveway. It was a Sunday. The party was as much for her as for me, a kind of release valve for all the tension of the last few weeks, a healing of sorts for the disappointment of having to break the Alpha Global Expedition. Sam arrived. I was glad of the chance to thank him. Ironically, he couldn't stay for long. He had a meeting in London with a group of Russians flogging gas to Britain.

My parents came, driving up from their house in Hampshire. My father had made one important inroad during the time I was sailing. In company with Admiral Sir James Ebberley, a one-time chief of NATO naval forces, he had orchestrated a meeting with Andrey Chupin at the

Russian Embassy in London. Following that meeting in the summer, I had written to Andrey Chupin while waiting in Nome. As First Minister, he was the main point of contact for the Foreign Office.

One week after the party, on 7th October 2006, a drive-by shooting in Moscow left a Russian journalist, Anna Politkovskaya, dead outside her apartment building. She had been an outspoken critic of the Russian government and in particular, the war in Chechnya. In London, Aleksandr Litvinenko claimed Politkovskaya's killing to be the work of the FSB. He had long been a thorn in the side of the Russian government. A former lieutenant-colonel in the FSB, Litvinenko fled Russia to Britain in 2001. The following year, he published a book, *Blowing up Russia: Terror from Within*. In his book, Litvinenko claimed that the FSB was behind the September 1999 bombings in apartment buildings in the southern city of Buinaksk, Moscow and Volgodonsk. The government blamed the atrocities on Chechen rebels, an allegation denied by separatist leader Shamil Basayev. In the wake of the bombings, Russian forces launched a second offensive on Chechnya.

I called Andrey Chupin on Wednesday 1st November to arrange a meeting at the Russian Embassy in Kensington Palace Gardens.

On the same day at 4.00 pm, Litvinenko met Russian businessman Andrei Lugovoy at the Mayfair Millennium Hotel near Grosvenor Square. Later, he met Italian academic Mario Scaramella at the Itsu sushi restaurant in Piccadilly. Scaramella had been investigating FSB-related espionage. After returning home that evening, Litvinenko became ill and was admitted to Barnet General Hospital.

On Wednesday 8th November, Louise and I drove to London. 'Embassy Row' is a grand avenue of grand houses, gated and secured at both ends. I parked up across the street from the Russian Embassy 20 minutes ahead of our allotted appointment. A junior staffer showed us to the Orangery overlooking the formal gardens of the residence, complete with tennis court. I was expecting a youngish, Armani-suited diplomat of the new order. Instead, Andrey Chupin was in his late fifties, reed-thin, wearing a tweed jacket, bespectacled and slightly stooping – more professorial than new generation egalitarian. The table was set with a bone-china service, pastries, hand-made Russian chocolates, silver cutlery and linen napkins. Andrey Chupin listened intently while I précised events that had led to my decision to delay the Alpha Global Expedition in Alaska. Despite everything that had gone

before, I needed to reapply for permissions to transit the NSR. Would
he, I asked, act as our liaison to ensure the application followed a
smoother path this time round?

'Well, you see, it's not possible for me to become directly involved.'

'Of course. I understand that various government departments in
Moscow act with a degree of autonomy.' Andrey Chupin cracked a
small smile at this reference to the FSB. 'But, I believe that were we to
gain the support of the ambassador, then the Foreign Office and your
Ministry of Foreign Affairs [MFA] might be able to have a more productive dialogue.'

The First Minister ruminated. 'Perhaps.'

'Rather than direct involvement, I am thinking more in terms of a
recommendation.'

We admired the room, spoke about the ambassador's prowess on
the tennis court and returned to the matter at hand.

'I will consider putting this to the ambassador. I see him daily.'

'Does His Excellency know of the Alpha Global Expedition?'

'Of course.'

We parted with the knowledge that Andrey Chupin had a fondness for English pubs and warm English beer and the promise that
he would table my request for some kind of intervention with His
Excellency, Yury Viktorovich Fedotov. I was to call the following
Tuesday to find out what, if any, result had materialised. Back in the
car and driving out of London, I realised I had put on mismatching suit
trousers.

On 11th November, Litvinenko spoke on the BBC Russian Service.
He claimed to have been the target of a 'serious poisoning'.

Three days later, on Tuesday 14th November, I waited anxiously
while somebody summoned Andrey Chupin to the telephone.

'I have spoken to the ambassador and I have to tell you, Mr
Flanagan, that His Excellency is fully in support of your expedition.'

'That's very good news, sir.' A cool wave of relief washed through
me. The Litvinenko affair was now commanding headline space on
front pages and news bulletins across the country. 'Can I ask you, Mr
Chupin, what's the next step?'

'I myself will prepare a document and this will be signed by the
ambassador and sent to the appropriate officials within the relevant
departments of the MFA. It is a matter for them to decide whether to
distribute the document to other relevant government departments
and agencies.'

'I am very grateful.' Pressing my luck, I said, 'May I ask, sir, what the document suggests?'

'The ambassador will be recommending that the relevant departments support the Alpha Global Expedition in granting clearances for a transit of the Northern Sea Route in 2007. Once we have heard back, I shall let you know the outcome.'

I followed the Litvinenko story closely. His dissident status was well known. So far, doctors had not been able to identify the cause of his illness. On 17th November, doctors transferred Litvinenko to University College Hospital. Suspicions mounted. Scotland Yard placed an armed guard outside his door. Any implication of subterfuge by the Russian government would strain diplomatic relations with Britain to breaking point. The consequences on the expedition might be terminal.

On 19th November, doctors concluded that thallium poisoning (a highly toxic metal once used to poison rats) was to blame. Litvinenko suffered a heart attack on the night of Wednesday November 22nd and died the following day. Doctors revised their diagnosis, discounting thallium poisoning. Scotland Yard's counter-terrorism unit began pursuing a rigorous investigation into Litvinenko's 'unexplained' death. Eventually scientists identified a radioisotope, polonium-210, as the poison that had killed Litvinenko. The police found traces of polonium-210 at the Mayfair Millennium Hotel, in cars and in a British Airways jet used by Lugovoy. The trail led directly back to Moscow.

I finally had the chance of meeting Ian Johnstone-Bryden and Henk de Velde at the London Boat Show in early January. Louise and I met up with Ian for breakfast in the hotel just outside the ExCeL exhibition centre in London's Docklands. Ian was losing me in his technical explanation of how website hit statistics are logged when my phone rang. I recognised the number.

'You father's fallen down the stairs.'

'Is he okay, Mum?'

'Yes, but I'm worried.'

So was I. He was 76 and recently out of hospital following surgery to his lower spine. 'Is his back okay?'

'It seems to be.'

'Did he trip or what?'

'He says not. His legs just gave way.'

'Is he dizzy?'

'No.'

'Well, Mum, there's not much I can do.' I explained where I was. 'Have you called an ambulance or the doctor?'

'No, not yet, I wanted to talk to you first.'

'Okay, look, call the GP, get him over there asap. A man doesn't just collapse for no reason.'

Henk de Velde was a large man with a mop of unruly, curly hair, arms like hams and a booming laugh.

'I have now my new boat. Ya! She is a catamaran, much different to *Campina*.' Henk was a wanderer who had never lost his appetite for wanting to know what lay over the horizon. We were sitting at the Kemp Sails' stand, trying to attract as much attention as possible to Rob and Matt's wares. 'Now I go on the islands expedition.'

'What's that?'

'I leave Holland for ever to sail to the unlived-on islands around the world. I make books and films of these. Here . . .' Henk fished in his bag and pulled out a DVD box. 'The voyage of *Campina*, for you.'

I wanted to know definitively which boats had made transits of the NSR. Henk started reciting names and dates, counting them off on his fingers.

'So, only seven yachts. I was in the water for the winter in Tiksi. The sea-ice damaged the rudders. Then in 2004, I got caught in ice. The only way out was to go on a ship with *Campina* on the deck, to Murmansk.'

'That was bad luck.'

'Ya! Maybe. But then you, number eight, but the first alone!' A great hand clapped down onto my shoulder.

'Chicken and eggs come to mind, Henk.'

Henk looked at me quizzically. 'Never mind,' I said. 'What about the inspection, was it thorough?'

'In my case, the harbourmaster of Provideniya inspected *Campina*. He looked at some technical drawings, he looked at the engine and the fuel tanks, drank his tea and was gone. It took 15 minutes.'

'And insurance? Monko's people were asking me about that, but I didn't have any.'

'I did not have insurance but I had a letter of credit from Campina (a Dutch dairy products company) covering costs up to US $100,000 for environmental damage and cost of icebreaker assistance.

'Of course I paid pilotage costs $5,000 but not the salvage costs.

Later, I heard that Campina made a deal but they never told me how much. I think some computers and other stuff for Mr Monko, but this is not official.'

I reckoned Campina probably didn't see a lot of change from the US$ 100,000.

Louise and I trawled the show and then drove back to Buckinghamshire. I called my father. He sounded unconcerned about his earlier fall. 'What did the doctor say?' I asked.

'Nothing much.'

'Did he find anything?'

'No.'

'Dad, I've got to tell you, I think you should be in hospital. Not to put too fine a point on it, you're 76 years old, you've just had reasonably major surgery and you're collapsing for no apparent reason. You should be under observation, 48 hours at least.'

My father brushed off my concerns and asked me about the boat show.

I decided to stay in the guest room at Louise's house. The phone rang at 3.45 am. I stirred awake. I could hear Louise's voice heavy with sleep coming from across the corridor, then the sound of a door opening and urgent footsteps.

'It's your mother.'

I grabbed the phone. My mother was hysterical. I tried to calm her. My father had taken ill. He couldn't breathe, collapsed on the floor of his bedroom. Neighbours were with her.

'Have you called an ambulance?'

'Roy has.'

'Right, put the phone near Dad's mouth so I can hear.'

She did. His breathing was rapid and shallow. He was hyperventilating. 'Mum?'

'Yes.'

'Put a pillow under his neck, not his head, his neck. Check he hasn't swallowed his tongue . . . do it now, Mum.' I waited.

'I think he's going.'

'Mum, I'm going to get dressed and drive down to you. When did Roy call the ambulance?'

'Ten minutes ago.'

'Okay. They'll be there anytime now. Just hold on. Call me when they're there.'

I handed the phone to Louise.

Forty minutes later, the phone rang. My father had died. Only later did we learn that an undetected abscess on his liver had ruptured, causing catastrophic septicaemic shock.

I heard back from Andrey Chupin in early February. The Ministry of Foreign Affairs had been in touch with him to say they would agree to distribute the ambassador's report to the appropriate departments within the Russian government: Interior, FSB, Defence, Transport and Northern Sea Route Administration.

'I am very grateful to you, Mr Chupin. I hope that the ice lets me through, but if it doesn't, the fact that I would be the first to enter the Northern Sea Route alone will make a small piece of history.'

'Yes, yes. I should say to you, Mr Flanagan, His Excellency believes that your voyage could make a positive contribution towards Anglo–Russian relations.'

I almost fell off my chair.

Louise, with a tenacity I came to admire even more, secured insurance for *Barrabas* against environmental pollution. Everything seemed to be in order. John Mann was still co-ordinating activity for the new per-mission in Moscow, liaising regularly with Nikolai Monko. Finally, he sent an email to say he would be in London in March. We arranged to meet at one of the hotels in Chelsea Village.

When John walked into the hotel foyer, I was surprised at his youth. More importantly, the rapport both Louise and I had developed with John through innumerable emails and telephone conversations, cata-lysed no doubt by the intensity and urgency of the situation that had thrown us all together, continued on without missing a beat. We went to a bistro across the road for lunch.

'This so just so weird,' I said to John. For a moment, his expression seemed uncertain. 'Sitting here in a restaurant in London with you.'

Of course, to John perhaps the encounter was not so surreal. He travelled extensively on business as head of Roman Abramovich's public relations and media management. To me, Russia was another country, unseen and ill understood. John was fluent in Russian, mar-ried to a Ukrainian and had made his home in Moscow. Meeting all types of people, from adventurers to politicians to corporate execut-ives, was all part of John's daily agenda.

'So,' I said, 'I guess you must have studied Political Science and Russian at Harvard.'

John looked startled. 'How did you . . .'

'Just a wild guess,' I said. It was an educated guess. I figured Roman Abramovich would only employ the best, and in the States that usually meant a degree from Harvard. John came from Washington DC, an African–American with a background as a former vice-president of US PR giant Burson-Marsteller, the company that represented Ford and Coca-Cola in the United States. Whatever his education, John was well schooled in circumspection. Dealing with Russia's labyrinthine bureaucracy required a practised hand and John agreed to continue liaising on behalf of the Alpha Global Expedition. Winning the requisite permissions for a transit of the NSR that summer would, we agreed, likely be a formality. How things might turn out in the hostile and unpredictable Arctic environment was less certain.

In the frantic race to get to and through the NSR the previous summer, I had not followed up on MDA's promise of providing satellite imagery to assist with navigation of the passage. I reprised that promise in an email to Simon Chesworth, MDA's sales director for Europe, the Middle East and Africa. He agreed to continue where we left off. I sent my anticipated timings to Simon:

- Fly from UK to Alaska: 25th June 2007
- Prepare Boat: 26th June – 10th July
- Sail to Provideniya for Boat Inspection (200 miles):   11th – 13th July
- Boat Inspection: 14th – 16th July
- Commence NSR Passage: 17th July
- Arrive at Vil'kitskiy Strait: 31st July
- Passage through Vil'kitskiy Strait: 1st – 10th August
- Vil'kitskiy Strait to UK via Murmansk: 4 weeks
- Arrival in Solent, UK: 28th August – 7th September

On 4th May 2007, John sent me a copy of the instruction from Nikolai Monko to the port authorities in Provideniya requesting that on completion of a satisfactory inspection of *Barrabas* they issue me with permit number 18/07 to transit the NSR. On the same day, I received the draft acquisition plan for satellite imagery from MDA.

To slot the final piece of the jigsaw, the visa, into place, I needed an 'invitation' from an appropriate organisation in Russia. John arranged for the invitation to come from the Administration of Chukotka

province, of which Roman Abramovich was still governor. After regis-
tering the invitation with the Ministry of Foreign Affairs in Moscow,
John sent me a copy and I in turn sent it on to Andrey Chupin.

Nikolai Monko had also copied his instruction to Nikolay Babych at
Western Marine Operations Headquarters, the traffic co-ordination
centre controlling shipping through the western part of the NSR, including the Vil'kitskiy Strait.

John said, 'The Murmansk Shipping Company operate the icebreakers under government contract. Western Marine Operations
Headquarters controls their activities, guidance, navigation, that sort
of thing.'

'And Babych?'

'He heads up WMOHQ.'

'So he works for MSCO?'

'I guess.'

'Do I need some kind of contract with MSCO then, in case I get into
trouble?'

'I spoke with Babych. He says an exchange of contact details is all
you need. If you get in trouble then they'll come help, presumably
with some cost. I'm not sure if Monko would go for that but it sounds
like an easier route.'

Adrian (to Simon Chesworth, MDA Geospatial Services): Thursday 14th June 2007

*I have been down with Tim in Portsmouth a number of times. We discussed
the best way to proceed with the ice routing. The plan is that Tim will use the
www.seaice.de website to get an overview, check on what the ice is doing on a
daily basis. He will cut the relevant section relative to my current position
and email the image (reducing file size as much as possible) so that I have a
general idea of what's happening with the ice edge. As I approach more ice-
congested waters – likely to be near Vil'kitskiy Strait, Tim will contact you
(with as much notice as possible) with requests for the satellite image needed
(long/lat/resolution etc). If you can then take the shot and pass it to Tim, he
will contact me for my current position and then plot the route and advise me
accordingly by either email or voice.*

*I have asked Tim to call you to discuss image formats etc and other
technical detail to max the accuracy of his interpretation.*

Meanwhile, John had finally received the vital authorisation from the
FSB. On Friday 22nd June, my last full working day in England, I drove

to the Russian Embassy in London to meet with the head of the Consular Section. I left an hour later with a three-month visa. On Monday 25th June, I flew from Heathrow back to the United States on United Airlines flight 931.

CHAPTER 23

Stamp of Approval

I stepped out of the small terminal building at Nome Airport. The muddied pick-ups in the car park, the distant buzz of quad bikes zipping along on the airport road and the treeless tundra surrounding the airfield were immediately familiar. Low grey cloud dropped sheets of drizzle. I lit a cigarette and waited for Tim to collect me.

As we turned onto the dirt road leading to the Crowley shop, I glimpsed *Barrabas* behind some earth-moving trucks that Rick had parked around her as protection. On board in the dim light, I made a quick inspection. No damp, just the dusty smell of disuse. The heater's fuel tank was full. The batteries had held their charge through the polar night. I fired up the heater and soon a wave of warm air began dispelling the scent of neglect.

I found Rick in the shop. 'So, Rick, what's that bloody huge dent doing in the side of the boat?'

He was wise to me now. 'Drove a truck into her, sorry 'bout that, you know how it goes, dark and that.'

We shook hands. 'How've you been?'

'Good, you know, not bad.'

'So no Eskimos camping in the boat.' That had been my biggest concern. Homeless Inuit found shelter beneath buildings, any nook or cranny to escape the bitter cold.

Later, I learned from Cam that Rick's wife was in hospital in

Anchorage, desperately ill, fighting cancer. She was due for major surgery to rebuild her spine, which the cancer had destroyed. How typical of Rick to bear it all with a grin.

I set straight to work, unwrapping the mast where it lay in the oil storage facility, overhauling the engine and installing the new Furuno Radar that DHL had air-freighted to Nome ahead of me. The radar was fitted with an integral GPS unit. I ran the cable below decks from the chart table to the aft frame. But how to mount it? Rick had a look.

He looked at me. 'What's d'matter widge you? You gotta problem with this?'

'Yeah, Rick. You got a solution?'

'Sure, no problem.' Off he went back to the shop. He reappeared fifteen minutes later. Using plastic plumbing pipe, Rick had constructed an angled support mount for the GPS receiver with a curved base plate that sat perfectly on the tubular structure of the aft frame. He tapped it in with two screws and for good measure bound it with Jubilee clips. I tested it for strength. Rock-solid. I reckon I could have hung off it with my full body weight.

Over the following days, while *Barrabas* sat squat in her trench, I organised the deck gear, set up the two laptops and rimmed out the mast radar cable outlet.

Adrian: Sunday 1st July 2007

Glad the boys have settled back quickly after I left. I have to confess to a mighty bout of depression when I left you at Heathrow but I'm okay now. I still wake with a heavy dread in the pit of my belly but it's easing slowly. Once I'm on the water I'll be fine . . .

On Wednesday 4th July, Rick came into work to help me. We lifted the mast horizontally with the crane, up and over the fence of the oil storage facility and 'walked' it towards the shop. Still suspended four feet off the ground, Rick welded reinforcing seams around the upper spreaders. As an Independence Day parade rolled by on the dirt road, Rick lowered the mast onto wooden blocks. I reattached the strops to the mast's upper part and Rick hoisted the mast vertically. I stood on *Barrabas*'s deck guiding Rick in the crane's cab with hand signals. We stepped the mast in a perfect operation. With the new radar scanner mounted on the mast, the mast electrics hooked up and the forestay and furling gear back on, we could now lift *Barrabas*.

With *Barrabas* held in slings, Rick locked the crane while I applied a fresh coat of antifoul. Cam, working as a mechanic with Crowley but an artist by training, temperament and inclination, 'tattooed' *Barrabas* on her starboard and port quarters with an image of a pal-ai-yuk, a mythical creature from Inuit tradition, half serpent, half crocodile and usually painted on hunting kayaks. Being fierce, the pal-ai-yuk would frighten other sea creatures away and protect *Barrabas*.

Later that afternoon, with *Barrabas* in the water and moored alongside the harbour wall, Rick left for Anchorage. It was a difficult farewell – Rick had been unstinting in his support for the expedition and me. Without him, this Alaskan hiatus would have been much more difficult.

On Sunday, someone tapping at the bow interrupted my routine of work and worry. Two young guys stood on the harbour wall. I recognised something distinctly non-American about them. It turned out they were French – Sébastien Roubinet and Eric André, who had just sailed in on a small, Kevlar catamaran, *Babouche*, so called because its shape was reminiscent of a Moroccan slipper. The boat's odd appearance was by design, the idea being to meet low pack ice at speed, climb up onto the ice and continue sailing on top of the pack. They were going to try the Northwest Passage. Sébastien and Eric, all lantern-jawed, tousle-haired, broken-nosed Gallic confidence, had no engine, no radar and only two hand-held GPS units for navigation.

While Sébastien and Eric made final preparations, tied up to the fishing boats' pontoon across the harbour, I bent on the mainsail, laid out the running rigging and filled the fuel cans lined up on the floor of the shop.

I learned from some of the crew on the local gold dredgers, barges and fishing boats about 'Splash Zone', a two-part underwater cement that set like rock to repair small holes in the hull. The risk of a hull rupture sat ever-present like an unwelcome guest long after the party is over. I ordered some Splash Zone from Katchemak Gear Shed in Homer.

Cam and his wife, Malinda, appreciating that I would not be sitting down to home-cooked food for a while, invited me to dinner several times – steak, pasta, salads, puddings, beer.

On Saturday 14th July, Malinda drove me to the A&C store out of town. I bought basic provisions: 60 litres of long-life milk, tins of fruit, chilli beef, creamed corn, cheese, salami, butter, jams, biscuits, tinned milk, energy bars, sweetener, fruit juices and paper towels (for mopping up oil and fuel spillage when I made filter changes on the engine).

I already had porridge oats, rice, tinned tuna and salmon, together with other supplies good for 30 days already on board, plus the essential coffee, tea and drinking chocolate and assorted nuts and confectionery.

The next day, I started loading the fuel and completing my list of final jobs. At dinner that evening, Malinda and Cam presented me with a box of food: Malinda's 'historic' fried bread, jams and wild Alaskan blueberries. Cam had made me a fishing line with a lure carved from bone and an amulet carved from moose antler.

'See, here's how it goes.' Cam leaned forward. The lid of the box was carved with a face. He pulled it away. 'This here's grizzly fur.'

'You shoot the bear?'

'Yep. See, when a grizzly meets a polar bear, the polar bear backs off.' He pushed the lock of fur back into the box and closed the carved lid. 'The idea's you hang it in the boat someplace. It'll ward off any polar bear attack.'

'Thanks. Really appreciate this, and everything else you two have done for me.'

Cam waved these sentiments away. 'How you feeling 'bout things?'

'Nervous. Colliding emotions, I guess. There's the desire to be under way and I'm eager for what lies ahead, but then there's fear, you know, fear of the unknown, the consequences of a misjudgement or of pure bad luck.'

'You can bet your ass the Russkis'll be watching you.'

'Good!'

I hung the amulet from the cabin headlining alongside the tea leaf lei from Hawaii.

I finally got away from Nome at 2.30 pm on Tuesday 17th July, three weeks to the day and almost to the hour since I'd arrived back in Alaska. Winds were light and out of the west. The next three days looked to be similarly fair. Provideniya lay 200 miles across the northern part of the Bering Sea so I expected to make port sometime on Friday, but crossing the International Date Line westwards would warp me forward 24 hours.

The Crowley team and Joy Baker saw me off. I discovered the boat's main GPS unit was not working. The instruments relied on signals from the GPS. With no signals, the displays were blank. I switched to a hand-held GPS back-up and then traced the problem to a section of cabling in the dark recesses of the lazarette. A sharp edge had abraded an area of the cable sheath and corrosion had broken the core connection. I cut, cleaned, spliced and soldered, tried the unit and bingo, we picked up six satellites and *Barrabas* and I were back in business. I followed this with a meal of fried eggs, Malinda's fried bread, salami and fresh wild Alaskan blueberries.

Barrabas settled comfortably on the open water. I kept the engine running but not engaged for 24 hours; after nine months of standing I wanted to make sure she worked well and that the fix to the cut-lass bearings had held true. I was close enough to Nome to return, if ignominiously, to sort out any problem. As it was, the engine ran sweetly.

Adrian (to Cam & Malinda): Wednesday 18th July 2007

I wrote a letter to Rick in Anchorage and I will repeat some of the things I said to him. Many people have taken inspiration from the journey I am attempting to complete. But really, the hallmarks of greatness lie within the simple courtesies of everyday life – generosity of time and spirit, concern and thoughtfulness, the expenditure of effort on behalf of others in return for no reward. All these things you have shown to me and I am deeply grateful to you both.

Louise had learnt from her previous experience of managing the expedition. This time round she had hired an au pair to help with the boys.

Louise: Wednesday 18th July 2007

All is well here – Rosanne took the boys out all day to give me time with my beloved computer. Rosanne is really working out way better than I expected. She has a lovely calm manner about her – she is absolutely on the boys' level which they love. Never tires of running around with them and playing tennis and football in the garden.

After making good progress, the wind came onto the nose. I tacked back and forth for six hours, going precisely nowhere. Then, the wind backed to the south-southwest and we were cruising. Provideniya lay 100 miles away. These winds held until late evening and we ticked off another 50 miles.

At 1.05 pm on Friday 20th July, we passed into Russian territorial waters, crossing the International Date Line at the same time. I raised the Russian courtesy flag on the starboard shroud.

Three large whales, brownish in colour, surfaced off the starboard beam. I heard their blowholes. When I came on deck, the mountains of the Russian coast loomed ahead, shrouded beneath eiderdowns of fluffy mist. *Barrabas* sailed on under an azure sky.

Louise: Saturday 21st July 2007

Off to see Harry Potter this morning then I have to go and buy some new jeans . . . seem to have crept from a size 10 to a size 12 – only temporary though! I must be feeling very relaxed . . . the Rosanne effect. Last time with no help I was in such a high state of anxiety all the time. I worried constantly how I was going to juggle the AGX and kids and took virtually no time for myself. It was all wrong and I see it very clearly now. Can't wait to hear what awaits you in Provideniya. Forget James Bond movies – this is the real deal!

I motored the last 10 miles to reach Provideniya's natural harbour carved from the mountains at the head of a deep-water fjord. Wreathed in layers of mist, precipitous scree slopes showed through like a massive granite and cotton millefeuille. I made it to the town at 6.00 am. Great rusted dockside cranes reached towards the sun-punctured sky like the curved talons of some long-dead prehistoric bird. Someone instructed me by radio to berth at number two – it turned out to be crane two. Three federal internal security guards ordered me to stay on the boat. Shaking hands seemed a somehow inappropriate gesture. After almost 30 hours with no sleep, the lure of the bag was too great to resist.

Loud banging brought me awake at 10.30 am. A posse of uniformed officials from various state departments instructed me to take *Barrabas* to another quay. It had been a jetty at one time, the concrete long since crumbled away leaving the twisted, rusty steel frame poking dangerously towards the hull. The guards produced a bevy of forms to fill, all in triplicate, then flanked by guards, we made our way across the dock to a neighbouring tug. In the relative comfort of the ward-room, I produced my wad of Russian permission letters. A brief discussion followed about the need for an ice pilot. I ruffled through more papers, incomprehensible documents in Russian. The answer seemed to be contained among them, rapid-fire Russian was followed by a consensus of nodding heads and any thoughts of an ice pilot quickly dismissed.

At noon, one of the uniforms gave me my permit to transit the NSR, numbered 18/07, stamped and approved. I was free to go!

I decided to stay the night alongside. Internal security allocated a two-man detail rotating in six-hour shifts to stay with the boat. We tried to communicate in the universal language of broken English, mime and gesticulation punctuated with groans of frustration as meanings were lost.

I needed to top up on fuel. The master of the tug called the oil terminal – no one answered so he gave me some of his at no charge. I gave him a bottle of rum and a bottle of sloe gin from *Barrabas*.

Uran, the tug's mate, spoke some English. He led me into town to buy onions. There was no shopfront as such, just a wooden door, bent by years of freezing winds. Inside, the place reeked of ancient wax and cabbage. A single, naked bulb cast a dull yellow light. The shelves were almost bare: a few tins here and there, some dusty bars of chocolate, candles, cooking oil. I imagined post-war rationing in a deprived area.

Back on the tug, Uran offered the use of their shower, which I readily accepted. The tug's master knew Henk de Velde, who had stopped here for an extended stay prior to his attempt at the NSR in 2003. So even in this strange forbidding land that time seemed to have forgotten, it was still a small world.

On Monday morning 23rd July, I was ready to leave. The FSB commissioner came to the dock at 10.45 am, handed my papers over, indicated for me to sign more documents in Russian and then I was free to go. I started the engine and slipped my lines at 11.00 am.

Barrabas passed Cape Dezhnava and crossed the 66° north parallel, the eastern entrance to the Northern Sea Route, at 00.50 am on Wednesday 25th July, the first yacht ever to do so single-handed. Under full sail during the night, *Barrabas* touched 6.5 knots despite her 6,000 lbs load of fuel and water. If ever a boat had real guts, it was this one. While she battled on, I slept for four hours. Our great adventure together into the unknown had begun.

CHAPTER 24

The Walrus and the Ice Bears

Louise: Thursday 26th July 2007

I almost killed your sons tonight. They were playing with the hand shower in their bathroom and managed to flood my office wiping out my external drive, my mobile phone, my cordless mouse and key pad. Thank God the computer is OK otherwise . . . as it is they are in their rooms for the rest of the evening (since 5.15). I have never been so angry in my entire life.

Winds built to 27 knots, not terrifically high, but in water depths of only 100 feet the seas kicked up without too much encouragement. The boat's stability concerned me. I dropped the mainsail and ran with reefed headsail. It was all about control – the feeling that the boat had control of the conditions.

By Saturday 28th July, we had covered 500 miles from Providen, Wrangel Island lay due north as we passed from the Chukchi Sea westwards into the East Siberian Sea. On deck, the weather was fine, a beautiful 'blue' day, the coast discernible eight miles off the port beam wreathed in mist but the air warm despite our latitude at almost 70° north.

I spent most of the afternoon constructing a jack to tension the alternator belts from two bits of wood, a bolt, a nut, a washer and some epoxy. The commercial fishermen based on Kodiak Island smothered their gloves in silicone sealant to keep them waterproof. I tried it, hanging the gloves to dry from the washing line in the galley.

Malinda: Monday 30th July 2007 (sent via Louise)
I hope that things are going well. We are checking Adrian's page daily. I just needed to relay a message to him. They are doing a huge recall on some canned chilli from Alaska and I think that he bought some when I took him shopping. Please let him know not to open the cans or eat anything inside. The cans could contain bacteria that cause botulism.

I had bought eight cans and already eaten one! I punctured the remaining seven and chucked them over the side, but the idea of botulin toxin on board outweighed my environment-friendly instincts.

On the last day in July, the easternmost of the four islands of the Ostrova Medvezh'i slid into view. I altered course to pass north of Chetyryokhstolbovyy Island (what kind of name is that!). Its neighbour, Leont'yeva Island, was lost behind a curtain of haze. The next island, Pushkova, sat dough-like on a flat, shimmering sea. Sea mist rolled in ahead of a depression. It had an icy look to it. I knew the land would be gone within minutes. The depression laid a mantle of thick cloud over this small part of the earth's apex, reducing visibility to half a mile. The light dimmed to grey. The sea became slate. Winds shifted to the northwest and built. We pushed into this wind for the next 24 hours, striking two precious miles off our track every hour.

Nikolay Babych, controller at West Marine Operations Headquarters, finally responded to my requests for weather information. The Maxsea GRIBs data did not extend much above 70° north. Tim provided forecasts by email, but I figured that WMOHQ would have access to more detailed reports specific to Russia's Arctic coast. Nikolay also sent through email contacts for two icebreakers operating on the eastern side of the Vil'kitskiy Strait with the instruction that I should copy the icebreakers on all communication to WMOHQ.

Barrabas bashed on through the night. I marked up the chart. In spite of the headwinds, we had reached the halfway point to Vil'kitskiy Strait.

Like a phantom echo, my appetite hovered somewhere distant. The mere thought of food, even a biscuit, vaporised the phantom completely. My body had shut down into some deep, primeval survival mode able to sustain itself with no obvious source of energy. The muscles of my belly became defined, my cheeks hollowed. I started heaping sugar into tea and coffee, the only sustenance I wanted or, it seemed, needed.

The land of northern Russia's remote wilderness scrolled slowly by, soft hills sliding gently to the sea, treeless and brown, mottled in places with snow, white flags as testament of surrender to the bitter winter cold.

Whenever *Barrabas* was happy sailing without me goading her on, I read, as much to hide from my anxiety as for the enjoyment on the page. I had already digested Paul Torday's *Salmon Fishing in the Yemen*. The thought of the dry heat of the Arabian desert seemed like Nirvana. By now, I was well into *The Road*, Cormac McCarthy's novel on the hell of surviving a post-nuclear world.

At 2.30 pm, Friday 3rd August, the radar registered a contact at two miles, 20° off the port bow. A patrolling icebreaker, perhaps? Tim had warned me to expect ice at 153° east. I glanced at the GPS. We were close, longitude 151.47° east. I grabbed the binoculars and went on deck. Apart from ships on the horizon, I couldn't see anything. I ducked my head below the companionway to watch the radar sweep. There it was again. I glassed to the fore. A massive chunk of sea-ice floated like a carcass abandoned by the herd. I played the binoculars along the line of the sea. More lumps of ice dotted the horizon, carved by wind and water into strange, alien shapes. I passed another one, a tiny island, streaked with blue and green. It looked like a swan the size of a family car, its head bent low on its icy neck as though being drawn inexorably into the melt. The ice edge stretched away to the north, intra-lit by the Arctic sun.

These were orphans, cut adrift from the southern bulge of the ice edge by the west wind, outriggers to the main pack. Climbing halfway up the mast did not help. I approached the edge of the pack southeast of Dimitriya Lapteva Strait, looking for a way round. Hummocks of ice stretched away in all directions, projecting cold like a solid wall. I estimated the ice at 30 per cent cover, the safe maximum in which *Barrabas* could manoeuvre. I was dressed warmly, helped by my heated mid-layer. A ski mask protected my eyes, preventing the frigid air from drawing tears and obscuring my vision. I edged forward along a narrow channel. The entire mass was moving and shifting on the currents, openings slowly closing, new channels widening, contracting and expanding as though the ice itself was drawing breath. I felt like a giant among a miniature archipelago. The wind-sculpted ice resembled landforms. Hills rose and fell, water lapped in small bays hewn between promontories. Within the ice perimeter, it was calm, the free water flat. Seals rested on level shards, curious at the low growl of the engine. Whiskery faces bobbed up around me at this unexpected interruption to their day. As I drew nearer, the seals' curiosity gave way to anxiety and they slid quickly to the sanctuary of the water. I stayed in the ice for six hours, steering cautiously. The ice was soft but submarine edges could still be razor-sharp. *Barrabas* nudged and bumped. My heart fluttered at each grinding contact. It was tense but exhilarating, this pristine world. I was the first man to be out here alone, this far from land along Russia's polar waterway. In that small footprint of the earth's surface, in that tiny fragment of time, I was discovering, if only of myself. I was eight years old when man first stepped onto the moon. I watched Neil Armstrong with a sense of wonderment and awe. Almost 40 years on, I was feeling that same sense in the ice.

Barrabas came through the ice field. Were there others close by? I managed a few hours' sleep. Like a siren, this icescape was as deadly as it was beautiful. The possibility of collision now became my central concern.

At some point while I was below, I heard the sound of something metallic falling on deck. The sound seemed half-real, half-imagined, as I dithered somewhere between sleep and wakefulness. Rousing myself from the warm innards of the sleeping bag, I clambered on deck and found a nut on the starboard side, nestled against the toe-rail, level with the mast. A jolt of panic zinged through me. I looked up. The split pin at the end of the through-mast bolt securing the lower shroud tangs had failed. The nut had worked its way off the bolt and dropped to the deck. The bolt was eking its way out too, the starboard shroud tang literally hanging on its very last thread. Had that gone with full sail set, the mast could have buckled in the middle! Part of the thread was damaged, so I drilled out the inside of the old nut (thank God I'd kept it from Honolulu) to use as a washer. Loosening the shrouds, I hefted the tang firmly up the bolt, slid the 'washer' home, tightened the nut and put in a new split pin. Freeclimbing the mast, I inspected the intermediate tangs and the cap shrouds at the mast top.

Cam: Monday 6th August 2007
Rick update. Hannah is doing better. She is up walking around (with some trouble), so that is a good sign. Rick is doing good, well as good as any guy that can't sit still more than two minutes can do sitting around.

Ever since reaching the halfway mark to Vil'kitskiy Strait, the wind had stayed stubbornly in the west at 25 knots, forcing us to bash into mounting seas. The wind-driven current reduced speed to little faster than a crawl. Ice gathered by the wind might bear down at any time. Sleep was difficult. Instinct, sharpened by time and experience, tugged at me. Something was about to fail. I could not afford to relax the ceaseless rounds of inspections and maintenance checks. I spotted a problem. The starboard forward lower shroud was unravelling! I gybed *Barrabas* onto port tack to take the pressure off the starboard rig and then went aloft to have a look. The damage was not so bad. One strand had broken. Still, a break was a break, and more worryingly, if one strand could break, others might follow. I called Louise and asked her to find out from Tim when this depression would blow over. She called back to say, 'The worst is over.'

The last 24 hours had been hellish. When was the last time I'd slept? With clear water all around and no contacts on the radar within a radius of 24 miles, I crashed into my sleeping bag. I woke six hours later to a thumping headache. The glass was rising. Was it air pressure or lack of food? The ice ahead at Vil'kitskiy Strait was at 90–100 per cent cover, impenetrable and impassable.

The engine demanded regular attention to ensure it kept running sweetly. In close ice conditions, loss of the engine would be catastrophic. I ran the engine routinely, to keep it warm and prevent any type of seizing. On 8th August, the engine suddenly cut out. My heart skipped a beat. I knew immediately it was a fuel problem – a sudden cut-out, no coughing and spluttering before dying, no blue, black or white smoke. I checked the fuel system. Everything appeared normal, no leaks or disconnected piping. The filters were clean. I called Louise. She called the engineers at Golden Arrow. Together we isolated the problem to a failed fuel solenoid. I switched the engine to a mechanical override and off she went. Nevertheless, the combination of events and conditions was enough. Seeds of doubt sprang from their pods and quickly took root. I found my thoughts turning as bleak as the sea around me. I had to snap out of this, give myself a talking to, which I did, aloud. There was a lot of shouting. I talked to *Barrabas*. Because of the impenetrable ice ahead, I put the idea to Nikolay Babych of finding an anchorage to wait for the ice to clear from the Vil'kitskiy Strait.

Nikolay Babych: Wednesday 8th August 2007

The passage through Vil'kitskiy Bay from the east at the present is not
available. Awaiting ice conditions improvement in the west part of the Laptev
Sea can be of long-term period – about 20–30 days. In the area of Begichev and
Peschanyy islands drift ice is observed. The place of stoppage for waiting of
best weather conditions is recommended to be area of Stolbovoy Island or to
make the call to port Tiksi.

Stolbovoy Island lay 30 miles north. Tiksi, the main port along the
NSR, was deep into the south of the Lena Delta. *Barrabas* answered.
The water rushed rhythmically against her hull like the passing of rail
track beneath a speeding carriage. Press on . . . press on . . . press on,
she seemed to be saying.

Strong westerlies howled in over the bow, crippling progress to an
agonising slowness. Sea and sky were a monochromatic continuum of
grey. The wind carried a bite, the sea clutched at *Barrabas*, pinching,
shoving, prodding. It was difficult to rest. With the horizon veiled by
curtains of mist and sea fog, the radar swept a constant vigil. Fatigue
and frustration began corroding my resolve, abetted by the cold.

Adrian: Friday 10th August 2007

How're things with you? Things here are dire. This is the eighth day with
strong headwinds. My average distance travelled towards my target is well
below one mile per hour. I could literally crawl faster. This last week has been
the most grinding, gruelling, soul-destroying section of the entire AGX. I am
on the verge of calling it a day – I won't of course, but I am very close. I am
getting maybe an hour's sleep per 24 and that's light and fitful. This is truly,
truly shit. Hope you're having a better time than me.

Just as my endurance had given out, the next morning broke clear and
blue. The wind backed south carrying with it the warmth of the land
close by. *Barrabas* barrelled along under full sail at over six knots, nose
to target, eager to make up lost ground. I fell into an exhausted sleep
for six hours. Two hundred and twenty miles remained to sail westwards and then we could turn north for the ice.

Louise: Saturday 11th August 2007

Benji starts his cricket course on Monday – and they both have their
swimming course next week as well. They have had a very active summer.
Has been wonderfully hot and sunny this week but forecast is for change . . .

more rain starting tomorrow. Ian says land temperatures in Russia are
unseasonably high right now. This is such good news for you . . .

I consulted my charts and found a promising anchorage in Bukhta
Pronchishchevoy on the eastern side of the Taymyr Peninsula. The
top, northern end of the peninsula formed the southern side of the
Vil'kitskiy Strait. From the chart, the anchorage appeared well protected and out of the tidal stream. I could hole up there for as long as
necessary, then as the ice allowed, inch northwards up the east coast of
the peninsula towards the Vil'kitskiy Strait, seeking out anchorages as
required. From our present position, Bukhta Pronchishchevoy was 75
miles west-northwest.

The great unknown in all of my reasoning was the ice. What was
the southerly extent of the landfast ice? How far south was the current
ice edge? Could I approach Bukhta Pronchishchevoy from the east?
Was there any drift ice north of Begichev Island? I put all these questions to Nikolay Babych.

By the evening of 12th August, I saw drift ice ahead, vanguards of
the main pack. This was a bad sign. We were still miles from the
peninsula. By 10.00 pm, we hit the edge of the pack ice, still 50 miles
offshore. My heart sank. The ice edge was much further south than I
had expected. With the engine on low revs and all sail down, I steered
Barrabas through these outlying regiments of drift ice. Ahead, a white
line looked like the leading edge of the solid ice sheet, but I knew that
as I drew closer, this line would break up revealing channels though
the pack.

I found a gateway in. Large pieces of ice formed an intricate mosaic.
Something moved in the water. At first I thought it was a bobbing ice
chip, but it was moving too fast. I looked again. Two black eyes stared
back at me. Now 20 metres in front of my bow, the polar bear lifted his
snout to sniff at this strange thing in its midst. He swam off to one side
checking repeatedly over his shoulder. I circled round. The bear
reached ice and lumbered up out of the water, a young male with an
immaculate coat. He shook himself and studied *Barrabas* from a better
vantage point. Everything was still, just the bear and me. He sniffed
vigorously, confused. As I came closer, he loped off to the other side of
the ice island and slid back into the water, swimming away though the
maze.

I carried on, passing through two more lines of denser drift before
getting to the edge of the main pack that curved away in a great arc to

the northeast, working my way in for a couple of miles until all around me the sea was covered by a solid carpet of white.

The sun dipped to kiss the horizon. Then, like a huge orange ball, it bounced back into the sky, climbing ever higher as *Barrabas* nosed her way gently between the massive floes, 24-hour daylight making this foray possible. Soon, periods of darkness would add another element of difficulty.

The ice thickened, too dense for me to go any further. My heart sank as I realised there was no way to get through to Bukhta Pron-chishchevoy. I thought of anchoring up to the ice, but worried that the shifting floes might pincer the boat. Sleep deprivation was making my eyes leaden. I worked *Barrabas* back to clear water and headed south. Anchorages along the north Russian coast were impossible to reach in a vessel drawing much more than three feet. In most places, mud banks extended up to 15 miles offshore covered only with waist-deep water. Where did I go now? The western side of Olenekskiy Zaliv (Bay) might be a possibility. The water was shallow but a five-metre contour pierced the western side of the bay, close to three small islands.

Clear of the main pack with open water to the south, I set the boat and went below. I had not slept for almost 30 hours. The prospect of a hot, strong cup of sweet tea was more appealing to me than anything else (with the exception of being teleported to a tropical island paradise). I never had the tea. I sat on the saloon banquette and immediately fell asleep.

A terrible screeching from the bow jerked me awake three hours later. *Barrabas* had collided with a chunk of drift ice. Dread surged through me like a cold rain. I grabbed a torch and went forward to inspect the forward part of the hull, stripped of insulation and fittings. I could see the inside of the hull plates: no gaping holes or splits, no ice-cold water rushing in. We pressed on. After a further 12 hours, I could evade sleep no longer. I laid out my sleeping bag on the floor of the galley because my starboard berth was on the high side of the heel and the port berth unserviceable, covered with 14 fuel cans full of diesel.

Sometimes, the most logically founded decisions are wrong. I believed I was clear of the drift. There hadn't been any at this latitude on the way up. I should have stopped the boat to sleep. Three hours later, I woke to the same screeching sound, a shudder and then no movement at all, not even the gentle side-to-side motion of a boat floating. I tore topside. We had collided again, only this time with a flat piece of ice. *Barrabas*'s bow had ridden up on to the ice. The wind had died. As the ice spun beneath us, pressed down by *Barrabas*'s weight, she slid off leaving smears of red anti-foul paint like blood on the ice.

Wind blew from the east as we entered Olenekskiy Bay, contrary to the forecast, which had the winds from the west and me sheltered in the lee of the land on the western side of the bay. We stole deeper into the bay along the narrowing finger of the five-metre contour. The wind stayed in the east and began to build. I had 13 feet of water beneath the keel and less than half a mile of similar depth on either side. Beyond that, *Barrabas* would ground. The anemometer touched 30 knots with no sign of the wind veering. This was dangerous, too dangerous. I needed to get the hell out.

Barrabas heaved under shortened main. I needed all the pulling power I could get. There was very little sea room and *Barrabas* was making leeway, sliding sideways towards oblivion. Over 24 hours had now passed since I had slept, with only a few hours in the last sixty. Thirty knots of wind does terrible things to water only 20 feet deep. The seas heap up. The frictional resistance of the seabed slows the lower portion of the waves. The upper parts keep moving and lose purchase, tumbling over to create the sailor's worst nightmare – breakers. They were marching towards us, line abreast. I didn't have much time before we ran out of depth. I needed to change direction eastwards and get more mainsail up to pull *Barrabas* as hard into the wind as she would go. I figured we had five minutes maximum before the keel touched bottom. If that happened, *Barrabas* would tip over onto her side and flood. Game over. I closed my mind to the shrieking wind and maddened water and went into the drill. Lock the wheel over to gybe. Sails across. Preventer on to stop the boom. Boom breaker off. Topping lift on to raise the boom's aft end. Clutches off the reefing lines. Dash to the mast. Drop the main six inches. Second reef cringle off the horn. Raise sail. First reef cringle on. Tighten the luff. Rush back to the cockpit. Tension the first reefing line. Preventer off, topping lift off to drop the boom. Unlash the wheel. Gybe round. Sails across. Boom breaker on. My back was soaked in sweat. The wind was biting. I had to make a course of 30° to run parallel to the contour line, more if I was to get eastwards to deeper water. Anything less than 30° and *Barrabas* would ground. 25°. Boiling crests crashed into the bow. 27°. Come on. 29°. Less than 50 metres behind the stern, the shoal would take the keel. A wave slewed the bow round. 30°. I punched the

driven air, screaming encouragement at *Barrabas*. The breakers lifted
her bow skywards then she plummeted down the back of the waves,
digging two feet into the troughs, water spuming over the foredeck.
Then up, then down, then up, then down. 31°. We fought together for
six hours, inching our way towards safety.

In 1933, the Russian schooner *Vasily Pronchishchevoy*, drawing three
metres, had made anchorage in a similar spot, creeping past the five-
metre line to within one mile of Ostrov Sylkay, the southernmost of
the three islands at the western end of Olenekskiy Bay. Had the wind
changed to the west I would have given it a go. As it was, we'd had a
close call. I was asleep on my feet. At one point, I fell in the cockpit,
gashing my forehead on the cuddy. Twelve miles offshore, I shortened
sail to slow the boat. The wind had veered south and lightened. I
decided to head northeast to greater safety, far enough offshore that if
the wind changed, I would have time to sleep before we were back in
the shallows. Heaving-to was not an option – the landward current
too strong. When I woke, 14 hours had passed. The wind had held.
Barrabas was still on a northeast track and close to the island of
Leykina.

Louise: Monday 13th August 2007
*How thrilling to see a polar bear. What a bummer about the ice. On the sea-
ice maps there has been a marked melting on the other side of Vil'kitskiy
Strait. Hope the rest follows suit and soon! We picked blackberries yesterday
and I made a huge crumble today. Thought how much you would have
enjoyed it. Hope you find good spot to stop soon.*

Too late, I received the reply from WMOHQ.

Nikolay Babych: Monday 13th August 2007
*Ice condition is very heavy to north from islands Begichev and Preobrezheniya
to Cape Cheluskin and you can't sailing to Pronchis'eva bay. I recommend to
wait betterment of ice condition in Anabarskiy Bay.*

The many ice scientists and organisations I had consulted, among
them America's National Ice Center, Russia's Arctic and Antarctic
Research Institute and the Scott Polar Research Institute in Cambridge,
agreed that the North Polar ice cap achieved its minimum extent on
15th September. I still had one month. The problem was where to wait
in the meantime.

Tim Thornton: Tuesday 14th August 2007

Looking at the satellite images over the last couple of weeks, the ice has definitely cleared on the west side during this period, but it is only over the last few days that there has been the beginning of a reduction in the ice on the east side. Prevailing currents on the east side are southerly, so ice is continually being pushed down towards the shore, which will delay its break up.

I scoured the charts for suitable anchorages in Anabarskiy Bay but found none. I decided to make for Leykina Island, listed in the British Admiralty sailing directions under its old name of Ostrov Osushnoy. Ominously, the pilot described the island's charted location as 'doubtful'.

A ring of small breakers marked the five-metre contour line as the seabed shoaled towards where the island should have been. Perhaps the island was just a sand bar long since washed away or submerged beneath the risen waters of the summer thaw. Whatever the reason, Leykina Island was not where it was supposed to be. After the disappointment at having the prospect of anchorage snatched away, I set a course west towards Peschanyy Island.

Tim Thornton: Wednesday 15th August 2007

Good news, the Uni Bremen ice image shows that the ice has thinned significantly. There appear to be two passages opening up: a narrow one right along the coast, and a much larger one further north.

Three days later, *Barrabas* nosed through scattered drift ice towards the low-lying Ostrov Peschanyy, not so much an island as an ovoid sand bar rising no more than two metres above sea level, enclosing a lagoon. The island measured four miles across at its widest and was home to a defunct light and walrus rookeries. I tried manoeuvring into the lagoon but *Barrabas* bottomed. I backed out and finally anchored off the northwestern side.

Tim Thornton: Sunday 19th August 2007

Definitely thinning out now and more so along the coastal passage than the one further to the north.

Barrabas dragged her anchor. Drift ice moved on the currents circulating around the island. Unseen beyond my horizons, the world moved on.

Louise: Tuesday 21st August 2007
Terrible weather system in Jamaica – many dead. Madeleine McCann still not found, presumed dead – forensics showed blood on the wall of their hotel room. House prices showing first signs of dropping.

According to an environmental congress in Norway, the North Polar ice cap was melting faster and earlier than at any other time previously. Ice bears and walruses were suffering. Permanent ice had disappeared revealing new islands.

My experience was different. Vanishing islands, the ice at Vil'kitskiy Strait stubbornly refused to yield and Peschanyy Island looked like market day in Hong Kong with the number of walruses snorting and hooting.

The shifting winds forced me to reposition *Barrabas* regularly. Storms and squalls were a daily occurrence. I moved to the east side of the island in anticipation of westerly winds. By the time I dropped anchor the wind was in the northeast. Within 15 minutes, wind speeds were touching 30 knots and six- to eight-foot waves were breaking as the seabed shoaled towards the beach a third of a mile behind me. *Barrabas*'s bow was lifting 10 feet into the air then digging in as she dropped down into the troughs. On a lee shore with little clear water beneath the keel, I decided to reposition. Try as I might, it was impossible to raise the anchor. Each time *Barrabas* lifted her bow, more anchor chain wrenched out, undoing the lengths I had managed to get inboard. There was no chance of pulling the anchor in by hand and the windlass was sapping the batteries. I could see drift ice on the horizon, massing like a wretched army. So began a long night vigil. My concern was whether the anchor chain would hold. I put the engine on in case *Barrabas* broke free. I even tried driving the boat forward to put slack in the anchor chain then wind in the slack using the windlass remote plugged in at the cockpit. The dire pitching made it impossible to see which direction to steer and at a certain length, the anchor chain became permanently taut and the wrenching out began again. I could either let go the anchor with a fender tied to the end of the chain so that I could retrieve it later under calmer conditions, or wait for the ice

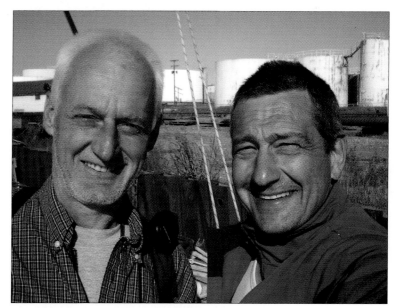

25. Me and Rick, a remarkable man, the kind of guy that makes the world turn. Nome, July 2007.

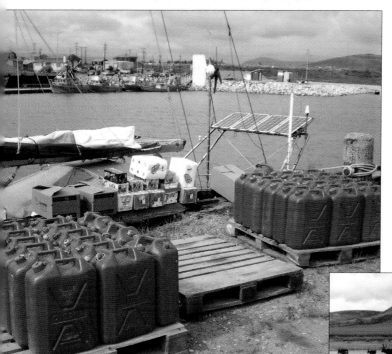

26. Stores and fuel ready for loading. Nome, July 2007.

27. Roman Abramovich in Chukotka where he is the provincial governor. His help was invaluable.

28. John Mann worked tirelessly to get me the permissions I needed from the Russian government.

29. Me and my guard in Provideniya, Siberia, July 2007.

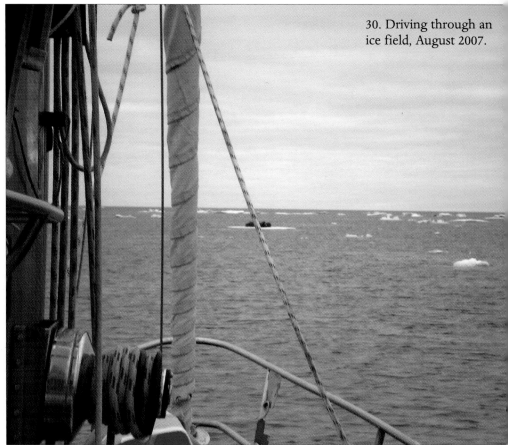

30. Driving through an ice field, August 2007.

31. My calorie intake soared in the cold Arctic conditions.

32. A polar bear checks our progress through a dense icefield.

Sep 15 2006
ASI ver. 5.2, AMSR-E, Grid: 6.25 km

Sep 15 2007
ASI ver. 5.2, AMSR-E, Grid: 6.25 km

33. The North Polar icecap on 15th September 2006.

34. The North Polar icecap on 15th September 2007 receded to its recorded historic minimum but a persistent 200-mile wide finger of ice blocked my path.

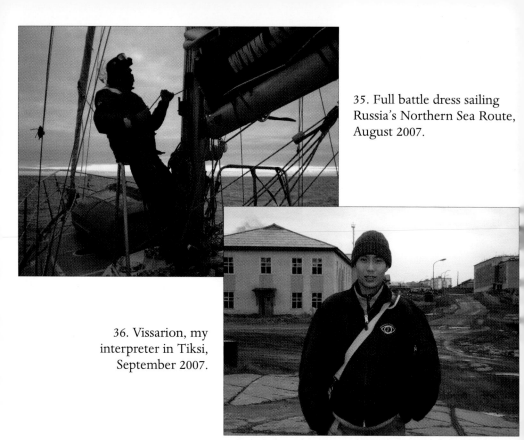

35. Full battle dress sailing Russia's Northern Sea Route, August 2007.

36. Vissarion, my interpreter in Tiksi, September 2007.

37. *Barrabas* loaded on the deck of the Russian cargo vessel, *Kapitan Danilkin* in Tiksi, September 2007.

38. Captain Zagorsky, me and Nikolay Babych, the ice expert, in Murmansk, October 2007.

39. Kåre Karlstad, an accomplished yachtsman, with *Barrabas* in Mehamn, April 2008.

40. *Barrabas* at the end of the small fishing boat pontoon in Mehamn on the morning of our departure and Louise's 47th birthday, 1st May 2008.

41. Keeping warm in the Barents Sea shortly after leaving Mehamn.

42. Taking a hot shower in the cockpit.

43. HMS *Mersy* welcomes *Barrabas* back to UK territorial waters, May 2008.

44. Back at last!

45. A welcome cup of tea from the Royal Navy on my arrival home, 21st May 2008.

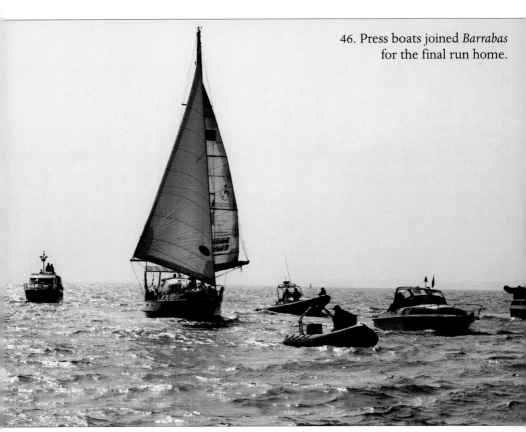

46. Press boats joined *Barrabas* for the final run home.

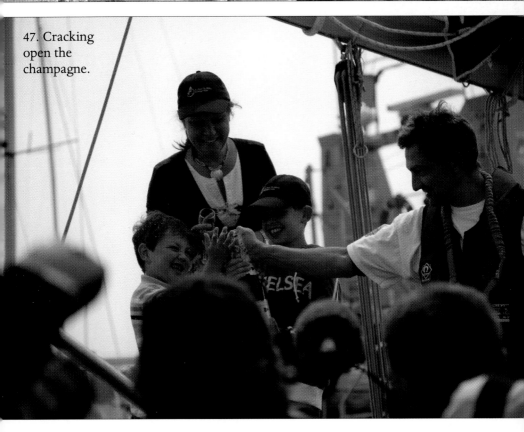

47. Cracking open the champagne.

48. Me and Benji take a rest on the pontoon after the media scrum has dissipated.

49. Reading *The Times* at breakfast the morning after my arrival back in the UK.

to advance. I figured the ice would act as a windbreak and calm the water between *Barrabas* and its advancing edge. I rigged the fender and waited through the stormy night. With the ice half a mile off and the wind still gusting to 30 knots, the hoped-for dampening effect happened and I got the anchor back on board then scuttled quickly away before the legions of ice sacked my position.

Nikolay Babych: Thursday 23rd August 2007
There is much drift ice in Vil'kitskiy Strait. Powerful and strong vessels having special ice class only under nuclear icebreaking assistance are able to sail through Vil'kitskiy Strait. As to your vessel, such sailing is not admissible even with nuclear icebreaker assistance. We have received more or less favourable forecast of improving ice condition in More Laptevych (Laptev Sea) in September.

I began to have serious doubts about the feasibility of getting through the Vil'kitskiy Strait. In 2002, Eric Brossier was through by 29th July.

In the respites between storms, I slept, attended to various ongoing jobs, read or watched the wildlife. The walrus, by now used to *Barrabas,* became more inquisitive, approaching the boat in pairs or trios. Their long tusks gave them lugubrious expressions and their eyes, situated shark-like at the sides of their heads, were small and mean, bloodshot and pedunculated, swivelling as if controlled by wire in need of fine-tuning.

A permanent ring of ice surrounded the island. Depending on wind direction, the ice either closed with the slender spit of sand or moved off like the bellows of some meteorological accordion. As the end of August approached, I needed a breakthrough.

Louise: Sunday 26th August 2007
Not long now to be patient. Both boys had the sick bug on Friday night so looked like a Chinese laundry here yesterday morning.

Tim had ordered up a Radarsat image. I emailed John Mann asking him to contact Nikolay Babych to get a more detailed prognosis of the ice and conditions at Vil'kitskiy Strait. While I waited for information, the island gained three new inhabitants, polar bears, a mother and two cubs.

John Mann: Tuesday 28th August 2007

OK, I had a long chat with Babych.

Right now, as Adrian noted, the temperature has dropped and winds turned to the north. That means ice is coming down from the north and nothing is opening up.

There is a 60 per cent chance that the winds will change to southerly. This would mean ice pushing north and a chance for Adrian to make a run through the Vil'kitskiy Strait.

BUT, the current view is this won't happen now until around 3 September. Then it would take a few days for the change to have its corridor-opening effect. The problem is that new ice will start to form around 20 September. In other words, the window is going to be very, very short.

There are three small ships in Tiksi waiting to travel. A Dutch yacht crew is waiting in Dikson wanting to go east. Right now, Babych isn't giving any of them clearance to make a run for it.

Drift ice had cleared from around Begichev Island and Preobrazheniya Island 50 miles west. Nikolay Babych recommended that I move there to await further developments. Meanwhile the American National Center for Snow and Ice published a comparison of the current melt with the previous minimum recorded in 2005. In October of that year, the North Polar ice cap shrank to 5.32 million km^2. On 22nd August, just a week before, the ice cap occupied an area of only 4.92 million km^2.

It was getting late in the season. The opportunity to get through the ice might remain for only a few short weeks.

I spent the whole of Wednesday 29th August on the west side of the island. Drift ice was moving on a northerly current. From 7.00 am until 11.00 pm I remained on watch, engine running, dodging the drift. One of the last pieces of ice to float by carried a small colony of walrus, grunting and snorting in the diminishing light. I went below to brew a cup of tea. Half an hour later and looking forward to a comfortable night I made a final check on deck. To my horror, the walrus were still there, inshore of *Barrabas* and moving in the opposite direction, southerly. The wind had changed, reversing the current, and 16 hours' worth of drift ice was now bearing back down on me. I decided there and then to set sail for Ostrov Preobrazheniya.

CHAPTER 25

A Slice of Chocolate Cake

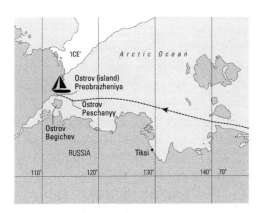

Sheer cliffs rose from the water on the east side of Ostrov Preobrazheniya. I rounded a long spit extending from the southern end. The west side of the island sloped to a gravel beach, the plain covered in cocoa-coloured tundra so the island sat like a giant wedge of chocolate cake laid on its side in the grey syrup of the ocean.

A disused polar research station was marked on the chart, but as I came into the bay I saw a small supply vessel resting at anchor and men moving about on shore. I coasted towards the other vessel and dropped anchor in the lee of a second spit, flat and straight like a man-made breakwater. A skiff broke away from the beach.

Through a combination of sign language, broken English and my Russian paperwork, I managed to establish my credentials and explain that I planned to stay for a few days while awaiting clearance to sail north towards Cape Cheluskina, Asia's most northerly cape and the eastern gateway to Vil'kitskiy Strait. I had no idea who these people were – maybe researchers, itinerant hunters, government employees. The two men in the boat, Valerie and Vladim, told me they were heading out the following day, Friday. They duly did, leaving me alone once more with my boat, the walruses, and my hopes that a sustained southerly wind would clear the ice and give me passage west to the Kara Sea.

Sitting at anchor off Preobrazheniya Island, I was isolated literally and figuratively. The Iridium could not support detailed satellite ice images and with no pictures to look at, I was relying completely on Tim's interpretations. The time delay between Radarsat taking shots and my receiving Tim's interpretations on board was too long. The information was out of date. Variable winds played havoc with the ice, blowing it onshore, pushing it off again, creating channels through the ice floes then closing them up too quickly for me to make any kind of plan.

'I've been in touch with AARI,' Louise said. Outside, strong winds were blasting the northern cliffs of the island and screaming down the southern slope into the bay. For a moment, I thought, 'Who the hell is Harry!' Then the acronym deciphered. I had managed to squeeze some information out of Russia's Arctic and Antarctic Research Institute but my requests for routing assistance had met with no response.

'How did you manage that?'

'It was Ian's idea. I called them up.'

'Just like that?'

'Yes. Anyway, I spoke to someone called Vasily Smolyanitsky. He's head of the climate laboratory. He's going to help. I've sent you some information.'

I couldn't believe this development. The elapsed time between a satellite snapping an image from space and the interpretation reaching me would be much closer to real-time.

'I need sustained southerly winds, three days minimum, five days would be better to blow the ice off the coast.'

'You're going to get them in a couple of days according to Vasily.'

Vasily corroborated Nikolay Babych's view that no south sector winds would appear before 3rd September.

AARI: Saturday 1st September 2007

The area of the Laptev Sea adjacent to Vil'kitskiy Strait is blocked by Taymyr ice massif, though the Vil'kitskiy Strait itself has only ice stripes and patches. According to the forecast for the next days (1st–3rd September) northeastern winds will preserve the ice near the coast of the Taymyr Peninsula. Not having high-resolution imagery, I cannot advise either going close to the coast or trying to use the stated weakenings.

The North Polar icecap had continued contracting and now covered only 4.42 million km^2, a 10 per cent decline within the last fortnight.

Despite this, a 200-mile-wide finger projected south from the main mass and clung to the eastern side of the Taymyr Peninsula, blocking my path. I favoured the inshore channel over any openings appearing among the offshore floes. If the ice blocked me, at least I had a chance of finding a place to anchor. Offshore, with nowhere to go, the ice would embrace *Barrabas* and then crush her to death.

The temperature plummeted. Freezing north winds dusted the rugged mound of the island with frost. Hail and snow fell steadily. Is this how an Everest mountaineer felt holed up at Camp 5, waiting for the weather to clear to make the summit push? Between me and the open water of the Kara Sea on the west side of the Vil'kitskiy Strait, 100 per cent ice cover in places presented as impenetrable an obstacle for a yacht as a mountain range, and yet the North Polar icecap had reduced to a staggering historic minimum. The only way through would come with sustained southerly winds.

AARI: Monday 3rd September 2007
Our expert strongly advises Adrian to wait where he is for changes in ice situation due to favourable winds. Pending stable south and southwesterly winds for a couple of days, the Taymyr ice massif will swiftly move in NE direction so that a good opening near the shore will form. Adrian still has three weeks before new ice formation and may wait for up to 10 days for changes in wind situations. Also, it is much more reasonable for the yacht to use near shore opening than try to use very risky seaward weakenings as due to winds and currents, the ice situation in the NW Laptev Sea may change too swiftly for the yacht.

At least the confirmation of using the inshore channel was heartening. Now I could eliminate any thoughts about an offshore passage. Vasily compressed the Envisat images he was receiving and sending them to Tim who forwarded them to me. I now had pictures. But until Nikolay Babych agreed the viability of the inshore passage, with the implication for icebreaker support, that route remained closed to me as well. I had to get agreement from West Marine Operations Headquarters.

Adrian (to: Nikolay Babych, WMOHQ): Monday 3rd September
The latest satellite ice image from AARI shows an open water channel inshore along the coast of the Taymyr Peninsula. Is this the best route? Please advise soonest.

The tension nestled in my shoulders. The route was fraught with danger. South winds had to open the channel and keep it open for long enough for me to make the 100 miles to open water in the Vil'kitskiy Strait. If Babych gave me a 'Go', I would need 48 hours. If the winds reversed before I was through, the ice could pin me to the coast. The Taymyr Peninsula was crawling with ice bears. If the boat foundered in the ice, I would be in real danger. I had the shotgun, but only 50 rounds of ammunition.

Louise and I discussed the option of transporting *Barrabas* through the ice on the deck of a ship, much as Henk had been forced to do two three years before. We called it 'Plan B'. It would mean getting to Tiksi, 400 miles east. She would talk to John and get him to float the idea to Nikolay Babych as a contingency.

AARI: Tuesday 4th September 2007
The ice situation remains completely unfavourable for the yacht going westward as Taymyr ice massif blocks the way to Vil'kitskiy Strait due to the prevailing winds of NW-N sector. The same unfavourable perspective is for the next 1–5 days. However, long-term synoptic forecast for the period 9th–15th September points out for a high probability of the SW/S/SE winds. If there will be such S-sector winds blowing for a couple of days the Taymyr ice massif would move swiftly NE, thus opening a free water channel near the coast. Based on the above we recommend you to wait till the stated period 9th–15th September.

'This is really desperate,' I said to Louise. 'I was supposed to get south winds today, but according to Vasily, I've got to hang around here until the 9th. There's a bloody cyclone bringing down a north wind and sub-zero temperatures. Things ain't looking good.'

'Vasily says wait.'

'And I will. But I reckon new ice could be forming. We've got to look at Plan B.'

John Mann: Tuesday 4th September 2007
Okay, I've spoken to Babych. There is a large cargo boat coming through in the next few days. It is picking up a load of timber in Tiksi and then heading west. If Adrian wants to get a ride, he would need to rendezvous with this boat in Tiksi (loading him at sea would be too complicated) and they would take him to Murmansk.

This boat is scheduled to arrive in Tiksi sometime around September 11.

The only chance of getting proper weather to get through the ice is also in the Sept 15th–20th range, but it's not a big chance.

In other words, Adrian has a few short days to make a decision. In the meantime, we can continue working out the details with Babych. He's working on costs, etc.

Now it seemed that south sector winds *might* materialise on Saturday 15th September. I waited at anchor, anxiety and tedium vying for supremacy. I read, slept, tried to eat, paced the deck and occasionally listened to music. Time was fast running out.

John Mann: Wednesday 5th September 2007

I have more information that changes things a little bit.

The transport boat will arrive in Tiksi on or about Sept 11 but not leave for 10 days. Adrian could, in theory, arrive as late as the 17th or 18th and still leave time for the whole loading process. I think this gives Adrian a few more days lead time, meaning he can stay where he is for now.

He quoted a cost of $10,000. Not as expensive as I thought, but not at all cheap.

I grappled with the options. If I waited for south winds, I could miss the ship and if I missed the ship, I would have to winter *Barrabas* in Tiksi. Worse, new ice might obstruct me on the way to Tiksi. Then what? The loss of *Barrabas*? A rescue at sea? And, where the hell was I going to find $10,000!

Vasily came through with confirmation that winds would veer south the next day and hold for at least two days. I bent over the charts. Eighty miles to the entrance to the inshore channel, one day's worth of sailing leaving me only a day to navigate 100 miles along the channel. Too tight. Or was it? How much drift would there be in the channel? I had no way of knowing. The other problem was that no one had looked in detail at the northern exit from the channel. Was it open or would I travel the entire length of the channel only to find myself blocked at the far end?

I had not heard from Nikolay Babych about the feasibility of the inshore channel, but on Friday 7th September, I got my answer.

Nikolay Babych: Friday 7th September 2007 (translated by John Mann)

AARI's information about the existence of a coastal route without ice along the Taymyr Peninsula coast is inaccurate. In reality, that area to the north from 75N, due to the long-term action of north/northwest and northeast winds, is blocked with very serious ice.

Inaccurate? How could AARI's information be wrong? Tim had looked at the US GFS weather model, which confirmed Vasily's opinion that south winds would blow from 8th September. Babych was telling me that forecasts predicted south winds on the 15th September. Who was I to believe? Both AARI and WMOHQ were experienced interpreters of ice-imaging, but AARI had no vested interest in me. Was Babych playing it safe?

I wanted to go for the inshore channel. I could leave the following morning at dawn. The south winds would drive me to the channel's southern entrance. I could cover the 100 miles inside the channel in 24 hours and even if the wind changed, I would still have several hours before the ice started closing with the shore. It would be damn tight, but could I escape the channel into open water and get west fast and out of danger? The critical piece of information was Babych's view that floes of impenetrable ice were blocking the northern exit of the channel. He was offering an alternative.

Nikolay Babych: Friday 7th September 2007 (translated by John Mann)

I want to inform you that a caravan of not large boats called Osipenko, Orekhovo-Zuevo *and* Novoulyanovsk, *led by Captain Valery Petrov, departed from Tiksi on September 6. These boats have been told to wait for an icebreaker at 7530/11700. We plan that the icebreaker* Taymyr *could go to these boats on the morning of September 10.*

The southern winds that we expect after September 8 could change the situation favourably, as long as it lasts for 3–5 days or more.

I can't give any guarantee that the three-boat caravan's attempt will be successful. In any case, I suggest you join up with this caravan.

Could I keep up with a convoy? The route would be offshore, in deeper water, a total distance of 250 miles from the rendezvous to open water. At a constant five knots, travel time would be a minimum of 50 hours, probably longer. At no point during the passage would I be able to sleep. This would be tough – doable, but tough. Even getting below to make a brew would be a challenge.

I never thought a single-handed transit of the Northern Sea Route was ever going to be a gimme, but this was now down to the wire. The winter re-freeze was imminent, ambient air temperature was falling and winds were regularly hitting 25 knots, creating wind chill. There was another factor to consider. In sub-zero temperatures, ice could accumulate on *Barrabas*'s deck and rigging, raising the boat's centre of gravity to a dangerously destabilising extent.

If the icebreaker decided to give it a go, I would emerge into ice-clear waters at the western end of Vil'kitskiy Strait with perhaps only hours to spare. I preferred the inshore route, but without WMOHQ's permission to try it, they might not send an icebreaker if I got into trouble – hell, they might not have an icebreaker available. Babych was not giving me any option. I had to try with the caravan.

Louise: Saturday 8th September 2007
Good luck for tomorrow – at least you will be moving again. Start eating, otherwise you have no chance of having the strength to stay awake whilst in convoy.

I weighed anchor at 10.00 am the following morning. A decent south-easterly put me on a fast tack towards the rendezvous with the nuclear icebreaker *Taymyr*. To the west, a dense line of sea-ice showed the southerly extent of the massive ice bridge reaching down from the polar cap. Beyond the ice, the snow-dappled mountains of the Taymyr Peninsula floated on a bed of ground mist. The inshore channel meandered somewhere between the ice and the coast, open or closed, navigable or not, I didn't know. The rendezvous lay 80 miles north-northeast. I made good progress, averaging six knots, but recent satellite pictures had clearly shown large tracts of drift ice south of the RV position.

At 6.00 pm, I went on deck to check my horizon as I had done regularly throughout the afternoon. A piece of ice was bobbing in *Barrabas*'s wake 50 yards astern! We had narrowly missed another collision. More alarming was the sight to the front. A small ship was passing right across my bow. Two similar vessels followed astern of her. These had to be the three boats that together with *Barrabas* and the icebreaker would make up the convoy! Four miles north, the horizon was phosphorescent with ice, extending as far as I could see along the horizon. This was ominous. We were all still 40 miles south of the rendezvous. I hove-to. The three-ship convoy passed without altering course. Were the ships heading west to find a way around the drift? Maybe operations HQ was routing them through to the RV. I judged their speed at six knots and thought about tagging along behind, but worried that I might not be able to keep up and, if I had to come back east again, I would be head to wind.

While *Barrabas* held station, I went below and called on the radio.

'No English, no English,' came the reply.

'Tiksi, Tiksi, Taymyr, Taymyr,' I said, hoping that someone among their combined three crews would assimilate the information and draw the conclusion that I was talking about the icebreaker. Surely Nikolay Babych had told Captain Petrov that a yacht might be joining the convoy? Static crackled from the radio and nothing else. I tried calling again several times but no one answered.

Daylight faded fast, the drift too thick to penetrate alone. The latest forecast from Babych indicated north sector winds from 11th to 16th September. I computed the options. The best alternative was to wait here south of the ice until daylight and get an update from Nikolay Babych in the morning.

Just before midnight, I went on deck. Three miles astern, I saw the lights of the three ships blazing brightly, but the small convoy was now sailing due east. They had failed to find a way through the drift ice to the rendezvous.

I called Louise and explained the situation. 'It can only mean that the three ships are not being routed by Babych.'

'What do you want me to do?'

'Can you email Babych? We're all here in the same place, so ask him to get the icebreaker to come to us. That way, we'll have a path cut through the drift.'

'I'll do it now.'

'Babych won't be in his office, but he'll get it first thing. The problem is I can't communicate with the ships. No one speaks English. If I could get them to agree to wait here with me . . .'

I slept for eight hours. The wind died to a zephyr, drift ice framed the eastern horizon, but by morning, the ships had gone. I set the radar to a 24-mile radius sweep, its maximum range. No trace of the three ships. The radio had been on at full volume while I slept. If anyone had tried the VHF, I would have heard it. I checked my email for any response to my suggestion of re-designating the RV. Nothing. Had the ships met up with the icebreaker or turned back for Tiksi? By 2.00 pm on Monday 10th September, I still hadn't received any communication from Operations HQ. According to forecasts from WMOHQ and

AARI, southerly winds would continue through the day. I had missed the RV and it was too late to try the inshore channel. Setting course for Tiksi meant battling head to wind. The only option for the moment was to wait.

Louise called me at 7.30 pm. John had spoken to Nikolay Babych. The other three ships had not made the rendezvous and were 'circling'. The icebreaker *Taymyr* was still escorting large ships through difficult ice, 100 per cent cover in places and up to three metres thick. New ice was forming between the floes. The cargo ship *Kapitan Danilkin*, en route to Tiksi to pick up her load of timber, was stuck fast in the ice, awaiting the *Taymyr* to break her out. Nikolay Babych's recommendations mirrored my own bleak assessment: either winter *Barrabas* in Tiksi or get her transported on the *Kapitan Danilkin*. The convoy option was dead. The *Taymyr* had not even gone to the RV.

'Please wait where you are,' Louise said, her voice cracking with emotion. 'AARI are holding an emergency meeting to look at the inshore channel. It might still be on.'

'Don't cry,' I said. 'It is what it is.'

'Just wait there, promise.'

'Okay, I can't go anywhere until the wind swings round anyway.'

'I've also sent AARI's satellite pictures to Babych. We'll see what he says.'

Nikolay Babych: Tuesday 11th September 2007 (translated by John Mann)

We have received the picture that Louise sent to us. As a comment, I would note that it's necessary to know how to decode such pictures. A lip of solid ice that moves on to the south following the contours of the coast is very visible in this picture. There is clean water between the massif and the coast up to latitude 75.35N . . . to the north from 76.03N parallel the ice is from 6 up to 8 points. In the area of Ostrov Petra (Peter's Island), extended strips of ice of 9–10 points attached to islands are observed.

As we said before, there is no through passage along the coastal route through clear water. It's also necessary to keep in mind that the coastal area has a wide zone with the depths less than 10 m. The icebreaker Taymyr *has a 9m keel and it's forbidden for it to enter into depths less than 10 m.*

Finally it's necessary to know that when eastern and northern winds blow, such a pass could close in just six hours and it becomes a trap from which it is impossible to escape neither to the south, nor to the north, nor to the east.

The yacht Campina, *which entered into this pass without our permission, crashed in a similar situation approximately at 75.45N latitude.*

I sent to John our picture dated September 10 on which it's possible to see a lip of solid ice pressed to the coast of Taymyr at the lat 7520-7530N. The trap has slammed. It's very good that there is nobody there at the moment.

Vasily Smolyanitsky studied the latest Radarsat images and AARI's own Envisat images of 11th September. His meeting came to a similar conclusion. Strips of ice at 100 per cent cover obliterated the northern part of the channel.

CHAPTER 26

The Shipping News

I turned for Tiksi beneath grey skies. Darkness reduced any prospect of spotting drift ice so, at 10.00 pm, I gybed *Barrabas* and backed the sails to let her drift while I slept until daybreak at 3.00 am.

The *Kapitan Danilkin* had broken free from the clutches of the ice and was now steaming for Tiksi. She would load her timber cargo over a ten-day period. I checked the chart – 250 miles to go.

I nibbled away at biscuits. One night, with *Barrabas* forereaching under the storm jib hanked onto the inner forestay, I cooked porridge. I felt nauseous for hours afterwards. As I lay on my bunk 'camping' on the pitching Arctic seas, another major concern began to evolve. Even though I was now under less time pressure, dictated by *Kapitan Danilkin*'s loading schedule, the idea of coming across the Norwegian Sea and North Sea in autumn carried a deep foreboding. The Norwegian coast bore the brunt of North Atlantic storms sweeping east from Iceland. These storms increased in frequency and ferocity with the approach of winter.

Tim Thornton: Friday 14th September 2007
I just looked at the last two Radarsat images from today and yesterday. These confirmed what the Russians said – the broken ice isn't too dense, but there is a lot of new ice forming in between and Adrian probably wouldn't have been able to get through. At least that confirms we made the right call.

Barrabas broke free of the storm-tossed seas and into the lee of the Olenek and Reka deltas. The wind calmed. Dense veils of cloud that had persisted for weeks finally cleared and by nightfall stars glimmered and moonlight struck a reluctant flame in the ocean. The cabin was snug and warm, lit by the dull glow of a single reading light. With no evidence of drift ice, *Barrabas* sailed on through the night under reduced canvas. I burrowed into my sleeping bag, too exhausted to concern myself further, and slid blissfully beneath the blanket of sleep.

My body weight had fallen substantially. I felt drained. That evening I forced myself to cook spaghetti with fish sauce (clams from Honolulu) and sardines. A wave strike sent everything loose in the cabin flying, including the pot on the stove. The concoction of hot, stinky fish went all over me. I threw the pot into the sink in disgust. Anger and frustration boiled within me. I wiped myself down and retreated to my bunk while *Barrabas* nudged southwards at three knots. Just as nature had thwarted me, the dawn cheered me with blue skies and sunshine at long, long last.

Studying my only chart of the area, I spotted a small cove 15 miles from the port of Tiksi. I could anchor in the bay and rest up before facing the inevitable avalanche of bureaucracy in port.

The smooth-sided hills sloped cautiously towards the sea, suggesting that the bottom would be sand and mud shoaling gently. I dropped anchor at 8.00 pm in the still waters of the bay. In the lee of the hills, *Barrabas* sat quietly at her chain, sheltered from the west wind. Two small huts stood at the southern end of the beach. I sat up on deck appreciating the tranquillity of the scene until the last light crept silently away.

I woke to the noise of an outboard engine buzzing around *Barrabas* like an angry hornet. The skiff came alongside, its floor tiled with freshly caught Arctic cod and its driver grinning widely and jabbering in Yakut. He introduced himself as Slava as he rummaged among the fish, selected the two biggest ones and offered them up. I took the gift and laid them out on the afterdeck. Keen to show me his world, Slava suggested coffee by pointing to the huts on the beach then making a drinking gesture whilst uttering, 'Koff' several times. I climbed down into Slava's boat and we sped off towards the beach.

Slava's cabin, hewn from logs and lined with dried seal skins, measured 12 foot square, contained a pair of bunks and a single cot, a table supporting a variety of radio equipment, an unplumbed sink and a wood-burning stove. An outboard engine suspended from a trestle outside the hut generated electric power to a single, naked light bulb dangling from the low ceiling. My efforts at internationalism gathered Slava's story. He owned seven knives, three guns, had a wife called Ola and two children – a boy, Ura 12, and a girl, Viola 10. A brother had died, shot through the heart during a hunting accident the previous season. Slava was 34. In the summer, he cut and sold wood and in the winter hunted reindeer. Of his two dogs, one was a sweet-natured Husky, the other a Cujoesque monster of indeterminate breed (thankfully chained to a tree trunk). We drank coffee, smoked a couple of cigarettes together and inspected the new hut Slava was constructing. Back on board *Barrabas*, I gave Slava a litre of long-life milk, two tins of fruit, a jar of jam and two bottles of olive oil. Our comradeship forged, we bade one another farewell and I was alone again with my ship.

I weighed anchor early the next morning and as I rounded the headland, a cargo ship operating three deck cranes came into view. I asked for identification on the radio. In fluent English, the chief mate responded that the ship was the *Kapitan Danilkin* of the Murmansk Shipping Line. They had been expecting *Barrabas* and arrangements were in process to transport the yacht through the ice and on to Murmansk. As I passed close to their bow, the chief mate, Dimitri, came back on the radio. The immigration authorities were on board and insisting that I was forbidden from entering port, that I did not have clearance, the border was closed and that I should instead sail out to 'international waters'.

'Dimitri, please tell the immigration authorities that I cannot do that. It is unsafe. I am not going to place myself or my yacht in danger.'

A pause as Dimitri conferred. 'They are insisting.'

'They can insist all they want, Dimitri, I'm not going out there. I'm going into port.'

'Okay, I will talk to the Captain.'

Louise had found out about the ship from her correspondence with the Murmansk Shipping Company. The captain, Alfred Zagorsky, was their most experienced skipper and he spoke good English.

'Adrian, hello.' Captain Zagorsky's voice was a growl, his words heavily accented. 'I speak with immigration people. They say is impossible for you go in Tiksi, but I have idea.'

I was intrigued. I was going into port whatever anybody said. 'Do the immigration people speak English, Captain?'

'No, no. So listen.' I heard a quick burst of Russian and then Captain

Zagorsky was back on the radio. 'If you have damage to you then you go to port.'

'You mean an injury?'

'Yes, yes. You have one, no?'

'Yes, yes I do. My wrist is dislocated, broken.'

Another burst of Russian. Captain Zagorsky sounded irritated with whoever he was speaking to, presumably an immigration officer. 'Okay, I tell them you break hand. They say you can get X-ray.'

They wanted to check? Fine. Any film of my right wrist would show the unstable scaphoid.

'They can check if they want to, Captain.'

'Okay, good. You go to port. They say is okay now. I call you on radio later.'

I grabbed a bandage from the first-aid box and quickly strapped my right wrist.

Piers radiated seawards from the town like splayed fingers. I slowed *Barrabas*, looking for a mooring place. Car headlights pierced the driving sleet. A figure emerged, then limped to the edge of a pier leaning heavily on a cane. He stared at me without expression then gave orders to another man, a stevedore, who directed me to the western pier. Someone was screaming over the VHF on Channel 16 in Russian. It sounded to me like invective. I discovered later that an unmarked wreck lay submerged between the two piers. I had sailed ominously close to it. The western pier was dilapidated, bristling with iron spikes that at one time had secured timber joists, long since decayed and broken off. I moored in a 'clean' spot. The man with the cane, who clearly viewed my arrival as a nuisance, turned out to be the harbourmaster. I protested about the dangerous, protruding spikes and the boat's exposure to west winds, but he brusquely dismissed these concerns.

The expected phalanx of uniforms quickly descended. A research vessel, *Petrov*, had followed me into port, berthing at the eastern side of the dock. Its complement of German geologists came to say hello. In unequivocal language, the authorities told them to get lost.

I was processed, then handed over to some branch of the military, expressionless faces, khaki camouflage, high-laced boots. They passed my papers around amid much discussion until eventually a slightly built local man of Yakut descent was brought to the boat. His name was Vissarion and he'd learnt his English at Oxford. I was delighted. Through Vissarion, I explained the nature of my situation, my need to come into port because of my 'injury', the plans to transport the yacht and my desire to leave just as quickly as possible. The following days brought repeated visits and more questions. Each time, Vissarion was present to translate. These Q&As took place either in a military vehicle parked dockside or on *Barrabas*. One of the officers, the designated photographer, began snapping the Russian chart open on the navigation table. Where did I get it? England, I explained. I opened the chart table and showed them the 30 or so others detailing the north Russian coast. He gave up taking pictures of the charts after that.

During the Soviet period, Tiksi's population had swelled to 30,000. Now, many of the buildings were derelict, windows broken, roofing tin torn off by the winds. Concrete tenement blocks housed the 2,000 diehards clinging to a meagre living. Military uniforms and vehicles predominated. There were no visible shops, only peeling signs of 'bread' or 'tomatoes' hung askew on doors that slatted on loose hinges in the constant wind.

I went to the bank to exchange some US currency. The bank teller handed most of my 20-dollar bills back with the exclamation, 'Niet!' Eventually, a hundred bucks was accepted and exchanged after careful scrutiny. I discovered some shops on the ground floors of the tenements – no windows, just doors off long, straight corridors. I wanted eggs. In one shop, I flapped my arms and made clucking noises. The babushka behind the counter gave me a blank stare and an apathetic shrug. I drew a picture of an egg. No translation. Then an arrow pointing to a fried egg. Still nothing. On the other side of the egg picture, I drew a chicken to illustrate the entire sequence: a chicken produces an egg, which is then fried. The rouble dropped. The babushka's face creased. She called other shopkeepers. They locked their doors and hurried to the impromptu summit. The babushka handed round my drawing and explained. It seemed that I had provided the amusement of the week. I left the 'arcade' some time later with eggs, bread, tomatoes, onions and bacon (I had to draw a picture of a pig). On the walk back to the docks, I bumped into the German geologists. Who are you? Where are you from? How far have you travelled? They invited me on board the *Petrov* to take a shower any time I wanted. The *Petrov* was in port for three days.

At Captain Zagorsky's instruction, I made drawings of *Barrabas* detailing approximate measurements to help him assess the logistics of getting *Barrabas* onto his deck and shoring her up for the passage through the ice. At 7.00 am next morning, a tug nosed into the pier and I handed the drawings over. The tug's skipper made little effort to guide his vessel gently towards the quay. He simply crashed his huge boat into the pilings. Later, on board *Barrabas*, I heard a thudding against the hull. When I went topside to check, I saw a great raft of timber floating past that the tug had dislodged from the pier.

At 10.00 am, I went to the *Petrov*. The ship ran to Moscow time. Everyone was asleep. The first officer was on duty. I drew a picture of a stick man taking a shower and he grudgingly led me below. The shower was fantastic – powerful and hot. The last decent shower I'd had was in Nome, in Rick's 'shop'.

Louise had been liaising constantly with the Murmansk Shipping Company. They in turn had agreed in principle to transport *Barrabas*, but the final decision would be down to Captain Zagorsky. On Thursday 20th September, Dimitri called me from the ship.

'We will take you, but we are waiting for authorisation from Murmansk.'

'I was under the impression they had left the decision to you.'

'Yes, it's true,' Dimitri said, 'but you must have a contract first. This you must agree with them.'

I called Louise. She had discussed the contract with a man called Antonov. Murmansk would email the contract to Louise. She could sign it on my behalf.

The weather deteriorated. I was becoming anxious about loading *Barrabas* onto the ship. Much of the discussion between the *Kapitan Danilkin* and me had centred on whether we could get *Barrabas* hoisted with the mast in situ. Captain Zagorsky thought it might be difficult with the limited height of his deck cranes. If the mast had to come off, then so be it. I was desperate to get out of Tiksi.

The wind kicked in from the west, gusting to 40 knots. By some fortuitous foresight, I had scavenged among the piles of debris on the dock – discarded marine engines, bits of crane, burnt-out hulks of buses and cars and skidoos – for old car tyres, and hung them from the quayside to cushion *Barrabas*'s hull. By Saturday lunchtime, the seas were hurling *Barrabas* against the dock. The tyres undoubtedly saved the boat from serious damage. I called Dimitri and asked him to contact the harbourmaster. I needed a tug to pull me off and get me to a more protected berth.

Eventually an ancient tug puttered around the corner, approached

Barrabas far too closely, lost control in the high winds and collided. The tug got away from *Barrabas's* side, spewing oil all over her deck from the exhausts. I threw the towing line. The tug then dragged *Barrabas* along the quayside. Metal spikes dug into her hull. The spikes would have ripped a fibreglass boat to pieces. I ditched the towline as soon as *Barrabas* was clear and motored to the other side of the quay, completely protected from the strong winds forecast to continue from the west over the next 48 hours. I tethered *Barrabas* to a rusted crane platform moored deep in the recess between two piers so she would rise and fall with the tides without me having to adjust her lines.

Louise: Saturday 22nd September 2007
I am so sorry – it sounds like hell but the best news is that next week you will be out of there! How will they lift you out with no sling or spreader? All well here.

Early on Sunday morning at 1.00 am, I was woken by someone on board *Barrabas* shouting, 'Sorry gentleman, sorry gentleman!' Who the hell was this? Drunkenness and vagrancy were rife in Tiksi. My hunting knife hung in its scabbard near the chart table. I kept the blade honed to razor-sharpness. With the knife in my hand, I opened the companionway hatch. The reek of stale alcohol made me retch. I recognised the man as one of the crew on the tug. He wanted to sleep on the boat! I got rid of him as diplomatically as I could with constant shrugs as though I did not understand what he wanted.

After 10 days in port, I had still not received permission from the military authorities to leave. Captain Zagorsky was concerned. The ship had to sail on the 26th September. She was to be the last vessel through the Vil'kitskiy Strait before Nikolay Babych closed the route for the winter. The gaps between the ice floes had now frozen.

I went to see Vissarion in his office just outside the docks. He called the border control guards. They had not received any instruction from their headquarters in Petropavlovsk. On top of this, Captain Zagorsky radioed me to say that the port authorities were refusing to help. He had requested timber to shore up *Barrabas* and hoisting straps but they were not prepared to assist.

Louise was in tears.

'Call Andre Chupin and the commercial people at the British Embassy in Moscow. I think the problem here is that no one wants to take responsibility, so they just keep passing the buck to the next guy along.'

'This is a nightmare!'

'Tell me about it. If I don't make the ship's sailing schedule, *Barrabas* is stuck here for the winter. I don't know how safe she will be, but it's academic. We both know I can't come back next year.'

Lack of money to winter the boat for another season, the slim chance of getting another Russian visa, the difficulties of regaining permissions from NSRA and my refusal to be away from the children for another extended period meant either *Barrabas* sailed with the *Kapitan Danilkin* or I faced the hideous prospect of abandoning her in this Arctic hellhole.

A light tapping came from somewhere on deck. It was lunchtime. Vissarion was throwing small pebbles to attract my attention. I motioned for him to come on board.

The head of the border guards in Petropavlovsk had sent the order to give me clearance to leave.

'But,' Vissarion said, 'you have to go into Murmansk to check out of customs.'

'Okay.' I expected this.

'The border guards told me that information about you is being sent to Murmansk. If you do not go into port, then they will intercept you at sea.'

This whole experience was rapidly deteriorating into an Orwellian drama. I immediately called Captain Zagorsky.

'You must to wait in port on standby for loading.' Sweet words. I was getting out of here!

'What time do you anticipate calling me, Captain?'

'I think 5.00 pm. The weather today is good, but not so good for tomorrow.'

'I'm ready when you are.'

I stayed on board, tidying the cabin and preparing *Barrabas*. At 5.00 pm, the radio crackled. The ship was standing me down!

'What's the problem, Captain?'

'There is no contract.' I heard Captain Zagorsky speaking Russian. Dimitri came onto the radio. 'The captain says that you must have a contract with the Murmansk Shipping Company.'

'I do.' Louise was dealing with this.

'Murmansk say they sent the contract but they have not yet received it back.'

'Bloody hell. Okay, Dimitri, I'll sort it out. I'll call Louise now.'

'Okay. There is something else. We need two sea containers to place either side of the yacht on the deck. The port is refusing to send them to the ship. They must have authorisation from Murmansk, but with no contract, Murmansk cannot do this.'

'Leave it to me, Dimitri. I'll get on it now.'

I called Louise. 'What's happening with this contract? I can't . . .'

'There's a problem. I wasn't going to tell you. John and I are trying to . . .'

'What problem? The ship's leaving.'

I had to sit down as Louise gave me the bad news. The cost of the transport quoted in the agreement recently sent to her by MSCO was $52,000!

'But Babych quoted $10,000 and that was three bloody weeks ago. Right at the death, with the ship leaving in 24 hours, they come up with this?'

It was impossible to raise $52,000. Suddenly, the prospect of abandoning *Barrabas* was real once more. Because of the time differences between Tiksi, London and Moscow, we only had a few short hours to try to resolve the situation. Was this simply a bleak collusion of circumstance or, more worryingly, confused or even contrived information or misinformation against the minutes ticking rapidly away before the ship weighed anchor?

I radioed the ship and explained the situation. Captain Zagorsky agreed to stand by until 11.00 pm, six hours, otherwise preparations would be made for sea and *Barrabas* would be left behind and me with no option but to fly out of Tiksi and abandon *Barrabas* to her fate.

John Mann: Tuesday 25th September 2007

Not good news. Antonov (MSCO) said that Babych was very wrong to have given us that $10K figure at the beginning. He insists that this was done without consultation with the commercial freight division (not what Babych told me before).

The $52K price includes taxes, fees, etc . . . in conclusion, Antonov said he couldn't do this operation for any less than the price listed in the contract. He insisted they are a commercial organisation, blah, blah.

Louise and John set to work making calls, exchanging opinions, revisiting history, recalling decisions, negotiating and finally reaching agreement with contracts written, exchanged, signed and returned. I interjected the to-ings and fro-ings with numerous calls on the satellite phone and settled to wait as the clock ticked through half past ten. At five minutes to eleven, Louise called with the outcome.

'They've cut the price of the transport!'

This was a face-saving compromise, a big pill to swallow but not so big it would stick in my craw. At two minutes to eleven, the deadline only 120 seconds away, I radioed the ship to tell Dimitri, standing by on the bridge for my call, that we had an agreement.

Adrian: Tuesday 25th September 2007

Hi there . . . you must be mentally on the rack. Well done! I am still pretty sick at the amount but still, it's 'doable'. I always believed you would be able to negotiate an acceptable solution and so you have . . . if the AGX has delivered anything it should be in you believing in yourself in a way that perhaps you have never done before.

Please pass this msg on to JM

Hi John
Once again, I am deeply indebted to you. I am beginning to understand how difficult it can be dealing with the Russians. I realised that the only solution was going to have to be a face-saving compromise on both sides. Whilst the amount is (in my opinion) steep, it was clearly the result of skilful negotiation on your part and Louise providing succinct appraisals of the situation on the ground here. What started out as a 'single-handed' expedition has become anything but that.

Dawn broke divinely calm, bronze and rose in the east, fading to pewter and holding the promise of stillness. The sea around the *Kapitan Danilkin* was plate-smooth. *Barrabas*, moored against the ship's port side, tugged gently at her lines, a tiny infant suckling a mother's protection.

She knew, I'm certain, exactly what would happen later in the morning. I had explained it to her as we motored from Tiksi docks the previous evening. The six-mile run to the ship required three course changes. Without touching the autopilot, *Barrabas* made the turns, 10 degrees to starboard on each occasion on the mark without any input from me. She knew where she was going like a trekking horse that has trodden the same path interminably and no matter what cajoling from its rider will not deviate. *Barrabas* was just as anxious to get away as I was.

On arrival alongside, I met Dimitri, the chief mate, a young, amiable seaman and then Captain Zagorsky. At 72, he scrambled down the rope ladder onto *Barrabas*'s deck, small but toughly built like a jockey. Despite the diminutive stature, his greeting was akin to having my hand slammed in a closing elevator door. He then immediately yelled for light in the gathering dusk and almost instantly, *Barrabas* was ablaze beneath the port-side floodlights mounted high on the ship's superstructure. I watched him carefully. Hooded eyes flicked across the yacht's deck, up the mast then down again, shrouds and stays tested for tension. Rapid-fire Russian peppered the chief mate, who fed the questions back to me in English. How strong was the mast? Could I disconnect the backstays? How? Was it possible to rig a jury stay leading aft from the mast? How quickly could I get it done?

I accompanied the captain onto the deck of his ship, watched by the assembled crew. He wanted to show me the arrangements he had planned for taking *Barrabas* on board. In a quick aside, the chief mate told me that the captain had not slept well for three weeks over the problem of how to stow *Barrabas* and get her through the ice. He had conducted brainstorming meetings with the ship's company, made scale drawings and tested different options. Two sea containers barged out to the ship by the port authorities and fixed on the port and starboard hatches of the central cargo wells provided lateral support. The yacht's keel would sit on wooden blocking laid in the central gallery running between the hatches, the sides of the gallery deepened with more wood blocking positioned between the containers.

By midday on Friday, with the hoisting straps in place beneath *Barrabas*, the crane swung outboard and the great block lowered precisely between the yacht's twin backstays. On my advice to the captain, the crane took up tension on the straps and lifted *Barrabas* 12 inches. The forward straps raked backwards to the hook either side of the mast. I had angled their paths between the shrouds to avoid any contact between the shrouds and the straps. *Barrabas* had to come out of the water completely level. She did. Slowly, the crane lifted her from the sea to her new resting place. The crew then set to work, evidently rehearsed, shoring up the yacht's sides. We lashed two of the ship's fenders, each 12 feet high and 4 feet wide, vertically in the spaces between *Barrabas*'s bows and the sea containers. To prevent any side-to-side or forward and backward movement, the crew tethered

Barrabas to the deck of the ship, attaching straps to her forward, midships and stern cleats. They fitted chains to the other ends of these straps and secured the chains to strong points on deck. The chains were then tensioned until the straps were almost bar tight.

The *Kapitan Danilkin* weighed anchor in the late afternoon, turned hard to port and nosed eastwards out of Tiksi harbour. I watched from the bridge. To the west, the pewter had burnished to silver. Feathery cloud moved listlessly aloft. From high on the bridge deck, I watched the cranes' derricks lowered to their sea-going positions, one of them crossing over *Barrabas*'s stern deck like a protective arm.

CHAPTER 27

From Russia with Love

My cabin comprised two adjoining rooms on the fifth level, part of the officers' quarters just below the bridge. One contained a drawing room with sofa, armchair, coffee table and large desk, and the other a bedroom with an en-suite shower room. After supper in the mess, Captain Zagorsky knocked on my door and came in carrying two glasses and two tins of Tuborg. He moved with repressed energy. The dome of his head was bare. Under different circumstances, the pale blue of his eyes might be cold and intimidating, but some inner zest set them alight.

'You know, the carriage of the yacht is illegal.' The captain poured beer carefully, gave a small shrug. 'No insurance, no papers.' He sipped. I sipped. 'Babych is my friend. He say to me you must to take the yacht to Murmansk, so I help you.'

'Thank you, Captain. I am very grateful.'

'But, why you do this thing?'

'Sailing around the world?'

'Yes. It's crazy. And in the ice, bah!'

'Well, lots of reasons but mainly because I wanted to.'

Captain Zagorsky looked baffled. He was a contradiction, a company man raised in the strictures of the Soviet regime yet a maverick who made his own laws and bent or simply ignored the dictates of others if that suited his purpose.

After a while he said, 'Okay. You know, I see this.' He nodded, not approval but certainly understanding. 'But I am seaman for fifty year. Is dangerous for small boat to sail with big ships, no?'

'Yes.'

'If you are only one on board, how can you see ships coming?' He told the story of a Danish fishing boat run over by a Russian ship with the loss of all hands.

'There is a risk which any single-handed sailor must accept, a responsibility.'

'And you children?'

'Two boys.'

'What they think of you do this?'

'What can I teach them? To work hard, to play hard, to be good, respectful, polite. But also to show them to be true to themselves, to do what they believe. Like you, Captain. To make their own rules.'

I learned later that the captain's nonagenarian mother had recently died. Normally, he would have been relieved of command and flown to St Petersburg on compassionate leave. Instead, he had chosen to stay with the ship to get *Barrabas* safely out of Tiksi.

'I have two daughter. One is married. He is painter.' The captain made brush strokes in the air. 'I not like him.'

'Why?'

'No job . . .'

'Like me.'

'You write book, no, this is your work, this why you make voyage.'

He was twisting the order of things to accept me more comfortably, bending his own rules this time to suit his purpose.

On 30th September just before midnight, the ship made its rendezvous with the icebreaker *Russiya*. I walked from the bridge in a snowstorm as we headed through early bands of progressively thicker drift ice. I wanted to see the ice. A question still hovered. Could I have made it through on my own? I stayed up into the early hours of Monday morning observing the ice from the freezing prow and the comfort of the bridge. Ice was at 100 per cent cover, three metres thick. I spent some time on the afterdeck with the captain. The reason for my vigil was to answer a second question. Could a ship, maybe one in the convoy, have towed *Barrabas*? The icebreaker crunched through the frozen sea seven cables ahead leaving a path strewn with ice boulders in her wake. The *Kapitan Danilkin*'s 38-mm-thick steel bows pushed this debris aside and in turn left a trail of open water. Captain Zagorsky explained that pieces of ice pressed beneath the bows could ride along the ship's keel and emerge at the stern. Ice chunks breaking the surface from the depths of the ship's draught, 25 feet, each weighing up to one ton, would cause devastating damage to a yacht following behind. As the captain and I stood in the warm lee of the funnel stack looking sternwards, I saw boulders of ice breaking the surface. A single impact from one of those would have sent *Barrabas* to the bottom.

My lingering sense of disturbance dissipated with the vindication of transporting *Barrabas* on the ship's deck.

My few days on board the *Kapitan Danilkin* quickly fell into a routine governed by rigid mealtimes and the two periods I spent with the captain: morning coffee (which usually ran on until lunch) and tea or a drink in the evening in the conference room annexed to the captain's cabin. Dimitri always joined us for coffee. Occasionally, the chief engineer dropped in to share a drink after supper. Between times, I checked on *Barrabas*, showered, rested, read, talked to Louise and spent time on the bridge with the officer of the watch, marking up my charts. Sleeping in a heated cabin was blissful. The food was unimaginative, but I still did not have much of an appetite anyway. Meals tended to be quiet, even silent affairs, more a refuelling pit stop than a forum for social interaction. The officers ate separately from the rest of the crew. Often the captain and I were the only ones who spoke. I made a light-hearted comment to the captain about the paltry breakfasts, usually a bland pancake or cold sausage and coffee.

'What you like?'

'Well, you know, English breakfasts, eggs, bacon, sausage, bread, jam and best of all, a glass of ice-cold milk.'

'Bah!'

Captain Zagorsky was interested in many topics and our conversations ranged widely: oriental philosophies, religion, future population migration and national cultural influences. The captain's favourite subject revolved around the concept of freedom. He was keen to delve further into my rationale for making the voyage and the consequences of it. He was, I think, using me as a sounding board, perhaps to better understand the artistic temperament of his son-in-law or in some way to reconcile that difficult relationship. The conversation continually returned here, to this blight.

'You have another daughter?' I asked.

'Yes.'

Perhaps his second daughter had married a better proposition. I noticed the Slavic lift of his eyes that usually lent his face a cunning expression had dropped, the mischievous blue light momentarily dulled. 'But she has died,' the captain said quietly.

'I'm sorry.' Hopeless words. 'What about grandchildren?'

The light returned. 'Twins. A boy and a girl. They are five. I walk them in St Petersburg and take them to the hut in the woods . . .'

'A dacha . . .'

'Hut. A small place. My son-in-law, he is doing the place up.'

We spoke about the hut in the woods. His mother had died. His wife was ill. His child had died. Captain Zagorsky needed to make sense of what he had left. I felt drawn in. Like a son.

I mentioned I wanted to wash some clothes. One morning after breakfast, I found Captain Zagorsky in my cabin stringing up a clothes-line. He then marched me along the corridor to the laundry room and showed me how to operate the washing machine.

I turned 47 at sea, with the ice safely astern and a 50-knot wind screeching across the deck. I got up late and went down to the mess hall on the first level. Everyone else had finished. The dining-room hostess came out of the kitchen, beaming. She set a tray down and placed a plate of fried eggs and sausage, bread, jam and a tall glass of very cold milk in front of me

'Kapitan!' she said triumphantly.

I pointed to the plate. 'Kapitan Zagorsky?'

'Da!' She replied, nodding happily.

'Speciba!'

At morning coffee in the conference room with Dimitri and the chief engineer, the captain presented me with a bottle of 18-year-old Chivas whisky. That evening after supper, the cook brought up my 'birthday cake', an apple tart on a sweet bread base. After the anxiety and exhaustion of the NSR, it was a happy time. I had been holding onto another worry. I decided to speak to the captain.

'I'm getting a bit anxious about going round North Cape in October,' I said to the captain at morning coffee the next day.

Dimitri was there. He had spent two seasons in Cape Horn, as chief mate on a passenger ship plying between Ushuaia and Antarctica. 'We call North Cape the Cape Horn of the northern hemisphere. In October is very bad, very dangerous place.'

The captain was not quite as fluent in English as the chief mate. He spoke fast, often tripping over English words, checking his step and continuing in Russian. I heard the word 'fjord' several times.

Dimitri was nodding, then turned to me. 'The captain says you can go through the Norwegian fjord system. He has done it once in winter. You go below North Cape.'

'I don't have charts.'

The captain got up from the table, a stream of Russian spilling over his shoulder. He picked up the telephone.

'The captain will call one of the cadets to get charts from the chart room for you to see.'

Fifteen minutes later, Captain Zagorsky and I bent over the charts laid out by the cadet.

'You go here,' the captain said, his finger tracing the route through the fjords down as far as Vestfjorden.

Adrian: Tuesday 2nd October 2007

I have a problem! The weather around northern Norway in Oct/Nov is horrendous – 60 mph winds common. This was why I wanted to get past the Vil'kitskiy Strait in August. I've checked my charts for Murmansk to home and they are not detailed enough. I will have to wait for suitable weather windows of 2–3 days then stop in port and wait etc all the way down the Norwegian coast. So can you contact Martin Amy. I need detailed charts along the Norwegian, Danish, German and Belgium coasts.

Two rules applied to every vessel entering or leaving the port of Murmansk, regardless of size: an onboard pilot and agency representation, primarily because of security issues surrounding the Russian North Atlantic Fleet based at Severomorsk, halfway along Kola Bay. Captain Zagorsky arranged representation for me through the MM agency, an affiliate of the Murmansk Shipping Company.

Louise: Tuesday 2nd October 2007

Martin Amy on the case and will DHL to Murmansk. Every time I think the nightmare is over – hey presto, you find a new one. Went to the bank today to transfer funds to Murmansk. All done and on the way to them.

In preparation for our arrival in port, I filled the water tanks on *Barrabas*. The captain organised a hose from the galley, but when this did not work, a crew member led the hose up the outside of the superstructure to the captain's galley on the fifth level and connected it to the sink. I also mended the clew of the headsail, stitching in a reinforcing webbing strap to counter the chafe inflicted by 30,000 miles at sea.

The *Kapitan Danilkin* dropped anchor a mile offshore from the port of Murmansk late on Friday night, 5th October. Transportation of *Barrabas* through the Arctic ice on a ship not designed for such work, with a makeshift hoisting rig and a deck support structure for the yacht cobbled from sea containers, timber and chain, was always going to be a risky business. Early on Saturday morning the wind stood still and, as in Tiksi, we had perfect conditions. The hoist was smooth. Captain Zagorsky and I discussed using an extra length of strapping to get the crane block above the twin backstays. From our experience of loading the boat, we knew we had sufficient clearance above the containers to use the extra strap and avoid possible damage to the yacht's rig by the massive crane block.

Captain Zagorsky barked commands, radioed instructions to the crane operator and pulled on tag lines to orientate *Barrabas* for her descent to the water. His men sprang into action and soon, *Barrabas* was once more bobbing gently alongside the ship.

My pilot, a quiet man called Yevgeny, boarded the *Kapitan Danilkin* at 9.00 am and he and I were soon under way. As my engine fired and the lines let go, a cheer erupted from the crew, led as always by Captain Zagorsky.

'I come to see you later,' Captain Zagorsky told me. His rotation on the *Kapitan Danilkin* was over and he would be returning to St Petersburg in the next day or two, back to look after his sick wife during four months of shore leave.

During the unloading procedure, Dimitri had worked up quite a sweat. He was suddenly incredulous at the successful delivery of *Barrabas* to Murmansk. We stood together on the side deck shaking hands before I scuttled down the rope ladder to the deck of my own ship.

Barrabas eased away. I turned hard to port as instructed by the pilot and then gave the wheel over to Yevgeny to steer us the two miles to the customs quay. Within minutes of arrival, uniformed officialdom descended. After an hour of questions, form-filling and document-stamping, we were done.

Yevgeny reappeared, directing me to a new mooring on Pier 16. A 300-metre quay jutted westwards and another protruded southwards, both occupied by 50,000-ton ships. A rag-tag assortment of floating pontoon barges, tugs and bunker vessels hovered in the crotch between these two limbs. I tied up to one of the floating barges. A doghouse enclosed a small office manned on a 12-hour rotation by 'watchmen'. Ura and Ghena were on duty. Ghena had one of those fascinating faces – the features unequal, lopsided, crunched, akimbo as though moulded from a softer, more pliant material. I showed him a long piece of flex with American plugs and asked (through various gesticulations and diagrams) if he had a Russian plug so I could get power to the boat. Ghena eventually got the picture (literally). He insisted on doing the splicing. To support the cable while he worked, he ran it through a small steel loop welded to the door (I did not see this at the time because I had retreated to the boat). He called for me when he'd finished. I made suitable expressions of pleasure, then saw the run of the flex and pointed out to him that the plug would not come back out through the steel loop. Ura thought this hilarious. Crimson patches bloomed on Ghena's ravaged face. We sorted it out second time round.

With heat and light on board, Captain Zagorsky eventually located me, pulling two loaves of bread and a carton of cigarettes from his small bag. I made tea and he promised to return the following day with his great friend, Nikolay Babych.

Captain Zagorsky arrived with Nikolay Babych at noon on Sunday, this time bringing a bottle of cognac, which we attacked with the eagerness of comrades who had shared a unique experience.

I pulled up satellite images on the laptop. Nikolay Babych interpreted them.

'Impossible for you to go ice,' he concluded, shaking his head solemnly from side to side. 'But you the first to be in North Sea Route alone. This is great honour for me to be on boat,' and with that he raised his glass and we all drank.

Captain Zagorsky said, 'I give you this.' He handed me a piece of paper, a number scribbled in pencil. 'This my telephone in St Petersburg. You to call when you in England. Then I sleep okay to know you are safe!'

We embraced, a bear hug. Somewhere, our hasty alliance had turned to affection. Later, nursing the kind of hangover that afflicts the unaccustomed, I took a stroll along the docks. When I got back to *Barrabas*, Ura pointed to a package in the cockpit.

'Mr Babych,' he said. Inside the bag, I discovered bread, cheese and various Russian salamis and sausages.

On Monday 8th October, Port State Control visited the berth to check my safety equipment. Having passed muster, I ordered a weather file. A vicious depression north of Murmansk would keep me pinned down for the next four days. The charts arrived from Louise. I pored over them, deciding a route. The small town of Vardo 100 miles west of Kola Bay on Norway's northeastern coast seemed like a good first stop.

Igor Melnikov appeared with a bright smile on his fresh 24-year-old face announcing himself as my 'new' agent from the MM agency.

At night, the temperature plunged. I needed an external heater. Igor disappeared, returning at 6.00 pm with a heater. He refused to take any money. When Igor arrived at the pontoon the next morning, *Barrabas* was as warm as toast and I was down to a T-shirt.

'I was talking to my family about you and your voyage last night.' Igor clambered down the companionway steps clutching packages. 'My mother made these for you.'

The packages, wrapped and tied with ribbons and bows, contained a freshly made mince pie and dried fish.

I was astonished. 'Please thank your mother.'

'I will, yes. This is no problem.'

'What's her name, your mother?'

'Lubov.'

I nodded.

'It means love,' Igor said.

He disappeared with my driving licence to get a pass for me to leave the high-security dock area. With two of my empty gas bottles in the trunk of his car, we eventually found a filling station, left the bottles and drove to his home for lunch with his brother, Dimitri. The apartment building was a featureless concrete box in a rank of many identical structures that constituted an estate, dilapidated and care-worn, its common areas pocked as if strafed by gunfire. Graffiti adorned the hall. This was 'middle-class' living by Russian standards. The flat was small: a hallway shared with another apartment, a sitting room, tiny kitchen, bathroom with a separate toilet and two bedrooms. The whole family lived here.

After lunch, Igor and I visited bookshops in search of something in English. I managed to find copies of *Lord of the Flies* and *Sons and Lovers*. At a supermarket, I stocked up on milk, biscuits, bacon, sugar and Nesquik, and after that, at his office I emailed 12 pictures to Louise on a high-speed internet connection.

A more recent weather file decided my departure date – Saturday 13th October. A 40-hour window of south winds would see me to Vardo. With high water at 9.30 am, I could make the 20 miles to the entrance of Kola Bay, going with the tide.

Two nights of sub-zero temperatures had left Murmansk sheathed in a cling film of white and *Barrabas* painted with a veneer of ice. Stepping carefully onto the treacherous deck, Alexandre Kondakov, a director of the Murmansk Shipping Company, and Sergey Minchenko, head of the MM agency, visited me on *Barrabas*, presenting me with a beautiful crystal polar bear on behalf of the company.

Igor drove me to a vantage point to the west of the city, the largest settlement north of the Arctic Circle. Descending to the urban sprawl, its centre ringed by sentinels of ugly, grey apartment blocks, we came across a shopping complex, newly opened, and inside, a revelation of European chic and modern design. The place was buzzing with young women. Their objective was clear – see and be seen. Collectively, these girls were monumentally attractive with an apparent genetic predisposition towards an extra six inches of leg length above standard proportions and a startling array of eye colour (either that or some wily entrepreneur was making a killing in the coloured contact lens business). The fashion: jeans so tightly fitting as to suggest aspirations towards painting them on rather than pulling them on and boots, winkle-picked and stilettoed to the limit of walkability. After months on a visual diet of water, tundra and Tiksi, this feast of eye-candy was hugely appetising.

By 3.00 pm, I was back on board from my city sojourn (during which, ironically, given the city's predilection for fashion consciousness, I was unable to find a comb) to meet the press. Two television crews and a clutch of print journalists, attracting with them a small crowd of bemused dockworkers, arrived at my berth. I showed them *Barrabas*, answered questions, posed and said 'Hello' to Murmansk on cue through several takes because the interviewer could not quite wrap her tongue around 'Flanagan'.

Louise's diary: Wednesday 10th October 2007

Sunk to the very bottom. Spent most of the day in tears, a cumulative effect of everything. Tired from the stress of the expedition, worried about what dramas may unfold next, desperate for Adrian to get home but with no clear sign of timings in sight, lost all tolerance and patience with the boys and it is so unfair on them. Wondering what my life is going to be all about when this is finished and pissed off that I spend my whole time looking after everyone else with no one looking after me.

I was talking to a journalist in England.

'Do me a favour. Louise is pretty down right now. Can you organise a bunch of flowers for her.'

'Consider it done. Anything on the card?'

I thought for a moment. 'From Russia with Love.'

CHAPTER 28

Mayhem in Mehamn

I slipped my lines on 13th October, a gusty, dismal Saturday morning. It would have been my father's 76th birthday.

The pilot on board was called Andrey. He spoke no English and we soon lost any reason to communicate. He'd joined me on *Barrabas* shortly after a small army of officials arrived from the immigration authorities to give me permission to leave.

Seven miles out, Murmansk radio ordered us to stop. 'Why?' I said to the pilot, palms upturned, arms outstretched, shoulders shrugging to get my question across. A Russian naval vessel was coming in to Severomorsk. This restriction came with no warning. We moored up to a buoy and sat down to lunch. After getting under way at 3.00 pm, we reached the pilot station two hours later. The pilot vessel, a powerful tug, drew close. I asked the helmsman to hold a steady course at four knots then brought *Barrabas* in on an elliptical sweep, coming alongside so that our decks were 12 inches apart and my pilot could step onto the tug.

Clear of the traffic separation scheme at the entrance to Kola Bay and the zones restricted for military use, I steered *Barrabas* around Rybachiy Peninsula beneath a wondrous display of the Northern Lights, green and blue illuminations seeping through the night sky like ink on wet paper.

Barrabas crossed the border into Norwegian territorial waters just after midday on Sunday 14th October. I stayed awake through the night.

Situated on a small island connected to the mainland by an undersea tunnel, Vardo is the oldest settlement in northern Norway, with a population of 2,000. I entered through the harbour wall into a merciful calm. Pretty, colourfully painted houses peppered the hillsides. Clean, modern cars zipped along unblemished strips of tarmac in contrast to the ancient jalopies coughing along the fractured roads of Murmansk. I moored *Barrabas* against a barge just inside the harbour wall. To get ashore, I had to step onto the barge and then, on the other side, onto a Norwegian search and rescue vessel and up a gangway. I introduced myself to the captain of the *Oscar Tybring IV*, Roger Pettersen. He invited me on board. Could I have a shower? No problem, he said. Further, he was cooking dinner and I was welcome to join the rest of the three-man crew, which I did for a traditional Norwegian dish of soupy cabbage and lamb chops followed by nutty custard with a fruit jelly sauce. I ate three servings of each. After almost 40 hours awake, I collapsed into my sleeping bag.

Next morning Roger came to have a look at *Barrabas*. We went over my charts. Roger gave me some useful local knowledge for sailing in these waters. The coast became a treacherous place when the wind blew from the north. *Oscar Tybring IV* belonged to Redningsskoyta (The Rescue Company). A fleet of similar vessels, powerful twin-diesel tugs, was located at strategic points along the Norwegian coast. The organisation was part-government funded and relied on public donations and membership fees to cover the rest of its operating budget. Unknown to me, Roger had been onto his head office in Oslo, explaining who I was and what I was doing. Redningsskoyta offered me free membership to the end of the year.

To be back in Europe felt wonderful. England had seemed so distant while I was in Russia. The 100-mile passage to Vardo had been a great leap homewards. I visited the town, wrote postcards to the boys, found a John Grisham novel in English and bought a few fresh provisions.

On Tuesday 16th October, with the promise of another 40-hour weather window, I set sail from Vardo. As Roger had warned, I soon discovered that navigating close inshore along the Norwegian coast was a hazardous business. The long, high-sided fjords amplified the wind. Crossing the mouths of the fjords took me into 50-knot maelstroms. During late afternoon, Vardo radio issued a gale warning of

Force 8. I gybed and reefed the main. Through another sleepless night, I put into the small port of Berlevåg at dawn. After a few hours' sleep and breakfast of coffee, eggs and bacon, I went in search of fishermen to tap them for some local knowledge. I told them I was heading for Gamvik before the weather closed in. Immediately and in unison they shook their heads.

'Gamvik's got a no good harbour,' one said.

'Ja,' the second agreed. 'Mehamn's better.' So Mehamn it was. I had enough time. With the wind light but steady from the northwest, I made good time under full sail around Nordkynhalvoya, an island bounded on the east by Tanafjorden and on the west by Laksefjorden. As I turned the corner into Mehamnfjorden and picked up the occulting white, red and green light providing guidance towards the harbour entrance, darkness had already descended with all the density of a speeding Arctic winter. I dropped all sail. *Barrabas*, ever true and seeming again to know my intentions, nosed gently round in tight circles as I tidied halyards and sheets and rigged mooring lines and fenders on both sides. Then with the engine humming sweetly, we eased round the headland and picked up the fixed green light of the harbour entrance. Within the safety of the breakwater, I steered *Barrabas* around the harbour perimeter. An assortment of fishing boats occupied all the quays and sidings, but in the northwestern corner I found a pontoon and tied up alongside in pouring rain just as the clock struck midnight.

By morning, the rain had stopped, to be replaced by a sleeting mist. I climbed a hill past neat houses and down the other side over tundra towards a small beach. Breakers goaded by the wind shattered onto rocks. A seagull watched silently from a narrow promontory. Together we surveyed the innocent violence of the sea. I thought of my sons. Today was Gabriel's sixth birthday. I should have been home by now.

I stopped at a supermarket and the town's bakery. When I returned to *Barrabas*, the wind was screaming. I set a bowl of fresh fruit on the saloon table, a visual reminder of domestic normalcy. Next to the bowl of fruit, six candles cast a soft, sputtering light. I'd bought a small cake. While the wind shrieked and the rain clattered down, I toasted Gabriel with a tot of Captain Zagorsky's French brandy.

Oddvar Jenssen owned Nordkyn Seafoods. The wood-clad office block and processing plant stood on the harbour's edge just up from the pontoon. Two fishing boats tugged angrily at their lines against a quay in front of the buildings. I climbed the stairs to the offices and introduced myself.

'My wife told me she met you,' he said.

'Your wife?'

'In the bakery, yesterday.'

'Otto Jenssen's bakery, is that you?'

'My father. Now my wife runs it.'

'So, Oddvar, you know the fjords?'

'Ja, I often go to Tromsø. That's my boat.' Oddvar pointed through the window. A cabin cruiser tied to a mooring buoy bobbed close to the pontoon. 'But now, this time of year . . .' He gave a few small shakes of his head.

'Can you show me anyway, on the charts?' I had brought them along. There was really only one way to go and Oddvar pointed out anchorages, chin tucked in, peering over the top of his glasses in the peculiar manner of spectacle wearers.

Outside, the weather was atrocious, constant gales howling in from the west. Oddvar logged onto a local weather site. Wind speeds just offshore were touching 50 knots. All the fishing boats had stayed in port. How far would I get bashing head to wind in open water against the prevailing southwesterlies?

Inshore, the step-sided fjords funnelled the wind so for the moment this route was not an option either. North Atlantic low-pressure systems travelled eastwards between Norway and Spitsbergen and as at Cape Horn, moved unopposed with no landmasses to break, slow or decay the depressions. Conditions would worsen going into November. England was so tantalisingly close, yet between northern Norway and the English south coast, I was facing the prospect of the worst sustained conditions of the entire voyage. Charts in hand, I wandered back to *Barrabas*, brewed a fresh pot of coffee and sat there for a long time, thinking.

All circumnavigations conform to a guiding principle: you hit the hotspots at the best time of year. I made it round Cape Horn just in time, at the end of the southern hemisphere summer. The delay in Honolulu meant I was late getting to the antipodal point and the risk from typhoons became very real. I was lucky to get away without a serious encounter with big weather. Sea-ice presented a unique aspect to the 'vertical' route, a physical barrier rather than a weather danger and (in my case) west of there, the Norwegian Sea and the North Sea. Delay at any critical point and the ramifications transmitted down the track. My plan had me past the ice by the end of August with September to get round Norway and home before conditions turned perilous.

Force 7–12 conditions plague the Norwegian Sea 30 per cent of the time in November and through the winter months. Unmarked rocks litter the coast south of Vestfjorden. Savage seas build quickly over the shoals and in the prevailing winds, the Norwegian coast is a lee shore. I watched the weather and waited. The conclusion was inescapable. I had missed my window.

Adrian: Friday 19th October 2007

Hello . . . I know you were not happy about our conversation earlier, but I'm afraid it looks like I will have to winter Barrabas in Norway. As I explained, the weather in this region and all the way down the Norwegian coast and the North Sea is horrific from October through to the end of January. I always knew this would be a problem area if I came through Vil'kitskiy Strait any later than end August. I pretty much figured that an over-winter in Norway was inevitable when I was still in Russian waters by end August. I didn't mention anything to you because I wanted to get to this area and see what it was like. I have sought out local knowledge here which also confirms my views.

I know you feel that your huge efforts will thus be extended for many more months, but last time I was back I was very edgy because of the whole Russian deal – the visa, the ice, Russian ports, the bureaucracy – none of that applies now. The distance home is very short. I can leave the boat fully rigged so no extended preparation time as was necessary in Nome.

My decision was not yet final. I waited through the weekend, popping into Oddvar's office to check out weather forecasts on the internet. Each day I downloaded fresh GRIB files and walked along the coast staring seawards.

Oddvar came to the boat on Sunday.

'So, what have you decided?'

I blew out my cheeks. 'Leave *Barrabas* here. Come back in April or May.'

Oddvar nodded. 'Good. The right decision.'

'Will *Barrabas* be okay?' There were no facilities to lift her out anyway.

'My boats stay in the water all through winter. It's no problem.'

The water was cold enough to preclude barnacles encrusting the hull but the warm Gulf Stream prevented the sea from freezing over. My concern about leaving *Barrabas* in the water for six months must have been obvious.

'Don't worry,' Oddvar said. 'You will show me how everything works, the bilge pumps, battery isolation, the windmill [wind generator] and I will come to the boat each day to check.'

Louise: Sunday 21st October 2007
You are right – no one apart from you knows the real sea conditions where you are at this time of year and I do understand. If it really means putting yourself in grave peril and still not being home for two months then it is more sensible to come home.

If Oddvar Jenssen dominated on the west side of the harbour – he also owned the Arctic Hotel in town and had bought up a group of dockside buildings – then Kåre Karlstad dominated on the east side. His company owned the main quay where the small cruise ships plying the fjords tied up, a trading company and shops. He came to have a look at *Barrabas*. A one-time naval officer, twice married (his second wife was a Russian model), Kåre spent the winter months in Thailand. We talked boats for a while.

'I had for many years a Baltic 43. I sailed her up to Spitsbergen but mainly near Oslo.'

We were driving west in Kåre's Mercedes. I wanted to see something of the countryside and he was happy to show me. Over lunch in a bistro in Kjøllefjord, I asked Kåre about the sense in trying to sail home at this time of year.

'I answer with a story,' he said. 'Some years ago, I sailed with a French couple to Spitsbergen, they in their 35-foot yacht and me and some crew in the Baltic. The French couple went down to Bergen. They wanted to go back to France. It was October, so I said to them it was crazy to try this now. Anyway, they went. In the North Sea, they were in many storms. Usually, they dropped the sails and drifted, lying ahull. Then, in big seas, their boat rolled over and they lost the mast. Scottish rescue services saved them, but they were lucky. For you, I think it is crazy to try this now.'

When I spoke with local fishermen, they all said pretty much the same thing. My main concern though was not the weather nor *Barrabas*'s ability to cope with extreme conditions. After all, we had both been round Cape Horn. I was physically and emotionally

shattered. The sea would ruthlessly exploit any weakness. To put to sea
in my state of deep fatigue would be a misjudgement and the consequences might easily be fatal.

I called Louise. My decision was final. I would fly home on 1st November. She was getting ready to go out to dinner.

Louise: Wednesday 24th October 2007
Benji was violently sick last night before I went to the Chapmans for dinner. It happened in the downstairs loo and it took me two full rolls of kitchen paper and 25 minutes to clean up – no area of the room was left unsplattered! He apologised profusely to me and I said, 'Don't be silly, this is what being a parent is all about Benji,' to which he replied, 'Thank God I've got about 30 years to wait then!'

Kåre's house stood alone on its own island, which enclosed the northern part of Mehamn's harbour, connected to the mainland by a man-made isthmus. I walked to the house. Across the dark waters of the harbour, Mehamn's twinkling lights banked up the shallow hills. Inside, the house was warm, floored and walled in polished pine. Another friend was there, Gunn Marie, a town councillor.

'We have something special for dinner,' Kåre announced. 'Whale meat.'

The cooking smell was meaty, but not quite beef. I bit into a texture somewhere between liver and lamb with a flavour of fishy beef.

I prepared *Barrabas* for her second winter alone. The sails came off and went into the attic of Oddvar's warehouse. I rinsed the water-maker with a biocide solution, flushed antifreeze through the engine cooling chamber, shut off the fuel, electrics and sea cocks, checked the stern gland, cleared the deck lines and finally, laced tarpaulin over the cockpit area. While *Barrabas* was alongside Nordkyn's quay (his boats were out fishing), I showed Oddvar how to operate the bilge pumps.

With the help of two local men, Roy and Marinius, who, under Oddvar's direction connected a new chain to the harbour bed, we set *Barrabas* to her mooring buoy. Below decks, I kissed my faithful yacht. As in Nome, I knew the people of Mehamn would keep her safe. Then they rowed me ashore.

PART III
Homeward Bound

CHAPTER 29

Port to Port

My time in England passed quickly, but as with the previous wintering, the burden of unfinished business weighed heavily. The last phase of the Alpha Global Expedition would be short. I wanted to enjoy it and to go back to *Barrabas* refreshed.

During the school holiday in April, Louise took the children to Mauritius, to the same resort they had visited during my first Christmas at sea in 2005. I drove them to the airport. Four days later and four weeks before flying back to Norway to sail the third and final leg of the Alpha Global Expedition, it dawned on me that I'd never enjoyed a proper holiday with the children. Despite my creaking finances, I called Louise and we agreed I would fly out to join them. The expedition had elevated my zest for life onto a higher plain and I wanted to pack this year, 2008, with lots of positive experiences.

Our time together in Mauritius was wonderful, filled with laughter and fun. Despite this, I still felt anxiety at what lay ahead. The Norwegian Sea can be unpredictable and treacherous. Across the North Atlantic there are no landmasses to corrode the low-pressure weather systems spawned by warm maritime air joining the cold polar air masses. These air masses twist together to form frontal depressions and are then catapulted eastwards by the earth's rotation. The weather patterns combined with the sudden shoaling of the Norwegian coast create the potential for rogue waves. The northeastern part of the

Norwegian Sea is one of the world's hotspots for these rampaging waves that can reach heights of 100 feet. I would be sailing right across this area. In the North Sea, prevailing southwesterly winds meant I was looking at the prospect of a slow, painful bash into headwinds all the way down the east coasts of Scotland and England. Given the extreme shallowness of water over the North Sea plateau, less than 30 metres in places, dangerous seas can erupt even in relatively modest winds. Hurricane-strength winds are uncommon in spring and early summer but they do occur. My old schoolfriend Roger, who had followed the progress of the expedition from day one, had sent me two emails much earlier in the voyage:

Roger: Tuesday 10th January 2006
If you are lying there hot and sweaty then things could always be worse. Tonight's shipping forecast:
'Hebrides, Bailey, Fair Isle, Faeroes, south veering southwest severe gale 9 to violent storm 11, <u>INCREASING HURRICANE FORCE 12</u> for a time, then veering west 7 to severe gale 9. Squally showers. Moderate or poor.'

Okay, but that was January. Precisely the reason why I'd kept *Barrabas* in Norway through the winter. In May of that year, 2006, Roger had sent another email:

Roger: Friday 19th May 2006
Lucky you're not sailing up the Channel this morning:

'Thames, Dover, Wight, Portland, Plymouth southwesterly 6 to gale 8, <u>OCCASIONALLY SEVERE GALE 9</u> at first, except Plymouth. Rain or showers. Moderate or good, occasionally poor later.'

Pretty bizarre for the middle of May.

Bizarre or not, that had been May! It could happen. Severe gale force 9 in the North Sea or the English Channel might easily spell disaster for a small yacht with an exhausted single-handed crew. In survival conditions, one mistake and it would be *game over*.

Trepidation was nothing new to me, but familiarity with fear makes it no easier to bear.

A few days before I returned to Mehamn, the phone rang. I was at Louise's house discussing final preparations. She had recently sent out a press release and spent the previous 48 hours fielding press calls. I listened distractedly from the kitchen while I loaded my laptop with the latest version of the Maxsea software that had proved invaluable.

'. . . Knox-Johnston . . . yes . . . delighted . . . sure . . . today . . . uh huh . . . no problem, he'll be thrilled.'

Louise bounced into the kitchen beaming. 'There's a new programme on BBC Radio Solent. You're not going to believe this!'

'They want to interview me and Sir Robin together?'

'Better than that! The show's called H2O. That was the producer. Sir Robin presents the show; it's all about sailing, water sports blah, blah. It's his show, Sir Robin's, he'll be interviewing you!'

'Wow! When?'

'This afternoon sometime.'

I did my interview with Sir Robin Knox-Johnston. Although Sir Francis Chichester had initially inspired my own circumnavigation, Sir Robin's 1969 feat of becoming the first single-handed yachtsman to circumnavigate without stopping and using navigation techniques similar to Magellan and Drake centuries before, fuelled my motivation further and propelled him, in my opinion, to rank as the most iconic solo sailor of all time. I seemed to have come full circle. To Sir Robin, I guess the interview was just another means to an end. To me it was an arrival of sorts. All I had left to do was sail 2,000 miles from northern Norway to the Hamble River and maybe, just maybe, I might earn a place at Sir Robin's table.

I arrived in Mehamn late on Sunday evening, 27th April 2008. Thick snow covered the mountainous sentinels protecting the town. The temperature was close to freezing. I'd spotted *Barrabas* from the air and my heart lifted at the sight of her. I spent the first night in the Nordic Safari Lodge then went aboard the following morning. *Barrabas* was as familiar as a well-loved armchair or a favourite coat. The first order of business was getting the engine started after her winter hibernation. I replaced all the fluids, oil, coolant, transmission oil and the oil filter. At initial start-up, the oil-warning light came on and the alarm sounded. I dashed below to eyeball the engine. Oil was spewing out from the attachment area of the oil filter. I immediately shut the engine off. The seal ring of the filter which had been on during winter had stayed adhered to the engine block so the new filter seal was opposing the old one and the oil was coming out between the rubber seals. It was a stupid mistake (and not for the first time!). I drained off the remainder of the oil – two litres, which meant four litres had been evacuated – and refilled the sump.

I brought *Barrabas* alongside and put the sails on, collecting them from the loft of the Nordkyn Seafood Company, Oddvar Jenssen's business – he had been looking after the boat. Preparing to depart is always a tense time for me so I was glad of Kåre's invitation to dinner at the Nordic Safari Lodge. He had just returned from a business trip to Moscow. We ate two local delicacies, cod tongues (sounded revolting – I was seriously dubious but it was delicious) and air-dried cod that was then boiled and served up with potatoes and mashed carrot.

'So, how long to get to England?'

'With a following wind all the way I could do it in two and a half weeks.'

Kåre nodded sagely. We were chasing our courses with shots of aquavit and my head was beginning to spin. 'It's possible. Now we have north winds.'

'It's not going to happen, not all the way to England. I'm figuring four to six weeks. I've set a target of 31st May.'

Kåre refilled my shot glass. 'We drink to this.'

The town's council members were dining at the neighbouring table. Kåre knew them all. He introduced me and I suddenly found myself standing up in the middle of the restaurant delivering a mini-talk on who I was and what I was doing. They all knew *Barrabas*.

Back on board, and preparing *Barrabas* for this last leg, it was as if I had never been away. Even the strain returned, a remnant of the past come to life like the phantom pain from an amputated limb. By midafternoon the next day I'd checked all the boat's systems: engine, rigging, electronics, heating, electrics, navigation, computers, Iridium. All that remained was to ship some provisions to bolster the stock already on board. In the Co-op supermarket, I asked the checkout lady whether she could call a taxi. Instead, she offered to deliver my groceries to the boat herself after work.

Although the engine had passed muster, I thought I would give it another run just to be certain. At start-up, the oil warning light came on and the alarm sounded. I was perplexed. I went over the engine again and noticed the junction box had vibrated loose. I figured excessive vibration in the electrics might be setting off the alarm. Working through the late evening, I re-secured the junction box and packed foam dampeners behind it. When I tried the engine, the problem disappeared, so I assumed my diagnosis had been correct.

Thursday 1st May was Louise's birthday and a national holiday in Norway. It seemed an auspicious date to leave. I filled the water tanks. A local man called Roy who together with Marinius had helped put *Barrabas* to her winter mooring came by with a gift of seagull eggs, warning that I had to boil them for 15 minutes. A friend of his disappeared and came back some time later with beer from Tromsø – apparently I had to have the beer and seagull eggs together, a Norwegian tradition. It was a beautiful day – blue sky, warm in the sunshine with light southerly winds to get me north out of Mehamnfjorden and into the Barents Sea. I set the ship's clocks to UCT and slipped my lines at 12.30 pm. The log showed 28,961 nautical miles. I could not know it then, but only 1,864 nautical miles separated me from the finish line in the Solent.

Leaving Mehamn on 1st May was auspicious for another reason. My weather information predicted that the southerly winds would give way to easterlies generated by a high-pressure system far to the north. The shipping lanes around northern Norway are close to the coast. As I passed northwards to clear them and hook onto the north-easterlies that were set to propel me all the way over the top of Norway, visibility dropped to less than half a mile. I tried the engine but the oil-warning alarm sounded. Not knowing the problem, I was effectively without an engine, which compromised my manoeuvrability in reduced visibility close to shipping. My morale tumbled.

Despite over-wintering the boat, time compresses. The following day at 8.38 am, *Barrabas* passed westwards across the longitude of Nordkapp (North Cape), the northernmost point of the European mainland. At 10.00 am, I dropped the mainsail and let out full headsail so *Barrabas* could bear away and introduce some south into our course. It was cold and grey. It felt like I'd been on *Barrabas* ever since I set off in October 2005, the intervening two winters at home just figments. In the same way that I was experiencing that peculiar sensation of intense familiarity with *Barrabas*, I seemed to have tuned into Louise's wavelength. At 4.00 pm, just as I was reaching for the Iridium to call her, the phone started to chirrup. It was Louise. She'd been checking with Golden Arrow, the Lombardini agents in England, about the engine problem. They reckoned it might be the oil-pressure relief valve.

By the early morning of Saturday 3rd May, the wind had settled in the east at 30 knots, more or less dead astern. I had managed only one hour of sleep since leaving Mehamn. I nestled down into the thick warmth of my sleeping bag, but sleep would not come. It had turned very cold with a thick blanket of grey cloud pasted over the ocean. By late afternoon the wind had lightened to 12 knots and going downwind felt like nothing at all. I took the opportunity to check the oil-pressure relief valve. This involved draining the engine coolant system and disconnecting coolant pipework to get access to the valve. By the time I had reassembled the pieces, three hours had vanished. I tried the engine. The dreaded oil-pressure alarm sounded. I was stumped.

Still, the fantastic winds more than offset my concerns about the engine and my concerns centred on manoeuvrability. If I got into a scrap and needed to extricate myself fast – I might fall asleep and find myself on a collision heading with a ship – no engine meant limited options. It was unsettling.

There was also a new source of anxiety on this leg of the voyage. I was going home to complete the journey. With every passing mile, the finishing tape was coming within reach. Any mistake, any calamity that forced me to quit so close to the end would be impossible to bear. This was generating its own unique pressure.

I'd been expecting a hard beat into prevailing westerlies to get around northern Norway, but here I was already sliding down the west coast towards Vestfjorden with following winds 48 hours after leaving Mehamn. Just after 8.00 pm that evening, we passed south of the latitude of Mehamn. We were now making south *proper* and truly homeward bound. My morale now rocketed skywards. The psychological relief at having made the first mark combined with the prospect of further favourable winds relaxed me, despite the nagging concerns about the engine. I drifted off to sleep and woke five hours later at 3.00 am on Sunday morning, refreshed and eager for the sailing ahead.

Louise: Sunday 4th May 2008

Sorry you still haven't managed to get to the root of the problem with the engine. All well here. Lovely day with the boys yesterday – football in the sun, movie (Nim's Island, the one about the little girl whose father gets lost on his yacht!). Went shopping for new summer jammies for the boys then lunch at the Chinese in Fairford Leys – had the most amazing dish of chicken in satay, coconut and lemon grass sauce – then I gave Benji a REAL treat . . . I bought him a pair of running spikes. He is completely ecstatic. He wrapped them up with a ribbon for bed. We vaselined the spikes before we put them in as the

lady had told us to do so in the shop. I have never seen him so excited by
anything before. He can't wait to get back to school on Tuesday. Also don't
forget safety harness!!!!!!!!!!

Dear Daddy
Hope you are having a grait time. Please come home soon. Love Gabriel.

Dear Daddy
I am really missing you and I hope you will be back soon. I can't wait for us
to play cricket and sport again. Mummy bought me 3 tennis balls and a pair
of spikes. I'm really missing you. Love Benji.

Periodically the wind abated, leaving *Barrabas* to loll on a dead sea, drifting back northeast on the Norwegian Atlantic current. Rain pattered the deck like the tiny feet of a thousand dancing fairies. But it was a lull; by afternoon, I'd be in 30–35-knot northeasterly winds.

I decided that the likely problem with the engine was an airlock in the oil pump. I'd exhausted all other possibilities, save one: that there was a faulty electrical connection in the alarm wiring. I figured that the heavy rolling going downwind might have dislodged an air bubble. If I started the engine and immediately cranked up the revs, the air bubble might work its way up through the cylinders and be dispelled altogether. I listened carefully over the roar of the engine watching the oil-warning light. The briefest tinkle sounded from the engine, the classic sound of air in the cylinders. The oil-warning light flashed then dimmed. The engine settled into its regular hum. I let the engine run for a while to charge the batteries, feeling ridiculously euphoric that all systems on board were now functioning normally.

Barrabas was at latitude 69° north, just above Vestfjorden on Norway's west coast. I put her on a heading due west in anticipation of west winds forecast to arrive at midnight, which I could harness to sail south. I also had to clear the shallow water over the Røst Bank off Vestfjorden, not the place to be with the winds driving the seas against the land. Warnings of dangerous waves crowded my charts. The bone-marinating cold of the last few days and the pitiless grey of the seascape put me in mind of the Russian Arctic. Not only were thoughts of home fuelling my quest to make south but my feet felt like blocks of ice, just as they did going around Cape Horn. With the short distance to the English south coast, I was less frugal with onboard power. I didn't ration the heater to the same extent as before. I sat on the floor with my feet against the hot-air outlet and luxuriated in the simple sensation of comfort. A school of large black porpoises swam around *Barrabas* at mid-morning and a little way further off, plumes of spray betrayed a solitary whale. I was back in the groove of sailing *Barrabas* with all my onboard routines re-established.

I slept. When I woke, the skies had cleared. For the first time since leaving Mehamn, I didn't feel cold. The 24-hour light of the polar day in the far north was rapidly changing even though we were only 120 miles south of Mehamn's latitude. It was still light at night but increasingly dimmer.

> **Log: Tuesday 6th May 2008, 8.00 am**
> *68.56 north, 09.55 east, COG 218, SOG 5.2, Wind SSW 16, BP 1025($\downarrow$)*
> *. . . gybed main at 1st reef onto starboard tack and put out headsail at 2nd reef as wind backed west. I have to stay west of longitude 10° east otherwise I'll be too close inshore further south and it gives me a better line to Scotland (Scotland!? I'm talking about the UK after 29,407 nautical miles! Great! Bloody fantastic!!)*

Louise: Tuesday 6th May 2008
It is a beautiful sunny day today and I am on top of the world thinking of all the richness the future holds! Yesterday we stayed at home all day and the boys were in the garden having water balloon battles.

While the boys got soaked, so did I. *Barrabas* was taking some mighty thumps – Cape Horn-quality bashings as the west wind built to over 30 knots. We punched into it to create sea room. Green water breaking over the decks was pouring in through the seals around the forward hatch. I couldn't sleep on the starboard bunk. The angle of heel was too acute and I slid off (the port bunk was covered with fuel cans). So, at night, I made my bed on the floor at the base of the companionway steps. I felt like an astronaut, looking up at the control panels studded with dials, read-outs, switches, lights, cocooned in darkness but for the orange glow of the panel.

The steering wheel was rocking on the binnacle. I knew *Barrabas* so well that I diagnosed the problem immediately – a nylon bearing had come loose. With that sorted, I changed all the split pins on the lower shrouds and finally set about sealing the forward hatch with silicone.

Louise: Thursday 8th May 2008
It is as hot as Hades here – I've just put out the outside furniture. Boys and I will eat tea outside this evening. All well and happy here and so pleased your eta seems to be getting shorter and shorter!

Adrian: Thursday 8th May 2008
Hi . . . my progress appears to be better than it actually is, the reason being that at higher latitudes a given distance i.e. 100 miles covers more of the map than at lower latitudes e.g. the equator. My progress will appear to slow as I get further south. Since Mehamn my av daily mileage is 89. During the Russian phase it was 100 and about 107 during the first leg. However, I set up a schedule and on current performance should be in the Hamble on 22nd May.

I'd been lucky with the weather so far. Luck is preparation multiplied by opportunity – who knows. Gary Player, the great South African golfer, once said, 'The more I practise, the luckier I get.' I hooked onto a band of east winds to ride over the top of northern Norway, then northeasterlies chased me down the coast as far as Vestfjorden. Since then the wind combos had been more or less kind. *Barrabas* had woven a track towards the Shetland Islands and out of the rogue-wave danger zone.

At the outset of the expedition, I figured *Barrabas* would have to cover 30,000 miles to circumnavigate the earth via Cape Horn and the Russian Arctic. The log clicked over to 29,700 miles.

Adrian: Thursday 8th May 2008
Still a nip in the air here. Made 100 miles nose to target over the last 24 hours. Just about 1,000 to go! Today is slow, maybe 60 miles south and west then should pull in another 100–120 tomorrow. The wind will be on the side so Barrabas will be sailing fast – always a good defence in biggish seas. Your banana cake is still alive and well. The first one is gone. Half the choc biscuit cake left. My diet is great. Coffee, tea, cigarettes, chocolate. Had a shave today but can you believe it, I haven't got a razor handle on board! Must have taken it home by mistake. Anyway, did an ok job just holding the blade between my fingers . . . kisses for u 3 . . . Ax

I expected heavy weather on Saturday evening but the storm's severity exceeded my worst fears. The winds were not overly strong, touching 40 knots at times, but somehow the collusion of wind and water conjured a monstrous demonstration of raw, unbridled power. I shortened sail to second reef – most boats would be down to storm sails, but I wanted to generate good boat speed as a defence. The light dimmed to a grey so resonant that it appeared blue. A bizarre band of pink striped the gunmetal sky. *Barrabas* ripped into the feast, insatiable it seemed. I was over-canvassed but *Barrabas* was talking to me. 'Let me fly, let me fly.' Green water spumed over her decks as waves bayoneted by her prow collapsed. She took some truly jaw-shuddering impacts. This storm certainly ranked in the worst five we'd experienced on the voyage but again, *Barrabas* performed magnificently. I could not sleep simply from the noise and pounding of the boat. I did try to get my head down, arranging cushions on the galley floor and snuggling down into the sleeping bag with my head by the companionway steps so I could see the instruments over the chart table. After 10 minutes, a massive wave strike sent water streaming through the gaps in the closed companionway hatch, soaking my head and the top half of the sleeping bag. I gave up on sleep after that.

Adrian: Sunday 11th May 2008

Hi . . . I can think of better ways to spend a Saturday night! Horrific storm for last 24 hrs – calm now – no sleep. Luckily, I was in deep water so sea state not desperate. This boat is truly magnificent – some of the slams were just too awful. I was standing below just waiting for the bow to break off. I had too much sail up but that gave me speed as a defence. Now 150 miles north of the Shetland Islands. Good winds for next two days then I am in really shallow waters. Will get forecast. If big winds coming, will hold off entering the North Sea plateau. Otherwise all ok. R boys ok? Tell them two weeks max then we're done! Ax

By midday on Sunday 11th May, the winds had calmed to 12 knots from the north. I downloaded a four-day weather file. My next obstacle was crossing the 200-metre depth contour 120 miles to my south from the deep water of the Norwegian Sea onto the shallow plain of the North Sea. Big winds would kick up murderous seas over the rapidly shoaling seabed. I needed light, downwind conditions and the forecast promised exactly that: north sector winds at 12 knots. Perfect! I did a little jig around the deck, feeling the first real twinges of gut-tingling excitement. The battle into headwinds that had been a distinct possibility in the North Sea had given way to a perfect scenario. It felt like a reward after the storm. We were entering another high-pressure system, this one centred over northern France. I was passing from one high-pressure system to another like a relay baton and this new system was providing the gentle following winds, blue skies and warmth – exactly what I wanted and needed to pass over the 200-metre contour line.

With the boat stable, I slept on the starboard bunk, crashing out for nine hours. It was luxury being able to stretch out fully and not be cramped on the floor with my knees bent.

I set the sails in a goosewing, an arrangement which had served me so well before on the voyage, with the headsail poled out on the port side adding one knot of boat speed. At 2.00 pm on Monday 12th May, we passed over the 200-metre contour. Shortly after at 2.09 pm, the log clicked onto 30,000. It read 30,041 when I sighted British land once more. In the pink-tinged dusk, I saw Unst, northernmost of the Shetland Islands, some 20 miles west – my first sighting of UK territory from the deck since the Cornish coast faded behind me in the mist on a drizzly November morning in 2005. Entering UK territorial waters brought a blessed comfort – even the place names on the Shetland Islands conjured a soothing familiarity – Sullom Voe, Muckle Flugga, Lerwick, no more grappling with unpronounceable Russian or tongue-twisting Norwegian (even though some of the names in the Hebrides may have Viking origins). Since departing UK shores, I heard my first British weather broadcast courtesy of Shetland Island Coastguard at 6.00 pm. Eight hundred miles were all that remained for *Barrabas* to complete her vertical circumnavigation, but this was no gimme. I had been fabulously fortunate with the weather but things can change quickly and disastrously at sea. I held the rising tide of excitement in check and concentrated on my plan to make for Kinnaird Head across the open space of the Moray Firth. Beyond there, I would hug the east coast of England and when I'd hugged it all I could I'd get off my boat and kiss the ground – that was the plan.

I needed sleep. I spoke to the coastguard on the Shetlands. Could they tell me what shipping was in the area? I'd spotted three trawlers and two ships during the day. Not every vessel showed up on radar, they said – I stayed awake through the night. It was a good time to think. My thoughts and feelings were changing, morphing, as the end neared. I sailed the boat, attended to routine maintenance, but I was preoccupied with the sensation of change. A hugely important chapter in my life was drawing towards its end and with it came a peculiar juxtaposition: a rising euphoria set against the ebb of impending loss. The euphoria was easy to understand, the loss less so. Perhaps it was the ending of this profound experience I had shared with *Barrabas* or the ending of that special relationship between a sailor and his craft that manifests on the open sea. Sir Francis Chichester apparently hated *Gipsy Moth IV*. Perhaps. It is difficult to know how a boat that has carried a man around the earth cannot then own part of his essence and that ownership given willingly with a dollop of love and gratitude. I wondered how Chichester, Knox-Johnston, Blyth or the grandfather of single-handed circumnavigations Joshua Slocum felt as they approached home, only days away from stepping ashore. Similar feelings I suspect, a kaleidoscope of competing emotion. These men and others were true pioneers, reaching into what was then the unknown in terms of human isolation and endurance. Today there is inevitably less opportunity for such discovery but *Barrabas* had carved her own unique track around the world. Perhaps that was where my sense of loss originated, in stopping doing what no one else had ever done before.

Past the Shetlands and Fair Isle with the Orkneys below the horizon on my right, I thought, 'I'm closer to London than some people in northern Scotland!' That raised morale, not that my morale needed too much feeding with the third day of following winds set to continue driving me south at a good lick.

I'd left the dense clusters of oil platforms of the Brent, Viking Bank, Bergen Bank and the Fladen Ground far to my left, but there were others closer inshore. I passed by the Buzzard platform at the southeastern end of the Moray Firth as I angled my course due south towards Bridlington on the Yorkshire coast.

Adrian: Thursday 15th May 2008
Hi . . . sleeping as much as poss. Weather kicks off tomorrow around 2.00 pm and goes on for 36 hours, otherwise all ok – I would say arrival on Wednesday 21st is now 'probable' . . .

The wind stalled, not completely, but enough to slow my progress to a leisurely walking pace. According to my onboard weather forecasting programme, nasty east winds would hit at about 2.00 pm the next afternoon with wind speeds of 26 knots. I knew from long experience that the programme consistently underestimated wind speeds. I could safely add five to ten knots. In shallow waters, the sea state could be dangerous. So, my plan between now and then was to get as much sleep as possible and prepare food in advance which I could reheat. Poking around the boat looking for food I might have forgotten about,

I found a stash in the forward storage bin below the starboard bunk –
stuff I had bought in Alaska, mainly tinned fruit (always good) and
wonder of wonders, a tin of 'American' baked beans with bacon and
cane sugar. I couldn't resist. I had one egg left so I quaffed the lot.

Louise: Friday 16th May 2008
Boys and I will come out to meet you with Tim on a Beneteau (44 ft).
Wow . . . almost there . . . I'm so excited for you. Lx

Adrian: Friday 16th May 2008
Good morning . . . latest weather shows winds moderated – agrees with
Tim's – a perfect window for the next four days (subject always of course to
change). I have exactly 400 miles to go. Things will be slow until midnight
today then good winds arrive. If I can do 100 miles + per day (24hrs) on Sat,
Sun, Mon, Tues then I should be off Isle of Wight by midnight Tues. I should
be able to do this and now assess the probability of making a Weds 21st May
landing at 80%+.

If this pattern held, it would be the perfect window to see me home –
375 miles was all that remained of the Alpha Global Expedition's
vertical track around the world. So far, magical winds had touched
this final leg from Mehamn. Yes, there had been one nasty storm and
at times I had stood still in breathless conditions but not for protracted
periods. While I waited for the winds to pick up, I cleaned the galley
and the heads and rigged up a deck shower. I'd been running the
engine to charge the batteries and generate hot water. With the
pressurized water switched on at the galley pump, I had a glorious
hot shower in the cockpit, the shower hose led up from below. Why
hadn't I done this before? I must have been daft, although there was
always the concern about conserving power. Without the need to keep
an eagle eye on fuel reserves any longer and with plenty left over from
the Arctic phase, I was being much more liberal now. I used cabin
lights at night instead of candles and oil lamps. The radar was on 24/7
– necessary now that I was in relatively congested waters and the VHF
was permanently on Channel 16. Even though there were only 375
miles to go, I had to stay focused and concentrate on the job in hand.
One octogenarian supporter in Holland who had been following my
journey warned me to stay vigilant. A lapse would be all too easy
while, as Bé Vonk put it, my mind was '. . . milling around the end of
the affair'.

It was a good thing I had a shower earlier. That evening I had some unexpected visitors. With the sea more like a lake on a calm day and only a zephyr to nudge *Barrabas* along at a couple of knots, I was lying on my bunk reading while waiting for the northeast winds. The radar was on. The alarm sounded. A contact had entered the guard perimeter I'd set at six miles. I went topside. A ship was heading north on my starboard side. I went back to my reading. A few minutes later at 7.30 pm, the alarm sounded again. Maybe it was the same ship. I watched the radar screen from my bunk. No, this was a second contact. I watched the blip for several minutes. Whatever it was, she was moving fast and coming towards *Barrabas*. I got up and set an electronic bearing line (EBL) onto the contact. If a contact stays on an EBL, then the collision risk escalates. This contact was staying on the EBL and closing quickly. I rushed up to the cockpit, grabbing the binoculars on the way. Magnified, the ship was grey, moustached by a great white bow wave. I must have been guilty of something because my first thought was, 'What have I done now?' Just then, the radio crackled to life. 'Sailing yacht *Barrabas*, *Barrabas*, this is Warship *Mersey*, Warship *Mersey*.'

I spoke to Lieutenant Commander Alan Wilson. 'How did you know I was here?'

'We have our spies,' he joked. They had checked out the Alpha Global Expedition website. Lieutenant Commander Wilson and the ship's company wanted to stop by and wish me well for the rest of the voyage home. 'We have a small gift and a donation from the ship's company for your expedition's charities, Save the Children and The Oxford Children's Hospital.'

I hove-to while HMS *Mersey* nosed to a stop 200 yards off. What a welcome back into British territorial waters! A rigid inflatable boat (RIB) was lowered into the water and buzzed alongside *Barrabas*. Her crew passed on the good wishes of the ship's company amid much smiling and hand-shaking. One of the RIB's crew asked to come on board. Reluctantly, I had to refuse. I'd made my vow that no one, other than myself, would be on board *Barrabas* while she was making her way around the world.

I joked and chatted with the RIB's crew. They then handed across a cheque for the charities and a bottle of Special Reserve port.

I really appreciated the gesture by the Royal Navy and said so to Lt Commander Wilson over the radio. Soon after HMS *Mersey* disappeared over the horizon, the winds came. It was as if the curtain of calm had fallen just so the warship could make the rendezvous with *Barrabas* and me. If there was any way that things could be turning out better, I couldn't think of it!

CHAPTER 30

Promises

I slept for a few hours, waking at 5.50 am on Saturday morning. I would not sleep again for another 56 hours as I navigated the crowded gas field installations off the East Anglia coast then picked my way through the shipping lanes around North Foreland and the Dover Strait. Two hours later at 7.50 am, I went on deck and for the first time since my departure on the Alpha Global Expedition, I saw the UK mainland – green hills somewhere between Hartlepool and Middlesbrough. I looked at *Barrabas* as she creamed the sea at fabulous speeds touching nine knots, at her tired decks, her paintwork broken and peeling from excesses of sun and ice. Now she was back, almost, to where she started.

Louise: Saturday 17th May 2008
Hello speedy! Boys and I will be setting off around lunchtime on Tuesday. We said tonight whilst watching Britain's Got Talent that this time next week you will be watching it with us! I also said to Benji that if Chelsea wins the Champion's League on Wednesday, it could turn out to be the happiest day of his life! Maybe we can watch it in the bar of the Royal Southern YC!

Far to the south at his home in Lisbon, Ricardo was tracking my progress home. He sent an email to Louise that she forwarded on to me.

Ricardo: Saturday 17th May 2008

For years I have looked at that stretch of ocean between Norway and Iceland and Scotland and wondered what it would be like to be up there so far away and so far north. It is so inhospitable and rough. The lowest of lows go through there and yet there he is blessed by unbelievable weather, a perfect direct course. Adrian will be only too aware how dangerous the last dash is. Dover sucks. It is a major shipping and navigation nightmare. I really hope he has the wind to get through there fast.

I looked at a fresh weather forecast. It showed north sector winds with moderated wind speeds to a maximum 16 knots. Ricardo was right. I was blessed. If the previous forecast was near ideal, it was perfect now. I recalled my dinner conversation with Kåre in Mehamn, '. . . *a following wind . . . it's not going to happen, not all the way to England . . .*'

The wind either on or behind the beam would put *Barrabas* on her fastest point of sail. By 4.00 pm, we came to the gas fields east of the Humber Estuary. They continued down along the coast of East Anglia.

Adrian: Saturday 17th May 2008

Going really well – in amongst the oil and gas platforms – Barrabas humming along at 7–8 knots and been at it since 5.00 am – would you believe the fastest sustained sailing of the entire AGX!

I called Humber Coastguard to request information about active exclusion zones around the platforms. They put me in contact with one of the standby vessels that protect the rigs. The instruction was not to venture within one mile of any installation. As I passed the Minerva platform two miles off my port side, I could see five other rigs at various points around the horizon, colossal alien-looking structures. I figured I'd be through the bulk of the rigs by 8.00 am Sunday morning – it was going to be a sleepless night.

Coming through the gas fields at night was a fascinating experience. Lit up, I could see them dotted all about the horizon. It's like Piccadilly Circus in there – not just the rigs – each platform has a standby vessel holding station close by to warn off possible interlopers. Busy ferry lanes criss-cross with commercial shipping routes. Just after 2.00 am, I counted 13 platforms and seven ships, four of which were within a mile of me. I fed myself rice and chilli. It tasted good at the time but within an hour had given me indigestion. We cleared the gas fields at dawn and worked our way closer inshore towards Great Yarmouth, to get out of the shipping channels and to avoid some shallow banks.

Adrian: Sunday 18th May 2008

Posn at 0800 UCT 52.49 north 01.41 east (basically east of Great Yarmouth on the Norfolk coast). There must be a massive current here (in my favour) or a bunch of dolphins has fed Barrabas steroids – she was cruising at 10 knots for a couple of hours just now – and that was with shortened sail! Tell Benji I want to watch the Champions League final with him – that's why I'm breaking my neck trying to get back in time. Ahead of schedule so far – I set my markers at midnight – at midnight yesterday I was right on the money to make the Isle of Wight IoW by midnight Tuesday!

Louise called on the Iridium.

'Are you sure you gave me the right position?'

'Of course,' I said, surprised. I always checked positions before I sent them by email.

'Well, I think you're wrong. I plotted it and according my workings you're in a field somewhere in Norfolk.'

'Pretty waterlogged field.'

'Ha, ha! So what is your position?'

'What I sent you.' I thought for a moment. 'I know what you've done. Common enough mistake . . .'

'What?'

'You've plotted my longitude as west instead of east.'

'Oh.'

'I'm about three miles off the Norfolk coast. I can see a beautiful stretch of beach with trees. It's a fabulous day here – blue sky, warm, 14-knot breeze – glorious sailing.'

'Okay. Well, you're right. Anyway, so you're not in Norfolk. Can you do something for me?'

'Yep.'

'I need you to write something for the Press Association. Keep it short and sweet.'

'You'll have it on your desk in the morning, by the time you wake up.'

I was in for a second consecutive night without sleep. That's the problem with single-handed sailing in congested inshore waters. Hazards pepper the East Anglia coastline (as testified by the amount of wrecks dotting my charts). I had a narrow escape, passing over the 10-metre contour line of a submarine bank with charted depths of 12 inches in places. I immediately turned hard to starboard and furled the headsail, going downwind under main until I came to a break in the bank. I was running up and down the companionway steps to check the chart plotter that showed the submarine contours in detail. I judged my moment then made a 90° turn to port, unfurled the headsail and steered steadily for a mile between the banks to get to deeper water and safety.

I made my turn south of Great Yarmouth putting the wind directly astern. Without a spinnaker, I resorted to my favoured goosewing sail plan, the headsail poled out on the port side. We were going along nicely at five and a half knots. I hadn't sailed *Barrabas* or navigated quite so intensely on the whole of the voyage.

As I approached the start line on that blustery October morning in 2005, someone on a press boat asked me for a comment. I yelled back, 'Two miles down, 30,000 to go!' Less than 200 miles now stood between me and the finish. After all *Barrabas* and I had been through together, it seemed implausible that the end was almost literally in sight. I glanced at the log – 30,608 nautical miles.

With darkness falling, I called Thames Coastguard to obtain clearances to enter the shipping traffic scheme offshore from Harwich and Felixstowe. The tide had turned in our favour and *Barrabas* was now surging ahead at seven knots. I sat for a while on deck as we passed through deep-water shipping anchorages and the turning areas where several traffic lanes converged. I was thinking about the Press Association bulletin. I did not like the idea of writing about completion of the voyage before I had actually crossed the line. I might tempt fate and fate could turn around at any time to let me know exactly who was calling the shots here, but I understood Louise's shore-based world. She had steadily involved the media in my imminent arrival home and forward planning was all part of the package. I went below, sat at the chart table and fired up the laptop.

Adrian: Monday 19th May 2008
Release for Press Association
Barrabas has carried me almost 31,000 miles around the world to complete the first 'vertical' single-handed circumnavigation westwards from the United Kingdom via Cape Horn and the Russian Arctic. I feel immense relief that I have succeeded in fulfilling a boyhood dream and huge pride in my yacht

Barrabas. Her place in sailing history is assured as the first British-flagged yacht to enter Russia's Arctic territorial waters. She has seen me through fair weather and foul. I owe Sir Francis Chichester a debt of gratitude. It was he who inspired me to make this voyage after I read 'Gipsy Moth Circles the World' as a 15-year-old schoolboy. The voyage has been long and hard, filled with moments of joy but terrifying at times. Facing down the challenge of rounding the notorious Cape Horn against wind and currents from the Atlantic Ocean to the Pacific Ocean presented the greatest physical peril. Together, Barrabas and I now belong to a small group who have accomplished this feat. True adventure requires a unique aspect, something pioneering, something that has never been done. To have become the first solo yachtsman to enter the Russian Arctic is irreducible. It is the crowning achievement of the voyage, not just for me but for everyone involved. I owe much also to Louise, my ex-wife, who has managed the Alpha Global Expedition. My dream became her dream and without her, I would not have succeeded. To live and not to dream is pointless, but to dream and not to live it is worse. I hope the legacy of the Alpha Global Expedition will be an inspiration to my two sons Benjamin and Gabriel and to anyone else to chase their own dreams, just as Chichester inspired me.

Despite the dangers, I really enjoyed the hazardous navigation through the busy shipping lanes. Monday broke clear and blue. Unbelievably, the winds veered from northeast to east, following me round as I progressively pulled my course up from southwest to due west past Dover, Dungeness and Beachy Head. Finally, at 2.00 pm and after 56 hours without sleep, I crashed onto my bunk and slept for four and a half hours. By 9.00 pm on the evening of Monday 19th May we were south of Selsey Bill and entering the eastern approaches to the Solent, that stretch of water which separates the Isle of Wight from the mainland south coast. *Barrabas* had covered almost 300 miles in 48 hours, her fastest sustained sailing of the expedition, and we had arrived in the Solent 27 hours ahead of my most optimistic prediction.

Louise had been gunning for an arrival date of Wednesday 21st May. I had two choices: either I sailed around in circles or hove-to for the next 36 hours or I found somewhere to anchor. I decided the most sensible option was to anchor, get some sleep and prepare myself for the ending of this hugely significant chapter of my life. Some part of me wanted to sail up the Hamble River, moor *Barrabas* and steal home on a train or in a taxi without fanfare. Instead, I navigated into the narrow confines of Chichester Harbour. It seemed somehow apt. It was past 2.00 am on Tuesday morning when I finally dropped the hook in the Chichester Channel. The air was still and cool. I stayed on deck for a while thinking irrational thoughts; 'I'm safe now,' 'I'm not going to die,' 'It's over.' The low-grade buzz of anxiety that had shadowed me for every one of the 30,808 miles so far recorded on the log lifted, dissipated and quietly vanished like a morning mist borne away on a gentle breeze. Below decks, I switched on the heating, cooked spaghetti and sardines then turned in, cocooned within *Barrabas*, who sat rock steady on the still waters of the channel. When I woke at 7.00 am, a bright sun warmed my face. My spirits soared with the fresh realisation that I would soon be home.

The Iridium trilled.

'You're not going to believe this!' Louise exclaimed. 'The Royal Navy are going to lay on an escort for you!'

'You're kidding.'

'Nope. HMS *Trumpeter* – good name, don't you think? It's a fast patrol boat. They'll escort you up the Solent.'

I was amazed. It was an honour.

'We'll see you at the waypoint.'

I'd emailed cordinates of the rendezvous where Tim should bring the yacht that would be carrying Louise and the children. It was the east cardinal mark at the eastern end of the Solent's north channel, two and a half miles from the finish line between Calshot Spit Buoy and Hillhead. The line crackled.

'Where are you?'

'In the car coming into Southampton. I'm going to the BBC Radio Solent studio for an interview, then on to the Royal Southern Yacht Club.'

The rest of that day was a mix, preparing *Barrabas* for her final steps home and enjoying the tranquillity of the Chichester Channel. Because of the shallow water inside the harbour and *Barrabas*'s 1.9-metre draught, the tides prevented me staying a second night. Before weighing anchor at 11.50 pm, I sent Louise a last email that she would pick up the following morning.

Adrian: Tuesday 20th May 2008

Good morning! So, if we'd known on 28th October 2005 that a) I'd finish and b) the time and date would be 10.00 am, Wednesday 21st May 2008, I wonder what we'd have thought. This has been a long, hard road for both of us but I am confident that the effort will reap great rewards if only in the knowledge that I can lay the ghost to rest and know that I have achieved something unique and that you can know that without your involvement it would never have happened. So, thank you. I'll see you at 10.00 am. Ax

I sailed to Gilkicker Point, anchoring on the west side in Stokes Bay. Being on station only three miles from where I'd planned to rendez-vous with Louise and the boys meant I could get some sleep.

HMS *Trumpeter* under the command of Lt. Will King found me at 9.00 am the following morning. I'd been up since dawn doing nothing much but savouring the moment, waiting. The sun had pulled back the curtain of night on this, the final scene in the drama of the Alpha Global Expedition. Snapshots of the voyage flickered through my mind: hugging the boys as I prepared to sail, being swept from the deck, fighting massive seas in Biscay, the tropical cyclone off the Canary Islands, beautiful blue sailing in the Atlantic trades, arming myself as suspected pirates tracked me off the Brazilian coast, the capsizes at Cape Horn and reaching in the southeast trades towards Hawaii. Honolulu, an ice-cold Guinness, Michael Roth, Ivan Chan Wa, Ernie Woodruff and Bobbie Jennings. Astro-navigation, making the antipodal point and turning for the ice; Nome, Rick, Cam, Malinda, the Russians, frustration at having to break the voyage, my noble vessel making history as she entered the Northern Sea Route. The ice, the danger, the cold, Tiksi. I smiled as the rugged face of Captain Alfred Zagorsky flashed and faded, Murmansk, Igor, Vardo. Relief. Mehamn. Almost home but too late. Disappointment. A second win-tering, but good people to look out for *Barrabas*, Kare and Oddvar. Then the final leg and the best sailing of the voyage in potentially one of the most dangerous seas on earth.

Now here, only a few miles left. I saw myself on my ship, reading, writing, eating, shaving, sleeping, studying, laughing, crying, quiet, screaming, joyous, terrified, bored, euphoric. I stood and looked along *Barrabas*'s deck then up to her mast, squinting in the sunlight. She knew. I knew. Only the two of us. Our secret. When I had fallen over the side, this boat had stopped. She had stopped in 50 mile-an-hour winds among waves as tall as houses. She had stopped. As sure as I had been of the certainty of death, I knew she had stopped and let me clamber back on board. My partner, my friend, my teammate, my protector, I owed *Barrabas* more than gratitude, more than love. I owed her my life. I walked to the foredeck, knelt, rested my forehead on her firm, steel skin and pressed my lips to her.

'Thank you,' I whispered in the gentle breeze. 'Let's go home now.'

I weighed anchor at 9.30 am. HMS *Trumpeter* took up station at my stern. With the wind behind, I goose-winged the sails for our final run home. At exactly 10.00 am, we made the east cardinal mark. Press boats and an eclectic mix of launches and yachts had swelled our small convoy. I could see Tim's yacht heeled over coming towards us. She went wide, tacked round and came up on our starboard side.

Sailing up the Solent under a warm sun seemed majestically surreal. I remembered sitting at my desk three years before thinking about a name for the expedition and coming up with Alpha Global and now here I was completing the first single-handed vertical circumnavigation of the earth. Thoughts made real – a dream made concrete. HMS *Trumpeter* pulled alongside and one of her crew handed me a cup of tea. I waved to my children and blew a kiss to Louise while journalists yelled questions and cameras clicked. *Barrabas* sailed on sedately at five knots. I didn't record exactly when we crossed the line between Calshot Spit and Hillhead. It was sometime around 10.30 am. Whenever it was, we'd 'tied the knot', completing the loop of our track around the surface of the planet. I dropped the sails at the mouth of the Hamble, then motored upriver with HMS *Trumpeter* leading the way. Two of the harbourmaster's launches flanked me, sirens blaring while a busy swarm of dinghies and inflatables buzzed all around.

30,825 miles. That's what the log read when I tied up at the Royal Southern Yacht Club on the Hamble River just after 11.00 am on Wednesday 21st May. Events had overtaken time – too much happening to take in, not enough space to accommodate all the images and emotions that time had swept and heaped and stored at this place, the end of the Alpha Global Expedition.

Tim had brought his boat in ahead of me. Louise and the boys emerged from among the throng of journalists and camera crews. They clambered aboard. I ushered them below into the cabin.

'We did it,' I said to Louise as we hugged.

'You did it.'

'We did it.'

I kissed Benji. He looked up at me. 'Will you watch the football with me tonight?'

'Of course,' I said. 'Why d'you think I arrived back today!'

Gabriel clung to me. I kissed his soft cheek. His blue eyes flicked uncomprehendingly over the 37 fuel cans lashed in the cabin. 'It's smelly in here,' he said.

Back on deck, Annette Newton, the Royal Southern Yacht Club's Commodore, gave a welcoming speech to the crowd of friends, well-wishers and journalists and surprised me with honorary membership. The most recent honorary member had been Sir Robin Knox-Johnston. Perhaps I really had come full circle.

Much later that evening, the boys tucked up in bed in the clubhouse and Louise asleep, I stepped back aboard *Barrabas* in the quiet of a still summer's night. Below decks, I sat in the golden glow of a single candle.

I had made two promises. I'd promised the child I had once been that I would sail alone around the world and I'd promised my sons that I would return to them safely. Relief bubbled gently, from somewhere deep within, rising to the surface, tingling my skin. After all, through the eyes of a child there is nothing worse than a father who does not keep his promises.

GLOSSARY

Abeam Perpendicular to the side of the boat

Aft At or towards the stern or back part of the boat

Ahull (or lying ahull) Condition of a sailing boat when all sail is down and the helm lashed to force the bows into wind

Anemometer Instrument which measures wind speed

Anode Sacrificial zinc blocks fitted to the outside of a boat to prevent corrosion through electrolysis. The anodes corrode first

Apparent wind The combination of actual wind plus the wind created through motion

Astern Behind

Back Winds back when they shift in an anticlockwise direction, i.e. from east to north. Sails are described as backed when they are deployed on the same side of the boat as the wind direction and are blown against the rigging

Backstay Wire rope leading from the masthead to the stern which prevents the mast falling forwards

Bear away To turn the boat away from the wind

Beating To sail close to the direction from which the wind is coming and make towards an objective by alternately tacking through the winds to create a zig-zag course

Bilge Lowest part of the hull where internal water collects. This bilge water can be evacuated by either manual or electrical pumps

Block A pulley through which a rope is passed and used to either increase the mechanical load applied to the rope or to lead the rope to a desired location

Boom The horizontal spar fitted to the mast and to which the foot of the mainsail is attached

Boom breaker A large pulley attached to the underside of the boom through which a rope is passed attached to the deck on each side and which can be tensioned to prevent the boom from swinging violently from one side of the boat to the other

Bow The front end of a boat

Bowline (pronounced 'bo-lynn') A type of knot that creates a loop in the end of a rope and is used to fit a rope to a sail

Broach When a boat turns broadside to approaching waves

Buoy A floating mark either to assist navigation or to warn of danger

Cabin Living area below deck

Capsize When a boat tips over to between 90° and 180°

Carabiner A spring-loaded link

Cardinal mark A type of buoy used to indicate a hazard and indicating in which direction a boat should pass

Catamaran A twin-hulled boat. The hulls are connected by cross-spars

Chine The angle where hull plates in one plane meet hull plates in another plane

Cleat A horned fastening around which ropes can be tied, looped or made off

Clew The lower, aftermost corner of a sail

Close-haul Sailing as closely as possible

to the direction from which the wind is coming

Cockpit The working area of a boat and from where the boat is steered

Companionway Steps leading down from the cockpit to the cabin

Cringle An eye in a sail

Cruising chute A large, lightweight sail

Daggerboard A board lowered vertically so that it protrudes below the hull and helps the boat to sail in a straight line without any sideways drift

Drogue An object towed behind a boat to reduce speed

EPIRB Emergency position indicating radio beacon

Foot The bottom edge of a sail

Foredeck Deck nearest the front of a boat

Forereach Make progress to windward or movement in the direction from which the wind is coming

Forestay Wire rope leading from the masthead to the bow which prevents the mast falling backwards

Freeboard The height between the deck and the surface of the water

Furl To roll up a sail on the stay on which it is set by means of a rotating spindle

Galley Kitchen

Gimbals Pivots around which objects such as a stove can swing and so remain upright

Gooseneck Universal-joint fitting fixed to the mast to which the boom is also attached

Goosewing Sail arrangement for running dead downwind where the mainsail is set out wide on one side and the headsail on the other

GPS Global Positioning System – an array of satellites which triangulate a signal to provide an accurate position on the earth's surface

GRIB Gridded Binary Data – a means of packing a lot of information into a small electronic file size used for transferring weather data and graphics

Guardrails Safety wires running around the deck edge supported by stanchions

Gybe Turning the boat in the direction the wind is blowing so that the stern passes through the wind

Halyard A rope used to hoist a sail

Head The top corner of a sail

Heads Toilet

Headsail A sail set forward of the mast

Heaving-to A technique for stopping a boat by steering through the wind with the sails set to windward so that they are blown back onto the rigging. The rudder is lashed to counter the effect of the wind on the sails. The opposing forces cause the boat to stop. Heaving-to is commonly used as a storm tactic

Heel The tilt of a boat while it is sailing

Helm The steering wheel or tiller

Jury rig Makeshift rigging to support the mast in the event of a rigging failure

Keel The lowest part of the hull, weighted to provide stability

Ketch A two-masted boat with a main mast and a smaller mizzen mast behind

Knot A unit of speed equivalent to one nautical mile per hour

Latitude Lines running east to west, parallel to the equator

Lazarette A large storage compartment in the stern

Lee shore Shoreline while the wind is blowing onto it

Leech The trailing edge of a sail

Leech line A line running along the leech of a sail which can be tightened to prevent the leech from flapping

Longitude Lines running north to south and passing through both the north and south poles

Luff The leading edge of a sail

Mainsheet The rope used to control the boom

Nautical mile A unit of distance equivalent to 1,852m (slightly longer than a statute or land mile)

Overfalls Areas of turbulent water

Point of sail The direction in which a boat is sailing relative to the angle of the wind. The fastest point of sail is usually a *beam reach* when the wind is coming from abeam

Port Left

Port tack Any point of sail when the wind is coming from the port side

Preventer A rope attached to the after end of the boom and led forward to prevent the boom coming across the deck in the case of an accidental tack or gybe

Pulpit Rigid railing at the bow

Reach Sailing with the wind approximately perpendicular to the boat

Reef Reducing the area of a sail by lowering the sail and, by use of reefing lines, re-tensioning the foot of the sail

RIB Rigid inflatable boat

Rig The arrangement of sails, masts and spars

Rigging The arrangement of wires and ropes used to keep the mast up and control the sails

Rudder A movable, underwater blade controlled by either a wheel or a tiller which steers the boat

Running Sailing with the wind coming from directly behind the boat

Running rigging The arrangement of ropes used to control the sails

Shackle A U-shaped link fitted with a screw pin

Sheet Any rope attached to the clew of a sail and to the boom which can be tensioned or eased to trim the sail

Shroud Wire ropes leading from the deck either side of the mast to various attachments on the mast and which support the mast

Skeg A fin attached to the hull and situated between the keel and the rudder which supports the rudder

Sloop A single-masted boat with only one headsail set at any one time

Sole Cabin floor

Spinnaker A large, lightweight sail flown when sailing downwind

Spinnaker pole Pole attached to the mast and projecting forwards and outwards to carry the clew of a spinnaker

Spray dodgers Weather cloths laced along the guardrails either side of the cockpit to provide additional protection

Spreader Struts or bars projecting laterally in pairs from the mast to spread the angle of the shrouds and hold the shrouds away from the mast

Stanchion Post supporting the guardrails

Standing rigging Arrangement of steel wires (stays and shrouds) which support the mast

Starboard Right

Starboard tack Any point of sail when the wind is coming from the starboard side

Staysail Smaller sail flown forward of the mast from an inner stay, a wire leading from the upper portion of the mast to the foredeck

Stem The structural member at the centreline of the boat where the bows join

Stern The back of a boat

Storm jib A small, strong sail flown forward of the mast and used in rough conditions

Tack To steer so the front of the boat passes through the wind

Tack (sail) The lower forward corner of a sail

Tiller A lever used to control the rudder

Tiller lines Ropes connected to the tiller to allow control of the tiller from a distance

Toe-rail Protruding upper edges of the hull above the deck

Topping lift Rope leading from the masthead to the aft end of the boom to hold the boom up

Transom The back end of the hull between the waterline and the deckedge

Trim Adjustment of the sails

Trimaran A triple-hulled boat

True wind Actual wind

UTC Coordinated Universal Time. Sometimes called World Time and formerly called Greenwich Mean Time. Coordinated Universal Time is at the prime meridian (0° longitude)

Veer Winds veer when they shift in a clockwise direction, i.e. from south to west

Washboards Boards that fit into the entrance to the cabin

Winch Device for pulling in ropes

Windlass Device fitted on the foredeck to raise and lower the anchor

Windward The same side as the wind (opposite of leeward)

APPENDICES

Appendix I – Single-handed westabout roundings of Cape Horn

There is no official register of single-handed roundings of Cape Horn, so the following list is the author's compilation and may not be complete.

	COMPLETION	MASTER	COUNTRY	VESSEL
1.	1934	Al Hansen	Norway	*Mary Jane*
2.	1958	Marcel Bardiaux	France	*Les Quatre Vents* (31 ft.)
3.	1971	Chay Blyth	UK	*British Steel* (59 ft.)
4.	1974	Edward Allcard	UK	*Sea Wanderer* (36 ft.)
5.	1974	Ambrogio Fogar	Italy	*Surprise* (38 ft.)
6.	1974	Kenichi Horie	Japan	*Mermaid III* (29 ft.)
7.	1982	David Scott-Cowper	UK	*Ocean Bound* (41 ft.)
8.	1994	Mike Golding	UK	*Group 4* (67 ft.)
9.	1996	Samantha Brewster	UK	*Heath Insured II* (67 ft.)
10.	2004	Jean Luc Van den Heede	France	*Adrien* (58 ft.)
11.	2006	Dee Caffari	UK	*Aviva* (70 ft.)
12.	2006	Adrian Flanagan	UK	*Barrabas* (40 ft.)

Appendix II – Yachts that have sailed Russia's Northern Sea Route

DATE	MASTER	COUNTRY	VESSEL	CREW	ICE PILOT
1991–1993	–	Russia	*Yakutia*	Full	Yes
Comment: 1991: Tiksi–Chukotka 1992: cargoed back to Tiksi 1993: Tiksi–Murmansk					
1998–1999	Nicolau Litau	Russia	*Apostle Andrew*	Full	Yes
Comment: East to west, wintering in Tiksi					
2000–2002	Sergei Cherbakov	Russia	*Sibir*	Full	Yes
Comment: West to east, including two winterings					
2002	Eric Brossier	France	*Vagabond*	Full	Yes
Comment: West to east, first passage without wintering					
2002	Arved Fuchs	Germany	*Dagmar Aaen*	Full	Yes
Comment: West to east					

DATE	MASTER	COUNTRY	VESSEL	CREW	ICE PILOT
2003–2004	Henk de Velde	Netherlands	*Campina*	2	Yes

Comment: East to west, wintered in Tiksi. 2004: Ice damage, cargoed to Murmansk

| 2004–2005 | Paddy Barry | Ireland | *Northabout* | Full | Yes |

Comment: East to west, wintered in Khatanga

| 2007 | Adrian Flanagan | UK | *Barrabas* | 1 | No |

Comment: East to west, first single-handed into NSR, cargoed Tiksi to Murmansk

Appendix III – Records set during the Alpha Global Expedition

1. First lone yachtsman to voyage vertically around the earth in a sailing yacht.
2. First UK to Hawaii, single-handed, unassisted westwards.
3. First British yacht to sail the Northern Sea Route.
4. First single-handed sailing of the Northern Sea Route.
5. First Provideniya to Tiksi, single-handed, unassisted westwards.

Appendix IV – Sponsors

Ampair
Arctic and Antarctic
   Research Institute
Barton Marine
Blakes Paints
Broadly Boats
Cadbury's
Clipper – Organic
   Beverages
C-Map
Creative Labs
Crewsaver
Crowley Marine Services
De Cecco
DHL Global Forwarding
Dial-A-Flight
DMSTech
Dubarry
Ecover
Exalto UK – Quality
   Marine Equipment
Fiorentino Para Anchors
Fluke
Furuno

Gallery Hadley
Gerbing's Heated
   Clothing
Gillette
Golden Arrow
GUL
Heinz
Hurricane Lamps
Hydrovane
John Bull Clothing
John Lewis Partnership
Katadyn Watermakers
Kelvin Hughes
Kemp Sails
Lightfoots
Marlow Ropes
MaxSea
MDA Geospatial Services
MDL Marinas
Mornflake
Musto
Ocens
Powerade
Princes Foods

Rank Hovis McDougall
Redningsselskapet
   (Norway)
Reflex Corporate Marking
Rescue Streamer
Robert Stanley Opticians
RS Components
Satcom Distribution
Smartcom Software
Sovag Insurance
Strings & Things –
   Rigging
Tack Tick Marine
   Instruments
Timberland
United Kingdom Sailing
   Academy
Veridian Nutritional
   Supplements
Waikiki Yacht Club
web-two.co.uk
Wellers Accountants

Appendix V – Beaufort Scale

Specifications and equivalent speeds

Beaufort wind scale	Mean Wind Speed		Limits of wind speed		Wind descriptive terms	Probable wave height in metres	Probable maximum wave height in metres	Seastate	Sea descriptive terms
	Knots	m/s	Knots	m/s					
0	0	0	<1	0–0.2	Calm	–	–	0	Calm (glassy)
1	2	0.8	1–3	0.3–1.5	Light air	0.1	0.1	1	Calm (rippled)
2	5	2.4	4–6	1.6–3.3	Light breeze	0.2	0.3	2	Smooth (wavelets)
3	9	4.3	7–10	3.4–5.4	Gentle breeze	0.6	1.0	3	Slight
4	13	6.7	11–16	5.5–7.9	Moderate breeze	1.0	1.5	3–4	Slight–Moderate
5	19	9.3	17–21	8.0–10.7	Fresh breeze	2.0	2.5	4	Moderate
6	24	12.3	22–27	10.8–13.8	Strong breeze	3.0	4.0	5	Rough
7	30	15.5	28–33	13.9–17.1	Near gale	4.0	5.5	5–6	Rough–Very rough
8	37	18.9	34–40	17.2–20.7	Gale	5.5	7.5	6–7	Very rough–High
9	44	22.6	41–47	20.8–24.4	Severe gale	7.0	10.0	7	High
10	52	26.4	48–55	24.5–28.4	Storm	9.0	12.5	8	Very High
11	60	30.5	56–63	28.5–32.6	Violent storm	11.5	16.0	8	Very High
12	–	–	64+	32.7+	Hurricane	14+	–	9	Phenomenal

Appendix V – Book List

Fiction

The Burden of Proof – Scott Turow

The Island of the Day Before – Umberto Eco

The House of Blue Mangoes – David Davidar

Absolute Friends – John le Carré

Hold Tight – Harlan Coben

The Lincoln Lawyer – Michael Connelly

Fierce Invalids Home from Hot Climates – Tom Robbins

No Second Chance – Harlan Coben

Villa Incognito – Tom Robbins

Little Infamies – Panos Karnezis

The Road – Cormac McCarthy

The Shadow of the Wind – Carlos Ruiz Zafón

Sons and Lovers – D H Lawrence

Lord of the Flies – William Golding

The Plot Against America – Philip Roth

Life of Pi – Yann Martel

Shalimar the Clown – Salman Rushdie

The Kite Runner – Khaled Hosseini

The Broker – John Grisham

Jigsaw – Campbell Armstrong

Critical Judgement – Michael Palmer

The Solitary Man – Stephen Leather

The Lasko Tangent – Richard North Patterson

Modern English Short Stories

Salmon Fishing in the Yemen – Paul Torday

Eddie's Bastard – William Kowalski

Jig – Campbell Armstrong

Sight Unseen – Robert Goddard

Traitor's Kiss – Gerald Seymour

Heat – Campbell Armstrong

Fade Away – Harlan Coben

Deadline – Campbell Armstrong

Pandora's Clock – John J Nance

The Client – John Grisham

The Partner – John Grisham

Medusa's Child – John J Nance

The Da Vinci Code – Dan Brown

Mambo – Campbell Armstrong

The Agony and the Ecstasy – Irving Stone

Non-Fiction

The World According to Clarkson – Jeremy Clarkson

Psycho-Cybernetics – Maxwell Maltz M.D.

Long Way Round – Ewan McGregor & Charley Boorman

Six Questions of Socrates – Christopher Phillips

Longitude – Dava Sobel

How to Get Rich – Felix Dennis

The Tao of Pooh – Benjamin Hoff

The Hynek UFO Report – Dr J. Allen Hynek

The God Delusion – Richard Dawkins

The Northeast Passage – from the Vikings to Nordenskiold – John Nurminen Foundation

Between a Rock and a Hard Place – Aron Ralston

Breaking the Spell – Religion as a Natural Phenomenon – Daniel C. Dennett

The Tibetan Book of Living and Dying – Sogyal Rinpoche

Singlehanded Sailing – Richard Henderson

The Illustrated Guide to World Religions – Michael D. Coogan

The Voyager's Handbook – Beth A Leonard

Northwest Passage Solo – David Scott Cowper

Heavy Weather Sailing – Peter Bruce

Complete Sailing Manual – Steve Sleight

Socrates Café – Christopher Phillips

Biography

Lawrence of Arabia – Jeremy Wilson

Navigation

Reeds Nautical Almanac 2005
Nautical Almanac 2006 – Commercial
  Edition
Rapid Sight Reduction Tables for Navigation
  Volumes 1, 2 & 3
Weather at Sea – David Houghton
The Weather Wizard's Cloud Book – Louis
  D. Rubin Sr. & Jim Duncan
Instant Weather Forecasting – Alan Watts
Celestial Navigation – Tom Cunliffe
Admiralty Arctic Pilot – Volume One 1985
Ocean Passages for the World – 4th
  Edition
The Mariner's Handbook – 7th Edition
  1999
Admiralty Bering Sea and Strait Pilot –
  5th Edition 1980
Admiralty Arctic Pilot – Volume 3, 7th
  Edition 2001
Admiralty South American Pilot

Technical

*Boatowner's Mechanical and Electrical
  Manual* – Nigel Calder
Marine Diesel Engines – Nigel Calder
The 12-Volt Bible for Boats – Miner
  Brotherton & Ed Sherman
Marine SSB Operation – J. Michael Gale

Reference

The Oxford Companion to Ships and the Sea
*Maritime Safety Information Services
  (Oceana, The Americas and The Far East)*
  – Volume 3 (2) 2005/06
*Maritime Safety Information Services
  (Europe, Africa and Asia (Excl the Far
  East))* – Volume 3 (1) 2005/06
*Global Maritime Distress and Safety System
  (GMDSS)* – Volume 5 2004/05
SAS Survival Guide – John Wiseman
A Seaman's Guide to the Rules of the Road
Pocket Guide to Knots and Splices – Des
  Pawson

Games

Brain Teasing Crosswords
The Word Search Book

ACKNOWLEDGEMENTS

I have been around the world twice, once at the helm of *Barrabas* and again, at my desk while I was writing *Over the Top*. Through both journeys, Louise and the boys have waited and I thank them for their patience and love.

When I arrived back in the UK, a journalist asked Louise, 'So, now Adrian's back, what is he going to do next?'

Quick as a flash, she answered, 'Lots and lots and lots of baby-sitting!'

I owe her that and much else besides. Without Louise as the expedition manager, I would not have succeeded.

My parents gave me a childhood filled with travel to mysterious, intriguing places, surely the food to nurture any future adventurer. And they gave me an education which taught me to think, to question, to dream. No parent could give their child a greater gift.

Any sailor alone at sea is never truly single-handed. Were it not for the many people who offered their time, help and encouragement, the voyage would have been so much more difficult.

In South Africa, my father made great inroads towards securing the permissions I needed from the Russian government.

In England, Ian Johnstone-Bryden, Sam Laidlaw, Roman Abramovich, the Rt. Hon. John Bercow MP, staff on the Russia Desk at the Foreign & Commonwealth Office, His Excellency Yuri Fedotov, Ambassador of the Russian Federation, and his Chief Minister Andrey Chupin between them got my message to where it needed to be heard in Moscow.

Tim Thornton was available to provide technical support at all times of the day and night and Mark Ripley's company, web-two.-co.uk, did a fantastic job on the expedition website.

Alan Samson at Orion Publishing has been unfailing in his enthusiasm. I only hope that I have justified that enthusiasm and that this will be the first of many projects together. My heartfelt thanks also to Lucinda McNeile and Helen Ewing at Orion. Rose Dale should give up providing medical advice and take up editing professionally. She took my manuscript and sandpapered it smooth. Her office is now covered with a layer of literary sawdust.

Tina Hadley gave up her valuable time as a professional photographer to capture wonderful images of my departure and arrival home. And on my arrival back in the UK, Annette Newton and her committee at the Royal Southern Yacht Club laid on a fabulous reception. My thanks also to the Royal Navy, especially to Lt. Commander Alan Wilson and the crew of HMS *Mersey* for giving me such a great welcome back to British territorial waters, and to Lt. Will King and the crew of HMS *Trumpeter* for escorting me those last few miles.

In Portugal, Ricardo Diniz guided me through some potentially dangerous situations with calm authority. Remember Cape Horn? Wow – we had the full experience down there – I'll repeat something to you which Sir Chay Blyth once said to me – 'Your turn next!'

In Honolulu, Ivan Chan-Wa, Michael Roth, Bobbie Jennings and the members of the Waikiki Yacht Club gave me a welcome I will never forget. Ernie Woodruff gave up work for a week to help me on the boat and show me something of Oahu. My thanks also to Ed Reinhart for entertaining me at his fabulous house and restocking my library.

In Nome, Alaska, Rick Kostiew needs to change his brand of beer to Carlsberg because he is *probably* the finest mechanic in the world as well as being one of the finest men I have ever met. Cam and Malinda Kristensen opened their home to me and made sure I was properly fed before my sojourn to the Russian ice. George Fullwood and Tim Shields made sure I had access to everything I needed.

In Washington DC, Marie Forsyth at the British Embassy smoothed a potentially difficult situation with calm efficiency.

In Russia, John Mann was unstinting in his efforts on my behalf. Without him, I'd probably still be waiting in Nome (and no doubt drinking Carlsberg with Rick, Cam, Malinda, George and Tim). Sergey Frank, Nikolai Monko, Nikolay Babych and Vasily Smolyanitsky got me as far as it was possible to go through the ice. And when I couldn't go any further, the indomitable Captain Alfred Zagorsky and the crew of the *Kapitan Danilkin* took me and *Barrabas* the rest of the way. Igor Melnikov in Murmansk made my short stay memorable.

In Mehamn, Norway, Kare Karlstad and Oddvar Jenssen showed me kindness and a generosity of spirit that became the hallmark of the voyage.

I have listed the expedition's sponsors in Appendix IV, but my particular thanks go to Rob Kemp and Matt Atkins at Kemp Sails – I will never use another brand of sails – why change from the best? John Curry at Hydrovane provided me with the best helmsman in the world! Plus, I could shout at my Hydrovane and he didn't answer back, he worked 24/7 and I didn't have to feed him or pay him and, through it all, he kept *Barrabas* heading exactly where I wanted her to go. Penny Darnbrook and her team at DHL Global Forwarding saved my bacon more than once. Niamh McEnery at Timberland decided to put some marketing dollars behind me and the expedition. Without this support, it really is doubtful I would have got to the start line.

In France, Chris Elliott was the first person outside my immediate family to know about my plans. He found *Barrabas* and, without the slightest need for persuasion, acted as my interpreter and negotiator in the months that followed.

Bernard de Castro built a truly magnificent boat. I hope that her journey around the earth has made him as proud of her as I am.

There are four other people whom I want to acknowledge not only for what they did but more especially for the *way* they did it – with positivity and a real 'can-do' attitude: Martin Amy at Kelvin Hughes in Southampton, Denis Rawle at Exalto in Derby, Les Vasconelles in Honolulu and Gary Feaster in Anchorage.

To the many, many people around the world who followed my progress and sent messages of support – thank you.

Finally . . . I want to thank you, the reader. I am being premature, of course, but if my story has moved you in any way towards taking that first step on the long, hard road towards your own dream, then every dollar spent, every sacrifice made, every effort expended and every danger faced in taking *Barrabas* around the world will have been totally justified. Only then, can the true success of the Alpha Global Expedition be measured.

Index